JOB 28 AS RHETORIC

SUPPLEMENTS
TO
VETUS TESTAMENTUM

EDITED BY
THE BOARD OF THE QUARTERLY

H. M. BARSTAD
PHYLLIS A. BIRD
R. P. GORDON
A. HURVITZ
A. van der KOOIJ
A. LEMAIRE
R. SMEND
J. TREBOLLE BARRERA
J. C. VANDERKAM
H. G. M. WILLIAMSON

VOLUME XCVII

JOB 28 AS RHETORIC

JOB 28 AS RHETORIC
An Analysis of Job 28
in the Context of Job 22-31

BY

ALISON LO

Society of Biblical Literature
Atlanta

JOB 28 AS RHETORIC

Copyright © 2003 by Koninklijke Brill NV, Leiden,
The Netherlands

This edition published under license from Koninklijke Brill NV,
Leiden, The Netherlands by the Society of Biblical Literature.

All rights reserved. No part of this work may be reproduced or transmitted in any form or by any means, electronic or mechanical, including photocopying and recording, or by any means of any information storage or retrieval system, except as may be expressly permitted by the 1976 Copyright Act or in writing from the Publisher. Requests for permission should be addressed in writing to the Rights and Permissions Department, Koninklijke Brill NV, Leiden, The Netherlands.

Authorization to photocopy items for internal or personal use is granted by Brill provided that the appropriate fees are paid directly to The Copyright Clearance Center, 222 Rosewood Drive, Suite 910, Danvers, MA 01923, USA. Fees are subject to change.

Library of Congress Cataloging-in-Publication Data
Lo, Alison.
    Job 28 as rhetoric : an analysis of Job 28 in the context of Job 22-31 / by Alison Lo.
      p. cm.
    Originally published: Leiden ; Boston : Brill, 2003. (Supplements to Vetus Testamentum, ISSN 0083-5889 ; v. 97)
    Includes bibliographical references and index.
    ISBN-13: 978-1-58983-197-1 (paper binding : alk. paper)
    ISBN-10: 1-58983-197-7 (paper binding : alk. paper)
      1. Bible. O.T. Job XXVIII–Criticism, interpretation, etc. I. Title. II. Series: Supplements to Vetus Testamentum ; v. 97.
BS410 .V452 vol. 97 2005
[BS1415.52]
221 s—dc22
[223'.106]   2005029681

Printed in the United States of America
on acid-free paper

CONTENTS

Acknowledgement xi
Abbreviations xii

CHAPTER ONE: INTRODUCTION 1
  I. The Issues of Job 28 1
  II. Commentators' Approaches to the Issues of Job 28 ... 2
    A. Accepting Job 28 as Job's Words 3
    B. Reasons for Rejecting Job 28 5
      1. Discrepancy in Style 5
      2. Oddity in Job's Mouth 7
      3. Bringing the Book to a Premature Climax 9
      4. The Problems of 28:28 11
        Conclusion 15
  III. The Approach of This Study 15
    A. Definition and Advantage of Rhetorical Criticism 17
    B. The Argument of This Study 20

CHAPTER TWO: JOB 28 IN THE WHOLE BOOK 22
  I. Incongruities in the Book of Job 22
  II. Different Approaches to the Incongruities 25
    A. The Historical-Critical Approach 25
    B. The Structuralist Approach 29
    C. The Deconstructionist Approach 35
  III. Job 28 Within the Plot Development of the Book 37
    A. Three Movements of the Plot 39
      1. Movement One (1:1-2:10) 39
      2. Movement Two (2:11-31:40) 45
      3. Movement Three (32:1-42:17) 51
        Conclusion 53
    B. Plot Development and Job's Characterization in
       Job 22-31 54
  IV. Job 28 Related to the Rhetorical Situation of the
    Book 57
    A. Definition of Rhetorical Situation 58
    B. Concept of the Audience 59
    C. Rhetorical Situation of the Book of Job 62
      1. The Exigency of the Rhetorical Situation 62

CONTENTS

        a) Blind Application of the Theodicies 62
           i) The Concept of Retribution 63
           ii) The Concept of Human Depravity 65
           iii) The Divine Chastisement 66
        b) Proud Claims to Knowledge 67
        c) Misconceptions of God 67
      2. The Audience of the Rhetorical Situation 69
      3. The Constraint of the Rhetorical Situation 70
    D. Job 28 in Relation to the Rhetorical Situation of the Book 71
  V. Job 28 Within the Overall Rhetorical Strategy of the Book 73
    A. Inadequacy of the Friends' Perspectives 73
    B. Inadequacy of Job's Perspectives 74
    C. Job 28 as Part of the "From Less to More Adequate Perspectives" Strategy 77
  VI. Conclusion 78

CHAPTER THREE: JOB 28 WITHIN JOB 22-31 79
  I. Introduction 79
  II. Contradictory Juxtaposition as Part of the Author's Rhetorical Strategy 80
    A. Definition of Contradictory Juxtaposition 80
    B. Functions of Contradictory Juxtaposition 81
    C. Positive and Negative Aspects of Gapping 82
  III. How to Discern the Author's Intended Impacts upon the Audience 83
    A. Assumptions for Approaching the Story 83
    B. The Author's Guide to Interpretation 84
      1. Evaluative Points of View 84
        a) God's Evaluative Point of View 84
        b) Narrator's Evaluative Point of View 85
      2. Use of Irony 86
      3. Literary-Rhetorical Markers 87
        a) Inclusio 87
        b) Repetition 87
        c) Rhetorical Questions 88
        Conclusion 91
    C. Dramatic Presentation and Its Interpretations 91
    D. God's Final Verdict in Job 42:7b as the Key to Interpretation 94

CONTENTS

IV. Job's Contradictory Sayings in Job 22-24............ 96
   A. The Content 97
   B. The Characteristics of Job's Contradictory Sayings
      in Job 24 104
      1. Job 24:18-24 in Comparison with the Friends'
         Sayings 104
      2. Job 24:18-24 in Comparison with Job's Other
         Sayings 105
         a) Job's Sayings in 21:1-34 105
         b) Job's Sayings in 24:1-17 107
   C. Commentators' Approaches to the Issue of
      Job 24:18-24 108
      1. Removing 24:18-24 109
      2. Considering 24:18-24 as an Independent
         Poem of the Author....................... 109
      3. Attributing 24:18-24 to One of the Friends..... 110
      4. Retaining 24:18-24 as Job's Speech in which
         He Quotes the Friends 113
      5. Treating the Entire Speech as Job's Speech 114
      Conclusion 117
   D. The Unity of Job 24........................... 119
   E. The Rhetorical Impacts of Job's Contradictory
      Sayings in Job 22-24.......................... 120
      1. The Flow of Argument 121
      2. The Rhetorical Impacts upon the Audience 123
V. Job's Contradictory Sayings in Job 25-26............ 126
   A. The Content 128
   B. The Characteristics of Job's Hymnic Material in
      Job 26....................................... 132
      1. Job 26:5-14 in Comparison with Job's Other
         Hymnic Passages 133
         a) Job 9:5-13............................. 133
         b) Job 10:8-13............................ 140
         c) Job 12:13-25........................... 142
         Conclusion 144
      2. Job 26:5-14 in Comparison with Job's Non-
         Hymnic Materials 145
      Conclusion 146
      3. Job 26:5-14 in Comparison with the Friends'
         Hymnic Recitations........................ 146

       a) Job 5:9-16 (Eliphaz's) 146
       b) Job 11:7-11 (Zophar's) 148
       c) Job 22:12-14 (Eliphaz's) 148
       d) Job 25:2-6 (Bildad's) 149
       Conclusion 152
    C. Commentators' Approaches to the Issue of
       Job 26:5-14 152
       1. Re-assigning from Job to Bildad 152
       2. Job as Speaking Satirically against God 155
       3. Job as the Speaker, Finishing Bildad's Speech
          for him 156
       4. Defending 26:5-14 as Job's Speech 157
       5. Assigning Both Job 25 and 26 to Job 158
       Conclusion 159
    D. The Unity of Job 26 159
    E. The Rhetorical Impacts of Job's Contradictory
       Sayings in Job 25-26 160
       1. The Flow of Argument 160
       2. The Rhetorical Impacts upon the Audience 165
VI. Job's Contradictory Sayings in Job 27 166
    A. The Content 168
    B. The Characteristics of Job's Contradictory Sayings
       in Job 27 172
       1. Job 27:13-23 in Comparison with the Friends'
          Sayings 172
          a) Job 4:8-11; 5:2-7 (Eliphaz's) 172
          b) Job 8:11-19, 22 (Bildad's) 173
          c) Job 11:20 (Zophar's) 173
          d) Job 15:17-35 (Eliphaz's) 174
          e) Job 18:5-21 (Bildad's) 174
          f) Job 20:4-29 (Zophar's) 174
          g) Job 22:5-20 (Eliphaz's) 175
          Conclusion 175
       2. Job 27:13-23 in Comparison with Job's Other
          Sayings 175
          a) Job 21 176
          b) Job 24:1-17 176
          c) Job 27:1-12 177
          Conclusion 177

C. Commentators' Approaches to the Issue of Job 27	178
1. Denying Both vv.7-10 and vv.13-23 to Job	178
2. Accepting vv.7-10 but Rejecting vv.13-23 as Job's Words	180
3. Treating the Whole of Chapter 27 as Job's Speech	183
Conclusion	186
D. The Rhetorical Impacts of Job's Contradictory Sayings in Job 27	187
1. The Flow of Argument	187
2. The Rhetorical Impacts upon the Audience	193
VII. Job's Contradictory Sayings in Job 28-31	196
A. The Content	197
B. The Characteristics of Job's Contradictory Sayings in Job 28	205
1. Job 28 in Comparison with Job 11:5-12	205
2. Job 28 in Comparison with the Yahweh Speeches	206
3. Job 28 in Comparison with Job 27 and Job 29-31	209
Conclusion	211
C. Commentators' Approaches to the Issue of Job 28	212
D. The Rhetorical Impacts of Job's Contradictory Sayings in Job 28-31	212
1. The Flow of Argument	212
a) The Wisdom Poem in Job 28	212
b) The Oath of Innocence in Job 29-31	216
Conclusion	221
2. The Rhetorical Impacts upon the Audience	221
VIII. Job 28 Within the Context of Job 22-31	223
A. Contradictory Juxtapositions as a Common Structure	224
B. Contradictory Juxtapositions in Job 22-31 as Part of the Rhetorical Strategy	229
C. Gap-Filling of the Contradictory Juxtapositions	230

CHAPTER FOUR: SUMMARY AND CONCLUSION ... 233

APPENDIX: CONTRADICTORY JUXTAPOSITION IN OTHER BOOKS ... 237
   I. Introduction ... 237

II.	Proverbs	237
III.	Psalms 9-10	239
IV.	Psalm 73	242
V.	Ecclesiastes	245
	A. Ecclesiastes 1:12-2:26	245
	B. Ecclesiastes 3:1-15	247
	C. Ecclesiastes 3:16-22	248
	D. Ecclesiastes 5:9-19 [10-20]	249
	E. Ecclesiastes 8:10-15	250
	F. Ecclesiastes 9:1-12	250
	G. Ecclesiastes 11:7-12:8	252
VI.	Conclusion	253

BIBLIOGRAPHY 254

INDICES 289
  Authors 291
  Biblical Texts 293
  Subjects 307

ACKNOWLEDGEMENT

This volume is a slightly revised version of my doctoral thesis presented to the Faculty of Arts and Humanities, University of Gloucestershire, in 2002. Without the aid and support of many, this work would never have come into being. I cannot sufficiently express my gratitude to those who have in some way contributed to the successful completion of my study.

Special heartfelt thanks must go to Professor J. Gordon McConville for his most inspiring, encouraging and competent supervision, which has left an indelible mark in my life, and to Dr. John J. Bimson for his kindness as my second supervisor in suggesting new angles on the text.

Thanks as well to the School of Theology and Religious Studies, University of Gloucestershire, for its provision of a studentship, and to all the research colleagues in the Biblical Studies Seminar, University of Gloucestershire, for their academic stimulation and discussions, which helped sharpen the arguments of my present study. I am grateful to Adrian Long for his meticulous care in proofreading the text and improving my style.

I thank Professor André Lemaire for accepting this work for publication in the Supplements to Vetus Testamentum series and for offering suggestions to improve the manuscript. Thanks are also due to the two examiners, Dr. Grace Emmerson and Rev. Dr. Craig Bartholomew, for their great encouragement and support in getting this work published.

I especially acknowledge my greatest indebtedness to my late parents, who had provided me with an excellent model of self-sacrifice and perseverance. To them, I owe an immeasurable debt I can never repay. My warmest appreciation must be extended to my five brothers and their families, who light up my life with lots of fun and joy.

Finally, I am humbly grateful for the privilege of standing in the awe of the divine truth. For all its blemishes and imperfections, may this work prove a worthy thanksgiving on the altar of God.

Alison Lo, Jerusalem

ABBREVIATIONS

AB	Anchor Bible
ABD	*Anchor Bible Dictionary*
AJBA	*Australian Journal of Biblical Archaeology*
AJSLL	*American Journal of Semitic Languages and Literatures*
ALUOS	*Annual of Leeds University Oriental Society*
ANET	*Ancient Near Eastern Texts Relating to the Old Testament*
AOAT	Alter Orient und Altes Testament
ASV	American Standard Version
ATD	Das Alte Testament Deutsch
BBR	*Bulletin for Biblical Research*
BDB	*The Brown-Driver-Briggs Hebrew & English Lexicon of the Old Testament*
BEATAJ	Beiträge zur Erforschung des Alten Testaments und des antiken Judentums
BeO	*Bibbia e Oriente*
BETL	Bibliotheca ephemeridum theologicarum lovaniensium
BHT	Beiträge zur Historischen Theologie
Bib	*Biblica*
BibInt	*Biblical Interpretation*
BibOr	Biblica et Orientalia
BIS	Biblical Interpretation Series
BJRL	*Bulletin of the John Rylands University Library of Manchester*
BKAT	Biblischer Kommentar: Altes Testament
BN	*Biblische Notizen*
BSac	*Bibliotheca Sacra*
BT	*The Bible Translator*
BZAW	Beihefte zur Zeitschrift für die alttestamentliche Wissenschaft
CalTJ	*Calvin Theological Journal*
CBQ	*Catholic Biblical Quarterly*
CH	Church History
CR: BS	Currents in Research: Biblical Studies
CurTM	*Currents in Theology and Mission*
ESV	English Standard Version
EvQ	*Evangelical Quarterly*
ExpTim	*Expository Times*
GNB	Good News Bible
Greg	*Gregorianum*
HAR	Hebrew Annual Review
HAT	Handbuch zum Alten Testament
HBT	*Horizons in Biblical Theology*
HS	Hebrew Studies
HSAT	Die Heilige Schrift des Alten Testaments
HTR	*Harvard Theological Review*
HUCA	Hebrew Union College Annual
IB	*Interpreter's Bible*
IBC	Interpretation: A Bible Commentary for Teaching and Preaching
ICC	International Critical Commentary

IndJT	*Indian Journal of Theology*
Int	*Interpretation*
ITQ	*Irish Theological Quarterly*
JB	Jerusalem Bible
JBL	*Journal of Biblical Literature*
JNSL	*Journal of Northwest Semitic Languages*
JQR	*Jewish Quarterly Review*
JR	*Journal of Religion*
JSNTSup	Journal for the Study of the New Testament Supplement Series
JSOT	*Journal for the Study of the Old Testament*
JSOTSup	Journal for the Study of the Old Testament Supplement Series
JSS	*Journal of Semitic Studies*
KAT	Kommentar zum Alten Testament
KHC(AT)	Kurzer Hand-Commentar (zum Alten Testament)
KJV	King James Version
KTU	*Die Keilalphabetischen Texte aus Ugarit*
lit.	literally
LXX	Septuagint
MT	Masoretic Text
NAB	New American Bible
NASB	New American Standard Bible
NCB	New Century Bible
NEB	New English Bible
NIB	*New Interpreter's Bible*
NICOT	New International Commentary on the Old Testament
NIDOTTE	*New International Dictionary of Old Testament Theology & Exegesis*
NIV	New International Version
NJB	New Jerusalem Bible
NKJ	New King James Version
NLT	New Living Translation
NRSV	New Revised Standard Version
NSBT	New Studies in Biblical Theology
OBT	Overtures to Biblical Theology
OT	Old Testament
OTE	*Old Testament Essays*
OTG	Old Testament Guides
OTL	Old Testament Library
OTS	Oudtestamentische Studiën
PEGLMBS	*Proceedings, Eastern Great Lakes and Midwest Biblical Societies*
PIBA	*Proceedings of the Irish Biblical Association*
PSB	*Princeton Seminary Bulletin*
RevExp	*Review and Expositor*
RSV	Revised Standard Version
RV	Revised Version
SBL	Society of Biblical Literature
SBLDS	Society of Biblical Literature Dissertation Series
ScrB	*Scripture Bulletin*
SJOT	*Scandinavian Journal of the Old Testament*
SJT	*Scottish Journal of Theology*
SR	*Studies in Religion/Sciences religieuses*
SVT	Supplements to Vetus Testamentum
SWJT	*Southwestern Journal of Theology*

TOTC	Tyndale Old Testament Commentaries
TToday	*Theology Today*
TynBul	*Tyndale Bulletin*
TZ	*Theologische Zeitschrift*
UF	*Ugarit-Forschungen*
VT	*Vetus Testamentum*
*VT*Sup	*Vetus Testamentum* Supplements
WBC	Word Biblical Commentary
WW	*Word and World*
WZ	*Wissenschaftliche Zeitschrift der Martin-Luther-Universität*
ZAW	*Zeitschrift für die alttestamentliche Wissenschaft*
ZDMG	*Zeitschrift der deutschen morgenländischen Gesellschaft*
ZTK	*Zeitschrift für Theologie und Kirche*

CHAPTER ONE

INTRODUCTION

I. *The Issues of Job 28*

Habel has made this remark: "Job 28 is a brilliant but embarrassing poem for many commentators. It has been viewed as an erratic intrusion, an inspired intermezzo, a superfluous prelude, and an orthodox afterthought."[1] Many scholars suspect the authenticity of this chapter mainly because of its inconsistency with its context and also the problem of Job 28:28.

Within its context, Job's saying in Job 28 sounds contradictory to Job's preceding speeches and his subsequent oath of innocence (Job 29-31) in terms of the content and tone of utterance. Throughout the dialogue, Job vigorously rejects his friends' explanation of his suffering. They use some of the ideas of mainstream Yahwism and wisdom traditions, which define wisdom as "fearing God" and "shunning evil" (cf. Prov 1:7; 9:10), and highlight blessings for obedience and curses for disobedience (cf. Deut 28:1-14; 28:15-68; Prov 3:33; 10:27; 10:30; 12:21; 15:29; Ps 1:1-3; 15:1-5; 33:18-19; 112:1-9; 119:1-2; Ps 1:4-6; 10:14-15; 37:35-36; 112:10). However, when the story comes to Job 28, Job's argument sounds quite similar to his friends' standpoint, which he used to strongly oppose, namely, expressing an attitude of trust, though humans do not understand everything. Then, all of a sudden, Job turns back to his defiant argument again in Job 29-31. Therefore, in terms of content, Job's standpoint in Job 28 seems to be inconsistent within its context. In addition, the tranquil and reflective tone of Job 28 contrasts drastically with Job's argumentative style of the preceding speeches and the strong emotional outburst in his subsequent oath of innocence in Job 29-31, especially the complaints in 30:20-23 and the final challenge to God in 31:35-37.[2] Therefore many scholars suspect the

---

[1] N. C. Habel, *The Book of Job* (OTL; London: SCM Press, 1985) 391.
[2] See S. R. Driver and G. B. Gray, *A Critical and Exegetical Commentary on the Book of Job* (ICC; Edinburgh: T. & T. Clark, 1921) 233; and H. H. Rowley, *The Book of Job* (NCB; Revised edition; Grand Rapids: Eerdmans, 1980) 14.

originality of this chapter owing to the discrepancy of Job's viewpoint and tone of utterance in the context.

Furthermore, some scholars also question the authenticity of 28:28.[3] They tend to remove v.28 on several grounds: 1) the introductory formula "And He said to man" is considered as a prosaic addition, and the lines seem to be out of balance;[4] 2) the divine title אֲדֹנָי occurs only once in v.28, nowhere else in the book; and 3) the theme of how man can gain wisdom in v.28 seems to contradict the theme of wisdom's inaccessibility in vv.1-27.[5] Commentators have attempted to resolve the problematic inconsistency of Job 28 within its context and 28:28 within its chapter in various ways.

II. *Commentators' Approaches to the Issues of Job 28*

Generally speaking, those scholars who accept Job 28 as an integral part of the book either read this chapter as Job's words (Childs, Janzen, Whybray and Good) or consider it as an interlude or an authorial comment rather than Job's words (Westermann, Andersen, Sawyer, Petersen, Newsom, Hartley and Habel). Those who reject Job 28 base their arguments upon four reasons: 1) the difference in the author's style; 2) its unsuitability in Job's mouth; 3) its bringing of the book to a premature climax; and 4) the internal contradiction caused by 28:28. There are various approaches to address the discrepancy caused by Job 28. Some regard it as a later addition (Rowley, Pope, Driver-Gray, Dhorme and Gordis). Instead of Job's speech, some scholars consider Job 28 as an interlude (Dhorme and Gordis) or an independent poem (Driver-Gray). Some reassign this speech from Job to Zophar (Clines). Some transpose Job 28 to right after 42:6 (Szczygiel, Tur-Sinai and Settlemire). Some deny the au-

---

[3] See C. Westermann, *The Structure of the Book of Job: A Form-Critical Analysis* (trans. Charles A. Muenchow; Philadelphia: Fortress Press, 1981) 138, n.5; and Driver and Gray, *Book of Job*, 244-5. Also E. Dhorme, *A Commentary on the Book of Job* (trans. Harold Knight; London: Thomas Nelson and Sons, 1967) 414, li; this work is translated from Dhorme's *Le livre de Job* (Paris: Gabalda, 1926).

[4] See Driver and Gray, *Book of Job*, 245; M. H. Pope, *Job* (AB; 3rd ed.; Garden City: Doubleday, 1973) 206; and J. E. Hartley, *The Book of Job* (NICOT; Grand Rapids: Eerdmans, 1988) 383, n.3.

[5] Concerning the issues of Job 28:28, see Habel, *Job*, 400-1; Hartley, *Job*, 383, n.1-3; and R. Gordis, *The Book of Job: Commentary, New Translation and Special Studies* (New York: Jewish Theological Seminary of America, 1978) 538-9, Special Note 24.

thenticity of 28:28 (Driver-Gray, Dhorme, Geller, Pope and Westermann).

A. *Accepting Job 28 as Job's Words*

To start with, Janzen, Childs, Good and Whybray read Job 28 as Job's speech. They treat this chapter as an integral part of the book, and study it in its present position. Whybray sees Job 28 as Job's final comment over the debate that neither he nor the friends nor any human being acquires wisdom, but God alone possesses it.[6] Whybray defends the position of Job 28 as the text stands. Some scholars reject this chapter because there are introductory headings in chapters 27 and 29, but there is none in chapter 28. Whybray appropriately argues that no separate headings in chapters 28 and 30 indicate that the author intended chapters 27-28 and 29-31 to be understood as Job's two distinct speeches.[7] Whybray tries to link chapter 27 with chapter 28 by pointing out one common topic between them. According to Whybray, the accumulation of wealth by the wicked in 27:16-17 is connected with the acquisition of silver and other precious objects in 28:1-11.[8] However, Whybray has not convincingly dealt with the relationship between chapters 27 and 28. Other than that, he does not even explain how the story can develop from chapter 28 to chapters 29-31.

Janzen points out the phraseological connection between 28:28 and 1:1, 8; 2:3. According to Janzen, such connection indicates that up to 28:28 Job has survived the test and continues to be God's faithful servant. He also brings out the relationship between chapter 28 and chapters 29-31. According to Janzen, chapter 28 highlights the search for wisdom, while chapters 29-31 present the form of wisdom's enactment—displaying the task of "fearing the Lord and

---

[6] R. N. Whybray, *Job* (A New Biblical Commentary; Sheffield: Sheffield Academic Press, 1998) 21.

[7] Whybray, *Job*, 18.

[8] Whybray points out that the word "dust" (עָפָר) employed in 27:16 also occurs twice in 28:2, 6. According to Whybray, the purpose of 28:1-11 is to emphasize the ingenuity of human technology and the lengths to which men will go to acquire these sources of wealth, and to point out in vv.14-19 that the most precious treasure of all, namely wisdom, is the one thing that they cannot obtain. Therefore 28:1-11 may be seen as a comment on the futility of those who, like the wicked of Job 27, value material wealth above all else. This is how Whybray links chapters 27 and 28 together. See Whybray, *Job*, 20-1.

shunning evil."[9] However, Janzen's viewpoint about the relationship between Job 28 and Job 29-31 is not convincing. I do not think that chapters 29-31 present the form of wisdom's enactment. It seems that Janzen has not dealt with Job's complaints and defiant utterances in 30:20-23 and 31:35-37.

Childs suggests a holistic reading of the book according to its final canonical shaping.[10] He points out that Job 28 is presented as Job's words in the final form of the book. According to Childs, the effect of placing Job 28 in Job's mouth is "to reinstate him as a sage."[11] He claims that Job 28 functions to express Job's recognition of the divine limitations set on human wisdom. This poem also provides a connection between the portrayal of the "patient Job" in chapter 2 and the "impatient Job" in the dialogue. Job loses his patience because of his lack of wisdom. Childs further adds: "The canonical shaping of these chapters suggests that these are not two irreconcilable portrayals, but a calculated tension marking the proper limits of wisdom for the community of faith."[12] In this way the sharp discrepancy between Job 28 and Job 29-31 is explained as a tension making a link between patient and impatient Job. However, Childs still has not fully explained why Job 28 should come at this point.

In response to the scholars' suspicion about the originality of Job 28, Good makes this remark: "I join them in doubting that the 'Hymn to Wisdom' was here in the earlier stages of the book's composition. But here it is now, and it makes a contribution to its context."[13] Although Good also suspects that this chapter was not originally composed as Job's speech, he considers that its insertion into the book makes it appear to be Job's speech. Therefore Good tries to interpret it as the text stands.[14]

According to Good, Job redefines and reverses some terms in chapter 27. He redefines God as the wicked enemy at 27:7.[15] "To

---

[9] J. G. Janzen, *Job* (IBC; Atlanta: John Knox Press, 1985) 187-9.
[10] B. S. Childs, *Introduction to the Old Testament as Scripture* (London: SCM Press, 1979) 526-44.
[11] Childs, *Introduction to the Old Testament*, 542.
[12] Childs, *Introduction to the Old Testament*, 543.
[13] E. M. Good, *In Turns of Tempest* (Stanford: Stanford University Press, 1990) 290.
[14] Good, *In Turns of Tempest*, 290-3.
[15] According to Good's interpretation, Job redefines God as the wicked enemy (27:7) and himself as the alienated and godless (27:8). Good claims that Job accepts the term "godless" that his friends have implicitly applied to him all along.

fear God" is parallel to "avoiding evil" at 28:28. Since "wicked" has become the term for God in chapter 27, "avoiding evil" is therefore understood as "avoiding God." Good views "fear" in its literal sense, which expresses the danger of God's power (27:14-23). As regards Good's interpretation, the value system of religiosity at 28:28 absurdly means its opposite, a matter not of making contact with God but of evading Him.[16] However, Good seems to read too much into the text. His interpretation of irony in chapters 27-28 seems to have gone too far, with the audience hardly able to understand it as he does, even if that was how the author intended it. Good's interpretation of 28:28 as Job's alienation from God also raises the question of how to connect that verse with Job's strong determination to confront God in the subsequent chapters.

In short, the above four scholars (Janzen, Childs, Good and Whybray) all treat chapter 28 as Job's speech. However, they do not convincingly explain the special function of this chapter in its present context. They are not able to explain the abrupt shifts of tone and content from Job 27 to Job 28, and then to Job 29-31.

B. *Reasons for Rejecting Job 28*

Now we come to discuss the reasons why some commentators reject Job 28 and their approaches to resolving the problem. As we have seen, four reasons can be summarized for the rejection of Job 28: 1) the difference in authorial style; 2) its inappropriateness in Job's mouth; 3) its bringing of the book to a premature climax; and 4) the problem of 28:28.

1. *Discrepancy in Style*

Driver-Gray regard Job 28 as an independent poem, and they deny its originality.[17] Driver-Gray state that the words עָדָה (to pass over; 28:8), סָלָה (to value; 28:16) and מֶשֶׁךְ (the price; 28:18), which could have been used elsewhere are not otherwise used in the book. Furthermore, according to Driver-Gray, the use of a refrain in 28:

Given Job's reversals of the meanings of terms in 27:7-8, the fate of the "godless" in 27:14-23 is referred to Job himself. According to Good, here Job depicts his expectation of destruction at the hands of a wicked God exactly as the friends have described their expectation of his destruction at the hands of a righteous God. See Good, *In Turns of Tempest*, 287-90.

[16] Good, *In Turns of Tempest*, 292.
[17] Driver and Gray, *Book of Job*, xxxviii.

12 and 28:20 is more natural to an independent poem than to a speech.[18] Therefore they deny Job 28 as original, and consider it an independent poem.

However, Driver-Gray's argument that עָדָה (to pass over; v.8), סָלָה (to value; v.16) and מֶשֶׁךְ (the price; v.18) could have been used elsewhere but are not, is not convincing. The verb עָדָה (to pass over) is one of many Aramaisms which are abundant in the Book of Job. As for the verb סָלָה (to value), the author does not use it again simply because there is no other context in which a verb meaning "to value" is required. Furthermore, no other usual words for "price" are used outside chapter 28 in the Book of Job. Therefore it seems valid to use מֶשֶׁךְ (the price) here, corresponding to מְחִיר (the price) in 28:15.[19] Settlemire ironically comments upon this argument of Driver-Gray, "Perhaps their point could have been made more clearly if they had indicated where these particular words could have been used."[20] Furthermore, the use of refrain in rhetorical question form in 28:12 and 28:20 also occurs elsewhere in the Yahweh's speeches. The following two are examples:

> 38:19 Where is the way to the dwelling of light?
> And as for darkness, where is its place?
> 38:24 Where is the way that the light is divided,
> or the east wind scattered on the earth?

Therefore it seems that there is no ground for Driver-Gray to consider that the use of refrain in Job 28 points to an independent work.[21]

Furthermore, I do not think that the author's style is an adequate criterion in itself to decide whether a passage is original or not. For instance, both Settlemire and Dhorme seek to prove that chapter 28 is a work of the author of the dialogue and the Yahweh speeches, by demonstrating the common styles, terminologies and themes they share.[22] However, they both deny chapter 28 as an integral part of the book. Settlemire considers this chapter should have been placed

---

[18] Driver and Gray, *Book of Job*, 232.
[19] C. C. Settlemire, "The Original Position of Job 28," *The Answers Lie Below: Essays in Honour of Lawrence Edmund Toombs* (ed. Henry O. Thompson; Lanham; New York; London: University Press of America, 1984) 298.
[20] Settlemire, "The Original Position of Job 28," 298.
[21] Settlemire, "The Original Position of Job 28," 296.
[22] Settlemire, "The Original Position of Job 28," 288-98; and Dhorme, *Job*, lxxxv-xcviii.

after 42:6, while Dhorme views it as a later addition although it is a work of the same author. Obviously, then, authorial style cannot stand as the single factor determining the originality of a chapter.

2. *Oddity in Job's Mouth*

Another reason arousing scholars' suspicion about Job 28 is its unsuitability in Job's mouth. There is a sharp discrepancy between Job's calm, settled temper in chapter 28 and his hot, bitter outburst in chapters 29-31.[23] Driver-Gray reject Job 28 as Job's words particularly because of this discrepancy. They point out that it is hard to imagine how Job can fall back from tranquility (chapter 28) to complaints (30:20-23) and dissatisfaction with not having been justified by God (31:35-37).[24] In terms of content, Job 28 also seems to be inappropriate upon Job's lips. Pope denies it as Job's words and regards it as a later addition "since the burden of its message—that wisdom, the secrets of the universe and of divine providence are inaccessible to man—does not comport with Job's desire to bring God into court, as it were, and question him."[25] Pope's interpretation at this point needs examination, and we will return to it in due course. In addition, the absence of direct address, personal references and an introductory heading from Job 28 makes this chapter distinct from its surrounding speeches, thus adding to the scholars' suspicion about its speaker and originality. No introductory heading dividing Job 27 and Job 28 might mean that Job 28 is a continuation of Job's speech. However, the sudden shift of tone, topic and imagery from Job 27 to Job 28 arouses doubt about whether the speaker is Job. The introductory heading in Job 29 leads some scholars to think that Job is "resuming" his speech. To them, this implies that Job 28 is not Job's speech.[26]

If Job 28 is not Job's words, scholars have to decide who it belongs to. Clines considers Job 28 as Zophar's speech because Zophar has made similar points in 11:7-20. However, he notes that even if this poem was originally spoken by Zophar, it still seems to lessen the effectiveness of the Yahweh speeches. To resolve the problem

---

[23] Rowley, *Book of Job*, 14.
[24] Driver and Gray, *Book of Job*, 233.
[25] Pope, *Job*, xxvii.
[26] Concerning the issue of the absence of introductory heading in Job 28, see C. A. Newsom, "The Book of Job," *NIB 4* (ed. Leander E. Keck et al.; Nashville: Abingdon Press, 1996) 528.

Clines suggests that "Zophar is speaking only about the impossibility of knowing the particular cause of a particular misfortune, whereas God is speaking about the impossibility of humans' knowing whether a misfortune was due to any human cause at all."[27]

Despite the similarities between Job 28 and Zophar's speech in 11:7-20, it seems that these two passages have different focuses. Job 28 seems to stress that human beings in general lack wisdom, while in 11:7-20 Zophar's focus is on Job, who he considers "an idiot" who lacks wisdom (11:12). However, Zophar himself claims to speak out of his understanding in his second speech (20:3). There is therefore a discrepancy between Job 28 and Zophar's view (Job 11 and 20) about human wisdom. This makes it difficult to regard this wisdom poem as Zophar's words. However, Clines rejects this wisdom poem as Job's speech on the assumption that Job's emotions and sayings must remain constant. In fact, as I shall argue, Job may use language that is similar to the friends' viewpoint and contradictory to his own stance elsewhere for special reasons.

In order to resolve the problem of inconsistency of emotion and content between Job 28 and its surrounding contexts, many scholars tend to treat Job 28 as the author's comment, an interlude in the book, instead of viewing it as a speech. Westermann denies this chapter as a speech by any one of the friends or by Job. He claims that chapter 28 in its present position functions as an intermezzo and "it plays the role of a *fermata*, a resting point, while at the same time being the conclusion of the cycles of discourse between the friends and Job."[28] According to Newsom, Job 28 "serves as a sort of meditative interlude, reflecting on the dialogue that precedes it, and preparing for the final section of the book, which will reach its climax in the divine speeches in chapters 38-41."[29] Interestingly enough, among those who treat Job 28 as an interlude, some accept it as an integral part of the book (Westermann, Andersen, Sawyer, Petersen, Newsom, Hartley and Habel),[30] while others do not

---

[27] D. J. A. Clines, *Job 1-20* (WBC; Dallas: Word Books, 1989) lix.
[28] Westermann, *Structure of Job*, 137-8.
[29] Newsom, "Job," 528.
[30] See Westermann, *Structure of Job*, 137-8; F. I. Andersen, *Job: An Introduction and Commentary* (TOTC; Downers Grove: Inter-Varsity Press, 1976) 222-4; J. F. Sawyer, "The Authorship and Structure of the Book of Job," *Studia Biblica 1978, 1: Papers on Old Testament and Related Themes [6th International Congress on Biblical Studies, Oxford, April 1978]* (ed. Elizabeth A. Livingstone; Sheffield: JSOT Press, 1979) 255; M. Petersen, "Job 28: The Theological Center of the Book of Job," *Biblical*

(Dhorme, Gordis and Driver-Gray).³¹ It seems that treating Job 28 as an interlude (the author's comment) is a popular way of resolving the issue of speaker, no matter whether its originality is accepted or not.

Basically, the above scholars, no matter whether they treat Job 28 as integral or not, deny this chapter as Job's speech and consider it as an authorial comment on the ground of its discrepancy in tone and content. Their arguments seem to be based on the common assumption that Job's mood, viewpoint and use of language must remain consistent all along. However, we should not exclude in advance the possibility that Job's emotion and speaking might change at different stages of the story's plot development.

3. *Bringing the Book to a Premature Climax*

The third reason for rejecting Job 28 is that some scholars consider this chapter as an anticipation of the divine speeches. Rowley objects,

> If Job had unaided reached the recognition that the wonders of the world surpassed man's understanding and that the way of wisdom lay in humble submission to God and obedience to him, the Divine irony in the speeches from the whirlwind would scarcely have been called for. If a Chorus had similarly anticipated the divine speeches and enlightened Job and his friends, the Divine speeches would not be the climax of the book.³²

Therefore Job 28 makes the Yahweh speeches an anticlimax. He further adds, "If this chapter is omitted, the Divine speeches, recalling Job from his anguished doctrinaire assumptions to the simple piety he once knew, are understandable."³³

Similarly to Dhorme, Gordis denies Job 28 as an integral part of the book, but believes that this poem is an early work of the same poet because of its affinities of vocabulary and style with the Yahweh speeches.³⁴ Gordis thinks that Job 28 should not be in its present position because it makes the Yahweh speeches anticlimactic, but

---

Viewpoint 29 (1995) 101; Newsom, "Job," 528; Hartley, *Job*, 26-7; and Habel, *Job*, 38-9.
   ³¹ See Dhorme, *Job*, xcvii; and Gordis, *Book of Job*, 298.
   ³² Rowley, *Book of Job*, 179.
   ³³ Rowley, *Book of Job*, 14.
   ³⁴ Gordis, *Book of Job*, 298; and Dhorme, *Job*, li and xcvii.

nor can it be put after the divine speeches. Therefore he suggests that this poem was later inserted into the book by copyists.[35]

To solve the problem of creating an anticlimax, Szczygiel suggests that chapter 28 should be placed after Job's repentance speech (42:2-6). He claims: "es gehört nach 42:6 als weitere Ausführung der rückhaltlosen Hingabe Jobs an Gott."[36] Following Szczygiel, Tur-Sinai also puts Job 28 after 42:6. According to Tur-Sinai, the purpose of Job 28 is to point out that man cannot understand the order of the world and has to trust God's wisdom. Tur-Sinai considers this poem as the answer to the primary question of the Book of Job, while the questions posed in Yahweh's speeches are intended to lead to the answer that man cannot find wisdom. Therefore he regards chapter 28 as the final answer to Job's doubt. In addition, Tur-Sinai also points out that God's utterances in chapters 38-41 seem to be incomplete, because they present questions about God's governance of the world and His struggle with Leviathan, and then break off inconclusively. Therefore he claims that chapter 28 should have been placed at the end of Yahweh's questions to Job (38:1-42:6), "expressing the idea at which the questions are aimed."[37]

In the same vein as Szczygiel and Tur-Sinai, Settlemire also does not accept the present position of Job 28, because of its irrelevance to chapters 27 and 29.[38] In addition, Job 28, preceding the Yahweh speeches, spoils the effect of the divine speeches.[39] She points out that it seems impossible to put this poem after the first Yahweh speech because Job has said that he is not ready to respond (40:4), and Yahweh's ironic tone seems to increase from 40:8-9 onwards.[40] According to Settlemire, 28:28 gives "a literary cue that chapter 28 originally belonged between the end of the poetry and the prose epilogue"[41] because vv.1-27 are in poetry form, but v.28 has a prosaic heading, "And He said to man." She translates כִּי in 28:1 as "for" rather than "surely" so that 28:1 can follow well after 42:6, and 28:

---

[35] Gordis, *Book of Job*, 298.
[36] English translation of Szczygiel's comment is: "It belongs after 42:6 as a further exemplification of Job's unreserved dedication to God." P. Szczygiel, *Das Buch Job* (HSAT; Bonn: Peter Hanstein, 1931) 20.
[37] N. H. Tur-Sinai, *The Book of Job: A New Commentary* (Jerusalem: Kiryath Sepher, 1957) 395.
[38] Settlemire, "The Original Position of Job 28," 299-300.
[39] Settlemire, "The Original Position of Job 28," 300.
[40] Settlemire, "The Original Position of Job 28," 303.
[41] Settlemire, "The Original Position of Job 28," 304.

28 can also flow smoothly into the prose epilogue. Settlemire further justifies her transposition of Job 28 as follows:

> By its position after the Yahweh Speeches, Job is demonstrating in chapter 28 that wisdom has been given to him by God through the encounter with God. Thus, the greatest possible significance is given to the theophany by the demonstration in the Wisdom Poem of Job's new awareness. The man who fears God as he should speak like this. The reader is not left to guess what effect the theophany had on Job's thinking. Job does not have the great wisdom of God, but he has a new comprehension which is a gift of God who has acted on his behalf. Job's problem has been solved.[42]

Similarly to Szczygiel and Tur-Sinai, Settlemire transposes Job 28 right after 42:6 in order to avoid the premature climax caused by the present position of this wisdom poem. Szczygiel, Tur-Sinai and Settlemire rightly see that chapter 28 is not the climax of the book in its present form. But they do not resolve the problem. Even though Szczygiel, Tur-Sinai and Settlemire seek to remove the oddity by transposing Job 28 right after 42:6, this only raises the question how this chapter could have got to its present position. I want to investigate whether the thrust of chapter 28 has a special function which leads to the further motion of the plot development. Therefore this study strives to read chapter 28 as original without displacing it, asking if one can make sense of it in its present setting.

4. *The Problems of 28:28*

The last factor leading to the rejection of Job 28 is the problem of 28:28. Some scholars raise doubts about the authenticity of 28:28 on several grounds: 1) the problem of the introductory formula "And He said to man"; 2) the use of the divine title אֲדֹנָי and 3) the discrepancy between vv.1-27 and v.28.

First, Pope finds that the introductory formula "And He said to man" (וַיֹּאמֶר לָאָדָם) is too short to form a poetic line, and declares it an editorial splice.[43] Verse 28a is considered as a prosaic addition, and the lines in v.28bc seem to be out of balance (9/6).[44] Secondly, Driver-Gray point out that the divine names regularly used in the dialogue (90 occurrences in all of אֱלוֹהַּ, אֵל and שַׁדַּי)[45] do

---

[42] Settlemire, "The Original Position of Job 28," 312-3.
[43] Pope, *Job*, 206.
[44] Driver and Gray, *Book of Job*, 245; and Hartley, *Job*, 383, n.3.
[45] Driver and Gray, *Book of Job*, xxxv and xlii.

not occur in Job 28, while אֲדֹנָי is used only once, in Job 28:28, occurring nowhere else in the book.[46] Thirdly, some scholars reject 28:28 because they find that the theme of how man can gain wisdom in v.28 seems to contradict the theme of wisdom's inaccessibility in vv.1-27. Pope considers v.28 as "an antidote to the agnostic tenor of the preceding poem."[47] Dhorme treats this verse as a later addition to bring a practical conclusion.[48] Westermann regards it as "a secondary and deliberately corrective addition."[49] Geller comments that v.28 was added to distract the reader from the unorthodox message of the chapter.[50]

In regard to Pope's argument about the introductory formula "And He said to man" (וַיֹּאמֶר לָאָדָם), Gordis correctly argues that it is an anacrusis, standing outside the meter. Similar cases can be seen in other Old Testament books, for instance Psalm 1:1, 4; 50:16 and Proverbs 4:4.[51] Habel also rightly points out that אָמַר (say) has been used in the preceding verses of the deep, sea, Abaddon and death in 28:14 and 28:22. Therefore it is not a problem to have this verb.

Concerning Driver-Gray's point about the divine name אֲדֹנָי being used only once in 28:28 and nowhere else in the book as evidence to deny the authenticity of Job 28, Settlemire correctly responds:

> It is difficult to follow their logic at this point since they view verse 28 as an addition to chapter 28. Therefore, if 28:1-27 is by an entirely different hand than 28:28, the use of any word which appears in verse 28 should not be considered in discussing the style of the author of chapter 28. If, however, this verse is a quotation then no elements of the author's style in general or vocabulary in particular should be expected to occur here even though the author was the one responsible for including this quotation at the end of the poem.[52]

As regards the use of the divine title אֲדֹנָי instead of Yahweh, it may be the poet's tactic to remind the reader that Yahweh is God's name

---

[46] Driver and Gray, *Book of Job*, 232. See also Pope, *Job*, 206.
[47] Pope, *Job*, 206.
[48] Dhorme, *Job*, li, 414.
[49] Westermann, *Structure of Job*, 138, n.5.
[50] S. A. Geller, "'Where is Wisdom?': A Literary Study of Job 28 in Its Settings," *Judaic Perspectives on Ancient Israel* (ed. J. Neusner, Baruch A. Levine and Ernest S. Frerichs; Philadelphia: Fortress Press, 1987) 174-5.
[51] Gordis, *Book of Job*, 538.
[52] Settlemire, "The Original Position of Job 28," 297.

without explicitly using it.⁵³ Habel rightly states: "Not only does the new title produce a striking contrast with the titles which have preceded, it allows the listening audience to hear a veiled reference to the name of Yahweh in that title because of their familiarity with the idiom 'the fear of Yahweh' (cf. Prov 10:27; 14:26, 27)."⁵⁴

Concerning the resolution to the discrepancy between the inaccessibility of wisdom in vv.1-27 and the availability of wisdom in v.28, two interpretations are noteworthy: a) there are two kinds of wisdom (Gordis and Whybray); and b) there are two modes of acquiring wisdom (Hartley, Newsom and Fiddes).⁵⁵

As for the first interpretation, Gordis defines "wisdom with a definite article" in vv.12 and 20 as wisdom of a higher order, which is accessible only to God; and defines "wisdom without a definite article" in v.28 as wisdom of a lower order, which is practical to human beings.⁵⁶

As far as 28:28 is concerned, Whybray claims that this verse does not contradict the rest of the chapter, but confirms it. He comments: "This verse indicates that much of the previous discussion has been misguided because it has not distinguished between human and divine wisdom."⁵⁷ According to Whybray, although God alone possesses divine wisdom, He has given human beings another kind of wisdom, which is practical through piety.

Basically, both Gordis and Whybray seek to resolve the difference between vv.1-27 and v.28 by defining two kinds of wisdom. Concurring with Whybray, I think that 28:28 does not contradict 28:1-27, but confirms it. However, in disagreement with both Gordis and Whybray, I view wisdom as of only one kind rather than two different kinds.

Following the second interpretation, Hartley states that the wisdom available to human beings is qualitatively the same as the wisdom God knows. He considers the "wisdom" in vv.1-27 and v.28 as the same kind of "wisdom." However, the "wisdom" without the definite article in v.28 is the practical side of wisdom that mankind can obtain.⁵⁸ To explain the contradiction between the inaccessibility of wisdom in vv.1-27 and the availability of wisdom in v.28,

---

[53] Hartley, *Job*, 383, n.2.
[54] Habel, *Job*, 401.
[55] Habel, *Job*, 401.
[56] Gordis, *Book of Job*, 539, Special Note 24.
[57] Whybray, *Job*, 21.
[58] Hartley, *Job*, 383-4.

Newsom views v.28 as a parallel with vv.25-27. "Fear of the Lord" and "turning from evil" in relation to humans parallel with "giving weight to the wind" and "setting a limit for the rain" in relation to God. Newsom also points out the two modes of gaining wisdom:

> God's acts are cosmos-creating acts, and God perceives and establishes wisdom in the midst of that activity. The human actions of true piety—fearing God and turning from evil—those too are acts of creation. They are cosmos-creating acts, not as acts of physical creation but as acts of moral creation. Humankind cannot find wisdom by searching for it as though it could be mined or purchased. One cannot possess wisdom; one can only embody it.[59]

In brief, according to the second interpretation, the difference between v.28 and vv.1-27 is due to the different modes by which wisdom can be acquired. That is to say, God gains eternal wisdom directly through His discovery in the act of creation, while human beings gain wisdom indirectly through submission to God.[60]

To account for the tension between the inaccessibility and availability of wisdom, Fiddes notably points out that God knows the way to wisdom because of His perfect knowledge and total vision of the vast creation. Wisdom is hidden to human beings, not because of the transcendence of wisdom, but because of the expansiveness, complexity and inexhaustibility of the world order, which are beyond human understanding. The primary meaning of the "fear of God" (v.28) is humility in the midst of all human calculations.[61] Humanity cannot find wisdom as only God is great enough to possess it. Therefore humans can only access wisdom by fearing God. God has determined it shall be so, hence "And He said to man, 'Behold, the fear of the Lord, that is wisdom; and to depart from evil is understanding.'"

Habel rightly points out the function of 28:28.[62] He maintains that Job 28 serves as a bridge between chapters 3-27 and chapters 29-31, and that 28:28 links with 1:1, forming an inclusio.[63] Accord-

---

[59] Newsom, "Job," 533.

[60] This is Habel's summary of the second interpretation. See Habel, *Job*, 401.

[61] P. S. Fiddes, "Where Shall Wisdom be Found? Job 28 as a Riddle for Ancient and Modern Readers," *After the Exile: Essays in Honour of Rex Mason* (ed. John Barton and David J. Reimer; Macon: Mercer University Press, 1996) 171-90.

[62] Despite my disagreement with Habel's point that Job 28 is an interlude or authorial comment instead of Job's speech, his insight about the function of Job 28:28 needs to be acknowledged. However, in contrast to Habel, this study seeks to demonstrate how Job 28 makes sense as Job's words in its context.

[63] Habel, *Job*, 38-9.

ing to Habel, the poet wants to show that the traditional orthodox answer in 28:28 is not acceptable to Job. Job no longer wants to seek traditional wisdom through piety, but to seek God and confront Him face to face. That is why right after 28:28 Job launches into a series of avowals of innocence to challenge God in chapters 29-31.[64]

Conclusion
I find the approaches to the issues of Job 28 discussed above unsatisfactory because: 1) they cannot convincingly explain the abrupt shifts of tone and content from Job 27 to Job 28, and then to Job 29-31; and 2) they tend to avoid difficulties caused by the contradictions between Job 28 and its surrounding context. Therefore a new approach is necessary.

III. *The Approach of This Study*

Those who reject Job 28 as Job's words all hold the same assumption that Job's language, ideas and emotion must remain consistent all the way through. But it may be that for special reasons Job uses language and ideas which are quite like his friends' rather than his predominant argument's. Despite the similarities between Job 28 and Job 38-41, I believe that Job 28 does not make the rest of the book an anti-climax. In fact, these scholars fail to realise the special rhetorical function of Job's saying in Job 28 within its surrounding context.

The hypothesis of this study is that Job's viewpoint, emotion and use of language do not necessarily remain constant all the way through the story. In addition, Job 28 is viewed as Job's words and also an integral part of the book. In fact, Job 28 is not the first time that Job uses contradictory sayings. Indeed, there is a series of Job's contradictory sayings in the third speech cycle, namely Job 23; 24:1-17 to Job 24:18-24 (25); Job 25 to Job 26; and Job 27:1-12 to Job 27:13-23. Similarly to the issues of Job 28, such contradictory juxtapositions in the third cycle have caused many scholars to consider that the third speech cycle has undergone dislocations. However, I would see such contradictory juxtapositions as part of the author's

---

[64] Habel, *Job*, 39, 392-3.

rhetorical strategy, designed to engage his audience in order to make a rhetorical impact upon: 1) the flow of argument in the story; and 2) the audience.

Concerning the rhetorical impact upon the flow of argument, Patrick-Scult state:

> Rhetoric...is an inherent function of language use: Any author must necessarily shape his or her language in one way rather than another, and insofar as we may assume artful deliberateness on the author's part, the shape and form of the discourse is an indication of how he or she means for us to take the message. It is thus through a text's rhetoric that a modern interpreter can recapture the possibilities for encounter the particular text holds.[65]

Therefore this study seeks to examine how Job's contradictory sayings in Job 22-31 hang together as part of the author's rhetorical strategy to transmit his thought through a text (the story of Job), and communicate a message. Before exploring the intended impact upon the audience, the first and foremost thing to do is to understand how Job's contradictory sayings contribute to the thrust of the story itself (i.e. the flow of the argument), because the text is the means of communication between the author and audience. This is the first level of rhetorical analysis.

In regard to the rhetorical impact upon the audience, Patrick-Scult further point out, "Rhetoric is that quality of discourse which does not allow it to 'stand still'; rather, it gives the discourse a voice which moves outward and gives it the capacity to address audiences, both immediate and more distant in time and place."[66] Furthermore, "Rhetoric is communication with a purpose, the purpose of persuasion, that is, moving the will by speech or by the written word. Thus it is no mere communication of knowledge. It aims at agreement and consensus."[67] Therefore Job's contradictory sayings in Job 22-31 serve as a rhetorical strategy to persuade the audience along the flow of argument in the story to adopt the author's evaluative points of view. Investigating how the author guides the audience to adopt his evaluative points of view is the second level of rhetorical analysis.

---

[65] D. Patrick and A. Scult, "Rhetorical Criticism and Biblical Exegesis," *Rhetoric and Biblical Interpretation* (JSOTSup 82; Sheffield: The Almond Press, 1990) 13.

[66] Patrick and Scult, "Rhetorical Criticism and Biblical Exegesis," 16.

[67] T. A. Lenchak, *"Choose Life!" A Rhetorical Critical Investigation of Deuteronomy 28,69-30,20* (Roma: Editrice Pontificio Istituto Biblico, 1993) 45.

A. *Definition and Advantage of Rhetorical Criticism*

Methodologically, some of the theories of rhetorical criticism will be applied in this study. Rhetorical criticism as a methodology for the study of the Hebrew Bible was first introduced by James Muilenburg in his 1968 Presidential Address to the Society of Biblical Literature, entitled "Form Criticism and Beyond."[68] The term "Muilenburg School" refers to a variety of works written by the students of Muilenburg throughout the 1970s and early 1980s. These writings make special reference to Muilenburg's "Form Criticism and Beyond" as a basis for discussing rhetoric or rhetorical criticism in the Hebrew Bible. Basically, the rhetorical criticism of Muilenburg and the "Muilenburg School" is mainly focused upon the stylistics of Hebrew prose and poetry.[69]

However, the recent trend of rhetorical criticism goes beyond the scope of descriptive study of stylistics, and seeks to explore the practical persuasive power of the texts in influencing action. Kennedy comments, "The identification of rhetoric with style...represents a limitation and to some extent a distortion of the discipline of rhetoric."[70] He regards rhetoric as "that quality in discourse by which a speaker or writer seeks to accomplish his purpose."[71] He further adds that rhetorical criticism looks at the text "from the point of view of the author's or editor's intent, the unified results, and how it would be perceived by an audience of near contemporaries."[72] Therefore, according to Kennedy, the focus of rhetorical criticism is not the study of descriptive stylistics, but the examination of practical persuasion upon the audience.[73] The rhetorical criticism employed in this study thus seeks to investigate the practical persuasion upon the audience rather than the descriptive stylistics of the texts.

My work is different from van der Lugt's *Rhetorical Criticism and*

---

[68] J. Muilenburg, "Form Criticism and Beyond," *Beyond Form Criticism: Essays in Old Testament Literary Criticism* (ed. Paul R. House; Winona Lake: Eisenbrauns, 1992) 49-69.
[69] T. B. Dozeman, "Old Testament Rhetorical Criticism," *ABD 5* (ed. D. N. Freeman et al.; New York: Doubleday, 1992) 712-5.
[70] G. A. Kennedy, *New Testament Interpretation Through Rhetorical Criticism* (Chapel Hill: University of North Carolina Press, 1984) 3.
[71] Kennedy, *NT Interpretation*, 3.
[72] Kennedy, *NT Interpretation*, 4.
[73] Concerning Kennedy's point, see also Dozeman, "Old Testament Rhetorical Criticism," 715.

the Poetry of the Book of Job.[74] Based on his understanding of poetic units and their identifying characteristics, van der Lugt advances a new theory about the speech cycles of the Book of Job. Rejecting the usual interpretation of Job 3-27 as three cycles of speeches by Job and his three friends, van der Lugt reconstructs the book as follows: the introduction in chapter 3; the first two cycles in chapters 4-14 and 15-26; then the third cycle in chapters 27-31 and 38-41; and Job's answer in 42:1-6 as its conclusion. The criteria of van der Lugt's study rest almost exclusively upon the theory of poetics and linguistics. Crenshaw has made this remark: "The entire discussion has a decidedly conservative theological bent..."[75] Obviously, van der Lugt's investigation is only "a total theory of stylistics."[76] Differently from van der Lugt's work, this study focuses upon the practical persuasive power of the texts in eliciting a transformed world view, rather than the stylistic description of the texts.

Although this study mainly focuses upon the practical persuasion upon the audience, it is not like some schools of reader-response criticism, which seek to interpret meaning in ways that encompass all of the possible effects that a text may have on those who read it in any different situation or context. In this study special attention will be paid to the author's intent and the text itself, which will in turn serve as crucial binding forces to constrain the freedom of interpreting the impact upon the audience. Fiore defines rhetorical criticism as follows:

> Rhetorical (or pragmatic) criticism considers a work of art chiefly as a means to an end, as a vehicle of communication and interaction between the author and the audience, and investigates the use of traditional devices to produce an effect in an audience. It is an internal criticism that focuses on the rhetoric of the text itself, but also works outward to considerations of author, audience, and their interrelationships.[77]

As mentioned above, rhetorical criticism seeks a balance of the in-

---

[74] P. van der Lugt, *Rhetorical Criticism and the Poetry of the Book of Job* (Leiden; New York; Köln: Brill, 1995).

[75] J. L. Crenshaw, "Book Review: Rhetorical Criticism and the Poetry of the Book of Job," *JBL* 116 (1997) 344.

[76] Crenshaw, "Book Review: Rhetorical Criticism and the Poetry of the Book of Job," 344.

[77] B. Fiore, "NT Rhetoric and Rhetorical Criticism," *ABD* 5 (ed. D. N. Freedman et al.; New York: Doubleday, 1992) 716.

terrelationships among the author, audience and the text.[78] Patrick-Scult point out: "Of course, the auditors are free to interpret the language of the discourse in any way they wish, but the speaker or author attempts to constrain that freedom and direct interpretation by giving the audience cues and indicators as to how he or she means the discourse to function for them."[79] Gitay expresses a similar view:

> Rhetorical study is a pragmatic method of analysis that integrates the three dimensions of a literary work: the author, the text itself, and the audience. The author/speaker establishes his or her thematic goal through the transmission of his or her thought into a text (speech). The listener's/reader's situation, ways of perception, and set of mind are also taken into consideration by the author/speaker. The discourse is structured and shaped thematically and stylistically in order to capture the audience's interest.... Rhetorical analysis reveals the speaker's strategy of appealing to or mastering the audience's mind.[80]

Therefore it is impossible to figure out correctly the intended rhetorical impact upon the audience without taking the author's intent and the text into serious consideration. Rhetorical criticism has an advantage of keeping a balanced relationship among the author, audience and text.

Another advantage of rhetorical criticism is its compatibility with other methodologies. Walton rightly points out that rhetorical criticism "provides *an* interpretative key, but not *the* interpretative key. In other words, it yields its most useful results when used in conjunction with other approaches..."[81] Renz also states: "rhetorical criticism is an approach rather than a method, or rather, that it is an approach in which several methods are applied. Rhetorical critics make the decision to look at a text as part of an act of communica-

---

[78] Thomas Renz also seeks to find the balanced interrelationships between author, audience and text. See T. Renz, *The Rhetorical Function of the Book of Ezekiel* (Leiden; Boston; Köln: Brill, 1999). He rightly points out that different scholars of rhetorical criticism have different degrees of focus on any one of these three elements. For example, James Muilenburg focuses on authorial intent in his "Form Criticism and Beyond." Phyllis Trible focuses on text in her *Rhetorical Criticism: Context, Method, and the Book of Jonah*. Dale Patrick and Allen Scult have special concern with reader response in their *Rhetoric and Biblical Interpretation*.

[79] Patrick and Scult, "Rhetorical Criticism and Biblical Exegesis," 15.

[80] Y. Gitay, "Rhetorical Criticism," *To Each Its Own Meaning: An Introduction to Biblical Criticisms and Their Application* (ed. Steven L. McKenzie and Stephen R. Haynes; Louisville: Westminster/John Knox Press, 1993) 136.

[81] S. Walton, "Rhetorical Criticism: An Introduction," *Themelios* 21 (1996) 6.

tion and to focus on the elements of persuasion in this act. Their approach is fed by many sources."[82] Therefore rhetorical criticism is a flexible approach that can adopt other approaches to help illuminate the communicative situation of texts. In this study rhetorical criticism is used in combination with narrative criticism. Normally "narrative criticism" is applied to narrative as a genre distinct from poetry. But here "narrative" is used in a different, broader sense, which defines "narrative" as "any work of literature that tells a story."[83] The Book of Job is a narrative in this broader sense. Therefore the devices used in narrative criticism are essential for the audience to understand the meaning of this text.

B. *The Argument of This Study*

In Chapter Two the main focus will be upon how Job 28 fits into the whole book. First, contrasting with the historical-critical, the structuralist and the deconstructionist approaches to the Book of Job, this study argues that Job 28 stands within the plot development of Job. Through the investigation of the plot development and Job's characterization, it shows how Job 28 can be read as Job's words and as an integral part of the book.

Secondly, this study proceeds to demonstrate that Job 28 relates to the rhetorical situation of the whole book, through the examination of the exigency, audience and constraint of the book.

Thirdly, it continues to show how Job 28 functions within the rhetorical strategy of the whole book. The author reveals his evaluative viewpoints to the audience by using the strategy of "from less to more adequate perspectives,"[84] which first exposes the inadequacy of the friends' perspective (the limit of theodicies) through Job's arguments from contradictory experience of reality, and then proceeds to disclose the inadequacy of Job's perspective (his misconceptions of God) through God's correction and instruction in the whirlwind. This is how the audience is directed from less adequate to more adequate perspectives throughout the book. Contradictory juxtapositions within the context of Job 28 (chs. 22-31) are part of

---

[82] Renz, *Rhetorical Function of Ezekiel*, 11. Renz stresses that literary approach forms the basis for a rhetorical analysis (p.8). He also points out the legitimacy and importance of form criticism in his study (pp.5, 12-14).

[83] M. A. Powell, *What Is Narrative Criticism?* (Minneapolis: Fortress Press, 1990) 23.

[84] I borrow this term from Newsom. See Newsom, "Job," 337.

the rhetorical strategy to expose the friends' inadequate perspective by highlighting the contradictions between traditional theology and actual experience.

In short, Chapter Two aims at arguing that Job 28 is Job's speech and can be understood in terms of the unity of the book. This chapter demonstrates that: 1) Job 28 is within the plot development of the story; 2) it relates to the rhetorical situation of the book; and 3) it is within the author's whole plan of rhetorical strategies to resolve the exigency.

Chapter Three mainly focuses on how Job 28 fits into the context of Job 22-31. Contradictory juxtaposition is the common structure knitting Job 28 and its surrounding chapters together. In this chapter we will investigate the rhetorical impacts of contradictory juxtapositions in Job 22-31 at the two levels of rhetorical analysis: 1) the flow of argument in the story; and 2) the audience. But before that, the methodology of how to detect the author's intended impact upon the audience will be examined. After discussing the rhetorical functions of the contradictory juxtapositions within Job 22-31 unit by unit at two different levels of rhetorical analysis, a conclusion will be drawn to show how Job 28 connects with Job 22-31 and the Yahweh speeches.

Basically, this study demonstrates how Job 28 functions within the whole book, and more specifically within the context of chapters 22-31.

CHAPTER TWO

JOB 28 IN THE WHOLE BOOK

I. *Incongruities in the Book of Job*

Polzin states: "Few books in the Old Testament have discrepancy and contradiction so central to their makeup as the Book of Job."[1] In Chapter One it has been shown that some scholars call into question the originality of Job 28 because they find that Job's sayings in this poem contradict Job's preceding speeches and the subsequent oath of innocence (Job 29-31) in terms of the content and tone of utterance. Similar to the case of Job 28, there is a great variety of incongruities and inconsistencies throughout the Book of Job. Such discrepancies have aroused many scholars' suspicions about the unity of the book.[2]

To start with, the prose section which contains both the prologue (chs. 1-2) and the epilogue (42:7-17) seems to be inconsistent with the poetic section of the book (3:1-42:6). One striking difference is that Job is depicted as a patient sufferer in the prologue, but as a verbose complainer in the dialogue. It has therefore been argued that the prose was written much earlier than the poetic section.[3]

In addition, the third speech cycle is considered to have suffered dislocations. Concerning the pattern of the speeches in the first two cycles, each of the three friends alternates with Job in the dialogue,

---

[1] R. M. Polzin, "The Framework of the Book of Job," *Int* 28 (1974) 182.
[2] For the detailed literary issues of the book, see Hartley, *Job*, 20-33; and Clines, *Job 1-20*, lvi-lix.
[3] Concerning this point, Clines rightly points out that Job's characterization shifts from a patient sufferer to a verbose complainer, simply because "it is dramatically satisfying that Job should change from his initial acceptance of his suffering to a violent questioning of it..." Clines also comments that the prologue-epilogue cannot be an independent whole. The introduction of the three friends (2:11-13) is to prepare for the subsequent development of the speech cycles. God's reprimand (42:7-8) does not make sense unless the three friends had spoken something wrong in the dialogue. If they merely remained silent and showed their sympathy with Job, Job would not have made atonement for them. Clines argues that the authors of the prologue-epilogue and of the dialogue are one and the same poet. See Clines, *Job 1-20*, lvii-lviii.

and the lengths of their speeches are more or less equal. However, the total silence of Zophar, the brevity of Bildad's speech (Job 25) and the contradictory sayings of Job (24:1-17 and 24:18-24 [25]; 26:1-4 and 26:5-14; 27:1-12 and 27:13-23) in the third cycle have caused many scholars to consider that this cycle has undergone some disruptions.[4]

The Elihu speeches are frequently regarded as a later addition. One reason is that Elihu is not mentioned in either the prologue or the epilogue.[5] Furthermore, Elihu adds nothing new to the theology of the three friends.[6] Therefore many scholars question the authenticity of chapters 32-37.

Concerning the Yahweh speeches, Driver-Gray deny the authenticity of the Behemoth and Leviathan sections (40:15-24; 40:25-41:26 [41:1-34]) on the following grounds: 1) the depiction of the beasts is much longer than the description of the animals in the first Yahweh speech; 2) the question form in this section is less frequently

---

[4] See Habel, *Job*, 37-8; Hartley, *Job*, 24-6; and Gordis, *Book of Job*, 531-6, Special Note 19, 20 and 21. Rowley has given a long list of reconstructions of the third cycle; see H. H. Rowley, "The Book of Job and Its Meaning," *BJRL* 41 (1958) 118-9.

[5] Clines also admits that the evidence showing the Elihu speeches as secondary is very strong. However, he carefully adds, "but it is nevertheless something of a difficulty to understand how an author wishing to expand the Book of Job would have inserted Elihu's speeches as chaps. 32-37 but failed to insert Elihu's name in chap. 42. Whatever the origin of the Elihu material, the interpreter of the book must of course come to terms with the shape of the book as we have received it, and must, if at all possible, explain the significance of Elihu's intervention..."; Clines, *Job 1-20*, lviii-lix. See also Hartley, *Job*, 28-30; Gordis, *Book of Job*, 546-53, Special Note 28; and Habel, *Job*, 36-7. Whybray argues that Elihu is better seen as a transitional figure. The lack of reference to Elihu in the epilogue is mainly because he has no further role to play in the author's scheme, just like the total disappearance of the satan. See Whybray, *Job*, 22-3.

[6] Habel rightly comments: "The approach of most interpreters has been to focus on the content rather than the context of Elihu's arguments, his thought rather than his function in the structure of the Joban narrative. They have tended to ask the question, 'What is Elihu saying that is new or profound?', rather than, 'What is Elihu doing that is significant in the design of the book?' Theological rather than literary considerations have usually prevailed." See N. C. Habel, "The Role of Elihu in the Design of the Book of Job," *In the Shelter of Elyon: Essays on Ancient Palestinian Life and Literature in Honor of G. W. Ahlström* (ed. W. Boyd Barrick and John R. Spencer; Sheffield: JSOT Press, 1984) 81-98, p.81. Habel argues that Elihu plays an important role in the design of the book of Job. According to Habel, Elihu acts as an arbiter. He appears to respond to Job's request for an arbiter to handle his case (31:35-37, 40c). For the details, see Habel, "The Role of Elihu."; and Habel, *Job*, 443-7.

used than in the first speech; 3) the frequent use of questions in the first speech has brought forth a sense of vividness, which is not obvious in the second speech; 4) the first speech describes the habits, actions and temper of the animals, while the second speech depicts the bodily parts of the beasts; 5) if the Behemoth and Leviathan are Egyptian animals (the hippopotamus and the crocodile respectively) or mythical monsters, they are different from the actual Palestinian animals described in the first speech; and 6) the two sections are linguistically and stylistically different.[7] The differences between the first and the second Yahweh speeches have prompted some scholars, like Driver-Gray and Westermann,[8] to conclude that there was originally only one Yahweh speech, which had attracted many additions until a later editor put it into two speeches.

To be sure, this study mainly focuses upon the function of Job 28 within the context of Job 22-31. However, the relationship between Job 28 and its nearest context cannot clearly and correctly be seen unless we have a panoramic view of the whole book. More importantly, the approach to the issue of Job 28 and other discrepancies of the rest of the book will decisively affect our conclusion about the function of Job 28 in its context. Therefore this study seeks to argue that the full significance of Job 28 cannot be seen unless we see it in the context of the whole book.

This chapter of the study is divided into three sections. In the first section three different approaches to the Book of Job—the historical-critical approach, the structuralist approach and the deconstructionist approach— will be investigated and the inadequacy of these

---

[7] Driver and Gray, *Book of Job*, 351-2. Gordis comments on Driver-Gray's grounds as follows: "Basically, these objections derive from a mechanical approach to the material. They fail to reckon with the poetic talents of the poet, who would utilize every resource available to him in order to introduce variety and avoid the cardinal sin of monotony"; Gordis, *Book of Job*, 567-8, Special Note 36, p.567. See also Hartley, *Job*, 30-3. Hartley also defends the two Yahweh speeches as integral parts of the book. He points out that the reason for two Yahweh speeches is that they address different issues. He states: "The first speech counters Job's accusation that Yahweh fails to administer the world justly, and the second speech challenges Job to surrender his case before the all-powerful ruler of the cosmos." (pp.32-3).

[8] Westermann, *Structure of Job*, 105-23. Using form-critical analysis, Westermann claims that a theophany, by its unique nature, can only have a single speech. If two speeches were delivered by Yahweh, each should have brought forth new ideas and a new sequence of events. He regards 40:15-24 and 41:4-26 [41:12-34] as later additions because the descriptive style in these two sections is quite different from the interrogative style of the Yahweh speech.

approaches to deal with the contradictions in the book will be discussed. Highlighting the significance of reading Job as an overall unity, the second section demonstrates how Job 28 fits within the plot design of the whole book. Beneath the surface incongruities throughout the book, this study seeks to demonstrate an underlying coherence which links Job 28 and the rest of the book together. Then the third section proceeds to show how Job 28 relates to the rhetorical situation of the book, which is the context or circumstance prompting the rhetor to tell the story of Job. Finally, the last section underscores how the rhetorical strategy used in Job 28 links with the author's overall rhetorical strategy in the book. That is to say, this chapter aims at viewing Job 28 within the book as a whole.

II. *Different Approaches to the Incongruities*

A. *The Historical-Critical Approach*

Seitz summarizes two major features of the historical-critical approach to the discrepancies of the Book of Job.[9] The first feature is to show the multilayered nature of Job. There is an historical-critical consensus regarding the nature of the book: that it is made up of various constituent parts. Basically, there are five constituent-pieces:[10] 1) the prologue-epilogue (chs. 1-2; 42:7-17); 2) the dialogue (chs. 3-27; 29-31); 3) the Yahweh speeches (chs. 38-42:6); 4) the Elihu speeches (chs. 32-37); and 5) the wisdom poem (ch. 28). In regard to how the notion of constituent parts resolves the issues of inconsistencies, Seitz makes the following remark: "Up to this point, it would appear that observations about the constituent nature of Job are theologically neutral. One could take issue with the notion of constituence only if it led to the suggestion that this or that section was secondary to a whole, otherwise unified book, or if the theological validity of the book depended on its having been composed by one individual."[11]

---

[9] C. R. Seitz, "Job: Full-Structure, Movement, and Interpretation," *Int* 43 (1989) 6-9.

[10] See the discussions in Seitz, "Job: Full-Structure, Movement, and Interpretation," 6-8; Hartley, *Job*, 20-33; Pope, *Job*, xxiii-xxx; Rowley, *Book of Job*, 8-18; and Good, *In Turns of Tempest*, 5-9.

[11] Seitz, "Job: Full-Structure, Movement, and Interpretation," 7.

The second feature is related to the compositional development of Job. It examines how these different constituent parts developed chronologically into the present text.[12] In the historical-critical treatment of Joban development, there is a consensus over the composition of the book. It is summarized as follows:[13]

1. An old folktale once existed and presented the ancient heroic Job as a patient sufferer. It formed the prologue-epilogue prose (chs. 1-2; 42:7-17).
2. Using the folktale as the narrative framework, a poet inserted the poetic dialogue between the three friends and Job (chs. 3-27; 29-31). The patient-Job episode was replaced by a much longer rebuttal, in which Job was portrayed as an impatient sufferer.
3. There then came the conversation between Yahweh and Job (38:1-42:6).
4. Next the Elihu speeches (chs. 32-37) were inserted.
5. The wisdom poem (ch. 28) was later added between chapters 3-27 and chapters 29-31.
6. During the transmission of the text, the third speech cycle had undergone dislocations. Zophar's final speech was missing. Bildad's final speech in Job 25 became too brief. However, Job's words were extraordinarily long and his standpoints were similar to the friends' arguments, which Job used to strongly oppose. Therefore it was believed that the third cycle had been in disarray.
7. Other trivial variations took place during the transmission of the text, for instance, the alteration of spelling, the correction of suspected mistakes, the loss or addition of some words and so on.

Clinging to this hypothesis, some scholars consider the Book of Job as the work of a single author over different stages of his life (e.g. Gordis and Snaith).[14] Some scholars claim that the book is a collec-

---

[12] Seitz, "Job: Full-Structure, Movement, and Interpretation," 8-9.

[13] A seven-stage hypothesis of composition of Job is examined in Andersen, *Job*, 41-55; and a simplified four-stage hypothesis of composition is summarized in Good, *In Turns of Tempest*, 8-9.

[14] Snaith claims that the author of Job presented his work in three editions: 1) the shortened prologue plus the shortened epilogue, i.e. without the three friends, Job's soliloquy, Yahweh's speeches with an apology and a submission of Job; 2) the present prologue, the present epilogue, the three friends, the miscellaneous pieces in chs. 24-28 and all the poetic pieces of the first edition; and 3) the book

tion of different independent pieces from different authors (e.g. Irwin).[15] Some scholars maintain that the bulk of the book was composed by the author, but as time passed other people added to it (e.g. Rowley).[16]

Seitz rightly points out the major problem with this developmental theory: that it just focuses on a simplistic view of Job, suffering and rewards. However, it does not "touch the difficult view of God that pervades all levels of tradition in the present book."[17] Greenberg states: "Reversal and subversion prevail throughout—in sudden shifts of mood and role and in a rhetoric of sarcasm and irony. The dialogue contains much response and reaction but no predictable or consistent course of argument."[18] In regard to the literary issues in the third speech cycle, expectations of simplicity, consistency and linearity characterize historical-critical scholars' presuppositions. In order to make the pattern of the third cycle similar to the first two cycles, and in order to keep Job consistently impatient and "unorthodox," reconstruction becomes a common approach. Therefore these scholars try to redistribute the speeches, so that Zophar has something to say and Job refrains from saying things that are considered inappropriate in his mouth (24:18-24; 26:5-14; 27:13-23; ch. 28).[19]

In Chapter One we saw how scholars deal with the discrepancy of Job 28 in its context. According to Good, 95 per cent of writers on Job come to the conclusion that Job 28 is not part of the original dialogue.[20] The way in which scholars deal with the incongru-

---

as it now stands, with the Elihu speeches inserted at the end of the dialogue and before the divine speeches. See N. H. Snaith, *The Book of Job: Its Origin and Purpose* (Studies in Biblical Theology; London: SCM Press, 1968) 8, 10. For Gordis' standpoint, see R. Gordis, *The Book of God and Man: A Study of Job* (Chicago: The University of Chicago Press, 1965) 100-3, 110-2, 209-15; and also Hartley, *Job*, 20.

[15] W. A. Irwin, "Job," *Peake's Commentary on the Bible* (Revised edition; ed. M. Black and H. H. Rowley; London: Thomas Nelson and Sons, 1962) 391; and Hartley, *Job*, 20.

[16] Rowley concludes that the original structure of the book was as follows: the prologue, Job's opening soliloquy, three cycles of speeches, Job's closing soliloquy, the first Yahweh speech, Job's submission (two parts joined together) and the epilogue. He considers chapter 28, the Elihu speeches and the second Yahweh speech as secondary additions. See Rowley, *Book of Job*, 17-8.

[17] Seitz, "Job: Full-Structure, Movement, and Interpretation," 9.

[18] M. Greenberg, "Job," *The Literary Guide to the Bible* (ed. Robert Alter and Frank Kermode; London: Fontana Press, 1997) 283.

[19] Seitz, "Job: Full-Structure, Movement, and Interpretation," 9.

[20] Good, *In Turns of Tempest*, 183.

ity of Job 28 is the same way in which they deal with other incongruities in the rest of the book, as mentioned above. For the historical-critical approach, there are two common ways to resolve incoherence.[21] The first is to remove the parts of the incoherence which originated at different times and places. The second is to change whatever makes a text incoherent in order to restore the coherent "original." The criterion that "the text means only what it used to mean"[22] has prompted many historical-critical scholars to trim the so-called secondary additions, like Job 28, the Elihu speeches and so on. This severely damages the message of the text.

Good has noticed historical-critical scholars' common presupposition that a text must be coherent all the way through, criticizing them as follows: "Incoherence is incompatible with the notion, derived from our entire tradition, that by definition a text is the coherent presentation of an author's views on something."[23] As mentioned in Chapter One, most commentators regard Job 28 as an independent poem to smooth the contradiction in its context. Good rightly comments that scholars who consider this poem an interpolation simply try to point out the unsuitability of its placement, but not the reason for its present position as the text stands. In this way denying the originality of a text becomes an adequate reason for them not to say anything about its presence.[24] Good interestingly remarks:

> That seems to me a pseudo-historical answer to a historical question. Because the "original" book supposedly did not contain the poem, people who hold this view of texts find it self-evidently stupid that someone inserted it. But if the historian's task is to explain historical change, to satisfy oneself with merely noting historical change ("This poem was not present in the original Book of Job") is to do only half of the historian's task ("This poem is now present in the Book of Job because").[25]

However, Good's comment still does not give the whole picture. In fact, while Childs accepts that various parts of the book are later additions, he also strives to explain why the texts are put together in their present, final shape. As we have seen in the preceding chap-

---

[21] Good, *In Turns of Tempest*, 183.
[22] Good, *In Turns of Tempest*, 177.
[23] Good, *In Turns of Tempest*, 183.
[24] Good, *In Turns of Tempest*, 184.
[25] Good, *In Turns of Tempest*, 184.

ter, Childs points out that Job 28 serves to provide a link between the "patient" Job of the prologue and the "impatient" Job of the dialogue.[26] Despite the fact that Childs still has not fully explained the inconsistency between Job 28 and its surrounding context, his recognition of this issue needs to be acknowledged.

B. *The Structuralist Approach*

As mentioned before, Polzin notes that "Few books in the Old Testament have discrepancy and contradiction so central to their makeup as the Book of Job."[27] Polzin treats Job as a unified work. Commenting upon the source-critical and form-critical approaches to Job, he claims that "Attempts to remove these inconsistencies can be characterized as academic 'failure of nerve' just as the platitudes of Job's friends are a 'failure of nerve' in the face of Job's problems. By removing the book's inconsistencies, some scholars have succeeded in removing its message."[28] Polzin adds: "Such attempts at analysis seem to me ultimately to destroy the message(s) of the book and moreover make impossible the first step toward understanding how, in its present form, it has affected men so profoundly down through the ages."[29]

According to Polzin, "A central concern of the book can be expressed in terms of a contradiction between what a member of society should believe and what he actually experiences."[30] Polzin figures out three major contradictions in the book. The first one concerns the words and actions of Job. After the Yahweh speeches (chs. 38-41), Job affirms what he denies in the dialogue (in total 18 chapters): although he still does not understand it, God must reward the good and punish the evil. On the other hand, after the vision of God Job denies what he affirms for all these chapters in the dialogue: his own experience of innocence and God's injustice.[31] The second inconsistency focuses upon Job's friends. They affirm the doctrine of divine retribution for 10 chapters, but after God's words in 42:7-8 they sacrifice to God "for not speaking of Him what is right" and God accepts their recanting. What the friends affirmed before the

---

[26] Childs, *Introduction to the Old Testament*, 542-3.
[27] Polzin, "The Framework of the Book of Job," 182.
[28] Polzin, "The Framework of the Book of Job," 183.
[29] Polzin, "The Framework of the Book of Job," 186.
[30] Polzin, "The Framework of the Book of Job," 184.
[31] Polzin, "The Framework of the Book of Job," 184.

vision of God, they deny after it.[32] The third inconsistency is that some of God's words sound contradictory to His actions. His statement that Job is right and his friends are wrong in 42:7 seems to contradict His rebuke of Job in the Yahweh speeches (chs. 38-41) and His reaffirmation of the retributive principle in the epilogue.[33]

Polzin pinpoints three key elements in a structural analysis of Job, namely the framework, the code and the message of the book.[34] As far as the framework is concerned, Polzin maintains that the story is a sequence of relationships between Job and God.[35] The narrative works out a series of contradictions by means of four major sequential functions, which separate the book into four movements (i.e. the four largest analyzable units).[36] The first movement (chs. 1-37) focuses upon God's afflictions on Job, setting up a conflict between the sphere of belief and that of experience. The friends hold the sphere of belief whereas Job holds the sphere of experience.[37] The second movement (chs. 38-42:6) highlights the theophany, which resolves the first contradiction, but sets up a new conflict—Job denies the validity of his own suffering experience after assenting to the vision of God.[38] The third movement (42:7-9) affirms that Job has spoken what is right. It resolves the second contradiction, but sets up a new conflict—the contradiction between God's rebuke of Job in Job 38-41 and His approval of Job in 42:7-8.[39] In the fourth movement (42:10-17) God's restoration of Job's fortunes affirms His words in 42:7-8 and Job 38-41. Thus it resolves the last conflict, and returns to the initial equilibrium. Finally, Job ends up where he began.[40]

The second element of Polzin's structural analysis of Job is the code of the text, which is the structure behind the framework. It is studied with the help of mathematical concepts of group structure, showing the interdisciplinary coordination of structuralism.[41] Ac-

---

[32] Polzin, "The Framework of the Book of Job," 184-5.
[33] Polzin, "The Framework of the Book of Job," 185-6.
[34] Polzin, "The Framework of the Book of Job," 187.
[35] Polzin, "The Framework of the Book of Job," 190.
[36] Polzin, "The Framework of the Book of Job," 199.
[37] Polzin, "The Framework of the Book of Job," 192-4.
[38] Polzin, "The Framework of the Book of Job," 194-6.
[39] Polzin, "The Framework of the Book of Job," 196-8.
[40] Polzin, "The Framework of the Book of Job," 198-9.
[41] R. M. Polzin, *Biblical Structuralism: Method and Subjectivity in the Study of Ancient Texts* (Philadelphia: Fortress Press, 1977) 89ff.

cording to Polzin, the framework of Job is made up of a set of transformations, which are the representation of a Klein group (i.e. an Abelian group with four members).[42] Each movement consists of a *before* and *after* element, and a sphere of belief (X) and that of experience (Y). Polzin lists out a series of transformations in the four movements as follows:[43]

Initial situation	+X+Y	
First movement	+X+Y	-X+Y
Second movement	-X+Y	+X-Y
Third movement	+X-Y	-X+Y
Fourth movement	-X+Y	+X+Y

By observing such mathematical symbols, Polzin perceives that one transformation is missing: the negation of belief and experience (-X-Y). Polzin claims that this is the state Job vehemently begs for—being sent down to Sheol. He further adds: "If there was a conflict between Job and God it was ultimately a conflict in which God represents the affirmation +X+Y, while Job keeps begging Him for -X-Y."[44] Finally, Yahweh wins the conflict, and therefore Job stops requesting Sheol, which denotes the negation of everything.

As a result, this clue—the denial of a way out through death—leads to a discussion of the message (the third element of the structural analysis of Job).[45] Polzin states: "The message of the book centers around the courageous affirmation of apparently irreconcilable spheres instead of the insane negation of those spheres to avoid conflict and contradiction. The Book of Job is a conflict between God, who affirms life however cruel, and Job, who wanted death to avoid that cruelty. It is the story of how God won."[46]

Polzin's structuralist approach seeks to read Job as a unified whole and to deal with the inconsistencies throughout the book.[47] However, it is difficult to see how the sequential story moves from the initial equilibrium through contradictions to its final equilibrium,

---

[42] Polzin, *Biblical Structuralism*, 91ff.

[43] Polzin, *Biblical Structuralism*, 96.

[44] Polzin, *Biblical Structuralism*, 100.

[45] With regard to the message of the Book of Job, see Polzin, *Biblical Structuralism*, 102-25.

[46] Polzin, *Biblical Structuralism*, 101.

[47] Polzin, *Biblical Structuralism*, 57-8; also Polzin, "The Framework of the Book of Job," 182-3.

especially when two of the largest analyzable units are found in three verses and eight verses respectively, in 42:7-9 and 42:10-17.[48]

Concerning the first major contradiction in the book, Polzin claims that in his second response to God Job affirms what he denies, and denies what he affirms in the dialogue. However, I see this as Job's transformation rather than a contradiction of his words and acts. It seems clear that Job has reached a new position and his horizon has been expanded. A likely reading of Job's second confession is that he repents of the whole line of argument based on retribution. Job 42:6 can give us a clue for this interpretation.

It is admitted that the meaning of 42:6 is uncertain and ambiguous.[49] The controversy is caused by the absence of an object for the verb מָאַס (repudiate).[50] Pope argues that מָאַס without an object does not necessarily mean "despise myself." Comparing 7:16 where מָאַס has no object in the Hebrew, he notes that the object need not be expressed when it is clear in the context. He thinks the context shows that what Job despises is the things he has said. Rowley rightly comments: "Whether Job is despising himself for the things he has said or recanting the things he has said does not need to be decided, since the one would involve the other."[51] It is likely indeed that in Job's final speech he admits that he was wrong, and that he has uttered what he did not understand (42:3b). He did accuse the friends exactly of this (e.g. 13:4-5; 26:2-4, 14; 27:5, 12). But exactly

---

[48] B. W. Anderson, "Biblical Structuralism: Method and Subjectivity in the Study of Ancient Texts (A Review)," *TToday* 35 (1979) 519.

[49] Driver and Gray, *Book of Job*, 373.

[50] The verb מָאַס is rendered in various ways: "despise myself" (RSV); "melt away" (NEB); "retract" (JB); "ashamed of" (GNB); "recant" (Pope); "sink down" (Dhorme); and "abase myself" (Gordis). Dhorme reads the root מאס as a parallel to the root מסס (melt away/sink down); see Dhorme, *Job*, 646-7. The controversy over the rendering of מָאַס is caused by the absence of an object for the verb. Patrick argues that this verb is not a genuine reflexive as *BDB* suggests. According to Patrick, מָאַס carries the sense of "reject" and thus an object is needed. Curtis holds that God is the object of Job's contempt; see J. B. Curtis, "On Job's Response to Yahweh," *JBL* 98 (1979) 497-511. Kuyper claims that the object is Job's words; see L. J. Kuyper, "The Repentance of Job," *VT* 9 (1959) 91-4. But Patrick takes the "dust and ashes" of 42:6b as the object and renders מָאַס as "repudiate." In agreement with Patrick's interpretation, Habel adds that the clue to the object of מָאַס can be found in Job 31:13, where Job did not dismiss the case of his manservant. According to Habel, in the context of 42:6, the implied object seems to be Job's case against God. For the argument of Patrick, see D. Patrick, "The Translation of Job 42:6," *VT* 26 (1976) 369-71; also Habel, *Job*, 576.

[51] Pope, *Job*, 62, 348-9; Rowley, *Book of Job*, 266.

in what way was Job wrong? Gutiérrez rightly points out that after the divine encounter, Job realises that his views of God are rigidly bound in the box of retributive principle, and that he has falsely made certain inferences from the doctrine of retribution that he has shared with the friends.[52] Thus he abandons his dejected outlook, and at the same time admits that in a certain respect he was wrong.

Patrick's interpretation of 42:6b also sheds new light on the understanding of Job's second confession.[53] If the verb נחם (42:6b) is taken as a Niphal it is normally translated as "to repent," but if it is taken as a Piel it is translated as "find consolation in."[54] The former rendering "to repent" seems to fit better in this context. According to Patrick, when the root נחם is used with the preposition עַל, it means "to change one's mind" or "to reverse a decision" (cf. Exod 32:12, 14; Jer 18:8, 10; Amos 7:3, 6).[55] "Dust and ashes," which is treated as the object, is an image of groaning and lamentation. Therefore "I repent of (change my mind about) dust and ashes" (וְנִחַמְתִּי עַל־עָפָר וָאֵפֶר) in 42:6b means that Job rejects his position of lamentation among the dust and ashes.[56]

In fact, 42:6b is in the same line with 42:6a, highlighting Job's abandonment of the dejected worldview. Before seeing God, Job cannot accept innocent suffering. In order to defend his own innocence, he puts God in the wrong. But after the divine encounter, he has a bigger view of God's justice than before. Now he realises that the innocent can suffer, but innocent suffering does not necessarily rule out the justice of God. Therefore the emphasis of 42:6 is that Job changes his mind about the whole line of argument based on retribution. In sum, I see Job's second confession as a transformation of worldview rather than simply a contradiction of Job's words and acts, although this transformed worldview involves repentance because of his attribution of wrong to God.

Furthermore, I am not convinced that Job is overwhelmed with

---

[52] G. Gutiérrez, *On Job: God-Talk and the Suffering of the Innocent* (trans. Mattthew J. O'Connell; Maryknoll; New York: Orbis Books, 1994) 87.

[53] Patrick, "The Translation of Job 42:6.".

[54] N. C. Habel, "'Naked I Came..': Humanness in the Book of Job," *Die Botschaft und die Boten: Festschrift Für Hans Walter Wolff Zum 70. Geburtstag* (ed. Jörg Jeremias and Lothar Perlitt; Neukirchen-Vluyn: Neukirchen Verlag, 1981) 388; also Habel, *Job*, 576.

[55] Patrick, "The Translation of Job 42:6," 370.

[56] Patrick, "The Translation of Job 42:6," 370.

a death wish.[57] Admittedly, the poetic dialogues start with Job's birthday curse (ch. 3). He at first appears to be a victim, who wants death as his comfort (6:3-11). But later he takes a new role of self-defence for his righteousness (6:29), with honest words (6:25). Brown pinpoints the transformation of Job's character: "As Job's words begin to reshape the contours of integrity, an uncompromising, even strident, honesty comes to possess Job, breaking the shackles that have suppressed all previous discourse (7:11). Contrary to the ideal of the quiet sage, Job's integrity loosens his tongue rather than restrains it."[58] In spite of the fear of divine intimidation in 9:33-35, Job's speech in chapter 10 marks a breakthrough in that he gives full vent to his complaint boldly before God. Job's outcry at 14:13 is certainly not a death-wish. Brown rightly states that "Job's character has changed remarkably from the one presented in his initial discourse. The rhetoric of victimization has become Job's impervious defense."[59] Job's self-defence before God reaches its climax in his final oaths of innocence (chs. 29-31). Obviously, Job's earlier death wish has been replaced by his fervent courage to confront God. Therefore Polzin's application of the mathematical group theory, which leads to the curious conclusion that the message of Job is represented by the one transformation (-X-Y) not attested in the text, seems to be rather arbitrarily imposed.

It is true that Polzin tries to deal with the major contradictions in the book. However, he has just dealt with the inconsistencies in general, without touching the particular contradictions in the text, especially Job's contradictory statements in Job 23-24, 26:5-14, 27:13-23, Job 28-31 and so on.

Pointing out the weaknesses of structural criticism, Patte correctly writes: "The limitations of a structural exegesis are clear. We have left out many features of the text. Actually, our structural study was limited to the study of a single meaning-producing dimension, and thus we bracketed out its other meaning-producing dimensions."[60]

---

[57] Anderson, "Biblical Structuralism (A Review)," 519.

[58] W. P. Brown, "The Deformation of Character: Job 1-31," *Character in Crisis: A Fresh Approach to the Wisdom Literature in the Old Testament* (Grand Rapids: Eerdmans, 1996) 72.

[59] Brown, "Deformation of Character: Job 1-31," 74.

[60] D. Patte, "Structural Criticism," *To Each Its Own Meaning: An Introduction to Biblical Criticisms and Their Application* (ed. Steven L. McKenzie and Stephen R. Haynes; Louisville: Westminster/John Knox Press, 1993) 165.

Seemingly, Polzin's structural approach has neglected other dimensions of the text. For instance, he does not study the Book of Job as a story which is characterized by the unfolding of its plot, or as a discourse through which the author seeks to affect his audience in certain ways.

C. *The Deconstructionist Approach*

As mentioned above, historical-critical scholars cannot accept inconsistencies which they always explain as secondary additions in an effort to eliminate all those materials which do not fit their context. Seeing the limitation of the historical-critical approach, deconstructionist scholars advocate their own approach to explain Job's incongruities. They maintain that a text has already undermined itself and means a whole host of contrary things.[61] According to Beardslee, "Deconstructive criticism is a way of reading that involves both discovering the incompleteness of the text and finding a fresh, if transient, insight made possible by the 'free play' or indeterminacy of the text."[62]

In his article "Deconstructing the Book of Job," Clines argues that the book deconstructs itself in several fundamental areas.[63] He tries to distinguish deconstructions from simple incoherence by quoting Jonathan Culler's strategy of deconstruction: "To deconstruct a discourse is to show how it undermines the philosophy it asserts, or the hierarchical oppositions on which it relies."[64] Clines points out that there are two conflicting philosophies in the prologue. The first philosophy, which stresses that only the wicked suffer, appears in the first section of the prologue, where both the narrator and God af-

---

[61] Good, *In Turns of Tempest*, 177, 181.

[62] W. A. Beardslee, "Poststructuralist Criticism," *To Each Its Own Meaning* (Revised edition; ed. Steven L. McKenzie and Stephen R. Haynes; Louisville: Westminster/John Knox Press, 1999) 253.

[63] In this article Clines pinpoints two arenas in which we may see the book of Job deconstructing itself. The first one is the issue of moral retribution, which is discussed in this section. The second one is its handling of the question of suffering. Clines states that when the readers are told the reason for Job's suffering, they are led to penetrate into the explanation of human suffering in general, but then start to realise that the book actually presents the unique case of Job's suffering. See D. J. A. Clines, "Deconstructing the Book of Job," *The Bible as Rhetoric: Studies in Biblical Persuasion and Credibility* (ed. Martin Warner; London; New York: Routledge, 1990) 65-80; and "False Naivety in the Prologue to Job," *HAR* 9 (1985) 133-5.

[64] Clines, "Deconstructing the Book of Job," 65.

firm Job's fear of God and avoidance of evil (1:1-8). There then comes the second philosophy when Job's suffering demonstrates that piety does not necessarily lead to prosperity and that the cause of suffering is not necessarily sin.[65]

Clines stresses that the second philosophy actually does not undermine, but confronts the first. They conflict with each other. The second philosophy is strongly asserted by the poem of 3:1-42:6, the core of the book as a whole. The poem proves over and over again that the doctrine of retribution is wrong. But, all of a sudden, the last eleven verses of the book, i.e. the epilogue (42:7-17), deconstruct the second philosophy. In that place Yahweh's rewarding of Job indicates that the most righteous man on earth is the most wealthy. According to Clines, what the book has been demolishing, the doctrine of retribution, is finally affirmed.[66] Clines explains why it is not called an incoherence, but an undermining. He states: "The very fact that the ending of the book of Job is not normally regarded as logically incoherent with what precedes it is an evidence that the contradiction is an *undermining*."[67]

However, during his discussion on the issue of moral retribution, Clines' reading seems to be overgeneralized. He divides the book into three blocks: 1) the two conflicting philosophies about the retributive principle in the prologue (chs. 1-2); 2) the second philosophy being asserted by the poetic sections (3:1-42:6); and 3) the second philosophy being undermined by the epilogue, while the first philosophy is affirmed by it (42:7-17). However, Clines does not pay particular heed to Job's contradictory statements about the retributive principle in Job 22-31. Clines maintains that the whole block of Job 3:1-42:6 backs up the second philosophy which highlights the falsity of the retributive principle. But he does not explain why Job returns to the first philosophy by asserting the retributive principle when the story comes to 24:18-24 and 27:13-23. Thus I am not convinced that Clines succeeds in showing that the book undermines itself.

Clines also does not mention how the deconstructive reading can be effectively applied in Job 28 which highlights the fear of God and the avoidance of evil again (28:28). Perhaps he still maintains that

---

[65] Clines, "Deconstructing the Book of Job," 68.
[66] Clines, "Deconstructing the Book of Job," 68-71.
[67] Clines, "Deconstructing the Book of Job," 71.

Job 28 is Zophar's speech, as he does in his commentary.[68] Therefore Clines' deconstructionist approach does not throw much light on the issue of Job 28.

Differently from the historical-critical, the structuralist and the deconstructionist approaches, this study seeks to investigate the entire plot design of the Book of Job, which highlights the coherence of each individual part of the work. It will demonstrate how one of the most ambiguous texts, Job 28, is connected with other parts of the book which may also be considered as inconsistencies. As Habel rightly claims, there is "a continuous narrative plot which underlies the book of Job and gives coherence to the text as a whole."[69]

III. *Job 28 Within the Plot Development of the Book*

This study examines the text in its final narrative form in the MT. The basic assumption here is that the message of a narrative such as the Book of Job is conveyed in two ways: 1) through the content of each individual section and the speeches of each character; and 2) through the design of the entire book.[70] Instead of rejecting the ambiguous texts, this study seeks to highlight how different parts of the book contribute to the author's entire plot design. In addition, Job's characterization is traced throughout the book. Through discussion of the plot development of the whole book and the characterization of Job, this study will demonstrate how Job 28 is an integral part of the book and makes sense as Job's speech. Special reference is made to Brown's investigation of character formation,[71]

---

[68] Clines, *Job 1-20*, lix.
[69] Habel, *Job*, 25.
[70] Seitz, "Job: Full-Structure, Movement, and Interpretation," 10.
[71] Concerning approaches to biblical wisdom, Brown notes that both anthropocentric and theocentric dimensions should be included, but that the anthropocentric framework is primary. He states: "Wisdom begins and ends with the self, in recognition that knowledge of God cannot be divorced from human knowledge of the self" (p.3). He suggests that character formation is the central framework of biblical literature, focusing on the development of the self in relation to the perceived world, and thus bridging the gap between the anthropocentric and theocentric framework in the wisdom literature (p.4). According to Brown: "In order to render a faithful interpretation of the book of Job, it is important to keep in mind that Job is *primarily* about Job and not someone else, even God, or something else, including theodicy. Job does not attempt to provide a solution to the universal problem of suffering. Rather, the book charts the journey of one person's

Habel's analysis of narrative plot development,[72] Alter's, Bar-Efrat's and Sternberg's principles of biblical narrative.[73]

According to Bar-Efrat, "the plot of a narrative is constructed as a meaningful chain of interconnected events. This is achieved by careful selection, entailing the omission of any incident which does not fit in logically with the planned development of the plot."[74] In addition, the plot functions to arrange a whole chain of events in a way that imbues the events with meaning and also stimulates the readers' emotional involvement and interest.[75] Therefore every individual incident has its own signficance in terms of its position and role in the plot system as a whole. Bar-Efrat adds: "The incidents are like building blocks, each one contributing its part to the entire edifice, and hence their importance. In the building which is the plot there are no excess or meaningless blocks. The removal of one may cause the entire structure to collapse or at least damage its functional and aesthetic perfection."[76] The true significance of Job 28 in its present position can only be seen when the rest of the book can also be read as the text stands. The defence of the integrity of Job 28 must ask whether it can contribute to the plot of Job according to these strict criteria.

The Book of Job is a biblical narrative, comprising both narration and dialogue. To detect the narrative plot, it is indispensable to examine the linkage between narration and dialogue. Alter explains as follows:

> A quick review of the main functions served by narration in the Bible will give us a better sense of the special rhythm with which the Hebrew writers tell their tales: beginning with narration, they move into dialogue, drawing back momentarily or at length to narrate again, but

---

character in response to an instance of seemingly inexplicable suffering, and in so doing, provides a new frame of reference and model of normative character that invites consideration for post-Joban generations" (p.51). Concerning Job's characterization, see W. P. Brown, *Character In Crisis: A Fresh Approach to the Wisdom Literature of the Old Testament* (Grand Rapids: Eerdmans, 1996) 50-119.

[72] In regard to the plot development of Job, see Habel, *Job*, 25-35.

[73] As for the principles of biblical narrative, see R. Alter, *The Art of Biblical Narrative* (London; Sydney: George Allen & Unwin, 1981) 47-130; S. Bar-Efrat, *Narrative Art in the Bible* (JSOTSup 70; Sheffield: The Almond Press, 1989) 13-140; and M. Sternberg, *The Poetics of Biblical Narrative: Ideological Literature and the Drama of Reading* (Bloomington: Indiana University Press, 1985).

[74] Bar-Efrat, *Narrative Art in the Bible*, 93.

[75] Bar-Efrat, *Narrative Art in the Bible*, 93.

[76] Bar-Efrat, *Narrative Art in the Bible*, 93.

always centering on the sharply salient verbal intercourse of the characters, who act upon one another, discover themselves, affirm or expose their relation to God, through the force of language.[77]

Alter argues that the primacy of dialogue and the highly auxiliary role of narration are the general traits of biblical narrative.[78] The primacy of dialogue means that direct speech plays the most important role in plot development because it may indicate an action, and may retard, complicate or resolve the plot.[79] The next section will demonstrate how the plot of Job is rooted in direct speech and how it is interwoven with the rest of the story.

Basically, narration serves the following three functions: 1) to convey actions essential to the unfolding of the plot; 2) to give expository data ancillary to the plot; and 3) to confirm assertions made in dialogue.[80] Therefore the prose materials (i.e. the narration) in the Book of Job (1:1-5; 2:11-13; 32:1-5), which introduce the major characters in the plot—Job, the friends and Elihu—provide very important background information for plot development. In addition, Job's restoration (42:12-16) balances the introduction (1:1-5) and makes the story a closure. Habel rightly demarcates the three movements of the narrative plot of Job (1:1-2:10; 2:11-31:40; 32:1-42:17) in light of these prose markers: 1) God afflicts Job—the hidden conflict; 2) Job challenges God—the conflict explored; and 3) God challenges Job—the conflict resolved.[81]

A. *Three Movements of the Plot*

1. *Movement One (1:1-2:10)*
The narration in 1:1-5 serves as an exposition, providing background information for the first movement and the entire story.[82] Job is profiled as a pious, wealthy and successful man. In 1:1 four

---

[77] Alter, *Biblical Narrative*, 75.
[78] Alter, *Biblical Narrative*, 65.
[79] N. C. Habel, "The Narrative Art of Job: Applying the Principles of Robert Alter," *JSOT* 27 (1983) 104.
[80] Alter, *Biblical Narrative*, 76-7.
[81] Habel, *Job*, 25-35, 26-7; and Clines, *Job 1-20*, xxxv-xxxvi.
[82] Bar-Efrat points out that in most cases the information communicated at the beginning of a narrative connects immediately and organically with the account of the events themselves. Such exposition serves as a natural point of departure for understanding actual plot developments. See Bar-Efrat, *Narrative Art in the Bible*, 111-6.

key traits of Job are highlighted by the narrator: Job is "blameless" (תָּם), "upright (יָשָׁר), "fearing God" (יְרֵא אֱלֹהִים) and "turning away from evil" (סָר מֵרָע). Job's piety is illustrated by a concrete example that he mediates for his family by sacrificing burnt offerings continually in order to avoid the punishment of cursing God. Job's overarching character "blamelessness" or "integrity" is the central focus of the whole book, as will be highlighted through later developments in the plot.

There then follows the first episode set in the heavenly council (1:6-22). In 1:8 Yahweh boasts of Job's integrity in the same way as the narrator: "For there is no one like him on the earth, a blameless (תָּם) and upright (יָשָׁר) man, fearing God (יְרֵא אֱלֹהִים) and turning away from evil (סָר מֵרָע)." Yahweh's boast about Job is "the catalyst" initiating the plot.[83] In response, the satan challenges Yahweh to test Job's alleged integrity (1:9): "Does Job fear God for nothing (חִנָּם)?" The satan questions Job's motive for fearing God, and at the same time accuses God of "having made it worth Job's while to behave in an ethically credible manner."[84] In this way both Job's and God's integrity are challenged. Yahweh consents to let the satan test Job, and the wheel of the plot starts moving. The verbal actions in the dialogue between Yahweh and the satan are central to the development of the plot. Yahweh's boast has evoked a conflict with the satan and the negotiation to test Job with afflictions. However, Job succeeds in enduring a series of disasters with an uncompromising acceptance of his fate. He is grateful for what God has given him and does not blame Him for taking it away. He blesses the name of Yahweh (1:20-21). At the end of Job's first test the narrator affirms Job's integrity: "Through all this Job did not sin nor did he blame God" (1:22). The conflict between Yahweh and the satan is resolved, but it is in fact a false ending.[85]

The second episode starts in the same heavenly scene (2:1-10). Yahweh repeats His boast of Job (2:3): "For there is no one like him on the earth, a blameless (תָּם) and upright (יָשָׁר) man, fearing God (יְרֵא אֱלֹהִים) and turning from evil (סָר מֵרָע). And he still holds fast (חָזַק) his integrity (תֻּמָּה)." Yahweh also accuses the satan of ruining Job "without cause" (חִנָּם; 2:3b). Then the satan further challenges

---

[83] Habel, *Job*, 27.
[84] Brown, "Deformation of Character: Job 1-31," 52.
[85] Habel, *Job*, 27; and Whybray, *Job*, 32.

Job's integrity by asking God to give Job a new test on his body. In response, God allows the satan to test Job again (2:6-7). As before, Yahweh's repeated boast of Job's integrity triggers a conflict with the satan. Job's wife challenges Job (2:9a): "Do you still hold fast (חָזַק) your integrity (תֻּמָּה)?" She also echoes the satan by urging Job to "curse God and die" (2:9b). However, Job rebukes his wife and accepts the cruel afflictions (2:10). Similarly to the first episode, the narrator also comments that Job has uttered no verbal sin. Once again, Job's acceptance of his fate resolves the conflict between God and the satan. The audience, who has been anxiously waiting to discover whether Job will survive the test, is now satisfied. But this resolution is merely apparent.[86]

In the first movement of the plot (1:1-2:10) Job is characterized by various means: 1) the narrator; 2) God; and 3) Job's own actions. Highlighting Job's righteousness, the narrator uses four terms to portray him as "blameless, upright, fearing God and turning away from evil" (1:1). God repeats twice Job's direct characterization with the same four terms (1:8; 2:3). In these two verses, He adds: "There is no one like him on the earth" (also twice) and "He still holds fast his integrity." In addition, the narrator also evaluates Job's response to his calamities: "Through all this Job did not sin nor did he blame God" (1:22) and "In all this Job did not sin with his lips" (2:10). Job has committed no verbal sin. The evaluations given by the narrator and God are trustworthy. Bar-Efrat rightly remarks: "These expressions of direct characterization are uttered by the narrator, who is the supreme authority, and by God, who is above authority."[87]

Job's indirect characterization is reflected by what he says and does. His piety can be seen through his sacrifice of burnt offerings for his sons at the end of the days of feasting (1:5). His unquestioning acceptance of his fate is demonstrated when he remarks after the first test, "Naked I came from my mother's womb and naked I shall return there. The Lord gave and the Lord has taken away. Blessed be the name of the Lord" (1:21), and when he rebukes his wife after the second test, "You speak as one of the foolish women speaks. Shall we indeed accept good from God and not accept adversity?" (2:10).

Why does the author use various means to illustrate Job's

---

[86] Habel, *Job*, 28.
[87] Bar-Efrat, *Narrative Art in the Bible*, 88.

overarching character-integrity in the first movement? The reason is that the primary ethical problematic of the book is the act-consequence nexus. The author highlights Job's integrity in different ways because the prologue tackles the question of whether prosperity is brought forth by piety. But the dialogue deals with the question of whether suffering is brought about by sin. These are actually the two sides of one coin. Clines points out that the above two questions are merged at 2:3, where Yahweh allows Job to be afflicted "without cause" (חִנָּם). Yahweh Himself breaks the act-consequence nexus. The prologue mainly focuses upon the piety-prosperity nexus, but the merging point at 2:3 indicates that the narrator is skilfully paving the path to the development of the dialogue, where the problematic of the sin-suffering nexus is fully addressed.[88]

Readers and commentators often raise the issue of the moral legitimacy of divine testing—how God could allow such things to happen to an innocent man. Brown is correct in pointing out that "the prologue's characterization of God is much more nuanced."[89] He disagrees with Habel's depicting God in the prologue as a "jealous king, who is apparently willing to violate human life to gratify personal ends."[90] Brown states that it is out of confidence that Job is worthy of Yahweh's approval, and that He allows the satan to test Job's integrity.[91] Brown further stresses that "the test becomes necessary only when such integrity is challenged, both Job's and Yahweh's."[92] If the narrator intends to portray God as a brutal tester, he does not need to bring in the second conversation between God and the satan. Brown adds: "In accordance with the dynamics of the plot, it is the boast and the protest in Job 2:3 that most vividly betrays a glimpse of the divine character, the struggling Tester."[93]

The key *Leitwort* that underscores Job's most distinctive character is "blameless" (תָּם) with its cognate term "integrity/blameless-

---

[88] D. J. A. Clines, "False Naivety in the Prologue to Job," *HAR* 9 (1985) 132-3.

[89] Brown, "Deformation of Character: Job 1-31," 55.

[90] N. C. Habel, "In Defense of God the Sage," *The Voice from the Whirlwind: Interpreting the Book of Job* (ed. Leo G. Perdue and W. Clark Gilpin; Nashville: Abingdon Press, 1992) 26.

[91] Brown, "Deformation of Character: Job 1-31," 55.

[92] Brown, "Deformation of Character: Job 1-31," 56.

[93] Brown, "Deformation of Character: Job 1-31," 57.

ness" (תָּמָה). Integrity reflects the wholeness or coherence of character.[94] The central concern of the prologue is Job's integrity, which frames the focus of the entire book.[95] Concerning the function of a *Leitwort* in the text, Alter writes:

> A *Leitwort* is a word or a word-root that recurs significantly in a text, in a continuum of texts, or in a configuration of texts: by following these repetitions, one is able to decipher or grasp a meaning of the text, or at any rate, the meaning will be revealed more strikingly. The repetition, as we have said, need not be merely of the word itself but also of the word-root; in fact, the very difference of words can often intensify the dynamic action of the repetition...The measured repetition that matches the inner rhythm of the text, or rather, that wells up from it, is one of the most powerful means for conveying meaning without expressing it.[96]

In the prologue the narrator profiles Job's character as "blameless" (תָּם; 1:1; cf. 1:22; 2:10) and Yahweh affirms Job as "blameless" (תָּם; 1:8; 2:3). Both the satan (1:9; 2:4-5) and Job's wife (2:9) challenge Job's integrity. "Integrity" is not only the focus of the prologue, it also foreshadows the thematic statements in the subsequent dialogue.[97] Eliphaz urges Job to find hope in the "integrity" of his past religious piety (4:6). Bildad regards Job as an evildoer, because he thinks that God would never spurn the "blameless" (8:20), but Job reaffirms himself as guiltless (9:21-22). It is again Job's integrity that motivates him not to agree with his friends' arguments (27:5-6). The climax of Job's defence of his integrity is fully expressed in a series of oaths of innocence in Job 31. How "integrity" interweaves with the rest of the book will be further discussed later in the chapter.

Superficially, the conflict between Yahweh and the satan seems to be resolved when Job holds fast to his integrity and utters no verbal sin. In fact, the real conflict has not been resolved yet. The audience knows the reason for Job's suffering, but Job is ignorant. Habel rightly states: "If the story ends with the first movement, that conflict is not even explored and its ironic complications are left as irrelevant mysteries."[98] The hidden decisions in heaven create sub-

---

[94] Brown, "Deformation of Character: Job 1-31," 53.
[95] For further details, see Brown, "Deformation of Character: Job 1-31," 58-60; and Habel, "The Narrative Art of Job," 103.
[96] Alter, *Biblical Narrative*, 93.
[97] Habel, "The Narrative Art of Job," 103.
[98] Habel, *Job*, 29.

sequent conflicts between Job and God, and the debates between Job and his friends. After the first movement heaven is sealed off and silent. God does not speak again until 35 chapters of human speech have finished. God's total silence has the most important function in the "play of perspectives." Sternberg makes the following remarks:

> The "characters' perspective" differs from all the others—God's, the narrator's, the reader's—in its multiplicity. Each character observes the world from his own perspective. And it is their divergence—in interest, interpretation, world view, scenario, hope and fear—that keeps the action going, just as their convergence makes for its resolution...What such diverse figural perspectives have in common is the inherent limitation of knowledge and liability to misjudgment, which motivate the progress of the tale.[99]

Concerning the requirement of the development of the plot, Sternberg further pinpoints:

> Like Greek tragedy in the dramatic genre, however, the Bible is the first narrative to develop this necessary condition for plot into a focus of interest and a compositional principle...Generally speaking, we have the new doctrinal load carried by the opposition between divine omniscience and human restrictedness; the two faces of "knowledge" as world viewing and world view; and the overall interplay of perspectival tensions. More specifically, where the minimal requirement for plot would be one "bewildered" agent or party vis-à-vis God, the Bible opts for the multiplication and complication of viewpoints on the human side.[100]

Therefore this "play of perspectives" is especially suitable for human talk about God. The ignorance of the heavenly plan generates "the multiplication and complication of viewpoints on the human side"—Job and his friends. Such human ignorance serves as the impetus to sustain the sequence of actions. As Sternberg highlights: "No ignorance, no conflict; and no conflict, no plot."[101]

In the Book of Job it is the "play of perspectives" which puts the audience into a situation where the audience knows better. According to Sternberg, such a privileged position enables the audience to observe the characters and their doings from an omniscient vantage-point, at the expense of the characters.[102] Sternberg adds: "The

---

[99] Sternberg, *Poetics of Biblical Narrative*, 172.
[100] Sternberg, *Poetics of Biblical Narrative*, 173.
[101] Sternberg, *Poetics of Biblical Narrative*, 173.
[102] Sternberg, *Poetics of Biblical Narrative*, 164.

narrator's disclosures put us in a position to fathom their secret thoughts and designs, to trace or even foreknow their acts, to jeer or grieve at their misguided attempts at concealment, plotting, interpretation."[103] Therefore the first movement of the plot has created a dramatic irony, which continues through the whole book, that the audience knows what Job does not, namely the hidden decisions in heaven.[104] In short, the audience-elevating strategy effectively engages the audience to view the whole development of the story, to wrestle with the characters, to experience a reformation of worldview and to venture on a new journey of character transformation.

The prologue plays the most important part in creating the next stage of the plot's development. The primacy of dialogue in moving the narrative plot is a significant feature of the prologue.[105] The conflict between Yahweh and the satan is in dialogue form, and their verbal actions initiate series of events on the earth. The conflict between Job and his wife is also a verbal action. Both conflicts are resolved by Job's verbal expression of integrity. "These dialogues provide important precedents for the extended dialogue conflicts, first between Job and his friends and then between Job and his God, and constitute further evidence of continuity between the so-called prologue and the chapters which follow."[106] Brown also notes that: "The downward turn in negotiations between Yahweh and the satan that results in further suffering for Job is precisely what generates the remainder of the plot, beginning with the wife's leading question and the consolation of the friends."[107] In the next movement the linkage between the prologue and the dialogue will be demonstrated.

2. *Movement Two (2:11-31:40)*

The second movement starts with an exposition, introducing the three friends, who come to sympathize (נוד) with Job and to comfort (נחם) him. They sit silently on the ground with Job for seven

---

[103] Sternberg, *Poetics of Biblical Narrative*, 164.

[104] For the notion of "dramatic irony," see Sternberg, *Poetics of Biblical Narrative*, 164; and Whybray, *Job*, 29.

[105] Alter, *Biblical Narrative*, 63-87; Habel, *Job*, 81; and Habel, "The Narrative Art of Job," 104-6.

[106] Habel, *Job*, 81.

[107] Brown, "Deformation of Character: Job 1-31," 57.

days and seven nights (2:11-13). This long time of total silence expresses the friends' genuine empathy for Job, but more importantly it serves a crucial rhetorical purpose. Habel claims that "This period of silence, however, is important in the plot of the narrative, for it allows time for bitterness and rage to build up within Job before they explode in the curses of Job's next speech (ch. 3). Thus the silence sets the stage for the violent verbal outburst of Job which follows."[108]

The word "afterward" in 3:1 marks the end of the silence. The suggestion of Job's wife serves as the latent catalyst for Job's birthday curse in chapter 3. After his two tests, his wife challenges him to "bless/curse" (ברך) God and die. His wife's use of ברך brings out a double irony: 1) responding to Job's blessing of God in 1:21; and 2) urging Job to curse God and die.[109] In the prologue Job refuses to curse in response to his fate, but now his mouth is full of cursing. Job's birthday curse lays the foundation for the subsequent nearly 40 chapters of discourse. From chapter 3 onwards, Job no longer remains silent. His verbal action generates further complications, which are not resolved until his final words in 42:2-6. Job's curse seemingly provokes the silent friends to indignation and to speech, because throughout Job's lament he presents himself as an innocent sufferer, not admitting his calamity to be consequence of sin. This seems to imply the falsity of the retributive principle. In addition, his curse gets close to being a complaint against God's injustice.[110]

From the very beginning, the friends are not false comforters at all. There is a clear movement in the argumentation of the friends.[111] In the first speech cycle Eliphaz starts with words of consolation (4:2-6), without questioning Job's integrity. He encourages Job to have confidence in his "fear of God" and hope in his "integrity" (4:6), for the innocent and the upright will never perish (4:7), and only those who plow iniquity and sow trouble reap the same (4:8). Although Bildad has cast some doubt upon Job's integrity by saying: "If you are pure and upright, surely now He would rouse Himself for you and restore your righteous estate" (8:6), he concludes that "Behold, God will not reject a man of integrity... He

---

[108] Habel, *Job*, 98; also Whybray, *Job*, 36.
[109] Greenberg, "Job," 285; also Good, *In Turns of Tempest*, 178.
[110] Whybray, *Job*, 37.
[111] Seitz, "Job: Full-Structure, Movement, and Interpretation," 11.

will fill your mouth with laughter, and your lips with shouting" (8:20-21). Finally, Zophar roundly states that God has forgotten a part of Job's iniquity, implying that Job has suffered less than he deserves (11:6). In the first cycle the friends describe both the blessings upon the righteous (Eliphaz 4:6-7; Bildad 8:20-21; Zophar 11:13-19) and the calamity upon the wicked (Eliphaz 4:8-11; 5:1-7; Bildad 8:8-19, 22; Zophar 11:20). In addition, the three of them also exhort Job to seek God (Eliphaz 5:8, 27; Bildad 8:5-7; Zophar 11:13-20) in order to restore his wellbeing.[112]

In the first cycle Job's accusation against God is first implicitly suggested in Job 3, is intensified through Job 6-7, and reaches its climax in Job 9-10.[113] In Job 3 the curse is directed against the one who gave life to Job (3:20-23). There then comes Job's indirect accusation against God about how God's arrows and terrors attack him (6:4). The real accusation is expressed in 7:12, stating that God has set a guard over Job and treats him like a sea monster. In Job 9-10 Job has broken the traditional theology by claiming that God has power and knowledge but misuses both in His governance of the creation. Job 12-14 shifts the focus from Job's complaint about God to his appeal for God's vindication. In 13:17-19, 23-27 Job makes his legal dispute with God.[114] Finally, Job points out God's decree of the universal human fate of death (Job 14).

"That this long speech of 12-14 represents a turning point in the whole drama is seen from the immediate reaction—for once to the point—of Eliphaz in chapter 15. Job's point of view is plain heresy. The 'doctrine of God' he has just unfolded is offensive to pious ears, represents rank impiety."[115] In the second speech cycle the friends make accusations against Job (Eliphaz 15:2-6; Bildad 18:2-4; Zophar

---

[112] Hartley, *Job*, 38-9; also Seitz, "Job: Full-Structure, Movement, and Interpretation," 11-2.

[113] Westermann states: "The accusation against God in chaps. 9-10 strikes one as a high point that is hard to surpass. The accusation against God only intimated in chap. 3 is so intensified through chaps. 6-7 and on into this zenith in chaps. 9-10 that one has to ask how the continuance of this theme in chaps. 12-14 is to be understood." See Westermann, *Structure of Job*, 53; also D. Cox, "A Rational Inquiry Into God: Chapters 4-27 of the Book of Job," *Greg* 67 (1986) 628.

[114] Westermann notes the change in style in chapter 13, where Job starts to turn from his friends toward God. See Westermann, *Structure of Job*, 53; and Cox, "Rational Inquiry," 634.

[115] Cox, "Rational Inquiry," 636. See also Pope, *Job*, 114, who notes that Eliphaz's attitude toward Job in the second cycle is "less courteous and less conciliatory than in his previous speech."

20:2-3), instead of giving him words of consolation. Furthermore, the friends do not even exhort Job to seek God any more in this cycle. In addition, they no longer defend Job's righteousness, but openly charge him with his sins by declaring the fate of the wicked to him (Eliphaz 15:17-35; Bildad 18:5-21; Zophar 20:4-29). Eliphaz says: "your guilt teaches your mouth" (15:5), and Zophar states: "This is the wicked man's portion from God, even the heritage decreed to him by God" (20:29). Based on the heavenly scene in the prologue, it is evident that the friends have spoken wrongly about Job and also about God, and they have moved toward folly.[116]

Taking the form of a lament-type accusation against enemies, Job launches an attack on God in chapter 16 by portraying God as a cruel, brutal deity (16:6-17).[117] In a cry of despair, Job expresses the avowal of a "witness in heaven" (16:19). Job 19 marks the crescendo of Job's violent accusation against God (19:7-22).[118] In line with 16:19, Job expresses his hope for a redeemer (19:25). To attack the friends' traditional theodicy, Job uses an argument from experience to show how the wicked prosper (Job 21). Thus Job reverses traditional theology, pointing out that there is no necessary link between piety and prosperity, wickedness and punishment.

In the third cycle Eliphaz, in order to defend his theology, falsely accuses Job of "great wickedness" (22:5-20), and concludes with a call to repentance (22:21-30). Then Bildad utters a brief hymn to contrast God's majesty and perfection with man's corruption (Job 25). The third cycle has been a puzzle to many interpreters. In the first two cycles Job strongly opposes his friends' viewpoint, but in the third cycle he begins to utter some statements which sound like his friends'. These passages are 24:18-25, 26:5-14 and 27:13-23. After expressing the ups and downs of hope and despair of seeing God in chapter 23, Job further underscores the contradiction between the experience of social injustice (24:1-17) and the belief in God's judgment upon the wicked (24:18-25) in chapter 24. By uttering a hymn to laud God's supremacy, Job primarily aims to bring out the limitation of human understanding (26:14) in order to mock the friends' lack of wisdom in explaining his case. In response to the friends' false allegations, Job condemns them as his enemies: "Let

---

[116] Seitz, "Job: Full-Structure, Movement, and Interpretation," 12; also Hartley, *Job*, 39.

[117] Westermann, *Structure of Job*, 45; also Cox, "Rational Inquiry," 638-9.

[118] Cox, "Rational Inquiry," 643.

my enemy be as the wicked, and let the one rising up against me be as the unrighteous" (27:7). Then Job declares the fate of the wicked upon his friends (27:13-23). In fact, Job's application of the fate of the wicked to his friends is not new in the third cycle. It is foreshadowed in 19:28-29, but it comes to its fullest expression in chapter 27. Apparently, "the friends-become-enemies are driven into silence."[119] The dialogue between Job and his friends ends and from now onwards Job's discourse is directed primarily to God.[120]

The wisdom poem of Job 28 comes after the collapse of the debate between Job and his friends. It functions as a bridge between the dialogue and the speeches that follow. In this poem wisdom is regarded as "the noblest divine trait."[121] Human beings do not know the abode of wisdom. Only God fully knows it and utilizes it in His ways. This is Job's judgment on the dialogue, following from his accusation of the friends in chapter 27. Neither Job nor the friends can give an account for Job's suffering.

"Fearing God and shunning evil" in 28:28 provides human beings with a practical avenue to wisdom. However, when Job ponders over God's promise in 28:28, it triggers his anger and drives him to re-examine his life then and now. When he recounts his past, he affirms that he did live a life of fearing God and shunning evil (Job 29). However, his fearing God and shunning evil do not save him from the present afflictions nor grant him any wisdom to know the cause of his suffering (Job 30). The failure of the friends' counsel presses Job to seek a hearing from God by making an oath of innocence (Job 31). Job's "bold tenacity, brutal honesty, righteous anger, and flagrant self-assertion" finds its full expression in Job 31.[122] The oaths mark the climax of Job's defence of his integrity and prepare him to have a confrontation with God.[123]

Readers and commentators may raise the issue of the inconsistency of Job's character. In the prologue Job is profiled as a flat character with a single trait—a pious man, who accepts his fate from God submissively—whereas in the dialogue the round character of

---

[119] Seitz, "Job: Full-Structure, Movement, and Interpretation," 12-3.
[120] Brown, "Deformation of Character: Job 1-31," 77.
[121] Hartley, *Job*, 373.
[122] W. P. Brown, "The Reformation of Character: Job 32-42," *Character in Crisis: A Fresh Approach to the Wisdom Literature in the Old Testament* (Grand Rapids: Eerdmans, 1996) 116.
[123] Brown, "Deformation of Character: Job 1-31," 81.

Job is portrayed—a man whose complexity of inner life is penetrated and revealed entirely. Unquestioning acceptance of his fate is replaced by bitter complaints. Brown notes that "Job is enfleshed with ambiguity and complexity as he begins to detail and assess his life."[124] To resolve the issue of the inconsistency of Job's characterization, Brown points out:

> Yet what holds the prose and poetic characterizations of Job together is Job's claim that he is able to maintain his hold on integrity throughout his passionate outbursts (27:6). In the poetry, Job's integrity is never jettisoned; it is reformulated, although the patient endurance that so characterized him in the prologue is subsequently overturned. Job the silent has become Job the verbose, full of bitter complaints. Indeed, the verbal excess with which Job complains gives expression to what is essentially unspeakable in the prose.[125]

The more Job challenges his friends and God, the stronger his anger against God, and the wider the gap between his integrity and "the kind of righteousness that requires unquestioning submission before God."[126] However, Sternberg appropriately points out: "Moral perfection no longer subsumes but opposes unquestioning acceptance."[127]

Habel is correct in noting that "Central to the book of Job is the conflict between God and Job, between the integrity of the Creator and the integrity of a particular mortal."[128] Job's ignorance of the hidden negotiation between God and the satan causes him to question God's character. Based on their traditional wisdom, the friends try to defend God's integrity by imposing the reasons of theodicy upon Job's plight, but at the expense of Job's integrity. As for Job, he tries to defend his own integrity, but at the expense of God's integrity. Therefore the divergence between Job's and the friends' perspectives provokes a series of verbal battles in the dialogue.

The central development of the plot in the second movement is Job's pursuit of vindication.[129] Because of God's silence, Job cannot comprehend the reason for his plight (9:11). He wants to engage directly with God, and present his case before Him, but God's

---

[124] Brown, "Deformation of Character: Job 1-31," 60.
[125] Brown, "Deformation of Character: Job 1-31," 60.
[126] Brown, "Deformation of Character: Job 1-31," 82.
[127] Sternberg, *Poetics of Biblical Narrative*, 346.
[128] Habel, *Job*, 60.
[129] Habel, *Job*, 31.

face remains hidden. Job's desire for vindication and God's silence urge Job to appeal to an arbiter, who can help present his case to God and protect him from divine intimidation (9:33-35; 13:20-22). Job's recurring plea for vindication provides an important linkage for the further development of the plot. It first emerges in 9:33a: "There is no arbiter between us" (i.e. Job and the creator). In 13:18 he proclaims his readiness to engage God directly: "Behold now, I have prepared my case; I know that I will be vindicated." However, God remains silent to him (13:24). Then Job's desperate plea is expressed in even more intense pathos in chapter 14. He requests God to provide him a shelter in Sheol to hide from His anger, so that a proper meeting will be established for his case (14:13-17). Job is aware that his only access to present his case is to appeal to the arbiter[130] who can arbitrate Job's lawsuit with God (16:19; 19:25). Job is confident that God will pay attention to his case if He can be located (23:6). But God remains hidden from him (23:8-9). The failure of the friends' counsels drives Job to seek wisdom and address to God directly (ch. 28). But when Job reflects on God's promise at 28:28, his calm emotion turns to anger. Such a promise drives Job to recall his past (ch. 29). But his "fearing God and shunning evil" in the past did not save him from his present suffering (ch. 30). In order to make a final defence of his own innocence, Job swears an oath of purity (ch. 31). He challenges his arbiter to hold a hearing and summon his accuser with a written document (31:35-37). The vindicator theme is clearly expressed in Elihu's words (33:19-33). Elihu speaks to Job: "Speak, for I desire to justify you" (33:32b). Job's pursuit of a mediator foreshadows the advent of Elihu as arbiter and the later appearance of Yahweh in the whirlwind.[131]

3. *Movement Three (32:1-42:17)*

Elihu is the "foreshadowed arbiter," whom Job calls for to process his case at court (31:35). Elihu takes up the role of arbiter and summons Job to present his case before Elihu and take his stand

---

[130] Patrick notes that there is a distinct decrease in Job's direct appeals to God after chapter 14. For a further discussion, see D. Patrick, "Job's Address of God," *ZAW* 91 (1979) 268-82. See also Hartley, *Job*, 40; Brown, "Deformation of Character: Job 1-31," 75; and Habel, *Job*, 31.

[131] Brown, "Deformation of Character: Job 1-31," 75; Habel, *Job*, 30-2; and W. S. Miller, "The Structure and Meaning of Job," *Concordia Journal* 15 (1989) 111-2.

(33:5).[132] However, the appearance of Elihu is not a real resolution. In fact, his advent retards the movement of the plot, and postpones the expected theophany.[133] Nevertheless, Elihu helps set the stage for Yahweh's appearance and discourse (37:2, 14, 23).[134] It prepares both Job and the readers to enter into the climactic stage of the plot's development.

Yahweh, in His twofold appearance in the whirlwind, counters Job's demand for vindication and challenges Job's accusation about God's misgovernance of the world (e.g. 12:13-25). "Job defends the veracity of his perception; Yahweh reveals his limitation of experience."[135] The first divine speech (chs. 38-39) aims at pointing out Job's fault that he darkens God's counsel by words without knowledge (38:2). God reveals His orderly governance over the universe and His providential care over the natural world. Suffering does not necessarily prove God's misgovernance of the world. The second divine speech (40:6-41:26 [34]) highlights divine justice and sovereignty, aiming at rebuking Job's putting God in the wrong in order to justify himself (40:8). Even though the forces of chaos, like Behemoth and Leviathan, exist in God's world, God is still the sovereign and in control.

In his first response to Yahweh Job admits his insignificance (40:4). In his second response he confesses that he has made ignorant accusations against God's governance of the cosmos (42:2-3). Now Job gains a new, vibrant and direct knowledge of God in comparison with the previous "hand-me-downs" wisdom.[136] Brown comments on the transformation of Job's character:

> His rejection of life is paralleled by the comfort achieved by Yahweh's revealing creation's inherent goodness, a radically expansive goodness that deconstructs and reforms Job's previously restricted worldview and, thus, ultimately his character.[137]

Job's final response to God resolves the conflict between Job's integrity and God's integrity. God is vindicated by Job's submissive responses (40:3-5; 42:1-6). God's appearance seems to be a sufficient vindication for Job, because Job withdraws his case without making further appeal to God. But God's affirmation of Job's innocence is

---

[132] Habel, *Job*, 32-3.
[133] Brown, "Reformation of Character: Job 32-42," 84; also Habel, *Job*, 33.
[134] Brown, "Reformation of Character: Job 32-42," 88-9.
[135] Brown, "Reformation of Character: Job 32-42," 90.
[136] Brown, "Reformation of Character: Job 32-42," 108.
[137] Brown, "Reformation of Character: Job 32-42," 110-1.

implicitly expressed by His address to Eliphaz, which is repeated twice in the epilogue (42:7, 8).[138] Brown adds:

> Such vindication affirms that Job's relentless quest and protestations have been legitimate and acceptable, at least provisionally. Throughout the dialogues, Job's character has progressed from resignation to protest to deep yearning, acceptance, and finally surrender, a veritable reformation of character.[139]

After resolving the conflict between Job and God, God appoints Job as the mediator to intercede for his friends. Finally, the conflicts between Job and his friends and between God and the friends are resolved.[140] What does Job speak rightly about God? And if Job speaks rightly about God, why does God rebuke him in the whirlwind? Nicholson correctly points out:

> Job exposed the yawning chasm between the harsh reality of life and what orthodox piety, as represented by his companions, declared to be the automatic harvest of the righteous. For this truthfulness he is commended by God as against his three friends who did not speak "what is right" about God (42:7-8). But disjunction is pressed by Job at the expense of the conjunction of realism and faith. Present experience is allowed to eclipse faith, and lament and plea grounded in hope and trust are replaced by the bitter accusation that God is unjust and his creation a travesty. It is for this that Job is rebuked and censured, and it is against this that God rouses himself to speak from the whirlwind—not to assert himself like a bully against Job, coercing him into humiliating submission, but to declare his mastery in and over creation, and so to renew his ancient pledge and in this way reawaken faith.[141]

Conclusion

The central issue of the Book of Job is the conflict between Job's integrity and God's integrity. Such a conflict is generated by Job's ignorance of the hidden negotiation between God and the satan. The formula for plot development is: "No ignorance, no conflict; and no conflict, no plot."[142] The three movements of the plot dem-

---

[138] Brown, "Reformation of Character: Job 32-42," 112; also Habel, *Job*, 34.
[139] Brown, "Reformation of Character: Job 32-42," 112.
[140] Habel, *Job*, 34.
[141] E. W. Nicholson, "The Limits of Theodicy as a Theme of the Book of Job," *Wisdom in Ancient Israel: Essays in Honour of J. A. Emerton* (ed. J. Day, Robert P. Gordon and H. G. M. Williamson; Cambridge: Cambridge University Press, 1995) 81-2.
[142] Sternberg, *Poetics of Biblical Narrative*, 173.

onstrate the coherence of the book, in which conflicts are developed, anticipated and resolved "within the framework of the eternal tension between the will of heaven and the happenings of earth, the plan of God and the program of mortals."[143]

"Job the silent" in the prologue becoming "Job the verbose" in the dialogue creates tension in Job's character. As Sternberg recognises, "The clash between Job's epithetic and dramatic characterizations threatens the unity of his character and lends some color to the friends' (and the satan's) insinuation that the upright Job is little more than the public image exposed by adversity."[144] However, Job's integrity brings these two different characterizations together. Brown writes:

> Both the silent and the verbose "Jobs" lay claim and hold fast to integrity. Integrity is presented as a dynamic component of character that can oscillate between complete adherence to moral norms and unorthodox honesty and tenacity. The poet's purpose consists by and large of reshaping the contours of Job's integrity....It is these unorthodox traits, not the traditional virtues, that constitute the raw material out of which God reforms Job's worldview and character.[145]

It is the conflict between Job's integrity and God's integrity, motivating the progress of the tale, that keeps Job going through the whole journey of character and worldview reformulation.

B. *Plot Development and Job's Characterization in Job 22-31*

Habel's plot analysis and Brown's character analysis have made important contributions to scholarship on the Book of Job. However, neither of them successfully deals with Job 22-31, which I consider as the most perplexing section in the book. Habel claims that "the narrative plot of the book of Job reveals an underlying structure which gives coherence to the work as a literary whole...The integrity of the work is evident in its overall construction, the setting of its characters, and the interrelationship of its several parts."[146] On the one hand, he stresses the unity of the book, but on the other hand, he does not thoroughly read the text as it stands. Realising

---

[143] Habel, *Job*, 35.
[144] Sternberg, *Poetics of Biblical Narrative*, 345.
[145] Brown, "Reformation of Character: Job 32-42," 115-6.
[146] Habel, *Job*, 35.

that Job appears to utter in the third cycle some orthodox statements which are contrary to his previous arguments in the first two cycles, Habel attributes them not to Job but to his friends: the whole of chapter 24 to Zophar; 26:5-14 to Bildad; and 27:13-23 to Zophar.[147] Habel's reallocation of Job's contradictory statements to other speakers reflects his presupposition that Job's thought has to remain consistent throughout the three cycles. Because of the theological tension, Brown holds that 24:1-17 is Job's speech, and that 24:18-25 represents one of the friends.[148] In addition, he thinks it doubtful that 27:13-23 is Job's standpoint. He has dealt with 27:1-12, but without discussing 27:13-23.[149] In his work Brown does not mention Job's other contradictory statements in the third cycle. In doing so he has, in my view, omitted the most crucial part of Job's characterization in the book. In my opinion, the complexity of Job's inner life gives its fullest expression in this section through his utterance of contradictory statements. Such complexity signifies another stage of Job's characterization, which prepares him to see God face to face.

As noted above, Job is portrayed as a flat character in the prologue and a round character in the dialogue. In the first two cycles the conflict between Job's integrity and God's integrity drives Job to wage a series of verbal battles with his friends in order to defend his own righteousness. He no longer restrains his tongue as before, but utters all his grievance and bitterness before God and his friends. I consider chapters 3-21 (from Job's birthday curse to the end of the second speech cycle) as the first phase of change in Job's indirect characterization. The poet seeks to examine Job's character "below the surface epithet" to reach the depths of his personality.[150] In the first two speech cycles Job the silent becomes Job the complainer. During the interchange of the arguments with the friends Job utters sceptical sayings to accuse God and blame his friends. Job's portrait as blameless and upright, one who fears God and shuns evil (1:1, 8; 2:3) seems to be "so categorical as to leave no room for the subsequent emergence of the bold inquirer into God's ways."[151]

---

[147] See Habel, *Job*, 351-63 on chapter 24, 364-75 on 26:5-14 and 383-7 on 27:13-23.
[148] Brown, "Deformation of Character: Job 1-31," 75, n. 49.
[149] Brown, "Deformation of Character: Job 1-31," 77, and n. 52 on the same page.
[150] Sternberg, *Poetics of Biblical Narrative*, 342.
[151] Sternberg, *Poetics of Biblical Narrative*, 345.

However, it is this very feature of his character—integrity or blamelessness—that drives Job to act counter to expectation, causing the high complexity of Job's characterization.[152]

In the third speech cycle the verbal battle is still going on, but the brief reply of Bildad and the total silence of Zophar signify the failure of the friends' arguments. Job's speech is getting extraordinarily long (Job 26-31). It is noteworthy that Job's character becomes even more complicated because he utters a series of contradictory statements in this cycle. The alternate expressions of hope and despair in Job 23 and the juxtapositions of Job's contradictory sayings in Job 24:1-17 and Job 24:18-24 (25); Job 25 and Job 26; Job 27:1-12 and Job 27:13-23; and Job 28 and Job 29-31 seem to be at odds. With Habel, many commentators reject the contradictory sayings of 24:18-24 (25), 26:5-14, 27:13-23 and Job 28 as Job's speech because they seem contradictory to Job's standpoints in the first two cycles. These scholars try to reallocate these passages from Job to the friends in order to keep Job's thinking consistent throughout the three speech cycles.

However, I would rather consider this stage as the second phase of change in Job's indirect characterization, in which the complexity of Job's inner life has come to its fullest expression—the fluctuation of hope and despair (Job 23), the contradiction between belief and experience (Job 24), the strongest condemnation of the friends' wrongdoings (Job 26-27), the deepest contemplation over wisdom (Job 28) and the firmest determination to confront God (Job 29-31).

In the third cycle Job's defiance of his friends is progressively intensified: exposing the inadequacy of their theology (Job 23-24); mocking their lack of wisdom (Job 26); swearing not to agree with their standpoints (27:1-12); and declaring the destiny of the wicked upon them (27:13-23). Job's growing determination to hold fast to his integrity has aggravated the conflict with the friends and Job 27 marks a final rift with them.

The collapse of the debate drives Job to pursue wisdom (Job 28). In this poem Job highlights that wisdom is unfathomable and inaccessible to human beings. Only God has access to wisdom. However, God promises that man can acquire wisdom through fearing God and shunning evil (28:28). In effect, such a promise triggers Job's anger and arouses him to re-examine his past and present. In his reflection, he realises that his life of living out the fear of God

---

[152] Sternberg, *Poetics of Biblical Narrative*, 346.

and avoidance of evil in the past (Job 29) does not save him from the present afflictions (Job 30), nor does it give him any understanding about the resaon of his suffering. Such pondering drives Job to make his final oath of innocence in Job 31, which marks the climax of Job's defence of his integrity and his determination to confront God.[153] Job's calm reflective tone (Job 28) has shifted to an angry outburst of complaint (Job 29-31).

At this stage Job's defence of his innocence in Job 27 and Job 29-31 reaches a crescendo. However, at the same time, the tension between him and the friends (Job 27) and between him and God (Job 29-31) also marks the high point of the story. Divine intervention is thus highly expected. In addition, the perplexity of Job's inner life is fully revealed by his conflicting views of God. Job swears his oath by the name of the God who has wronged him (27:2; 30:20-23; 31:35-37). He has become Job the ambiguous.

The above plot and rhetorical analyses have begun to show how Job 28 might make sense as Job's words. It also demonstrates how this chapter is interrelated with different parts of the book. It is not only important to treat Job 28 as an integral part of Job's last speech, it is also equally important to read the whole book as an overall unity, because all elements are structured within the plot strategy. Job 28 is within the plot development of the whole book, serving as a conclusion to the previous speech cycles, and also a deliberate foil to the subsequent oaths of innocence (Job 29-31). It marks a dramatic change in Job's emotion and characterization within its context, and paves the path to the climactic expression of Job's defence of his integrity (Job 29-31). This leads to the expectation of divine intervention. Job's contradictory statements in chapters 22-31 are the culmination of Job's honest righteousness. They serve "not just to modify our view of a certain righteous man but to redefine the concept of righteousness itself."[154]

IV. *Job 28 Related to the Rhetorical Situation of the Book*

There must be certain circumstances or contexts, which contribute to the origin of a communication act. This is the notion of rhetori-

---

[153] Brown claims: "The final series of oaths in ch. 31 reaffirms Job's own sense of integrity and equips him for the impending confrontation with Yahweh." See Brown, "Deformation of Character: Job 1-31," 81.

[154] Sternberg, *Poetics of Biblical Narrative*, 346.

cal situation. After studying how Job 28 is a part of the entire narrative plot of Job, this section focuses on how that chapter relates to the rhetorical situation of the book.

A. *Definition of Rhetorical Situation*

Before discussing how Job 28 relates to the rhetorical situation, we must first define what a rhetorical situation is. Bitzer defines the term as follows:

> A rhetorical situation may be defined as a complex of persons, events, objects, and relations which presents an exigency that can be completely or partially removed if discourse—introduced into the situation—can influence audience thought or action so as to bring about positive modification of the exigency.[155]

Before a discourse is presented, according to Bitzer, there are three constituents of a rhetorical situation:

> First, there must be an exigency—a problem or defect, something other than it should be. Second, there must be an audience capable of being constrained in thought or action in order to effect positive modification of the exigency. Third, there must be a set of constraints capable of influencing the rhetor and an audience.[156]

A particular discourse occurs in the situation where there is an urgent need, because such need invites utterance to make modification. "An exigency is an imperfection marked by some degree of urgency; it is a defect, an obstacle, something to be corrected. It is necessarily related to interests and valuations."[157] It is important to note that an exigency exists when factual conditions are related to felt interests.[158] If there is no exigency, no rhetorical communication is needed to bring forth change upon the audience. Therefore exigency is the indispensable condition of a rhetorical situation.

Rhetoric always needs an audience who are capable of being changed in line with the discourse's intent. The audience must be

---

[155] L. F. Bitzer, "Functional Communication: A Situational Perspective," *Rhetoric in Transition: Studies in the Nature and Uses of Rhetoric* (ed. Eugene E. White; University Park: The Pennsylvania State University Press, 1980) 24; and L. F. Bitzer, "The Rhetorical Situation," *Rhetoric: A Tradition in Transition. In Honor of Donald C. Bryant* (ed. Walter R. Fisher; Michigan State University Press, 1974) 252.
[156] Bitzer, "Functional Communication," 23.
[157] Bitzer, "Functional Communication," 26.
[158] Bitzer, "Functional Communication," 28.

capable of modifying the exigency positively through the influence of the rhetorical message.[159]

Every rhetorical situation contains some constraints which have the power to influence decision, thought and action required to modify the exigency. Such constraints may include beliefs, attitudes, documents, facts, traditions, images, interests, motives, persons, events, objects, relations, rules, principles, laws, emotions, arguments and so on. In order to influence the audience effectively, the speaker has to discover and use the constraints appropriately in his message.[160] Arnold regards constraints as opportunities and limitations within which and through which the rhetor must work to evoke change.[161]

To sum up, prior to the creation and presentation of a message, there must be an exigency, which specifies the audience to be addressed and the change to be effected. The speaker has to properly use the constraints to invite the audience to modify the exigency.

B. *Concept of the Audience*

The key focus of rhetorical criticism is to study the impact of a text upon the audience. Therefore it is indispensable to grasp a clear understanding of the concept of the audience. Although rhetorical criticism seeks initially to find out the audience to whom the work was first addressed,[162] it is difficult, even impossible, to trace the historical audience of the Book of Job. The narrative world in this book is a fictive domain, in which the characters are located in a distant patriarchal world outside Israel. Throughout the rest of the Old Testament there are only two references to Job in Ezekiel 14:14, 20, where Job is mentioned along with two other ancient heroes, Noah and Danel. This sixth-century reference in Ezekiel is made to the ancient hero Job, but not to the Book of Job. Suffice it to say, there is no reference to the historical background or the original audience of the book.

---

[159] Bitzer, "Functional Communication," 23; and Bitzer, "Rhetorical Situation," 253-4.

[160] Bitzer, "Functional Communication," 23-4; and Bitzer, "Rhetorical Situation," 254.

[161] C. Arnold, *Criticism of Oral Rhetoric* (Columbus: Charles E. Merrill, 1974) 28-9.

[162] Powell, *What Is Narrative Criticism?* 19.

As regards the date of Job, there is a great divergence of views in the Rabbinic tradition. In Baba Bathra 14b and 15a of the Talmud, for instance, Moses is regarded as the author of Job. But in 15a and 15b, later dates are proposed for Job, ranging from the time of the Judges (15b), the Babylonian Exile (15a), to the generation of Ahasuerus (15b). Seemingly, no consensus is reached among the rabbis.[163]

Some scholars note that the theme of innocent suffering in Job is also found in Jeremiah and Deutero-Isaiah, both of which came out of the sixth century B.C. In addition, the Babylonian exile is considered to have provided the milieu for this work on suffering. Therefore the Book of Job is sometimes regarded as a sixth century work. However, based on the limited grounds of literary affinity and foreign captivity, different scholars have different speculations about the dates for Job.[164]

For instance, Gordis holds the view that Job is later than Deutero-Isaiah. According to Gordis, the author of Job has picked up the idea that suffering is not necessarily the result of sin from the prophet of the exile. Therefore he supports a 500-300 B.C. date for Job, i.e. the era of the second temple, which marked the heyday of wisdom literature.[165] Based on the same ground of literary affinity, Pfeiffer, however, argues that Job could be interpreted as having priority over Deutero-Isaiah. If Job was composed before Deutero-Isaiah, it will lead to a date for Job not later than the sixth century.[166]

Hartley argues against the factor of Babylonian exile to set the date for Job. He finds it impossible that Job was composed to address the issue of suffering under foreign captivity, because the Book of Job focuses upon the suffering of an innocent person, while the Exile is viewed as the national punishment for the iniquities of the previous generation.[167] Seemingly, it is difficult to reach any consensus about the date of Job. Clines rightly points out: "But the author has so convincingly located his narrative in the patriarchal

---

[163] Concerning the date of the Book of Job, Pope has given a summary of these Rabbinic opinions. See Pope, *Job*, xxxii.

[164] For a full discussion of Job's date of composition, see Habel, *Job*, 40-2; Clines, *Job 1-20*, lvii; Andersen, *Job*, 61-4; Hartley, *Job*, 17-20; and Dhorme, *Job*, clxix-clxxii.

[165] Gordis, *Book of God and Man*, 216.

[166] R. H. Pfeiffer, "The Priority of Job Over Is. 40-55," *JBL* 46 (1927) 202-6.

[167] Hartley, *Job*, 18-9.

world that there are no clear contemporary allusions of any kind to the period contemporary with the author."[168]

Greidanus points out that in some narratives, "the historical reference is hermeneutically inconsequential...Thus, in the case of Job, the question of historicity is hermeneutically of no consequence."[169] "Consistent with the orientation of traditional wisdom thinking, the author of Job has created an artistic work with universal dimensions rather than a text directed at a particular historical situation or theological issue alive in Israel at a specific time."[170] This is because the author of Job does not intend to tell a historical event, but aims at persuading the audience to view suffering in a new perspective through the story he tells.

Although tracing the original audience is inconsequential in the Book of Job, the notion of the implied reader can be of help. The term "implied reader" parallels " implied author", which was coined by Booth. The latter notion can help us grasp a clearer understanding of the former. According to Booth, "the author's judgment is always present, always evident to anyone who knows how to look for it."[171] He further adds, "As he writes, he creates not simply an ideal, impersonal 'man in general' but an implied version of 'himself' that is different from the implied authors we meet in other men's works."[172] Booth further elaborates the sense of the implied author as follows:

> Our sense of the implied author includes not only the extractable meanings but also the moral and emotional content of each bit of action and suffering of all of the characters. It includes, in short, the intuitive apprehension of a completed artistic whole; the chief value to which this implied author is committed, regardless of what party his creator belongs to in real life, is that which is expressed by the total form.[173]

The notion of the implied reader parallels that of the implied author. Booth explains, "The author creates, in short, an image of himself and another image of his reader; he makes his reader, as he makes his second self, and the most successful reading is one in

---

[168] Clines, *Job 1-20*, lvii.
[169] S. Greidanus, *The Modern Preacher and the Ancient Text* (Grand Rapids: Eerdmans, 1988) 195.
[170] Habel, *Job*, 42.
[171] W. C. Booth, *The Rhetoric of Fiction* (Chicago; London: The University of Chicago Press, 1961) 20.
[172] Booth, *Rhetoric of Fiction*, 70-1.
[173] Booth, *Rhetoric of Fiction*, 73-4.

which the created selves, author and reader, can find complete agreement."[174] Therefore the implied reader is the one who responds to the expectations of its implied author. Powell highlights the advantage of using this concept: "The concept of the implied reader is a heuristic construct that allows critics to limit the subjectivity of their analysis by distinguishing between their own responses to a narrative and those that the text appears to invite."[175] In this way the concept of the implied reader and implied author maximises the constraints of the text in interpretation.

As mentioned above, the notion of the implied reader can help reconstruct the audience of the book. However, the concept of "audience" is somewhat different from that of "implied reader." This study mainly focuses upon the rhetorical audience which must be distinguished from a body of mere hearers or readers. The rhetorical audience consists only of those who are capable of being influenced and persuaded by the discourse and of being mediators of change. Not every discourse requires an audience to produce an end. Some discourses may simply serve to give information, knowledge, amusement, aesthetic experiences and so forth, but without persuading another's mind. Their audience is not necessarily rhetorical.[176] "But the rhetorical audience must be capable of serving as mediator of the change which the discourse functions to produce."[177] In order to distinguish the rhetorical audience from a body of mere hearers or readers, the term "audience" is preferred in this study.

C. *Rhetorical Situation of the Book of Job*

1. *The Exigency of the Rhetorical Situation*

The exigencies can be reconstructed by tracing the problems of the characters in the narrative. A number of exigencies are revealed in the debate between Job and his friends.

a) Blind Application of the Theodicies

A clue to the rhetorical exigency may be found in the problems of

---

[174] Booth, *Rhetoric of Fiction*, 138.
[175] M. A. Powell, "Narrative Criticism," *Hearing the New Testament: Strategies for Interpretation* (ed. Joel B. Green; Grand Rapids: Eerdmans, 1995) 241.
[176] Bitzer, "Rhetorical Situation," 253.
[177] Bitzer, "Rhetorical Situation," 254.

the friends. In fact, the friends have the problem of misinterpreting the relationship between suffering and the nature of God. They do not know how to reconcile innocent suffering with the goodness and justice of God. Based upon the belief that God always judges rightly between the righteous and the wicked, the friends do not accept that the righteous can suffer. To defend God's justice they accuse Job of being a sinner. More seriously, they even invent false allegations against Job in order to justify God (22:6-9). In response to the friends' arguments, Job criticizes them as liars (13:4a, 7), miserable comforters (16:2-3), worthless physicians (13:4b) and false accusers (19:2-3; 27:5).

Bound by their religious background, the friends employ the theodicies to explain Job's case. By definition, "a theodicy seeks to acquit God of the evil that befalls his servants."[178] Eliphaz, in his opening speech, has already set out each of the three theodicies, which are further advanced by himself and his two companions later in the debate with Job.[179] These three theodicies are the concept of retribution, the depravity of human beings and the chastisement of God.

i) The Concept of Retribution
This theodicy receives the greatest emphasis from all of the friends (Eliphaz 4:7-11; 15:17-35; 22:5-20; Bildad 8:8-22; 18:5-21; Zophar 11:13-20; 20:4-29).[180] In regard to this theodicy, Clines rightly notes that each of them argues from a different perspective, though their arguments share the same presupposition of a causal nexus between sin and suffering. Eliphaz sets suffering in the context of Job's evidently near-blameless life and his intention is to encourage Job to have patience and hope (4:6; 5:8). Bildad sets suffering in the context of the fate of Job's children and his intention is to warn Job to seek God's face in order not to be guilty of sins and struck dead as Job's children were (8:5-6). As for Zophar, his words are least sympathetic and sin is the principal issue in his argument. He argues

---

[178] Nicholson, "Limits of Theodicy," 72. Crenshaw defines theodicy "as the attempt to pronounce a verdict of 'Not Guilty' over God for whatever seems to destroy the order of society and the universe"; see J. L. Crenshaw, "Introduction: The Shift from Theodicy to Anthropodicy," *Theodicy in the Old Testament* (ed. James L. Crenshaw; Philadelphia: Fortress Press, 1983) 1.
[179] Nicholson, "Limits of Theodicy," 74.
[180] Nicholson, "Limits of Theodicy," 74-6.

from the suffering of Job in order to denounce Job and to urge him to repent of the sins that he has already committed (11:6c).[181]

In the first speech cycle Eliphaz sets up this theodicy to exhort Job to be patient and to put his confidence in his fear of God (4:6). It is meant to give hope and comfort to Job, because no innocent person has ever perished (4:7-8). Job's innocence is not questioned at this stage.

In his first speech (ch. 8) Bildad holds the assumption that God does not pervert justice (v.3). He argues from the contrast of the fate of Job's children (v.4) with Job's own prospects (vv.5-7) in order to give warning.[182] The death of Job's children is a proof of punishment (v.4). Since Job is still alive he is probably innocent of any sin deserving death. If Job is "pure and upright," God will deliver him (vv.6-7). In vv.21-22 Bildad concludes that "He (God) will yet fill your mouth with laughter, and your lips with shouting. Those who hate you will be clothed with shame; and the tent of the wicked will be no more." Bildad's conclusion seems to leave the question of Job's innocence open.[183]

Then, in his first speech (ch. 11), Zophar starts his argument with the assumption that suffering is deserved. He states that God punishes Job less than his iniquity deserves (v.6). Zophar points out that God's wisdom is beyond human understanding (vv.7-9), and God's superior knowledge reliably detects evils (vv.10-11). In view of God's immense wisdom, Zophar advises Job to reorient himself to God, and reform his conduct (vv.13-14). Then his troubles will be gone, and he will enjoy a secure and blessed life (vv.15-19). However, the wicked will have no security and hope (v.20).[184]

In the second cycle, to refute Job's claim that God's world is morally incoherent, Eliphaz employs the traditional concept of the fate of the wicked as evidence for the moral order of the world (15:17-35).[185] In his second speech Bildad's reply begins with the

---

[181] D. J. A. Clines, "The Arguments of Job's Three Friends," *Art and Meaning: Rhetoric in Biblical Literature* (JSOTSup 19; ed. D. J. A. Clines, David M. Gunn and Alan J. Hauser; Sheffield: JSOT Press, 1982) 210.

[182] Clines, "Arguments," 210.

[183] Clines, "Arguments," 206.

[184] Clines, "Arguments," 206-7.

[185] Clines points out, "how Eliphaz's affirmation of Job's piety in the first cycle (chs. 4-5) requires us to read his description of the fate of the wicked in the second cycle (ch. 15) as a depiction of what Job's fate is certainly not." According to Clines, the fate of the wicked in vv.17-35 is not describing Job's destiny. Since

objection to Job's words and attitude (18:1-4). The rest of the chapter focuses upon the descriptive account of the fate of the wicked (18:5-21).[186]

Like Eliphaz and Bildad before him, Zophar's speech in the second cycle focuses almost wholly on the description of the fate of the wicked in chapter 20. Three themes can be found here: 1) the brevity of the joy of the wicked (vv.5-11); 2) the self-destructive nature of evil through a striking series of metaphors pertaining to eating (vv.12-23); and 3) the inescapable destruction of the wicked by all the elements of the earth and the heavens (vv.24-29).

In the third speech cycle the application of the retributive concept reaches its climax when Eliphaz accuses Job of "great wickedness" (22:5) and falsely attributes flagrant misdeeds to him (22:6-9). Then he declares the fate of the wicked upon Job (22:10-20). But Eliphaz's conviction of Job's piety surfaces again, and the restoration of Job is assured (22:21-30).[187]

As mentioned above, the concept of retribution is characteristic of all the friends' speeches. Based upon the retributive principle, the friends' logic is that all sinners suffer. Job's suffering prompts them to conclude that Job is a sinner. The friends' elemental compassion has finally turned to cruel judgment upon Job so as to defend their doctrinaire interests. However, the author of Job wants to underscore that suffering does not necessarily prove the sinfulness of the sufferer.

ii) The Concept of Human Depravity

The second theodicy[188] set out by Eliphaz in his opening address is that all human beings are by birth and nature inherently morally flawed in God's eyes (4:17-21). Since God even puts no trust in His servants and charges His angels with error (4:18), "how much more those who dwell in houses of clay" (4:19). Eliphaz argues that perfect innocence, "purity" or "righteousness" (4:17) is not to be found

---

Job is not wicked, he is not doomed for ultimate destruction or prolonged suffering. Eliphaz just defends the religious ideology, but does not accuse Job as the wicked. See Clines, "Arguments," 211.

[186] Clines points out, "Bildad's exhortation to Job in his first cycle speech (ch. 8) to search his heart and take warning from the fate of his children becomes the hermeneutical clue for the reading of his second cycle speech (ch. 18): the fate of the wicked is a possibility that confronts Job, but may yet be avoided by him." See Clines, "Arguments," 211.

[187] Clines, "Arguments," 207-8, 211.

[188] Nicholson, "Limits of Theodicy," 76-7.

among human beings. It implies that not even Job is fully righteous in God's eyes, and so he cannot hope to escape God's judgment. Therefore even the most innocent, like Job, must expect to suffer deservedly on occasion.

In his second speech Eliphaz returns to this theme in 15:14-16, where he reminds Job of the truth about human nature, its inherent corruptness in the eyes of God. Once again, Eliphaz points out that God puts no trust in His holy ones, and even the heavens are not pure in His eyes (15:15; cf. 4:18). How much less is man, who is born of a woman (15:14, 16; cf. 4:19). In this section men are described as "detestable" and "corrupt" and their innate tendency to do evil is depicted as "drinking iniquity like water" (15:16).[189]

The climax of the concept of human inherent corruptness as a theodicy is reached in Bildad's final speech in chapter 25. Bildad declares that nothing in the created order, including man, can show any kind of cleanness (25:4-6). He emphasizes that mortals are "born of woman" (25:4; cf. 15:14), thus subject to corruption. Human beings are counted as no more than "maggots" or "worms" (25:6), which are the symbols of death, decay and the underworld in the Book of Job (7:5; 17:14; 21:26; 24:20). Therefore Job's claim to be innocent before God is preposterous. According to Clines, Bildad's focus upon the "uncleanness" of all created things echoes with his previous affirmation that since God does not pervert justice (8:3), sin must be punished.[190] In short, Bildad's speech in chapter 25, along with Eliphaz's speeches in 4:17-21 and 15:14-16, highlights the inherent corruptness of human beings as a theodicy to account for Job's suffering.

iii) The Divine Chastisement
Eliphaz proposes the third theodicy to interpret suffering as divine disciplining.[191] That means that Job has erred in some way, but not deliberately sinned against God. Therefore he needs corrective chastening from God, which will result in blessing and renewed wellbeing (5:17-27). This theodicy is not mentioned by the friends again in the dialogue until Elihu picks it up with great emphasis later (33:13-30; 34:31-33; 36:7-12, 15-16). Its assumption is that the sufferer is in some way blameworthy, and that God's correction is out

---

[189] Nicholson, "Limits of Theodicy," 76.
[190] Clines, "Arguments," 212-3.
[191] Nicholson, "Limits of Theodicy," 74, 77-78.

of mercy, not out of anger (33:14-33). Like the other two theodicies, Eliphaz also sees suffering as the evidence and proof of Job's wrongdoing when he applies the principle of divine correction to Job.

The theodicies mentioned above provide the reasoning behind the friends' rejection of the possibility of innocent suffering, and explain why they cannot resolve the conflict between innocent suffering and God's goodness and justice. The audience is assumed to have the same problem of misapplying the theodicies to account for suffering. The misapplication of the traditional theodicies is the exigency that the author needs to rectify in order to elicit changes from the audience.

b) Proud Claims to Knowledge
Another problem illustrated by the friends is the way in which they authorize their claims to knowledge.[192] It is in regard to their knowledge of the nature of God, the moral order of the world and the meaning of what has befallen Job that they authorize their claims to such understanding. In their argument they cite anecdotal evidence (4:8; 5:3) or even personal visions (4:12-16) as the authority of their claims to knowledge. They greatly rely upon the authority of tradition. They authorize their claims to knowledge by appealing to ancestral tradition (8:8-10; 15:17-19), and filling their speeches with traditional religious language, such as sayings, didactic examples and doxologies. The ground of their claims is confirmed by careful investigation (5:27). They boast of their wisdom and comprehension of the truth (15:8-10; 20:3). More precisely, they assume omniscience (12:2-3; 13:2, 5), playing God and passing judgment upon Job through their authorized claims to knowledge.

In sum, the friends' problems provide a clue to the rhetorical exigency. It is this sort of uncritical judgment of the religious tradition, blind application of theology, proud claims to knowledge and unauthorized right to play God that the author intends to challenge and break down.

c) Misconceptions of God
A trace of the rhetorical exigency may be found in the problems of Job. Similar to the friends' problem, the crux of Job's dilemma is that he cannot reconcile his own undeserved suffering with God's justice. In fact, Job holds the same theological assumption as the

---

[192] Newsom, "Job," 335.

friends that only the guilty suffer. However, based on the same presupposition, Job goes to another extreme to interpret his case.

This faulty theological presupposition has resulted in Job's misconceptions of God. Confident that he is innocent, Job claims that his undeserved suffering must be the fault of God. In contrast to the friends' conventional views that affirm God's goodness and justice (8:3), Job questions God's nature and His governance of the world.[193] Job depicts God as a violator of justice (27:2), who acts out of malicious curiosity (7:17-20) or in sadistic rage (16:9-14). Job highlights God's violent, capricious and fickle character by pointing out that God uses His cosmic power in a disruptive way (9:5-13). He also alleges that God's providential care and tender love to him are just a façade to trap him in sin (10:8-13). In addition, Job claims that God uses His wisdom and might for creating chaos rather than order in nature and society (12:13-25). To further attack God's "moral" governance over the world, Job underscores the prosperity of the wicked (21:30-33), widespread social injustice and the pervasive abuse of the poor (24:1-17). Job wants to bring out the point that there is a tremendous contradiction between his experience of reality and his belief about God's nature.

However, Job's speeches set up a even more complicated theological issue: he has two conflicting concepts of God. Despite the evidence of his experience and his observation of the reality, Job cannot give up the idea that God is a God of justice (13:15-22; 23:3-7).[194] Job makes an oath of innocence by the name of God whom he accuses of taking away his right and embittering his soul (27:2-6). His final vow of innocence reflects his strong desire to present his case before God, in order that he might be vindicated by Him (Job 29-31). These two oaths have brought Job's contradictory views of God to the fullest expression—seeking justice from a God who wrongs him unjustly. Newsom remarks: "The theological and emotional power of the book is due in large measure to the apparently insoluble nature of this contradictory experience."[195] Job's excruciating dilemma and his misconception of God originate from his faulty theological presupposition that only the guilty suffer. This is the nub of the problem that the author needs to work through in order to evoke modifications of the exigencies.

---

[193] Newsom, "Job," 335; also Habel, *Job*, 366.
[194] Newsom, "Job," 335.
[195] Newsom, "Job," 335.

To sum up, neither the friends nor Job can reconcile suffering with God's justice. Basically, both of them share the same paradigm of understanding. They all take as unquestionable the assumption that only the guilty suffer. However, based upon such an assumption, they go to different extremes to interpret Job's suffering. Proudly claiming to knowledge, the friends choose to defend God's integrity by applying three theodicies to Job's case, but at the expense of Job's integrity. They conclude that Job's suffering is the evidence and proof of his wrongdoing. Job seeks to defend his own integrity by condemning God as unjust, but at the expense of God's integrity. Job maintains that his undeserved suffering is the evidence of divine injustice and misgovernance over the world. Job's and his friends' misunderstanding of the relationship between suffering and God's nature are the signs of the rhetorical exigencies, which prompt the author of Job to compose this discourse so as to bring transformation to the audience.

2. *The Audience of the Rhetorical Situation*
Although the historically original audience cannot be traced, the previous discussion of the problems of Job and the friends leads rightly to the question: who is the audience of this story? The audience must be assumed to share some of the misconceptions of Job and the friends. They must be interested in probing the mysteries of man's relationship to God in the issue of human suffering, and the mysteries of the existence of evil in God's world. An exigency specifies the audience to be addressed. Job and the friends are deeply influenced by some of the concepts of mainstream Yahwism and wisdom traditions that the righteous will be rewarded and the wicked punished. The problems of the characters revealed in the narrative imply that these are the exigencies existing among the audience. In the Book of Job both Job and his friends are corrected by God's particular perspective of reality. Similarly, the author also expects the audience to accept God's vision of reality and to have their worldview transformed through listening to the story of Job, because the rhetorical audience "must be capable of modifying the exigency positively."[196]

---

[196] Bitzer, "Functional Communication," 23.

3. *The Constraint of the Rhetorical Situation*

As we have seen, constraints are the limitations and opportunities within which and through which any rhetor must work to induce change.[197] The constraint of the rhetorical situation can be drawn from all the speakers in the Joban story. It is the broad religious situation which sets the parameters of the debate. Certainly, the sayings of the protagonists cannot be taken at their face value, but need to be interpreted in the context of the dialogue as a whole. Even so I think that certain basic shared beliefs can be deduced by this means. In fact, the basic beliefs in Job are also broadly shared with other Old Testament writers and theology.

The most important constraint of the rhetorical situation is the traditional religious background. The audience is assumed to share the similar religious background with the characters in the Joban story. It is immediately clear that a description of this constraint lies close to a description of the exigency. However, it is possible to keep the two ideas apart.

Concerning the concept of God, the Book of Job is dominated by the idea of One God (cf. Deut 4:35, 39; Isa 44:6-8; 46:9). The names of Yahweh, Elohim, El-Shaddai, Eloah[198] refer to the same God, who creates and sustains the universe (5:8-18; 9:4-13; 12:13; cf. Ex 6:2-3). For example, human life comes from God (3:4-5, 20), who moulds, fashions and creates the embryo in a mother's womb (10:8-12).

A crucial factor is the belief that the relationship between man and God is governed by justice. God is the Judge (23:3-7; 37:23). It is believed that God Himself is absolute righteousness and that He does not pervert justice (8:3; 34:17-18, 23-28; cf. Jer 23:6).

It is true that Job questions God's justice. For example, he complains that God is elusive (9:14-16); He strikes him without cause (9:17-19); He destroys both the righteous and wicked (9:22); He gives him up to the ungodly (16:11-18); and He refuses to do him justice (19:6-12; 27:2-3). However, Job's continuous appeals to God's judgment (10:2-7; 13:3, 15-24; 16:19-21; 19:25-27; 23:3-7) reveal his presupposition of the divine justice, which comes to its fullest expression in his final oath of innocence (chs. 29-31).

---

[197] Arnold, *Criticism of Oral Rhetoric*, 28-9.
[198] Concerning the divine names in different parts of the book, see Driver and Gray, *Book of Job*, xxxv-xxxvi.

The fear of God/the Lord is a loyal response toward God (cf. Deut 6:2, 13, 24). Job is a man who fears God (1:1, 8; 2:3). This fear of God is wisdom (28:28; cf. Prov 1:7; 9:10; 15:33; Ps 111:10). It also implies the practical acts of piety and religious duties (4:6; 15:4). Fear of God is always associated with shunning evil (1:1, 8; 2:3; 28:28; cf. Prov 3:7). Those who fear God and shun evil are usually regarded as the "blameless", "upright", "innocent" and "righteous". However, those who forget God (8:13), reject His direction (21:14-16) and protection (22:15-18) are the sinful/wicked. To do good is wisdom (28:28), but to do evil is folly. Sin is seen as stupidity (1:22; 2:10) and the sinner as senseless (5:2, 3).

Based on the presupposition of the divine justice, it is believed that there is a connection between moral good and prosperity, moral evil and calamity (4:8; 5:6; cf. Prov 22:8; 10:27). This leads to the conviction that the righteous ought to be rewarded and the wicked punished. God ought to reward those who are loyal to Him. There are traces of this expectation, e.g. in Job's words in 13:23-28. Thus, in trying to describe the "constraint" of the rhetorical situation, one inevitably comes close to a description of the exigency.

In short, the constraint of the rhetorical situation is the traditional religious background, which can be traced throughout the story. The audience is assumed to be influenced and shaped by such a background. The protagonists believe in One God, who is the creator and sustainer of the universe. The relation between God and man is governed and regulated by justice. Fear of God and shunning evil are the loyal response to God, and He ought to reward those who are loyal to Him.

D. *Job 28 in Relation to the Rhetorical Situation of the Book*

Job 28 relates to the rhetorical situation of the book in terms of the constraint, the exigency and the audience. In regard to the constraint, Job 28 reflects the traditional religious background of the protagonists. Throughout vv.1-27, the poem highlights the unavailability of wisdom to human beings. Only God can have access to it. The only avenue for mankind to acquire wisdom is to fear God and shun evil (v.28). Job 28:28 is very much in the vein of some of the ideas of mainstream Yahwism and wisdom traditions, which define wisdom as "fearing God" and "shunning evil" (cf. Prov 1:7; 9:10), and highlight blessings for obedience and curses for disobedience (cf.

Deut 28:1-14; 28:15-68; Prov 3:33; 10:27; 10:30; 12:21; 15:29; Ps 1:4-6; 10:14-15; 37:35-36; 112:10; Ps 1:1-3; 15:1-5; 33:18-19; 112:1-9; 119:1-2). God's promise in Job 28:28 is the religious belief that Job and his friends hold tightly. This belief leads to their common presupposition that only the guilty suffer. The author will further reveal the inadequacy of such theology to explain Job's case through the Yahweh speeches.

In addition, Job 28 also relates to the exigency of the rhetorical situation reflected through the problems of the characters. Here the problems of the friends are treated as exigency. After the total collapse of the debate, Job utters this poem to pinpoint the limitation of human wisdom. The friends claim to have wisdom, but they fail to give an account for Job's suffering. They misunderstand the relationship between suffering and the nature of God. Their rigid imposition of the theodicies upon Job's case is proved to be wrong when Job points out the contradiction between experience and belief. Therefore this poem serves as a judgment upon the friends' misinterpretation of Job's suffering and their proud claims to knowledge throughout the three cycles of dialogue. Job 28 marks the confirmation that Job's problem needs to be resolved through channels other than human wisdom. His pondering over the issue of wisdom in Job 28 gives new impetus to Job's drive to seek God in person. This paves the way to the resolution of the other exigency illustrated by Job's problems later in the divine encounter.

Job 28 relates to the audience of the book too. It reveals the traditional religious contexts that deeply influence the audience's worldview. This wisdom poem provides some space for the audience to reflect over and evaluate the validity of their traditional theology—fearing God and shunning evil as the way to acquire wisdom. Seemingly, Job 28 points out the inadequacy of such theology to account for the innocent suffering. This chapter serves to engage the audience to seek the ultimate resolution for Job's bitter dilemma.

To sum up, Job 28 is closely related to the rhetorical situation of the book. It reflects the exigency, the constraint and the audience of the rhetorical situation that urge the rhetor to tell the story of Job so as to elicit a transformation of the exigency. In the next chapter this study will also show, in a closer analysis of chapters 22-31, that it is best to place Job 28 in Job's mouth.

V. *Job 28 Within the Overall Rhetorical Strategy of the Book*

The friends' theodicies and Job's argument from experience reveal that both positions actually depend on the same paradigm of understanding, which comes from their traditional religious background. As we have seen, both Job and the friends take for granted the assumption that retributive justice should be the central principle of reality. They all believe that only the guilty suffer.

To correct this, as Newsom states, the book appears to have been directing the audience "from less to more adequate perspectives."[199] She rightly remarks: "Within the dialogues, the friends' moral perspectives are shown to be inadequate by the compelling power of Job's words. The inadequacy of Job's perspective, however, is disclosed by the extraordinary speeches of God from the whirlwind. Surely one is supposed to adopt and endorse the perspective articulated by none other than God."[200] Newsom has notably pointed out how the author discovers and properly uses the constraints, within which or through which he works to evoke changes. This is an indispensable process in persuading the audience to modify the exigency.

A. *Inadequacy of the Friends' Perspectives*

The author demonstrates the inadequacy of the friends' theodicies through Job's arguments from his experience of reality. As mentioned above, the friends have proposed three theodicies to explain Job's case: 1) the reward/retributive concept; 2) the depravity of human beings; and 3) the divine corrective chastening. In regard to the reward/retributive concept, the friends stress God's just governance of the world. However, the author manifestly exposes the inadequacy of this theodicy by juxtaposing Job's ample evidence of the prosperity and security of the wicked.[201] Job points out that God seems to favour the plans of the wicked (10:3). Their homes are at peace (12:6). They enjoy longevity, die in peace, and are blessed with offsprings (21:7-13). In chapter 24 Job daringly pinpoints the contradiction between the reality of social injustice (24:1-17) and the traditional belief in God's judgment upon the wicked (24:18-25).

---

[199] Newsom, "Job," 337.
[200] Newsom, "Job," 337.
[201] Nicholson, "Limits of Theodicy," 75.

The prosperity of the wicked and the existence of social injustice indicate the inadequacy of the friends' retributive concept in interpreting Job's case and reality.

To counter the friends' concept of human depravity, which abases human worth before God, Job utters the passage in 7:17-21 to parody the teaching of Psalm 8:5-6 about human beings as God's noblest creation. Job charges that God's creative and providential deeds are but a façade to trap him in sin (10:1-17). Despite Job's misconception of God's nature, his argument aims to show the friends that "there is a jarring disjunction between what a text such as Psalm viii declares about human worth and the actual lot of many like Job in God's world. It is not that the creature is flawed in the making, but that for many God's world seems to be such that human beings are the victims of apparently arbitrary evil."[202] Again, Job's argument discloses the inadequacy of the friends' concept of humanity's sinful nature.

As regards the third theodicy—the notion of suffering as divine disciplining—Job attacks the rationale that God corrects wrongdoing out of merciful love by pointing out that he sees no fatherly correction from God. What he experiences is God treating him as His primordial enemy—the sea or the sea monster (7:12). Job's personal experience is evidently incongruent with the theodicy of loving divine correction. Job's argument is so powerful that the point remains untouched from Eliphaz's first mention until it is raised again by Elihu later in the story.[203]

To conclude, seeing that the friends' perspectives are bound by their traditional theological beliefs and presuppositions, the author of Job deliberately makes use of Job's own experiences of reality to expose the limitations of their theodicies in explaining Job's suffering. In this way the audience is invited and even challenged to make a critical judgment over their own theology from within another vision of reality.

B. *Inadequacy of Job's Perspectives*

Like the friends, Job has his misconception about the relationship between suffering and God's nature. Such misunderstanding also originates from the bounds of his theological presupposition that

---

[202] Nicholson, "Limits of Theodicy," 77.
[203] Nicholson, "Limits of Theodicy," 78.

retributive justice should be the central principle of reality, and that only the guilty suffer. Therefore he cannot reconcile his own undeserved suffering with the justice of God. The author skilfully exposes the inadequacy of Job's perspectives by using the two divine speeches from the whirlwind. Gordis appropriately comments that the purpose of the Yahweh speeches is "not the glorification of nature but the vindication of nature's God."[204]

The first Yahweh speech (38:1-39:30) focuses upon the divine "counsel" or "plan" (עֵצָה; 38:2). Here God first speaks of cosmological and meteorological phenomena (38:4-38), where He demonstrates His secure and well-ordered cosmos. He does not mention the place of human beings in the cosmos.[205] The universe was not created exclusively for human beings. Therefore man cannot judge the universe and its creator solely by human standards and measures.[206] Then God parades five pairs of animals (38:39-39:30) and shows His providential care over these creatures.

The first speech of Yahweh aims at pointing out Job's fault that he darkens God's counsel by words without knowledge (38:2). By means of rhetorical questions God speaks of His own wisdom and power in regard to the creation of the universe and nature, and Job's relative weakness and ignorance. Fox rightly states:

> God overwhelms Job by showing him the obvious, by opening his eyes to what he already knows. If the theophany had been a revelation of something new or hidden, the book would not be so relevant for people who do not receive such a revelation. On the other hand, if God had merely tried to shut Job up by demonstrating Job's ignorance, he would be saying that there was no possible way for Job to see God's equity and orderly rule and thus would in effect be excusing him for speaking of God as arbitrary and immoral.[207]

Therefore, on the one hand, God reminds Job of the limitations of his human understanding by asking him "Can you...?" (e.g. 38:31-35). On the other hand, God reminds Job of the potential of his wisdom by asking him "Who... since you know?" (e.g. 38:5, 25, 36, 41; 39:5). Although the universe and natural world are beyond man's power to fully comprehend, Job is still able to recognise God's orderly governance over the universe and His providential care over

---

[204] R. Gordis, "The Lord Out of the Whirlwind," *Judaism* 13 (1964) 49.
[205] Newsom, "Job," 336.
[206] Gordis, *Book of Job*, 435; also Newsom, "Job," 596-7.
[207] M. V. Fox, "Job 38 and God's Rhetoric," *Semeia* 19 (1981) 59-60.

the natural world. God rebukes Job for not living up to the potential of this wisdom. God criticizes Job for darkening His counsel with words without knowledge (38:2). This implies that God's plan (עֵצָה) for the world is so essentially manifest that Job is blameworthy for obscuring a truth that he has already known.[208] Suffering does not necessarily prove God's misgovernance over the world.

The second speech of Yahweh (40:6-41:26 [34]) highlights divine justice (מִשְׁפָּט; 40:8). This speech concerns a single pair of animals, Behemoth (40:15-24) and Leviathan (40:25-41:26 [41:1-34]). Behemoth and Leviathan are legendary creatures with mythic overtones. Leviathan is a symbol of threatening force, associated with primeval chaos.[209] These texts reveal the tension between the existence of evil and God's absolute justice. Here God acknowledges that there is evil existing in the world order. He affirms the complexity of the universe and its conflicting forces.[210] "But the declaration of these speeches...that the power of chaos, though not eliminated, is confined, and that God has given his pledge to his creation, renders evil less absolute than it would otherwise be."[211] Although evil exists in God's world, God is still the just God and He is in control.

The second divine speech aims at rebuking Job's justification of himself by putting God in the wrong (40:8). God points out that the existence of evil in God's world is a paradox. The righteous may suffer. However, innocent suffering does not necessarily mean that God and His world are evil. This message challenges Job to cling to his faith in the ultimate goodness of the living God, even though he experiences evil in God's world. It is the heart of God's answer to Job.

Apart from these points, the Yahweh speeches also serve to refute second-hand experiences of God. Job's arguments have demonstrated the inadequacies of the traditional religious consolations articulated by the friends. The parental, national, traditional teaching about God is inadequate to resolve Job's problem. Only the first-hand encounter with God brings Job to total submission (42:5). This divine encounter makes Job admit that he has hidden God's counsels without knowledge (42:3).

---

[208] Fox, "Job 38," 58-60.
[209] Newsom, "Job," 597.
[210] Gordis, "The Lord Out of the Whirlwind," 50.
[211] Nicholson, "Limits of Theodicy," 82.

To conclude, in order to effectively rectify the exigencies, the author has to discover and work through some constraints to evoke changes. In the story of Job the constraint for the friends and Job basically comes from the bounds of their traditional theological beliefs and presuppositions—especially about justice. The friends defend God's justice in governance, but Job accuses God of injustice. Within the dialogue the author exposes the inadequacies of the friends' perspective by juxtaposing Job's contradictory experience of the reality. Then he proceeds to demonstrate the limitations of Job's perspective by using God's challenge and correction in the Yahweh speeches.

C. *Job 28 as Part of the "From Less to More Adequate Perspectives" Strategy*

As illustrated above, the author has used the strategy of "from less to more adequate perspectives" to guide the audience from truth to whole truth so as to resolve the exigency of the rhetorical situation. The inadequacy of the friends' perspectives is revealed through Job's argument from his experience, whereas the inadequacy of Job's perspective is exposed through Yahweh's teaching. Job 28 serves as a transitional chapter to link these two parts of the strategy. On the one hand, it draws a conclusion upon the collapse of the debate. The total silence of the friends symbolizes their failure to convince Job. On the other hand, Job 28 functions as a deliberate foil (especially 28:28) to trigger Job's final oath of integrity before God (chs. 29-31), which provokes God to vindicate Himself in the theophany (chs. 38-41). Then, through Yahweh's correction, Job's inadequacy of perspective is pointed out.

Within the context of chapters 22-31, Job 28 shares a common structure of contradictory juxtaposition with its surrounding chapters. This section is characterized by Job's series of contradictory sayings, which highlight the contradictions between reality and belief, thus serving as the most powerful weapon to expose the inadequacy of the friends' theology. Job 28 within the context of the rhetorical strategy of contradictory juxtaposition in chapters 22-31 will be fully investigated in the next chapter of this study.

VI. *Conclusion*

This chapter seeks to argue that Job 28 is Job's speech and an integral part of the whole book. However, the true significance of this chapter can only be seen when the other parts of the book are also treated as a unified work. Although the Book of Job is full of incongruities and discrepancies—Job 28 among them—there is still a continuous narrative plot to give coherence to all of these inconsistencies. Job's characterization and the plot development of the story indicate that Job 28 is Job's speech and it fits well in the author's entire plot design. In addition, this wisdom poem also relates with the rhetorical situation of the book, reflecting the three constituents of the situation—the exigency, constraint and audience. Furthermore, it serves as a transitional chapter in the author's "from less to more adequate perspectives" strategy to rectify the exigency of the rhetorical situation. The next chapter will focus on how Job 28 functions within the context of Job 22-31.

CHAPTER THREE

JOB 28 WITHIN JOB 22-31

I. *Introduction*

In Chapter Two we saw how Job 28 makes sense as Job's words, and how it is related to the whole book. Through an examination of plot development and Job's characterization in the story, it was argued that Job 28 plays a key part in linking its preceding and subsequent chapters. In addition, Job 28 is also closely related to the rhetorical situation of the book—the exigency, the audience and the constraint—which motivates the author to tell the story of Job. Furthermore, Job 28 is also within the author's overall rhetorical strategy—"from less to more adequate perspectives"—to achieve transformation of the exigency.

In this chapter it proceeds to examine how Job 28 functions within the immediate context of chapters 22-31. Many scholars reject 24:18-24, 26:5-14, 27:13-23 and Job 28 as Job's words, because these passages are not quite like Job's other sayings, but are instead rather similar to the friends' arguments. Such discrepancy has prompted many scholars to claim that the third speech cycle has undergone disruptions and that Job 28 is a secondary addition. However, this study seeks to argue that the juxtaposition of Job's contradictory sayings in chapters 22-31 is part of the author's rhetorical strategy, intended to elicit a transformation of the exigency. Suffice it to say, this chapter aims at pointing out how Job 28 fits well in the context of chapters 22-31, which is frequently regarded as the most perplexing section in the book.

This chapter presents four major concerns. First, it introduces contradictory juxtaposition as part of the author's rhetorical strategy. Special reference is made to Sternberg's methodology. Secondly, it investigates how to discern the author's intended impacts upon the audience by discussing the presuppositions needed for the audience to approach the story, the author's guide to interpretation, the interpretation of dramatic presentation and God's final verdict in 42:7b as the key to interpretation. Thirdly, it explores the rhetorical functions of Job's contradictory sayings in chapters 22-31. Here rhetorical analysis is addressed to the rhetorical impacts of Job's contradictory sayings in two respects: 1) the flow of argument in the story; and 2) the audience. Fourthly, after the study of each individual unit of speech, there are further discussions of how Job 28 is connected with its surrounding chapters by the common structure of contradictory juxtapositions in chapters 22-31, and how the gaps generated by such contradictions can be closed. As regards the gap-filling process, special attention is drawn to the relationship between Job 28 and the Yahweh speeches.

II. *Contradictory Juxtaposition as Part of the Author's Rhetorical Strategy*

This section aims to define the notion of contradictory juxtaposition, underscoring its functions and paying attention to the positive and negative aspects of gapping.

A. *Definition of Contradictory Juxtaposition*[1]

According to Sternberg, a literary work is a system of gaps which need to be filled.[2] Contradictory juxtaposition appears when "the narrative juxtaposes two pieces of reality that bear on the same context but fail to harmonize either as variants of a situation or as phases in an action."[3] Its common phenomenon is that "event clashes with event, speech with event, speech with speech, or interior with vocal discourse."[4] In addition, the two opposite pieces are juxtaposed in such an abrupt succession that it widens their semantic distance.[5] Semantically, "the fuller the opposition, the more incongruous the juxtaposition."[6] Therefore contradictory juxtaposition "opens gaps, gaps produce discontinuity, and discontinuity breeds ambiguity."[7] By definition, a gap is "a lack of information about the world", which may be an event, motive, causal link, character trait,

---

[1] The term "contradictory juxtaposition" here is equivalent to Sternberg's idea of "opposition in juxtaposition." For further details, see Sternberg, *Poetics of Biblical Narrative*, 242-7.

[2] Sternberg, *Poetics of Biblical Narrative*, 186.
[3] Sternberg, *Poetics of Biblical Narrative*, 243.
[4] Sternberg, *Poetics of Biblical Narrative*, 243.
[5] Sternberg, *Poetics of Biblical Narrative*, 243.
[6] Sternberg, *Poetics of Biblical Narrative*, 245.
[7] Sternberg, *Poetics of Biblical Narrative*, 236.

plot structure or law of probability.[8] Sternberg further points out: "Gaps...and their expression heighten our sense of disharmony: they bring out the missing link in the chain, the oddity of conduct, the inconsistency or looseness of the official record."[9]

Proverbs 26:4-5 is one of the most interesting examples of contradictory juxtaposition. Here the sage exhorts us in diametrically opposite directions: "Answer not a fool according to his folly, lest you be like him yourself. Answer a fool according to his folly, lest he be wise in his own eyes."[10] In fact, contradictory juxtaposition is very frequently employed in wisdom literature and lament psalms. Ample examples are provided in the appendix.

B. *Functions of Contradictory Juxtaposition*

As discussed above, contradictory juxtaposition creates gaps. Therefore to examine the functions of contradictory juxtaposition means to find out the functions of those gaps. According to Sternberg, a "gap" (omission into relevancy) refers to what is omitted for the sake of interest, whereas a "blank" (omission into irrelevancy) refers to what is omitted for lack of interest.[11] Therefore gaps establish "the relevancy of absence."[12] With a "permanent gap," the lack of information will open an ambiguity for the audience to puzzle over throughout without resolving it. But with a "temporary gap," such incongruity will engage the audience to fill in the gap to the best of their ability, until the play of ambiguity is finally resolved or fixed.[13] Since gaps need to be filled, they direct the audience to move between the truth and the whole truth, to finally achieve a fullness in

---

[8] Sternberg, *Poetics of Biblical Narrative*, 235.
[9] Sternberg, *Poetics of Biblical Narrative*, 242.
[10] Bartholomew treats Prov 26:1-12 as a section and tries to interpret it in its context. He points out that 26:1 is the central theme of this section, which highlights "what is fitting" and "what is not fitting". Under this theme, 26:4-5 reminds us that we need to discern when it is fitting to answer a fool and when not. In some situations we should not answer a fool according to his folly lest we are contaminated by his folly. But in other situations we should answer a fool according to his folly lest he remain in his folly. There is no quick and easy way to know what is fitting. Therefore we need to know wisdom, which is acquired through submission to God. See C. G. Bartholomew, *Reading Proverbs with Integrity* (Grove Biblical Series; Cambridge: Grove Book Limited, 2001) 13-4.
[11] Sternberg, *Poetics of Biblical Narrative*, 236.
[12] Sternberg, *Poetics of Biblical Narrative*, 235.
[13] Concerning the difference between temporary and permanent gapping, see Sternberg, *Poetics of Biblical Narrative*, 237-40.

the reading.[14] Contradictory juxtaposition, which opens gaps, thus "pinpoints the incongruity and launches the quest for harmony by gap-filling."[15]

Gaps create ambiguity, which serves to generate curiosity, suspense and surprise.[16] Curiosity keeps the audience happily busy resolving the gaps.[17] Suspense polarizes the clash between hope and fear to "make a certain resolution desirable and its retardation enjoyably frustrating."[18] Surprise corrects the earlier false understanding and brings the pleasures of the unexpected.[19]

C. Positive and Negative Aspects of Gapping

Gaps are employed for the sake of interest. However, there is another side of the coin. Gaps "establish the relevance of withheld information on pain of incoherence."[20] Sternberg rightly claims: "The centrality of a gap accordingly becomes proportionate to the havoc it plays with (or the other way around, the contribution its filling would make to) the intelligibility of the plot."[21] Contradictory juxtaposition may create "a nagging discomfort about the plot."[22] But by threatening the plot value, a gap will in turn rouse the audience to take notice of its implication for theme and judgment.[23] To sum up the pros and cons of gapping, Sternberg states: "If the negative face of gapping consists in its operations as a disruptive force, demanding attention by threats of incoherence, then its positive face extends an invitation to synthesis beyond the bare necessities of reading and offers a point of maximum convergence."[24]

---

[14] Sternberg, *Poetics of Biblical Narrative*, 230. For detailed discussion of gaps and the reading process in biblical narrative, see Sternberg, *Poetics of Biblical Narrative*, 186-263.
[15] Sternberg, *Poetics of Biblical Narrative*, 243.
[16] Sternberg, *Poetics of Biblical Narrative*, 258-63.
[17] Sternberg, *Poetics of Biblical Narrative*, 259, 263.
[18] Sternberg, *Poetics of Biblical Narrative*, 259.
[19] Sternberg, *Poetics of Biblical Narrative*, 259, 263.
[20] Sternberg, *Poetics of Biblical Narrative*, 247.
[21] Sternberg, *Poetics of Biblical Narrative*, 247.
[22] Sternberg, *Poetics of Biblical Narrative*, 248.
[23] Sternberg, *Poetics of Biblical Narrative*, 248.
[24] Sternberg, *Poetics of Biblical Narrative*, 249.

III. *How to Discern the Author's Intended Impacts upon the Audience*

Before we explore the rhetorical impacts of Job's contradictory sayings in Job 22-31, it is important to grasp the principle of how to discern the author's intended impacts upon the audience. Therefore in this section we seek to examine the presuppositions needed for the audience to approach the story, the author's guide to interpretation, the criteria of interpreting dramatic presentation and God's final verdict in 42:7b as the key to interpretation.

A. *Assumptions for Approaching the Story*

To detect effectively the author's intended impacts upon the audience, four assumptions for the audience to approach the story have first to be recognised.[25] First, the audience is assumed to go through the story as a whole sequentially and completely, without skipping any part of it. They are assumed to prefer consistency, making efforts to resolve the tensions in the text.[26] Before telling the story, the speaker already has in mind an entire plan of how to hang different parts of it together in order to produce a smooth and convincing flow of argument. Therefore, when chapters 22-31 are studied, the audience is expected to examine the entire book sequentially and completely.

Secondly, the audience is assumed to know certain things, or sometimes even not to know certain things.[27] For example, they are supposed to have a certain knowledge about the concepts of different theodicies, traditional wisdom and the natures of God and the satan. The audience is also supposed to know that the aged are traditionally regarded as wiser. That is the reason why Eliphaz (the eldest one) speaks first among the friends, and Elihu is the last to speak (32:4, 6). In addition, the audience is supposed to have knowledge of the scene in the prologue, but not to know how Job will respond to his suffering after the prologue.

Thirdly, the audience is assumed to accept the dynamics of the story world that are established by the author, so that the audience can be fully involved in that story world.[28]

---

[25] Powell, "Narrative Criticism," 242-4.
[26] Powell, "Narrative Criticism," 242-3.
[27] Powell, "Narrative Criticism," 243.
[28] Powell, "Narrative Criticism," 243.

Finally, the audience is expected to be willing to accept the value system that the author intends them to adopt.[29] In these four ways the author exerts his influence upon his audience.

B. *The Author's Guide to Interpretation*

In order to explore the intended rhetorical impact upon the audience, it is necessary to discern how the author guides the audience to understand a text and take its message. Guiding an audience to interpret his message correctly is the most important rhetorical step for an author trying to influence others in order to modify an exigency. The author's guiding of interpretation can be spotted in several phenomena: 1) evaluative points of view; 2) use of irony; and 3) literary-rhetorical markers within the text.

1. *Evaluative Points of View*

To start with, in order to achieve successful persuasion, the author must guide the audience to "adopt the evaluative point of view consistent with that of the narrative."[30] Powell defines the evaluative point of view as follows:

> This refers to the norms, values, and general worldview that the implied author establishes as operative for the story. To put it another way, evaluative point of view may be defined as the standards of judgment by which readers are led to evaluate the events, characters, and settings that comprise the story.[31]

In biblical narratives authors expect the audience to adopt divine and narratorial points of view as the standards from which to evaluate events, characters and the settings of a story.

a) God's Evaluative Point of View

The audience is assumed to accept the author's evaluative point of view, but they have to detect which evaluative point of view the author wants them to adopt. In the biblical narratives authors always make God's (including His messengers') evaluative point of view a standard of judgment in governing the interpretation of a text. "What God thinks is, by definition, true and right."[32] On the

---

[29] Powell, "Narrative Criticism," 243-4.
[30] Powell, *What Is Narrative Criticism?* 23.
[31] Powell, *What Is Narrative Criticism?* 24.
[32] Powell, *What Is Narrative Criticism?* 24.

other side, negative or evil characters in the narrative, the satan in Job for example, provide evaluative points of view in a negative sense. This means that what the satan says is wrong and untrue.[33] Interestingly enough, the audience tends to empathize with those characters who express God's point of view and seeks to distance itself from those characters who do not.[34]

Therefore, when the rhetorical impacts of Job's contradictory sayings in Job 22-31 are explored, God's evaluative point of view in the prologue, Yahweh speeches and epilogue is the most important standard of judgment that the audience is expected to adopt. The audience can judge whether Job's or his friends' evaluative points of view are true by comparing them with God's or the satan's. For example, God regards Job as "a blameless and upright man, fearing God and turning away from evil" in Job 1:8 and 2:3. This can be used as a point of reference to check whether the friends' accusations against Job in the dialogue are true or not.

b) Narrator's Evaluative Point of View

Another guide to the author's evaluative point of view is the use of a narrator—the voice used by the author to tell the story. As for biblical narrators, the privilege of omniscience is obvious, making his viewpoint an authoritative standard of judgment. Ska notably states, "He is almost like God: he knows everything and speaks with an unabashed authority. This 'privilege' is felt especially when he reveals the thoughts of the characters through 'inside views'."[35]

"The process of storytelling, however, may involve an implicit contract between author and reader in which the latter agrees to trust the narrator."[36] In biblical narratives the points of view of the narrator are always consistent with those of the author. Therefore the narrator is so reliable that the audience is expected to believe what the narrator says.[37] In other words, the audience has to pay special attention to the narrator's direct narration, comment and explanation because the author usually guides the audience to un-

---

[33] Powell, *What Is Narrative Criticism?* 24-5.

[34] Powell, *What Is Narrative Criticism?* 25. In regard to the author's device of creating empathy, sympathy and antipathy within the audience, see Powell, *What Is Narrative Criticism?* 56-7.

[35] J. L. Ska, *"Our Fathers Have Told Us": Introduction to the Analysis of Hebrew Narratives* (Rome: Pontifical Biblical Institute, 1990) 44.

[36] Powell, *What Is Narrative Criticism?* 25; also Booth, *Rhetoric of Fiction*, 3-4.

[37] Powell, *What Is Narrative Criticism?* 26.

derstand the story and to adopt his points of view through the voice of the narrator.

For example, when the narrator says "that man (Job) was blameless, upright, fearing God and turning away from evil" in 1:1; "Through all this Job did not sin nor did he blame God" in 1:22; and "In all this Job did not sin with his lips" in 2:10, his comments are true and reliable. The audience can judge whether Job's or his friends' evaluative points of view are true or not by comparing them with the narrator's. Therefore the narrator's narration and points of view in the prologue and epilogue have set a very important foundation for us to explore the author's expected rhetorical impact upon the audience.

2. Use of Irony

The second way of detecting the author's guidance to interpretation is by observing his use of irony, which means that true interpretation is opposite to literal meaning.[38] Irony presents further levels of meaning.[39] It is an effective rhetorical device to encourage the audience to reject the literal meaning of the words with the help of internal and external clues, and to try out other, alternative interpretations. In addition, the audience also needs to evaluate irony in terms of what they believe about the author, and to make a decision based on the author's assumed intentions.[40]

In the dialogue both Job and his friends employ a number of ironies to mock each other. Job's polemical expressions in Job 12:2; 21:3 and 26:2-4 are good examples of rhetorical irony. The audience has to discern their true meaning, which is contrary to the apparent one.[41] "Irony is incongruity of knowledge. Characters think they know what they are doing when in fact they may be doing something rather different. They think they understand the way the

---

[38] Powell, *What Is Narrative Criticism?* 30.
[39] D. N. Fewell and D. M. Gunn, "Narrative, Hebrew," *ABD 4* (ed. D. N. Freedman et al.; New York: Doubleday, 1992) 1026.
[40] Powell, *What Is Narrative Criticism?* 27, 31.
[41] Hoffman identifies four categories of irony in the Book of Job: 1) ironic remarks voiced by the different characters, which they direct at each other and are discernible by all: Job, his friends and the reader; 2) the ironic attitude of the author toward his protagonists, which is understood by the reader but not by Job or his friends; 3) irony which the author directs against the reader; and 4) irony which the author directs against his work or against himself. See Y. Hoffman, "Irony in the Book of Job," *Immanuel* 17 (1983) 7-21.

world is when in fact it is different."[42] In Job's case, the audience is in a privileged position to see the cause of Job's suffering in the heavenly scene. Irony is present when the audience knows what the characters do not. "Awareness of irony" is an important matter for directing the audience's point of view.[43]

3. *Literary-Rhetorical Markers*
The last way to guide the audience to interpret a text is the author's use of literary-rhetorical markers. Inclusio, repetition, rhetorical questions and so forth are important literary-rhetorical indicators by which the audience must discern the rhetorical impact expected by the author.

a) Inclusio
"An inclusio is a repetition of words and/or a theme at the beginning and end of a section, or the beginning and end of a book...Such repetition demarcates a section, and indicates the main theme of that section."[44] For instance, the portrayal of Job as the one who "fears God" and "shuns evil" in 1:1 is echoed with the thematic expression "the fear of the Lord" and "the shunning of evil" in 28:28. Such an inclusio serves as a bracket, alerting the audience to the envelope structure of the book.[45] This is a crucial guide for the audience to interpret the text and discern the place of Job 28 within the book.

b) Repetition
The use of repetition is also an important indicator for the audience to detect the author's key emphasis in the story. Alter considers biblical narratives as creative writings with persuasive intent to move the audience to discern a particular perspective on reality. He claims, "it is altogether likely that they were written chiefly for oral presentation...to some sort of assembled audience...rather than

---

[42] Fewell and Gunn, "Narrative, Hebrew," 1026.
[43] Fewell-Gunn point out that irony is often produced by setting up a conflict of facts or values. Awareness of irony is thus a matter of point of view. See Fewell and Gunn, "Narrative, Hebrew," 1026.
[44] Bartholomew, *Reading Proverbs with Integrity*, 8.
[45] See K. Möller, "Presenting a Prophet in Debate: An Investigation of the Literary Structure and the Rhetoric of Persuasion of the Book of Amos," Ph.D. Dissertation. (Cheltenham and Gloucester College of Higher Education, 1999) 35-6; and Habel, "The Narrative Art of Job," 107.

passed around to be read in our sense."[46] He points out that the use of repetition is strong evidence for the oral context of biblical narrative.[47] If the speech or the text is read aloud it is presented in linear progression, and the audience does not have the possibility of hearing it again. Therefore "an orally recieved text is characterized by a greater degree of repetition than is a text intended to be read privately."[48]

A great variety of repetition can easily be found in the Book of Job.[49] For example, the term "blameless" (תָּם), which is used to describe Job's character at 1:1 is a key term, or *Leitwort*, connecting the theme of the whole book (1:1; 1:8; 2:3; 2:9; 4:6; 8:20; 9:21-22; 27:5-6).[50] Alter adds that by following the repetitions of *Leitwort*, "one is able to decipher or grasp a meaning of the text, or at any rate, the meaning will be revealed more strikingly."[51] In addition, scene-types are another kind of repetition. In the prologue, for example, the fourfold repetition of the scene of reporting Job's disasters gives the audience a sense of increasing intensity (1:13-19).[52] To sum up, the use of repetition clearly demonstrates the rhetorical nature of the book and is an important marker for interpretation.

c) Rhetorical Questions

Furthermore, the use of rhetorical questions can also bring forth the rhetorical effect of addressing both the ostensible (the characters in the narrative world) and implicit auditors (the audience or reader) of the story.[53] Koops defines "rhetorical questions" as follows:

> In an ordinary conversation...a question is assumed to be a request for information. When it becomes evident to the hearer that the "information" in question is already well known to both of them, he

---

[46] Alter, *Biblical Narrative*, 90.
[47] Alter, *Biblical Narrative*, 88-113.
[48] Kennedy, *NT Interpretation*, 37.
[49] For more examples, see Habel, *Job*, 49-50; and Habel, "The Narrative Art of Job," 106-7.
[50] Habel, "The Narrative Art of Job," 103.
[51] Alter, *Biblical Narrative*, 93.
[52] Habel, "The Narrative Art of Job," 106-7.
[53] Fox, "Job 38," 58; also D. E. Loyd, "Patterns of Interrogative Rhetoric in the Speeches of the Book of Job," Ph.D. Dissertation. (The University of Iowa, 1986) 1-12. Loyd's dissertation aims at studying the rhetorical effects of using the interrogative questions in the Book of Job. He points out that the poetic section 3:1-42:6 contains 991 verses, among which there are 253 interrogatives. Rhetorical questions are the most dominant type of questions in the book.

understands that the speaker must be deliberately flouting the expected pattern, and thereby doing something else, namely emphasizing a point.[54]

The use of a rhetorical question implies that the audience knows the answer, and that they will concur with the speaker's viewpoint. De Regt rightly comments: "A rhetorical question can be a persuasive device. Because the speaker implies more than the words as such and expects no response, the hearer is impressed by the thought processes that would logically lead to the kind of answer the speaker intends the hearer to reach."[55] Rhetorical questions can often make stronger statements with greater emphasis and implication than a straightforward assertion can bring about. In short, rhetorical questions "have the form of a question but are not designed to elicit information. The intent, therefore, is not to ask for a response but to make an emphatic declaration."[56] Therefore rhetorical questions are always found in contexts, where the discourse aims at persuading the audience.[57]

There are several pointers to the correct interpretation of questions as rhetorical in Job. First, there are unmarked rhetorical questions, which do not have an interrogative particle (e.g. Job 2:10; 10:9; 11:11; 17:4b; 38:8; 40:24, 25 [41:1]; and probably 12:12). The recognition of such unmarked rhetorical questions depends on the preceding context. For instance, Job 38:8 is the continuation of 38:5a.[58]

Secondly, to correctly interpret the meaning of rhetorical questions it is necessary to make distinctions between different stages of their implied meaning. According to Koop, rhetorical questions carry three layers of implied meaning: 1) the rhetorical level, in

---

[54] R. Koops, "Rhetorical Questions and Implied Meaning in the Book of Job," *BT* 39 (1988) 418.

[55] L. J. de Regt, "Implications of Rhetorical Questions in Strophes in Job 11 and 15," *The Book of Job* (BETL 114; ed. W. A. M. Beuken; Leuven: Leuven University Press, 1994) 321; also J. Frank, "You Call That a Rhetorical Question? Forms and Functions of Rhetorical Questions in Conversation," *Journal of Pragmatics* 14 (1990) 726.

[56] E. A. Nida et al., *Style and Discourse: With Special Reference to the Greek New Testament* (Cape Town: Bible Society, 1983) 39.

[57] Frank, "You Call That a Rhetorical Question?" 726; and Regt, "Implications of Rhetorical Questions," 321-2.

[58] L. J. de Regt, "Functions and Implications of Rhetorical Questions in the Book of Job," *Biblical Hebrew and Discourse Linguistics* (ed. Robert D. Bergen; Dallas: Summer Institute of Linguistics, 1994) 362.

which the negative-positive polarity is reversed; 2) the conventional level, in which a connection is made between a physical state (old or young), an attitude (you limit wisdom to yourself), and a mental state (wise, foolish or proud); and 3) the pragmatic level, in which the conclusion is drawn that certain behaviour should follow from certain conditions.[59]

Thirdly, some of the rhetorical questions in the Book of Job serve to open or close a section, and thus play a significant role in the structuring of the text. They can provide a reason or answer, or constitute an opposition or conclusion.[60] Therefore this kind of rhetorical question is a crucial marker for the audience to break down the chapter into different sections. Thus when chapters 22-31 are studied it is important to note that Job 24:25 and 28:12, 20 carry such a structuring function.

In short, the use of rhetorical questions is a powerful rhetorical device to make a strongly emphatic declaration. The unmarked rhetorical questions, which do not have the interrogative particle, are normally the continuation of preceding rhetorical questions. Rhetorical questions can include three layers of implication: the rhetorical, conventional and pragmatical levels. They also play an important part in the structuring of a text. Therefore the occurrence of rhetorical questions is a significant literary-rhetorical indicator for the interpretation of a text.

---

[59] Koops, "Rhetorical Questions and Implied Meaning," 420. De Regt quotes 38:8 as an example to illustrate these three levels of implied meaning. At the rhetorical level it is made clear that it is God who shut in the sea with doors. At the conventional level this implies that Job or any other human could not possibly have done it. At the pragmatic level the rhetorical question functions as a challenge. See Regt, "Functions and Implications of Rhetorical Questions in Job," 364.

[60] De Regt uses Job 21 to illustrate how rhetorical questions play an important role in the structuring of a text. Rhetorical questions (RQs) here serve to divide this chapter into different sections: vv.1-3; 4-6; 7-16; 17-26; and 27-34. In 21:28-34, de Regt points out that RQ in v.29 forms an opposition to RQ in v.28; RQs in v.30 and vv.32-33 are the answers; and then RQ in v.34 is a conclusion to vv.29-33. In Job, other examples of rhetorical questions with a structural function, either starting a section or closing one, are 3:11-12; 4:6-7, 17, 21; 6:11-13; 8:2, 10-11; 9:12; 10:18; 11:2-3, 7; 12:11-12; 13:7-8; 15:7; 18:2-3; 19:2, 22; 22:2-3, 12; 24:25; 28:12, 20; 35:2; 38:2; 39:5, 9, 19, 26. For the details of the function of rhetorical questions in the structuring of a text, see Regt, "Functions and Implications of Rhetorical Questions in Job," 368-71.

Conclusion

All in all, in order to make a rhetorical impact upon the audience the author must manage to guide his audience to interpret a text correctly and take the message so that the exigency can be removed. The author's evaluative points of view through God's and the narrator's comments, the use of irony and literary-rhetorical markers are major clues for detecting the author's intended impacts upon the audience. Combrink rightly points out: "It is therefore important to see that in the case of sacred texts rhetoric affects the interpretation because interpretation is actually a part of the rhetorical act."[61] A correct interpretation of a text is the most fundamental step for the audience to take the message and thereby to elicit its own transformation.

C. *Dramatic Presentation and Its Interpretations*

In a narrative the author conveys his message through the interplay of the characters. In order to correctly take the message, it is essential to observe how the author reveals characters. Booth rightly points out that the author may reveal characters either by telling the audience directly about them through the words of a reliable narrator, or by showing them what the characters are like directly through their dialogue in the story.[62]

Alter asserts the "primacy of dialogue"[63] in the biblical narrative: "By and large, the biblical writers prefer to avoid indirect speech....The rule of thumb is that when speech is involved in a narrative event, it is presented as direct speech."[64] Sternberg also highlights that "the Bible's free recourse to exegetical 'telling' [does not] preclude a mastery of the art of dramatic 'showing'."[65] Showing characters through recourse to direct speech can produce the "effect of bringing the speech-act into foreground" and give the audience a sense of "immediacy" and "complicating ambiguity."[66]

---

[61] H. J. B. Combrink, "The Rhetoric of Sacred Scripture," *Rhetoric, Scripture and Theology: Essays from the 1994 Pretoria Conference* (JSNTSup 131; ed. Stanley E. Porter and Thomas H. Olbricht; Sheffield: Sheffield Academic Press, 1996) 102.
[62] Booth, *Rhetoric of Fiction*, 3-20; also Powell, *What Is Narrative Criticism?* 52-3.
[63] Alter, *Biblical Narrative*, 65.
[64] Alter, *Biblical Narrative*, 67.
[65] Sternberg, *Poetics of Biblical Narrative*, 122.
[66] Alter, *Biblical Narrative*, 67.

Although showing is less precise than telling, it is a more interesting way of engaging the audience.[67]

The technique of telling and showing is very evident in the Book of Job. Comparatively speaking, the use of narration appears to be minimal in the narrative frame of the prologue (1:1-2:13)[68] and the epilogue (42:7-17), while recourse to direct speech turns out to be maximal in the central part of the story (3:1-42:6). The technique of showing produces an effect of dramatic presentation, reenacting Job's story as a drama and transforming the audience into spectators of the event. In the dramatic dialogues of the story of Job (3:1-42:6) the intervention of the narrator is kept to the minimum. His only role is to introduce the characters, mostly by giving a brief introductory formula, like "Then Job [Eliphaz, Bildad, Zophar] answered and he said." Therefore, when chapters 22-31 are studied, it is important to bear in mind that in this section the author has used the technique of dramatic showing to present his message. Chapters 22-31 as a dramatic presentation require us to pay special attention to some important interpretive criteria.[69]

First, the narrator's brief introductory formula functions to divide the text into rhetorical units[70] according to the speech of different characters. In Kennedy's model the first step of doing rhetorical analysis is to identify the rhetorical unit, i.e. to delimit the unit for study. A rhetorical unit is a convincing unit, which has a beginning, a middle and an end, and which can be large or small. The smallest units may comprise parables, metaphors, simple sayings, blessings, hymns and brief commandments. A combination of smaller units form a larger unit, which can in turn combine with other such units. The largest rhetorical unit achieved through such combination is the text as a whole.[71] Through dramatic presentation, the author of Job arranges the speeches of different characters in a very

---

[67] Powell, *What Is Narrative Criticism?* 52.

[68] The prologue is not purely narration. There are also many dialogues among the characters, but the role of the narrator in this section is very dominant in linking those dialogues together. Apart from the prologue and epilogue, there is also a narration in the brief introduction of Elihu (32:1-5).

[69] J.-P. Sonnet, *The Book Within the Book: Writing in Deuteronomy* (Leiden; New York; Köln: Brill, 1997) 12-21.

[70] Kennedy, *NT Interpretation*, 33-4; Walton, "Rhetorical Criticism: An Introduction," 5; and W. Wuellner, "Where Is Rhetorical Criticism Taking Us?" *CBQ* 49 (1987) 455.

[71] Kennedy, *NT Interpretation*, 33-4; and Walton, "Rhetorical Criticism: An Introduction," 5.

orderly way. Basically, each character's speech forms a complete rhetorical unit, within which there is a combination of smaller units. Therefore, in the study of Job 22-31, Eliphaz's speech in chapter 22 forms the first rhetorical unit. There then follow Job's speech in chapters 23-24 and Bildad's speech in chapter 25. In order to effectively address the issues of Job's contradictory sayings, Job's whole unit of speech in chapters 26-31 is broken down into smaller rhetorical units, namely Job 26, Job 27, and then Job 28-31.

Secondly, in the dramatic speech the narrator will not provide any details of the scene, or give any comment upon the characters or events. Everything is provided directly in the dialogue itself. Without the help of the narrator, dramatic showing compels the audience to judge by themselves the reliability of the character's point of view. The audience has to gather, compare and evaluate all kinds of evidence to make their own judgments. They also need to establish the author's point of view, by making reference to God's and the narrator's evaluative points of view in the book.[72] In this way dramatic presentation is a powerful rhetorical device, fully engaging the audience to wrestle vigorously with the issue. Therefore, when chapters 22-31 are investigated, God's and the narrator's evaluative points of view in the prologue, epilogue and Yahweh speeches serve as the most authoritative standard of judgment to evaluate the reliability of Job's and his friends' viewpoints.

Thirdly, in dramatic presentation, speech and narrative correspond to the unfolding impact of the argument in linear time. Sonnet rightly explains:

> Dramatic speech highlights the link of linguistic representation with the linear temporality of hearing and reading. When extensive recourse is made to direct speech, both the narrator behind the scene and the *dramatis persona* in the limelight concur in bringing everything home according to the sequential order of language.[73]

In Job 3:1-42:6 the flow of argument is developed according to rhetorical progression. The audience's understanding is sequentially and progressively accumulated, at the pace of the progression of speeches. The audience is supposed to stick patiently to this linear process of reading, without skipping any part of the story.[74] There-

---

[72] Powell, *What Is Narrative Criticism?* 52-3; and Sonnet, *The Book Within the Book*, 14-5.
[73] Sonnet, *The Book Within the Book*, 15.
[74] Sonnet, *The Book Within the Book*, 15.

fore, when Job 22-31 are studied, we cannot jump to any conclusion without looking at the entire flow of the argument, which is developed sequentially and cumulatively from the very beginning of the book.

Finally, dramatic speech gives the audience the advantage of being able to systematize the viewpoint of a character. Sonnet points out that "Systematization of direct speech in a given narrative amounts to systematization of point of view."[75] Basically, a character's point of view is reflected through his speech. The audience can then evaluate whether this point of view is true or untrue, by gathering, systematizing, comparing and analysing the speech of the character.

All in all, the above principles of interpreting dramatic presentation help us to interpret correctly the direct dialogue of the characters when we seek to explore the author's intended rhetorical impact of placing Job's contradictory sayings into chapters 22-31.

D. *God's Final Verdict in Job 42:7b as the Key to Interpretation*

In Job 22-31 Job and his friends carry on their debate, which has been progressing through the first two speech cycles. When the intended rhetorical effect of Job's contradictory sayings in this section is examined, it is indispensable to investigate how the audience is expected to be impacted through their own evaluation of Job's and the friends' standpoints. Such an evaluative process can prepare the audience to adopt the author's evaluative worldview in the narrative. Therefore the audience has to ask a question: are all Job's viewpoints right, and all his friends' wrong? As mentioned before, in order to detect the author's intention correctly, the audience is supposed to experience the whole story sequentially and completely, and to be able to search for all the evidences to support their evaluation.

Job 42:7b[76] is key to the above question. Porter correctly remarks that it is crucial to the interpretation of the entire book.[77] This verse will give the audience the most important clue to evaluate Job's and

---

[75] Sonnet, *The Book Within the Book*, 16.
[76] The comment in 42:7b is repeated by Yahweh in 42:8b.
[77] Porter discusses the ambiguity of this verse and evaluates all the scholars' suggested resolutions to its interpretation. For further details, see S. E. Porter, "The Message of the Book of Job: Job 42:7b as Key to Interpretation?" *EvQ* 63 (1991) 289-304.

the friends' standpoints. In 42:7b God rebukes Eliphaz (representative of the three friends), saying "you have not spoken of Me what is right as My servant Job has." This verse carries a certain ambiguity. Does the verdict mean that all Job's viewpoints are right and all the friends' are wrong? If all Job's arguments are meant to be right, then God's rebukes and ironical statements to Job in chapters 38-41 (e.g. 38:2; 40:2; 40:8) would certainly appear unnecessary and pointless. It is reasonable, therefore, to conclude that Job has spoken something right, which is commended by God in 42:7b, and something wrong, which is rebuked by God in chapters 38-41. But which is which? Nicholson rightly points out:

> Job exposed the yawning chasm between the harsh reality of life and what orthodox piety, as represented by his companions, declared to be the automatic harvest of the righteous. For this truthfulness he is commended by God as against his three friends who did not speak "what is right" about God (42:7-8).[78]

Job is said to be right in raising the question of divine justice, while the friends are said to be wrong in allowing an ideology—only the guilty suffer—to override the experience of undeserved suffering.[79] In Job 38 God points out the limitations of Job's human wisdom. However, He also shows Job the potential of the wisdom he has. With such wisdom, he is able to view God's orderly governance in the expanses of the universe. It is for not living up to the potential of this wisdom that Job is rebuked. In fact, God declares that His plan for the created order is so obvious that Job has no reason to condemn God as arbitrary and immoral.[80] Job is thus blameworthy for obscuring God's counsels that he is really aware of (38:2), and for justifying himself by putting God in the wrong (40:8). Therefore Nicholson adds:

> But disjunction is pressed by Job at the expense of the conjunction of realism and faith. Present experience is allowed to eclipse faith, and lament and plea grounded in hope and trust are replaced by the bitter accusation that God is unjust and his creation a travesty. It is for this that Job is rebuked and censured, and it is against this that God rouses himself to speak from the whirlwind—not to assert himself like

---

[78] Nicholson, "Limits of Theodicy," 81; also Porter, "Message of the Book of Job," 302.
[79] Porter, "Message of the Book of Job," 302; and B. Z. Cooper, "Why, God? A Tale of Two Sufferers," *TToday* 42 (1986) 420.
[80] Fox, "Job 38," 59-60.

a bully against Job, coercing him into humiliating submission, but to declare his mastery in and over creation, and so to renew his ancient pledge and in this way reawaken faith.[81]

A correct understanding of 42:7b can help the audience evaluate Job's and the friends' standpoints properly. Engaging the audience to judge the reliability of Job's and his friends' viewpoint is a persuasive device to guide the audience to adopt the author's evaluative point of view through Yahweh's correction and teaching later in the story. In due course the exigency can be modified through the telling of this story.

To sum up, when the rhetorical impact of Job's contradictory sayings in chapters 22-31 is examined, it is necessary at the outset to recognise the basic assumptions needed for the audience to approach the story, the author's guide to interpretation, the principles of interpreting dramatic presentation and God's final verdict in 42:7b as the key to understand the whole book.

In what follows, Job's contradictory sayings in Job 22-31 will be investigated in full detail. The whole block of Job 22-31 will be broken into four smaller units (Job 22-24, Job 25-26, Job 27 and Job 28-31). First, the content of each unit will be introduced. Next the characteristics of Job's contradictory sayings in each unit will be examined. Then the commentators' approaches to the issue of Job's contradictory sayings in each unit will be analysed. Finally, it will be argued that the juxtaposition of Job's contradictory sayings is part of the author's rhetorical strategy in order to make a rhetorical impact upon the audience.

IV. *Job's Contradictory Sayings in Job 22-24*

Chapter 22 and chapters 23-24 belong to Eliphaz and Job respectively. We group these three chapters together as a unit, so that we may discern how Job's contradictory sayings are linked with their nearest preceding context. Job 24 is frequently regarded as a dislocated passage. On the one hand, textual obscurities make the interpretation of the individual verses difficult. On the other hand, some scholars find that 24:18-24 seems to be inappropriate from Job's lips because it sounds like the arguments of Job's friends, that Job

---

[81] Nicholson, "Limits of Theodicy," 81-2.

otherwise strongly repudiates. Therefore 24:18-24 is often reallocated from Job to one of the friends. To resolve this contradiction, RSV and ESV add "You say" at the beginning of 24:18 (unlike NRSV or NIV).

However, this study seeks to argue that the juxtaposition of Job's contradictory sayings in 24:18-24 and 24:1-17 is part of the author's rhetorical strategy. In addition, it will demonstrate that 24:18-24 is not Job's first utterance of contradictory statements. In fact, many scholars have left out a series of contradictions in chapter 23. More importantly, Job's use of contradictory sayings can even be traced throughout the first two speech cycles, though its frequency reaches a climax in the third cycle. First, however, the content of chapters 22-24 needs to be outlined.

A. *The Content*

In response to Job's last speech in chapter 21, in which he turns the principle of retribution upside down, Eliphaz adopts a harsher tone in his final speech of the third cycle. Responding to Job's saying that the wicked dismiss piety because there is no benefit in it (21:15), Eliphaz argues that God does not receive any benefit from human righteousness (22:2-3). To counter Job's claim to be innocent (9:21; 16:17), Eliphaz defends God's impartiality that He does not punish the piety (22:4). But ironically, it is exactly Job's fear (יִרְאָה) of God causing his devastation. Since God gains no advantage from human righteousness (22:2-3) and He does not punish piety (22:4), Eliphaz concludes that Job's punishment proves his guilt (22:5). Eliphaz's accusation of Job's great wickedness (רָעָתְךָ רַבָּה; 22:5a) has reached its climax.[82]

Believing that God punishes the wicked, Eliphaz holds firmly that anyone who suffers must be very wicked. In order to fit his theology to Job's case, Eliphaz even twists the facts to falsely accuse Job. With the accusations introduced by כִּי (because/for; v.6), Eliphaz invents the social crimes (vv.6-9) that Job is supposed to have committed: the heartless treatment of his brother, the naked (v.6), the weary, the hungry (v.7), the widow and the fatherless (v.9). These crimes are forbidden in the Old Testament laws, and in chapter 31 Job makes his "negative confession" about them. Then, by using

---

[82] Newsom, "Job," 500.

עַל־כֵּן (therefore), Eliphaz concludes that Job has been punished for just these sins (vv.10-11).

In his second argument Eliphaz accuses Job of denying God's knowledge and judgment—sins that have led to ruin since ancient times (vv.12-20). Eliphaz claims that Job is mistaken in denying God's loftiness and omniscience (vv.12-14). He proceeds to ask Job whether he intends to walk in the paths of the ancient sinners, who were snatched away and whose foundation was poured out as a stream (vv.15-16). Eliphaz quotes the impious remark of those sinners, who ordered God to depart from them so that they could do their evil without divine interference (v.17). He agrees that God filled their houses with good things, but just for a short time (v.18). The righteous will triumph over the wicked after all (vv.19-20).

Eliphaz's sayings in 22:16-18 are very similar to Job's description of the wicked in 21:14-16.[83] Both Eliphaz and Job agree that the wicked dismiss God. However, Job depicts them as denying that God can do anything "for" them, while Eliphaz depicts them as denying that God can do anything "to" them. Job sees the prosperity of the wicked as the evidence that God favours the wicked. Eliphaz points out that the prosperity of the wicked does come from God, but they reject God without showing gratitude to Him.[84]

Despite the conviction that Job's punishment proves his great evil, Eliphaz does not despair of Job's restoration. He concludes his final speech with an appeal to Job, exhorting him to return to God (vv.21-30).[85]

In response to Eliphaz's false accusation in Job 22, Job's speech starts with a note of bitter defiance (23:2). Despite Eliphaz's counsel to seek God in repentance (22:21-30), Job insists on seeking a legal hearing that he may gain personal vindication from God (23:3-7). In fact, the idea of a lawsuit with God remains in his imagination because Job does not know how to search God out (23:3). Job imagines himself laying his case and stating his arguments before God (23:4), and then considers what God would reply to him (23:5). He even imagines God's restraint (23:6), rather than God's overwhelming power, which hinders his envisaging of a trial (9:32-35;

---

[83] The parallels of these two passages are 22:17a=21:14a; 22:18a=21:16a (not identical); 22:18b=21:16b. See Hartley, *Job*, 330, n.15.

[84] Newsom, "Job," 501-2.

[85] Concerning the analysis of Job 22, see Newsom, "Job," 500-3; Whybray, *Job*, 104-6; Good, *In Turns of Tempest*, 271-6; and Hartley, *Job*, 323-36.

13:20-21). Job is confident that God will "pay attention to" him (אַךְ־הוּא יָשֵׂם בִּי, lit. "He would fix upon me"). He imagines having a fair trial so that he can reason with God and have a just verdict from Him.[86]

However, Job's confidence is frustrated by the elusiveness of God (23:8-9). Job looks for God in all directions (קֶדֶם "forward", אָחוֹר "backward", שְׂמֹאול "left" and יָמִין "right" should be read as "east", "west", "north" and "south"),[87] but he cannot find Him.

Previously, Job described God's scrutiny and testing as hostile and unwelcome (7:17-19; 10:4-7). But now Job's hope returns when he affirms God's knowledge of his integrity (23:10a). Job is convinced that God's judgment of him (i.e. God's assurance that Job will prove to be gold when tested) will be the same as his testimony to his uprightness (23:10b-12).

At the peak of Job's hope, terror and dread plague him again (23:13-16). "What He desires, that He does" (23:13) brings out a negative sense of God's omnipotence—His arbitrariness. Whatever God has planned He will carry out, because He pleases none but Himself (23:14). Therefore (עַל־כֵּן) Job is overwhelmed by dread when he thinks of a confrontation with God (23:15-16; cf. 3:25-26; 9:34-35; 13:21). However, Job is not reduced to silence (כִּי־לֹא נִצְמַתִּי)[88] because of the darkness, nor because of the thick darkness that covers his face (23:17). In turn, he projects his own experience upon the world of humans, which opens the second half of Job's speech (Job 24).

Job 24:1 raises the question: "Why are not times of judgment (עִתִּים) kept by the Almighty, and why do those who know Him never see His days (יָמָיו)?"[89] Both "time" (עֵת) and "day" (יוֹם) signify the doom appointed for the wicked. However, the faithful ones do not

---

[86] Newsom, "Job," 508.

[87] Whybray, *Job*, 108.

[88] The verb צמת can either mean "be destroyed" or "be silenced." See the discussion in L. Koehler and W. Baumgartner, *Hebräisches und Aramäisches Lexikon* (3rd ed.; Leiden: Brill, 1983) 970; and L. Koehler and W. Baumgartner, *The Hebrew and Aramaic Lexicon of the Old Testament: The New Koehler-Baumgartner in English* (trans & ed M. E. J. Richardson; Leiden; New York; Köln: Brill, 1996) 1036. NRSV favours "be destroyed", but it changes לֹא to לוּ "if only." ESV reads "be silenced." It seems that the context favours the latter reading. Job's reluctance to remain silent paves the way to his further protest in Job 24. See also Newsom, "Job," 509-10; Dhorme, *Job*, 352; and Pope, *Job*, 173.

[89] According to Gordis the first line is the subordinate clause of condition, and מַדּוּעַ mainly governs the second line. Therefore he renders this verse as follows:

see God's judgment upon the wicked. To back up his rousing challenge at v.1, Job proceeds to bring out a series of evidence (vv.2-17) to justify his argument that not only he himself is suffering unjustly at the hands of God, but also that the weakest of the world are victims of God's refusal to bring the wicked to justice.[90] In vv.2-17 there is a constant oscillation between the acts of the evildoers (vv.2-4; v.9; vv.13-17) and the plight of the oppressed (vv.5-8; vv.10-12).[91] The structure of vv.1-17 is as follows:

v.1	Job's lament about the delay of God's judgment
vv.2-4	The acts of the evildoers
vv.5-8	The suffering of the poor
v.9	The robbery perpetrated by the wicked
vv.10-12	The plight of the poor
vv.13-17	The crimes of the evildoers

To start with, vv.2-4 depicts the evil deeds of the wicked. Land for agriculture and herds for pasturing are the bases of life in the ancient Israelite economy. The wicked remove the boundary markers (גְּבוּלֹת יַשִּׂיגוּ; 24:2a) in order to engulf their neighbour's lands into their own, and also seize the flocks of the weak (עֵדֶר גָּזְלוּ) and pasture (וַיִּרְעוּ) the plunder as their own (24:2b). The removal of boundaries is a violation of biblical law and wisdom teachings (Deut 19:14; 27:17; Prov 22:28; 23:10). The theft of animals is not only prohibited, but a person is required to return his neighbour's straying animal (Deut 22:1-3). Laws were also set to protect orphans and widows (Deut 24:17, 19-21). However, Job complains that the wicked take away the necessities for living from the most helpless—

"Since the times of judgment are not hidden from the Almighty, why do those who love Him never see the days of retribution." Gordis supports his translation by referring to the syntactic parallel in Isa 5:4 (cf. RSV's rendering). See the discussion in Gordis, *Book of Job*, 263-4. Hartley and Newsom also adopt Gordis' translation. See Hartley, *Job*, 343; and Newsom, "Job," 510. Following LXX, Dhorme omits לֹא and reads "Why have times [ ] been hidden from the Almighty?" See Dhorme, *Job*, 353. Seemingly, Gordis' grammatical explanation and Dhorme's ommission of לֹא reflect the incongruity between v.1a and 1b. However, perhaps they miss the point that צָפַן can either mean "to be concealed, hidden" or "to be kept, stored up." I favour the latter rendering. Then the meaning of Job 24:1a is: "Why does not God reserve fixed times (for judgment)?" See Rowley, *Book of Job*, 162 (cf. ESV's translation).

[90] D. J. A. Clines, "Quarter Days Gone: Job 24 and the Absence of God," *God in the Fray: A Tribute to Walter Brueggemann* (ed. Tod Linafelt and Timothy K. Beal; Minneapolis: Fortress Press, 1998) 245.

[91] Gordis, *Book of Job*, 253; and Whybray, *Job*, 109.

the orphan's ass and the widow's ox (24:3). They even thrust the poor from the road, and the poor have to hide themselves (חֻבְּאוּ) from the threat of the violence (24:4).

There then comes a description of the plight of the poor (24:5-8). Concerning the interpretation of פְּרָאִים (wild asses) and עֲרָבָה (the desert) in v.5, Joüon points out that these substantives are used as predicatives, thus adding "in" or "as/like" to them (cf. NASB, RSV and NRSV).[92] The general sense of this verse is that like wild asses wandering in the wilderness to search for food, the poor who have no land to cultivate, seek wild food in the wilderness to maintain themselves and their families. They harvest their fodder in the field, and glean the vineyard of the wicked (v.6). However, their labour is so laborious, unrewarding and soul-destroying that they have to find food for themselves and their families in the wilderness (v.5). They do not even have a warm garment to resist the cold (v.7) or a shelter to protect them from the rain (v.8). In short, vv.5-8 depicts how the oppressed work hard, but still suffer from hunger and live without a warm cloak or shelter.

Then the focus switches back to the description of the oppressors' evil deeds (v.9).[93] The wicked snatch (גָּזַל) the fatherless child from the breast and take a pledge against the poor.

Next the poet shifts the focus back to the suffering of the poor (vv.10-12). It highlights the alienation of the workers from their production. The poor have no means of clothing themselves while working (v.10a). Although they spend their days working on the land, they are not allowed to partake of the grain (v.10b), olive oil and wine (v.11) they are producing, but go naked (v.10a), hungry (v.10b) and thirsty (v.11b). This violates the ordinance in Deuteronomy 25:4, which forbids muzzling an animal while it is threshing. In Deuteronomy 23:24-25 a passer-by is allowed to enter a field or vineyard to eat of its produce. The panorama of wretchedness ends with the groaning and cry of the dying and the wounded (v.12a). Seemingly, the misery of the oppressed contradicts the covenant law. In Job's eyes the real injustice is not the social

---

[92] P. S. J. Joüon, *A Grammar of Biblical Hebrew* (2 vols.; trans. T. Muraoka; Rome: Editrice Pontificio Istituto Biblico, 1996) 457.

[93] Some scholars relocate v.9 after v.3 in order to avoid the sudden switch from the victim to the culprit (Driver-Gray, Dhorme, Hartley and Pope). However, Habel rightly comments that this destroys the poetic interplay of oppressor and oppressed (cf. Andersen). See Habel, *Job*, 354.

evil in itself, but God's indifference to it. He does nothing to vindicate the oppressed or to punish the oppressors. The crux of the problem, then, is that "God charges no one with wrong" (וֶאֱלוֹהַּ לֹא־יָשִׂים תִּפְלָה, lit. "but God pays no attention to wrongdoing"; v.12b).[94] Job's initial question about why those who know God never see His days of judgment (v.1) finds an ironic answer: God does not perceive anything wrong with the world.[95]

Job 24:13-17 returns to the acts of the evildoers again, describing the breakers of the sixth, seventh and eighth commandments—the murderer, adulterer and burglar—who prefer to operate in the dark. These criminals are "rebels against the light" (בְּמֹרְדֵי־אוֹר; v.13a), which is associated with God and goodness, and turn away from the ways and paths of light (v.13b). The murderer arises with the light and kills the poor and needy. And at night (וּבַלַּיְלָה), he is like a thief (v.14). The eyes of the adulterer wait for the twilight (נֶשֶׁף) when there is insufficient light for others to discern him (v.15). Similarly, burglars dig into houses in the dark (בַּחֹשֶׁךְ) when others do not work, and they shut themselves up during the day when others go out to work (v.16). Finally, Job concludes his account of the criminals with an ironic comment: deep darkness (צַלְמָוֶת) is morning to all of these perverted beings, and they are friends with the terrors of deep darkness (בַּלְהוֹת צַלְמָוֶת; v.17). In short, 24:13-17 highlights the activities of the murderer, adulterer and burglar, who operate in the dark and rebel against the light.

In sum, 24:2-17 displays the evidence to support Job's angry conviction that there are actually no days of judgment (24:1). Job enunciates that not only he himself suffers because of God's lack of responsibility for the moral governance in the world, but also that there are other people who suffer social injustice because of God's indifference.

After exposing social injustice through the interplay of the oppressor and the oppressed (24:1-17), Job utters a statement concerning the destiny of the wicked (24:18-24). The wicked are swift (קַל) and they are gone like something carried away by the waters (v.18a). Their portion (חֶלְקָתָם) in the land is cursed (תְּקֻלַּל; v.18b) and they

---

[94] MT (NIV, NASB, ESV, KJV and NKJ) reads תִּפְלָה (wrongdoing/ unseemliness/ folly) while Syriac (RSV and NRSV) reads תְּפִלָּה / תְּפִילָה (prayer). Dhorme follows Syriac to adopt תְּפִלָּה / תְּפִילָה and he also emends יָשִׂים (pay attention to) to יִשְׁמַע (hear). See Dhorme, *Job*, 361-2.

[95] Clines, "Quarter Days Gone," 249; and Newsom, "Job," 511.

do not turn toward the vineyards (v.18c) because they know that the vineyards are unfruitful.[96] As drought and heat snatch away (גָּזַל) the snow waters, so Sheol snatches away those who have sinned. Ironically, those who "snatch away" (גָּזַל) the flocks of the poor (v.2b) and "snatch away" (גָּזַל) fatherless infants from the breasts of their mothers (v.9a), will be "snatched away" (גָּזַל) as rapidly as drought and heat consumes the snow waters (v.19). Furthermore, the wicked pass out of all remembrance. Even their mothers, who bore them forget (שָׁכַח) them (v.20a). Only the worms feed sweetly (מָתֹק) on their dead bodies (v.20b). They are no longer remembered (עוֹד לֹא־יִזָּכֵר; v. 20c), so wickedness is broken down (תִּשָּׁבֵר) like a tree (v.20d).

Job 24:21 returns to the anti-social crimes of the wicked, who exploit and oppress the weakest of the society. They feed on (רָעָה) the barren childless woman and do no good (לֹא יְיֵטִיב) to the widow. Verse 22 asserts that although God may prolong (מָשַׁךְ) the life of the wicked and allow them to rise up for a while, there will come a time when they will lose confidence in their own survival (וְלֹא־יַאֲמִין בַּחַיִּין, lit. "they are not sure of life" or "they despair of life"). No matter how much security and support they appear to have achieved, God has their ways under His eyes (v.23). The wicked are exalted just for a little while (רוֹמּוּ מְעַט) and then they are no more (וְאֵינֶנּוּ; v.24a). They are doomed to be brought low (הֻמְּכוּ; Hophal of מָכַךְ) and gathered together (יִקָּפְצוּן; v.24b). They will wither (יִמָּלוּ; Qal of מָלַל) like the heads of grain (v.24c): Finally, the speech concludes with a rhetorical question: "If it is not so, who will prove me a liar (מִי יַכְזִיבֵנִי) and show that there is nothing in what I say (וְיָשֵׂם לְאַל מִלָּתִי)?" (v.25). The Hiphil of כָּזַב carries a factitive, declarative sense "who will convict me of lying."[97] אַל is used as a substantive here, meaning "nothing, worthlessness."[98] Job challenges whoever has been listening to dismiss his preceding speech as falsehood or worthless.

---

[96] Dhorme vocalizes דרך in 24:18c as דֹּרֵךְ ("the one who treads the grapes in the vat" or "wine-presser/treader"; cf. RSV). Dhorme also follows LXX to read כַּרְמָם (their vineyard) rather than כְּרָמִים (vineyards) in order to gain a parallel to חֶלְקָתָם (their portion). Hence Dhorme's emendations render v.18c as "No wine-presser turns towards their vineyard." The meaning is, then, that there are no grapes to tread. See Dhorme, *Job*, 387; and Rowley, *Book of Job*, 167.

[97] Hartley, *Job*, 352, n.15; and Dhorme, *Job*, 367.

[98] Dhorme, *Job*, 367; Gordis, *Book of Job*, 272; and Hartley, *Job*, 352.

B. *The Characteristics of Job's Contradictory Sayings in Job 24*

24:18-24 is very perplexing on the lips of Job, because it describes the ultimate punishment of the wicked. This very theme is the hallmark of the speeches by Eliphaz, Bildad and Zophar, whose viewpoints are explicitly challenged by Job in the first and second speech cycles, especially chapter 21. In addition, 24:18-24 is also at odds with its immediate context, because Job's statement here sounds contradictory to 24:1-17, where Job complains about God's delayed judgment upon the wicked. The juxtaposition of 24:18-24 and 24:1-17 is abrupt and dissonant.

To fully understand how like the friends' argument 24:18-24 sounds, provoking commentators' claims about it contradicting Job's previous standpoint, a thorough investigation comparing it with the sayings of the friends and the other sayings of Job is required. Such comparisons will show the characteristics of Job's contradictory sayings in chapter 24. The more we know about those characteristics, the more we may understand the commentators' different approaches to such sayings.

1. *Job 24:18-24 in Comparison with the Friends' Sayings*

Before comparing 24:18-24 with the sayings of Job's friends, it is important to know what viewpoints the friends hold throughout the speech cycles. As we have seen in the preceding chapter, their main arguments are contained in three theodicies: 1) the concept of retribution; 2) the inherent sinful nature of human beings; and 3) suffering as a divine disciplining.

Job's sayings in 24:18-24 focus mainly on the fate of the wicked. This passage is divided into three parts: 1) the punishment of the wicked—curse, descent into Sheol, oblivion after death (vv.18-20); 2) the evildoings of the wicked as the causes of their misfortune (vv.21); and 3) the brevity of the prosperity of the wicked (vv.22-24). Basically, 24:18-24 shares the idea of the three friends' first theodicy, mainly focusing on the destiny of the wicked with no reference to the blessing of the righteous. The comparison between Job's saying in 24:18-24 and the sayings of his three friends can be summarized as follows:

Job 24:18-24	*Sayings of Job's Three Friends*
1) Punishment of the wicked (24:18-20)	Eliphaz 4:8-11; 5:2-7 Bildad 8:11-19, 22 Zophar 11:20 Eliphaz 15:20-35 Bildad 18:5-21 **Zophar 20:12-18, 20-29** **Eliphaz 22:10-16**
2) Causes of their misfortune (24:21)	**Zophar 20:19** **Eliphaz 22:5-9**
3) Brevity of their prosperity (24:22-24)	**Zophar 20:4-11** **Eliphaz 22:18-20**

The similarity of Job's speech in 24:18-24 to his friends' viewpoint—which he strongly repudiates in the first two cycles—is the reason why many scholars find this passage inappropriate on the lips of Job and seek to reallocate it to one of his friends. Particularly noticeable is the fact that 24:18-24 shares all three themes with Zophar's speech in chapter 20 and Eliphaz's speech in chapter 22. Seeing that Zophar's final speech is missing in the third speech cycle, some scholars attribute 24:18-24 to Zophar rather than Job (Dhorme, Pope and Habel [1985]).[99]

To sum up, one distinctive characteristic of Job's contradictory sayings in 24:18-24 is that it shares common points with the three friends, expectations of the fate of the wicked, one of the theodicies the friends employ to account for Job's suffering.

2. Job 24:18-24 in Comparison with Job's Other Sayings
a) Job's Sayings in 21:1-34
Throughout the second speech cycle, Eliphaz (15:20-35), Bildad (18:5-21) and Zophar (20:4-29) have given extensive descriptive accounts of the fate of the wicked. In chapter 21 Job closes the second speech cycle with a disputation against his friends' views about the destiny of the wicked. In chapters 16-17 and 19, Job focuses upon his own struggle with God and ignores his friends' doctrine of retribution. According to this retribution, Job's afflictions seem to testify against him as a sinner. Therefore, in chapter 21, in

---
[99] Discussed further in the next section.

order to prove his innocence and uprightness, Job tries to argue from the opposite side of the thesis—a person's prosperity does not necessarily mean that he is righteous. Job develops his claim in four parts:

1) The happiness of the wicked (vv.7-16)
2) No calamity for the wicked (vv.17-21)
3) Randomness of fate and common end awaiting all people (vv.22-26)
4) The splendid funeral and memorial of the wicked (vv.27-33)

Job's response to Zophar in chapter 21 is a direct attack on the friends' retributive concept too, contradicting Zophar on the fate of the wicked as follows:

Chapter 21 (Job)	*Chapter 20 (Zophar)*
Longevity of the wicked (21:7, 13)	Brevity of their prosperity (20:5, 11, 21)
Blessings to their offspring (21:8-9)	Disaster to their offspring (20:10)
No calamity for the wicked (21:17)	Calamity for the wicked (20:28-29)
Same fate for all people (21:23-26)	The fate for the wicked (20:11)
Their abodes never disappear (21:28)	Their abodes will disappear (20:26-28)

In chapter 21 Job points out from his actual experience that many evildoers are secure and prosperous. They enjoy a rich and long life with lots of blessings although they rebel against God. Job finds that this contradicts the principle of retribution. If this is true, then by the same token those who suffer are not necessarily sinners. If under God's providence the wicked can prosper, the upright may definitely suffer.[100]

Job's speech in 24:18-24 contradicts his speech in chapter 21. The contradictions between these two passages are listed as follows:

Job 24:18-24	*Job 21*
The fleeting life of the wicked (24:18a)	The long life of the wicked (21:7, 17)
Their portion being cursed (24:18b)	Their children being blessed (21:8,11-12)
Their vineyards being barren (24:18c)	Their animals flourishing (21:9-10)

---

[100] Hartley, *Job*, 310.

Oblivion after death	Splendid funeral and memorial
(24:20)	(21:32-33)
Destruction after short uplifting	Peaceful death after a full life
(24:22-24)	(21:13)

Obviously, the viewpoint in 24:18-24 is diametrically opposed to the stance enunciated in chapter 21. Moreover, in 24:18-24 Job utters some statements which are like his friends' arguments in regard to the fate of the wicked. For instance, the wicked are swift (קַל) on the surface of the water (24:18). They are exalted (רֹמּוּ) just for a while (מְעַט) and they are gone (אֵינֶנּוּ; 24:24). This contradicts Job's previous standpoint that the wicked spend their days in prosperity (בַּטּוֹב; 21:13); they live a full life (עָתְקוּ גַּם־גָּבְרוּ חָיִל; 21:7); and go down to the grave peacefully (21:13). Job further points out the reality that the lamp of the wicked (נֵר־רְשָׁעִים) never fails (21:17).

In 24:20 Job states that the wicked will no more be remembered (עוֹד לֹא־יִזָּכֵר), but in 21:32 he says that they are buried in honour and their tombs are carefully guarded (עַל־גָּדִישׁ יִשְׁקוֹד). In 24:18 the portion of the wicked (חֶלְקָתָם) is cursed (תְּקֻלַּל). But in 21:8-12 the offspring of the wicked are established (זַרְעָם נָכוֹן); their houses are safe (בָּתֵּיהֶם שָׁלוֹם); their animals multiply; their children rejoice (יִשְׂמְחוּ). Seemingly, Job's speech in 24:18-24 is totally opposite to that in chapter 21.

b) Job's Sayings in 24:1-17
Job 24:18-24 also contradicts Job 24:1-17. Job 24:1-17 highlights the absence of God, which leads to social injustice and delayed judgment upon the wicked (v.1). In fact, it is the continuation of chapter 23, where Job points out the absence of God as the cause of his personal suffering. Thus Job argues that the absence of God is not only the cause of his personal affliction (Job 23), but also the source of widespread social injustice in the world (24:1-17). He sees that the evildoers successfully afflict others and reap the profits, while the righteous are poor and suffer. God's delayed judgment seems to aggravate the situation. By arguing the opposite side of the retributive thesis, Job's detailed presentation of the evil deeds in the world serves to "refute the easy, categorical answers of his friends."[101]

However, in 24:18-24 Job utters a statement about the fate of the wicked which highlights their short-lived prosperity and God's ulti-

---

[101] Hartley, *Job*, 342-3.

mate judgment upon evil. The juxtaposition of 24:18-24 to 24:1-17 is abrupt and dissonant. The contrast between these two adjacent sections can be seen in the following comparison:

Job 24:1-17	*Job 24:18-24*
Time of judgment not kept by God (1a)	The wicked perish swiftly (18a)
His faithful servants never see His day (1b)	The wicked's portion is cursed (18b)
	They go to Sheol (19b)
	They are forgotten and broken (20)
God charges no one with wrong (12b)[102]	God's eyes are upon the wicked (23)
	They are exalted for a while (24a)
	They are brought low and wither (24b)

In 24:1-17 Job questions why the times are not kept (לֹא־נִצְפְּנוּ עִתִּים) by God, and why His faithful servants do not see His day (לֹא־חָזוּ יָמָיו; v.1). When the oppressed groan (יִנְאָקוּ) and the wounded cry out for help (תְּשַׁוֵּעַ), God charges no one with wrong (אֱלוֹהַּ לֹא־יָשִׂים תִּפְלָה; v.12).

However, in 24:18-24, Job utters the opposite. The wicked are swift (קַל) to be carried away by the currents (v.18a), and their portions are cursed in the earth (תְּקֻלַּל חֶלְקָתָם בָּאָרֶץ; v.18b). Though they are given security (בֶּטַח), God's eyes are upon their ways (עֵינֵיהוּ עַל־דַּרְכֵיהֶם; v.23). Although they are exalted for a while (רוֹמּוּ מְעַט), they are no more (אֵינֶנּוּ) and they wither (יִמָּלוּ; v.24). The discrepancy between 24:1-17 and 24:18-24 has prompted many scholars to attribute the latter speech from Job to one of the friends.

In short, another distinctive characteristic of Job's speech in 24:18-24 is that it is not quite like Job's other sayings, contradicting his position in the first two speech cycles, especially chapter 21 and its nearest context of 24:1-17.

C. *Commentators' Approaches to the Issue of Job 24:18-24*

The scholars address the issue of Job 24:18-24 in various ways.[103] Basically five approaches are employed: 1) removing these verses because they are regarded as a pious gloss to make Job sound more orthodox; 2) considering them as an independent poem of the au-

---

[102] I follow MT (NIV, NASB, ESV, KJV and NKJ) to read וֶאֱלוֹהַּ לֹא־יָשִׂים תִּפְלָה as "God charges no one with wrong" (lit. "God pays no attention to wrongdoing"). But RSV and NRSV follow Syriac to adopt תְּפִלָּה / תְּפִלָּה rather than תִּפְלָה, rendering this clause as "God pays no attention to prayer."

[103] Andersen, *Job*, 213; and Habel, *Job*, 357.

thor; 3) treating the passage as the speech of one of the friends; 4) retaining it as Job's speech, but regarding certain portions as a quotation of his friends' standpoints; and 5) attributing the entire speech to Job.

1. Removing 24:18-24

To start with, Peake views 24:18-21, 24 as a pious gloss added to correct the views of Job and make him more orthodox than he is. When Peake comments on vv.18-21, he writes: "It would be simplest to regard the verses as an interpolation intended to modify Job's assertions of God's immoral government, or as a misplaced portion of the friends' contribution to the debate."[104] In response to the incongruity of v.24, he claims: "The immediate impression of the verse is that the prosperity of the wicked is brief, and if so the verse, since the contrary of what Job maintains, must be a mitigating gloss."[105] Peake denies that these verses are Job's words because he assumes that Job should have spoken unorthodox sayings all the way through the dialogue.

2. Considering 24:18-24 as an Independent Poem of the Author

Habel recognises the difficulty of accepting 24:18-24 as Job's speech too, because this section is opposite to Job's position in chapter 21. He further points out that if this is Job's speech, then he has already found an answer to the problem of injustice in the world, which is his friends' viewpoint. This would certainly make the responses from Elihu (chs. 34 and 36) and Yahweh (38:12-15, 35) totally redundant.[106] In his earlier commentary (1975)[107] Habel regards 24:18-24 as an independent poem which gives an answer to the problem of theodicy. However, he realises that the question still remains— why should an independent poem be inserted here when the position it reaches in its conclusion is that of the friends?[108]

---

[104] A. S. Peake, *Job* (The Century Bible; Edinburgh: T. C. & E. C. Jack, 1905) 228.
[105] Peake, *Job*, 230.
[106] Habel, *Job*, 357.
[107] N. C. Habel, *The Book of Job: Commentary* (Cambridge Bible Commentary; Cambridge: Cambridge University Press, 1975) 126-7. Here Habel regards the whole of chapter 24 as an anonymous discourse.
[108] Habel, *Job*, 358.

3. Attributing 24:18-24 to One of the Friends

In his later commentary (1985) Habel seeks to explore evidence which might support assigning 24:18-24 to the friends. He notes the parallels between Job 20 and Job 24 as follows:

Terminological and Thematic Connections Between Job 20 and Job 24

20:5	// 24:18	The prosperity of the wicked is fleeting
20:6	// 24:22, 24a	The wicked may grow as high as the sky
20:7-9	// 24:20, 24a	The wicked will disappear
20:10, 19	// 24:2-12	The poor in society
20:27	// 24:23	Heaven will expose the iniquity of the wicked
20:28a	// 24:18a	The wicked will be swept away
20:28	// 24:1	The appointed day of God's wrath
20:29	// 24:18	The allotted portion of the wicked

Common Motifs in Job 20 and Job 24

1) The appointed day of God's wrath
2) The allotted portion of the wicked
3) The exploitation of the poor

According to Habel, Job 24 continues the themes of Zophar's speech in Job 20 and answers Job's counterclaims in Job 21. He thinks that Job 24 is out of place, and that Zophar's name is deleted. In light of the above evidence he attributes Job 24 as a whole to Zophar.[109]

However, this still does not solve the problem. The contradiction between 24:1-17 (the complaint about God's delayed judgment) and 24:18-24 (the certain downfall of the wicked) still cannot reasonably be explained. In addition, Habel's parallel between 20:10, 19 and 24:2-12 is false because it does not bring out that quite different things are being said about the oppression of the poor in those places. Therefore he does not succeed in showing the unity of chapter 24 as Zophar's speech.

Habel's failure is also pointed out by van der Lugt, despite his agreement that Job cannot be the speaker in chapter 24, and that the speaker is most probably one of his friends.[110] He disagees with Habel's attribution of this chapter to Zophar because:

> Habel actually takes the question of v.1 as a reflection of "a claim of the protagonist which requires refutation"...In vv.2-17, then, the friends are supposed to make concessions to Job's standpoint, and not to take a hard line throughout! This interpretation, however, is as unthink-

---

[109] Habel, *Job*, 358.
[110] Lugt, *Rhetorical Criticism and Job*, 284.

able as the view that Job might have spoken the words of vv.18-24. Habel's view does no justice to the overall design of the book of Job...and much harm to the fact that the discussion between Job and his friends reaches a deadlock. When we take into consideration the preceding speeches, a hardening of the mutual positions can be observed. We must therefore assume that the first canto as a whole (vv.1-12) is meant as a reflection of Job's position.[111]

According to van der Lugt, in chapter 21 Job quotes his friends' views to reject them. In chapter 22 Eliphaz directly accuses Job as the wicked, and in chapter 23 Job holds onto his innocence. Then, in chapter 24, van der Lugt states, "the friends settle scores with Job by first quoting his position and then refuting it."[112] He considers that v.1 formulates Job's standpoint, which is then elaborated in vv.2-12. According to van der Lugt, the second canto (vv.13-25) is a refutation of Job's claim that there is no justice in the world. He attributes chapter 24 to Bildad and considers chapters 25 and 26 as Job's speech. He further points out that with the statement about the destiny of the wicked in 24:19-25, Bildad responds to Job's complaint about God's arbitrariness in 23:13-14 and Job's observations about the prosperity of the wicked in chapter 21.[113]

Furthermore, van der Lugt considers the introductory formula at 25:1—"then Bildad the Shuhite answered saying"—as the lost heading of chapter 24. He observes that the beginning of Bildad's second speech is connected with the beginning of his first speech by עַד־אָן (how long) in 8:2 and עַד־אָנָה (how long) in 18:2. Similarly, the end of Bildad's third speech is linked with the end of his first speech by אֵינֶנּוּ (no more) in 8:22 and 24:24. Another connection is שָׁחַר (seek eagerly) in 24:5 and 8:5. Van der Lugt justifies his allocation of chapter 24 to Bildad on the ground of these catchwords.[114] In addition, based on his theory of poetic formula, he denies chapter 24 as Job's speech because it displays cantos of thirteen lines, while chapter 23 displays cantos of five lines. He argues that if both are Job's speech, the number of lines of the cantos in these two chapters should have been the same.

Van der Lugt's reassigning of chapter 24 to Bildad is not convincing either. The catchwords "how long," "no more," and "eagerly

---

[111] Lugt, *Rhetorical Criticism and Job*, 284.
[112] Lugt, *Rhetorical Criticism and Job*, 284.
[113] Lugt, *Rhetorical Criticism and Job*, 284-5.
[114] Lugt, *Rhetorical Criticism and Job*, 507.

seek" that he singles out are not strong enough evidence to prove this chapter contains Bildad's words. Job uses the words אֵינֶנִּי and שָׁחַר in 7:21 too. Additionally, van der Lugt's criterion for determining the speaker is based almost exclusively upon poetic stylistic features, rather than the natural flow of the story. His methodology shows a high degree of rigidity and superimposition upon the interpretation of the text.

Dhorme attributes both 24:18-24 and 27:13-23 to Zophar. However, he places 24:18-24 between 27:13 and 27:14.[115] According to Dhorme, the alternation of the singular and plural in 24:18 becomes quite natural in this newly reconstructed position. In 27:13 there is an alternation of the singular אָדָם רָשָׁע (the wicked man) and the plural עָרִיצִים (the tyrants). Dhorme points out that 24:18 contains a clause in the singular, קַל־הוּא, which refers to אָדָם רָשָׁע, and two clauses in the plural referring to עָרִיצִים.[116] He finds that such alternation of the singular and plural in 24:18 seems to fit well with that in 27:13.

In addition, Dhorme finds the flow of content after his reconstruction very coherent too. He restores the introductory formula (20:1) before 27:13 to introduce Zophar as the speaker. Job 27:13 is followed by 24:18-24 to bring out the punishment and death of the guilty. Then there come the ills of those who survive him in 27:14-17.[117] According to Dhorme, Job's speech concludes at 27:12, with 27:13 being a renewal of Zophar's speech from 20:29. Dhorme outlines the close connection between 27:13 and 20:29 as follows:

27:13	זֶה חֵלֶק־אָדָם רָשָׁע עִם־אֵל וְנַחֲלַת עָרִיצִים מִשַּׁדַּי יִקָּחוּ׃
20:29	זֶה חֵלֶק־אָדָם רָשָׁע מֵאֱלֹהִים וְנַחֲלַת אִמְרוֹ מֵאֵל׃

Thematically, he points out that Zophar highlights the theme of the punishment of the wicked in chapter 20, a thesis to which he returns and further develops in the reconstructed passage—27:13; 24:18-24 and 27:14-23.[118] Dhorme's reconstruction reflects his assumption that the pattern of the speech cycles should have remained the same—Job alternating with each of his friends. Therefore he seeks to reconstruct the third speech for Zophar. He also rules out

---

[115] Dhorme, *Job*, xlv-xlvi; 386-93.
[116] Dhorme, *Job*, xlv-xlvi; 386-7.
[117] Dhorme, *Job*, xlvi.
[118] Dhorme, *Job*, 386.

the possibility that Job may use language similar to that of his friends.

Pope considers 24:18-20, 22-25 as the friends' speech rather than as Job's. According to Pope, the purpose of this displacement is to deliberately "confuse the issue and nullify Job's argument."[119] He places 24:21 within 24:1-17 in order to group "the evil acts of the wicked" together. Job's reply is reconstructed in this way: 24:1-3; 9; 21; 4-8; 10-14b; 15; 14c; 16-17.[120] Pope reassigns 24:18-20, 22-25 and 27:8-23 to Zophar. Slightly differently from Dhorme, however, he transposes 24:18-20, 22-25 right after 27:8-23.[121] Dhorme's and Pope's different ways of reconstructing 24:18-24 reveal the difficulty of reaching a consensus, even between those who agree that this passage should be placed upon Zophar's lips.

4. *Retaining 24:18-24 as Job's Speech in which He Quotes the Friends*

Driver-Gray regard 24:18-24 as "corrupt, difficult, ambiguous or unintelligible verses."[122] They point out that this passage is "most open to suspicion of interpolation."[123] According to Driver-Gray, this passage describes the unhappy fate of the wicked, which is a constant theme of the friends. To resolve the contradiction in vv.18-24, they claim that "Job admits at most and by way of concession that some wicked men meet with an unhappy fate, but only as rare exceptions to the general rule that the wicked prosper."[124] They maintain that it is necessary to assume either that these verses are out of place, or that Job is quoting his friends' standpoint in vv.18-21 to reject them in vv.22-24.[125] Therefore Driver-Gray add the words "(ye say)" in their translation at verse 18.[126]

Similarly to Driver-Gray's approach, RSV (cf. ESV) treats 24:18-20 as Job's citation of his friends' views by adding "You say" (this is not in the Hebrew text) and 24:21-25 as Job's reply. Rowley comments upon such interpretation: "But they are not really a reply, for they end with the assurance of retribution on the wicked,

---

[119] Pope, *Job*, xx.
[120] Pope, *Job*, 174-9.
[121] Pope, *Job*, 187-96.
[122] Driver and Gray, *Book of Job*, 211.
[123] Driver and Gray, *Book of Job*, 206.
[124] Driver and Gray, *Book of Job*, 211.
[125] Driver and Gray, *Book of Job*, 211.
[126] Driver and Gray, *Book of Job*, 211.

whereas Job is arguing that experience does not justify this assurance."[127]

Gordis believes that part of Zophar's speech is to be found in 27:13-23. However, if 24:18-24 is assigned to Zophar it would mean that Zophar's speech is broken into two separated parts—the first part (24:18-24) occurring before Bildad's hymn (Job 25) and the second part (27:13-23) after this hymn. Then 24:25, which is seemingly Job's, would become a single isolated verse, creating another textual problem. Instead of assigning 24:18-24 to either Bildad or Zophar, Gordis considers the orthodox sayings as Job's speech, but a quotation of the friends' position.[128] Gordis' argument is based on the following reasons. First, the style of 24:18-24 is consistent with that of 24:1-17. Secondly, the style of 24:18-24 is greatly different from that of Bildad's and Zophar's speeches. Thirdly, 24:25 is appropriate to Job in both style and spirit. Finally, Job makes use of quotations from his opponents in each cycle of the dialogue and after the Yahweh speeches. Examples can be found in chapters 12, 21, 40, and 41:2-6.[129] Although Gordis gives these four reasons to support his argument, he does not specify and elaborate any of these points. However, according to Habel, if Job 24:18-24 is considered a quotation of the friends' view as Gordis suggests, "then the quotation hangs as a limp ending with no reason, response, or reaction from Job."[130] In fact, Gordis does point out that after Job's citation of his friends' view, there usually follows Job's rebuttal (chs. 12 and 21). But in Job 24 only one verse of Job's refutation, 24:25, survives after the dislocation of the third speech cycle.[131] Seemingly, Gordis also realises the difficulty of connecting 24:25 with 24:18-24. In my opinion, Gordis' interpretation shows his attempt to keep Job's viewpoint consistent all along. This only raises the question: what does the text mean if 24:18-24 is Job's own viewpoint?

5. *Treating the Entire Speech as Job's Speech*

Newsom considers 24:18-24 as Job's speech. However, she argues that if translated as declarative sentences, as it is in most translations, the passage is completely incongruous in Job's mouth, becom-

---

[127] Rowley, *Book of Job*, 167.
[128] Gordis, *Book of Job*, 532-4.
[129] Gordis, *Book of Job*, 533.
[130] Habel, *Job*, 357.
[131] Gordis, *Book of Job*, 272.

ing a statement about the certainty of God's judgment against the wicked. Therefore she prefers the translation of LXX, the Vulgate and the Peshitta, which translate those verses as optatives—expressing Job's wish for what should happen. According to Newsom, Job's struggle with the absence of evident divine judgment leads him to a demand—Let it be done.[132] However, long before Newsom's interpretation, Driver-Gray had already pointed out the difficulty of translating 24:18-24 optatively (e.g. "let them be swift", etc.). Such a translation would require the jussive forms in Hebrew, for instance, קַל יְהִי for קַל הוּא and אַל יִפֶן for לֹא יִפְנֶה.[133] Newsom admits that this interpretation is not without its problems. However, she finds it justified in order to resolve the tensions created by the juxtaposition of 24:1-17 and 24:18-24.

Andersen argues that 24:18-24 should not be removed from Job's lips simply because it does not sound like Job's previous arguments. He is not convinced that Job could not have uttered these words,[134] adding that:

> Job has never maintained that the wicked never come to the bad end described by Eliphaz (5:2-7; 15:17-35), Bildad (8:8-19; 18:5-21) and Zophar (20:4-29). When he asked, "How often is it that the lamp of the wicked is put out?" (21:17), his implied answer is not "Never". Rather his impression is that God treats good and bad alike...In the end, death takes them all (21:23-26). In other words, Job does not counter the friends by a one-sided exaggeration of his own, claiming that God is hostile to the upright and an accomplice of the crooked. His position is more balanced, but more baffled. He simply cannot see how God's justice works out in his own case, which he realises is only one of many.[135]

Andersen's explanation shows his tendency to smooth the contradiction caused by the juxtaposition of 24:18-24 to 24:1-17. In trying not to push Job's standpoint to a one-sided extreme, Andersen in fact mirrors the presupposition of those who reject 24:18-24 as Job's words—the need to keep Job's viewpoint consistent throughout all three speech cycles.

Hartley also retains 24:18-24 as part of Job's speech. He disagrees with those scholars who reassign these verses as part of either Bildad's or Zophar's third speeches. Hartley argues that if they are

---

[132] Newsom, "Job," 511-2.
[133] Driver and Gray, *Book of Job*, 211; also Hartley, *Job*, 350-1. Like Newsom, Hartley translates 24:18-24 optatively.
[134] Andersen, *Job*, 207-8; 213-4.
[135] Andersen, *Job*, 213.

correct, 24:18-24 in its present location may have resulted from the displacement of the third cycle. According to Hartley, the style of this section seems to be more consistent with Job 24 than either with Bildad's speech in 25:1-6 or with the reconstructed speech of Zophar from 27:14-23. However, Hartley does not demonstrate the comparison of style between 24:18-24 and these passages. He further writes that Job's questioning about God's ways of governing does not necessarily mean that he puts aside all his belief in retributive punishment. Job's serious consideration about the exception to the rule does not mean that he denies his belief about justice.[136] Hartley interprets 24:18-24 as follows:

> Since Job wants God to execute his justice against these wicked as proof that he will act justly in his own favour, he utters a series of curses against the lawless, as the imprecatory style of v.18 suggests (Andersen). Cautiously accepting this interpretation, one can retain these verses as part of Job's speech.[137]

Basically, Hartley's interpretation is similar to Newsom's and Andersen's. He reads vv.18-24 as an imprecation rather than a statement, and hence he translates this section optatively to express Job's anguished demand for God's retribution upon the wicked. However, as commented above, an optative translation needs a different form of Hebrew. In addition, Hartley's interpretation also demonstrates his attempt to smooth the sharp discrepancy between 24:1-17 and 24:18-24.

Good reads chapter 24 as a whole as Job's speech, but with a very different interpretation. He points out that the emphatic plural pronoun הֵמָּה (they) in v.13 refers to human evildoers, while the subject at v.18 should be the deity.[138] Instead of reading the emphatic singular pronoun הוּא (he) as the collective name of the wicked, he considers it as referring to God. According to Good, Job gives an account of the further effects of the deity's absence in vv.18-20 and of His arbitrariness in vv.21-24.

At v.18 God's character of swiftness is brought out.[139] Because

---

[136] Hartley, *Job*, 352.
[137] Hartley, *Job*, 352-3.
[138] Good, *In Turns of Tempest*, 280.
[139] According to Good, the image of a god "swift across the waters" is reminiscent of the divine "wind" blowing "across the waters" at his creation (Gen 1:2). Therefore he considers these "waters" as the cosmic waters of chaos rather than lakes or streams. See Good, *In Turns of Tempest*, 280.

God has swiftly departed from the scene and does not turn toward the vineyards, He leaves behind chaos in nature where the fertile land is cursed (v.18) and where drought and heat consume life-giving water (v.19). The chaos even goes into society, where God reverses life and death and social structures are turned upside down (v.20). Not only the weak (v.21) but also the strong (vv.22-24) become the targets of God's oppression. The mighty are lifted up temporarily (vv.23a, 24a), but are then brought down in His renewed absence (vv.23b, 24b). Then Job repeats his earlier complaint about God's absence איננו (He is not there; v.24). In short, differently from other scholars, who read 24:18-24 as a statement about the destiny of the wicked, Good claims that this passage is Job's account of the effects of God's absence (vv.18-20) and of His arbitrariness (vv.21-24).[140]

I disagree with Good that the subject הוא at v.18a is to be understood as God. Verse 18a is most naturally read as a parallel to v.18b, c. The interplay of the singular and plural can also be found elsewhere in the book (e.g. 27:13). Generally speaking, Good's interpretation also shows that he seeks to portray a Job who consistently uses the same language to defiantly accuse God. His reading of 24:18-24 as a statement about the effects of God's absence and arbitrariness seemingly avoids the contradiction, which is evident if it is read as the fate of the wicked.

Conclusion
All in all, the scholars differ considerably in their identification of the speaker of 24:18-24. Their approaches to the issue can be summarized as follows: 1) this section is removed because it is treated as a pious gloss to make Job more orthodox than he is (Peake); 2) the speech is an independent poem of the author (Habel [1975]); 3) the passage is assigned to Bildad (van der Lugt) or Zophar (Dhorme, Pope and Habel [1985]); 4) the speech belongs to Job, but certain portions are a quotation of the friends' viewpoints (vv.18-20, RSV and ESV; vv.18-21, Driver-Gray; and vv.18-24, Gordis); and 5) the entire speech is attributed to Job (Newsom, Andersen, Hartley and Good).

Basically, those commentators who deny 24:18-24 as Job's speech presuppose that Job's expression of ideas may undergo no change

---

[140] Good, *In Turns of Tempest*, 280-1.

during the dialogue. They do not accept that Job can utter some sayings which are similar to his friends' viewpoint and contradictory to his own previous statements. Therefore they seek to reconstruct the speech in order to keep Job's use of language consistent throughout the speech cycles. In the last two decades both literary and canonical scholars have advocated reading the text in its final form in order to try to make sense of it as it stands. Seitz rightly comments:

> In order to make three full rounds of speeches, with a static, impatient Job throughout, critics have had to resort to speech-redistribution here. Yet if the full-structure is left alone, we have a very different effect. Job moves to a position of defending the moral order, but this does not happen in such a way as to slacken his complaint. In fact, he is all the more resolute in defending his innocence and demanding a fair trial (27:1-6).[141]

Quite appropriately, Patrick-Scult point out that "the less one 'reconstructs', the more objective one's interpretation."[142] Concerning the interpretation of Job, they further suggest:

> If we decide to interpret the extant text, we honour the text that it is at the expense of coherence and elegance. If we decide to reconstruct the original dramatic poem, we can concentrate on recreating the best text; but this Job can be at the expense of the text that it is. It is very hard to see how any compromise could be struck between the alternatives, but we can be clear about the costs and benefits of each.[143]

Those scholars (like Gordis, Andersen, Hartley, Newsom and Good) who defend 24:18-24 as Job's speech attempt to resolve the contradiction caused by the juxtaposition of this passage with its context in various ways. In fact, however, they also hold the same presupposition as those scholars who reject this passage as Job's words—that Job's expression of ideas should remain constant throughout the speech cycles. They have still not solved the problem: that the statement in 24:18-24 is really quite unlike Job's other sayings.

---

[141] Seitz, "Job: Full-Structure, Movement, and Interpretation," 12-3. See also P. L. Redditt, "Reading the Speech Cycles in the Book of Job," *HAR* 4 (1994) 205-14.

[142] D. Patrick and A. Scult, *Rhetoric and Biblical Interpretation* (JSOTSup 82; Sheffield: The Almond Press, 1990) 90.

[143] Patrick and Scult, *Rhetoric and Biblical Interpretation*, 91-2.

D. *The Unity of Job 24*

This study retains 24:18-24 as Job's speech and considers Job 24 as an integral part of the book. Quite properly, Habel pinpoints the coherence and unity of chapter 24. The language, thematic and terminological links indicate that 24:1-17 and 24:18-24 belong to the same unified chapter.[144]

24:11 יְקָבִים דָּרְכוּ they tread the winepresses
24:18 דֶּרֶךְ כְּרָמִים the way of the vineyards

24:2 וַיִּרְעוּ and they pasture
24:21 רֹעֶה feeding on

24:2 גָּזָלוּ they snatch away
24:9 יִגְזֹלוּ they snatch away
24:19 יִגְזְלוּ they snatch away

24:3 שׁוֹר אַלְמָנָה the ox of the widow
24:21 אַלְמָנָה the widow

24:14 יָקוּם רוֹצֵחַ יִקְטָל־עָנִי וְאֶבְיוֹן the murderer rises up and kills the poor and needy
24:22 יָקוּם וְלֹא־יַאֲמִין בַּחַיִּין they rise up but are not sure of life

As Habel shows, the catchwords show evidence of the literary unity of chapter 24. Among the thematic and terminological links listed above, two examples are noteworthy. First, גָּזַל is used twice to describe the evil deeds of the oppressors (v.2 and v.9). Then, ironically, such evil acts are linked with the destiny of the wicked (v.19): they are snatched away as the snow waters are snatched by drought and heat. Secondly, the verb יָקוּם is also used in an ironic way. In 24:14 the wicked arise (יָקוּם) to kill the poor and the needy, while in 24:22 the wicked rise up (יָקוּם), but they are not sure of life (וְלֹא־יַאֲמִין בַּחַיִּין).

As shown above, despite the disparity and tension between 24:1-17 and 24:18-24, a certain internal unity can be demonstrated for the chapter by an array of catchwords. However, the evidence of such thematic and terminological links cannot stand as the single factor supporting 24:18-24 as Job's speech because Habel in fact seeks to argue that this is Zophar's speech, not Job's, on the basis of it.[145] In the following section I will present further evidence to

---

[144] Habel, *Job*, 355-6.
[145] Habel, *Job*, 355-7.

back up my argument that 24:18-24 is from Job's lips, and that the juxtaposition of Job's contradictory sayings is the author's strategy to make a rhetorical impact upon the audience.

E. *The Rhetorical Impacts of Job's Contradictory Sayings in Job 22-24*

Concerning the interpretation of the Book of Job, Patrick-Scult rightly remark:

> But the commitment to interpret the entire work as it stands may sacrifice coherence and elegance. The interpreter must account for the tensions, disruptions and seeming incoherences as a part of an intentional design. Interpretive history shows that this quest for unity will smooth the sharp edges and harmonise the clashing perspectives of the book. Frequently there will be recourse to what can be called "third term" arguments, the supplementation of the text with ideas which fill in the gaps. All reading requires some filling-in, but we must count it an exegetical flaw to impute to a work a message which it nowhere states or implies only because a particular line of interpretation requires it for coherence.[146]

This study will not remove Job's contradictory sayings in Job 23-24. Instead, I believe that such contradictory juxtapositions serve its rhetorical function, that by which "a text establishes and manages its relationship to its audience in order to achieve a particular effect."[147] Patrick-Scult define rhetoric in this way:

> Rhetoric...is an inherent function of language use: Any author must necessarily shape his or her language in one way rather than another, and insofar as we may assume artful deliberateness on the author's part, the shape and form of the discourse is an indication of how he or she means for us to take the message.[148]

A proper interpretation of Job's contradictory sayings in Job 23-24 is key for detecting the author's intended impacts upon the audience. Therefore this study first examines how Job's contradictory sayings contribute to the flow of argument within the story itself, examining the meaning and function of those sayings in their context, before moving into a second level of investigation, where their intended impacts upon the audience will be explored.

---

[146] Patrick and Scult, *Rhetoric and Biblical Interpretation*, 91.
[147] Patrick and Scult, *Rhetoric and Biblical Interpretation*, 12.
[148] Patrick and Scult, *Rhetoric and Biblical Interpretation*, 13.

1. The Flow of Argument

Clines rightly notes that there is a sequential movement between Job's previous speeches and this speech in chapters 23-24: Job's desire to have a lawsuit with God. In the agony of his suffering, Job imagines a lawsuit with God so as to declare his innocence (9:3-4). Then he starts to realise that no one can argue with God and succeed (9:4, 19), and that he does not even know whether God will listen to him (9:14-16). Although the issue of God's overwhelming power deters Job from envisaging a trial (9:32-35), he does not give up the notion of legal disputation.

In chapter 13 Job fluctuates between confidence that he will gain personal vindication in God's presence, and fear that God's power might destroy him. Although he realises that his case is a hopeless one (13:15), he still strongly desires a confrontation with God (13:3). Again, God's overwhelming power blocks Job from envisaging a trial (13:20-21). In his subsequent speech Job seems to give up the notion of defending himself, envisaging an advocate (עֵד; 16:19) who would argue his case even after his death (16:20-22). His thought of having an advocate continues in chapter 19, envisaging a heavenly defender (גֹּאֵל) who would plead for him (19:25-26a). However, having a spokesman in God's presence is just a second-best idea. What Job most desires is to confront God face to face, "yet in my flesh I shall see God, whom I shall see for myself, and my eyes shall behold, and not another" (19:26b-27). While Job's speech in chapter 21 makes no allusion to the idea of legal disputation with God, his intention to carry his case forward is clearly shown in chapters 23-24.[149]

From the flow of theme mentioned above, it is evident that 24:18-24 is not Job's first contradictory statement in the dialogue. Even in the first two cycles, despite the strong defiant complaint against the deity, Job's positive view of God can be traced, especially the notion of seeking God's vindication (9:3, 32-35; 13:3; 16:19; 19:25-27). These positive aspects to Job's concept of God reveal his deep perplexity and ambiguous thinking about the nature of God. The notion of seeking God's vindication exposes Job's innermost conflict: he yearns to seek justice from the one who wrongs him unjustly.

When the story comes to the third speech cycle, the frequency of

---

[149] Concerning the development of the notion of a trial with God, see Clines, "Quarter Days Gone," 243-5; and Newsom, "Job," 508-9.

Job's contradictory sayings increases rapidly. As far as chapters 23-24 are concerned, many scholars only point out the single contradiction in 24:18-24, failing to realise that there is a series of contradictions in these two chapters.

Contradictory Juxtapositions in Job 23-24

	Introductory complaint	23:1-2
+ve[150]	Hope: A trial with God	23:3-7
–ve	Despair: Inability to find God	23:8-9
+ve	Hope: God knows his innocence	23:10-12
–ve	Despair: Job's dread of God	23:13-16
	Determination: Not being silenced	23:17
–ve	Social injustice	24:1-17
+ve	The fate of the wicked	24:18-24
	Conclusion: Speaking the truth	24:25

From the structure shown above, chapter 23 aims at bringing out Job's personal pain of facing the fluctuation between hope (vv.3-7; 10-12) and despair (vv.8-9; 13-16) about seeing God. Such contradictory juxtapositions highlight the tension between theological belief, which views God as judge and upholder of justice, and the experience of suffering, which results from the absence of God and the absence of His justice. On the one hand, Job believes that he can gain vindication from the just God. But on the other hand, the elusiveness and overwhelming power of God block Job's faith. Therefore we can see two pairs of contradictory juxtapositions in chapter 23, which underscore the alternation of Job's hope and despair.

Then Job proceeds to "project his own experience upon the world of humans generally and to ask what his own experience signifies for religion and theology; to ask also whether his own experience coheres with that of other humans of his own kind."[151] In chapter 24, when Job observes the world, he discovers the conflict between reality (vv.1-17) and theology (vv.18-24) which forms another abrupt juxtaposition within Job's contradictory sayings. The rhetorical question in 24:25 serves as a conclusion to the whole speech of chapters 23-24. Job has brought out the truth that there is a sharp

---

[150] Here +ve means "positive" and -ve means "negative."
[151] Clines, "Quarter Days Gone," 245.

discrepancy between experience and theology, clearly revealed through his own suffering (chapter 23) and widespread social injustice (24:1-17). In 24:25 Job claims that the exposure of such contradictions is the truth. If the facts are not as he has described, he challenges those who have been listening to dismiss his speech as falsehood or worthless.

Verse 25 is generally accepted as Job's words.[152] However, this verse is very often considered as the conclusion only to its adjacent preceding passage vv.18-24 (e.g. Whybray). Some scholars find it especially difficult to accept that Job can affirm the retributive principle which he used to strongly reject, prompting them to deny 24:18-24 as Job's words. In my view, it seems more reasonable to view v.25 as the conclusion to Job's whole argument in chapters 23-24, rather than as a conclusion just to vv.18-24.

Concerning the ambiguity of 24:18-24, Seitz rightly states that "Job moves to a position of defending the moral order, but this does not happen in such a way as to slacken his complaint."[153] In fact, using an opponent's viewpoint to refute his own case is a most powerful form of argumentation. In 24:18-24 Job defends the moral order, but with the purpose of supporting his own position and arguing against his friends.[154] Job appears as a righteous sufferer to declare judgment upon the wicked. Such a declaration of the fate of the wicked effectively exposes the inadequacy of the friends' retributive principle as an explanation of Job's personal injustice and the widespread social injustice in the world. For Job, the broader truth is that God is to be blamed for withholding the days of judgment and His indifference to injustice. Job's powerful argument starts to reduce the friends to silence. Bildad only utters six more verses (Job 25), in which the retributive principle is no longer mentioned, and Zophar fails to speak at all.

2. *The Rhetorical Impacts upon the Audience*

After examining how Job's contradictory sayings in Job 23-24 contribute to the thrust of the story itself, we now explore how such

---

[152] Driver-Gray states: "With the exception of v.25, the whole or a large part of this chapter has been regarded by many as interpolated." See Driver and Gray, *Book of Job*, 204. Gordis also points out that 24:25 is appropriate to Job in both style and spirit. See Gordis, *Book of Job*, 533, Special Note 19.

[153] Seitz, "Job: Full-Structure, Movement, and Interpretation," 12-3.

[154] Seitz, "Job: Full-Structure, Movement, and Interpretation," 13.

sayings serve to make an impact upon the audience. Contradictory juxtaposition is part of the author's rhetorical strategy to engage the audience in evaluating the events, characters and settings of the story. To motivate the audience to make a judgment is a powerful way of transforming its worldview.

The author juxtaposes Job's utterances of hope (23:3-7; 10-12) with his expressions of despair (23:8-9; 13-16), and his exposure of social injustice (24:1-17) with his declaration of judgment upon the wicked (24:18-24), guiding the audience to perceive the perplexities of real life. However, the audience has to judge how much Job has spoken rightly of God, and how much he has not.

First of all, the audience is expected to discern that Job is right in pointing out the discrepancy between the realities of suffering and social injustice and the belief in God as an upholder of justice. With respect to Job's suffering, the audience is supposed to have knowledge about the dialogue between the satan and God, which is concealed from Job and his friends. The audience knows from the beginning that Job's experience is a test case. Therefore they will concur that the traditional theology of retribution is not the answer to Job's suffering, because Job's case is an exceptional case. Concerning the experience of social injustice, the audience is expected to recognise that the theory of punishment and reward (24:18-24) cannot easily resolve such a problem, otherwise that problem would not exist. Similar to Job's case, the causes of social injustice might also be multiple and complicated. Life demonstrates that there are exceptions to any model answer. Therefore when Job asks a rhetorical question (24:25), challenging his friends to refute him and prove him a liar, the audience can affirm that Job has spoken the truth—there is a contradiction between reality and belief. This broadens the audience's horizon, showing that traditional retributive theology is inadequate to account for the existence of evil in the world.

On the other hand, the audience is also supposed to figure out that Job has not always spoken rightly of God. He considers God's absence as the reason for suffering. Job's problem is his inadequate perception of God. Job's motive in pointing out the conflict between reality and belief is to justify himself by putting God in the wrong. Having viewed the scene in the prologue, the audience knows that God's absence is part of the test to see whether Job's faith can endure. A faith which is not tested is not fully valid. After Job's first disaster God rebukes the satan: "You have incited Me against him, to ruin him without cause" (2:3). This remark vividly demonstrates God's laments over the irreparable damage that has been done to Job. From this the audience can recognise that "Yahweh's passionate protest gives voice to the theological dilemma of divine testing."[155] The audience can check God's evaluative point of view upon Job later, when the story comes to 40:8: "Will you condemn Me that you may be justified?" Seemingly, God rebukes Job for justifying himself by putting God in the wrong. Therefore the audience may discern that Job's accusation of God's absence as the cause of injustice is untrue.

Furthermore, when Job declares the judgment upon the wicked in 24:18-24, the audience is expected to recognise his contradictory views of God, which lay bare the complexities of Job's inner life. On the one hand, Job charges God with injustice (24:1-17). But on the other hand, he affirms His justice (24:18-24). The recognition of Job's misconceptions of God prepares the audience to receive Yahweh's teaching in due course.

After analysing the right and wrong viewpoints of Job's words, the audience will realise that the crux of Job's dilemma is the clash between undeserved suffering and the nature of God. Such evaluation prepares the audience to get a clear answer from God later in the Yahweh speeches, with the persuasive intent to rectify the exigency. There God acknowledges the complexity of the universe and its conflicting interests through the illustration of cosmic chaotic forces, Behemoth (40:15-24) and Leviathan (40:25-41:26 [41:1-34]). "The evil is not dismissed as illusory or unimportant, but neither is it permitted to usurp a position of dominance in the universe."[156] Although evil still goes unpunished in God's world, God remains the good God and He is in control. Similarly, Job's undeserved suffering does not necessarily have to rule out the justice and goodness of God. This is a particular vision of reality that the author expects the audience to take in due course.

Furthermore, Job's honest quest concerning the validity of punishment and reward theology and his strong challenge to the justice of God in Job 23-24 forces the audience to compare it with Eliphaz's approach to dealing with Job's suffering and apparent innocence.

---

[155] Brown, "Deformation of Character: Job 1-31," 56.
[156] Gordis, "The Lord Out of the Whirlwind," 50.

In 22:6-9 Eliphaz falsely accuses Job of great sins, which could have been recognised publicly. From the narrator's comment (1:1) and God's appraisals (1:8; 2:3) in the prologue, the audience knows that Job is a "blameless, upright man, fearing God and turning away from evil." Therefore they can see that Eliphaz is not speaking the truth. Gordis rightly comments: "Finding his theory of Divine justice contradicted by the facts, Eliphaz proceeds to the time-honored device of adjusting the facts to the theory."[157] When Job asks his rhetorical question in 24:25: If he has not spoken the truth, who can gainsay him and prove him a liar?, the audience is able to tell who is the real liar. Involving the audience to evaluate Job's and Eliphaz's different approaches to interpreting human suffering prepares them to adopt God's final verdict in 42:7-8 as their evaluative point. There God commends Job for his truthfulness in pointing out the contradiction between reality and belief. It is the truth that evil does exist in God's world. Eliphaz is said to be wrong because he twists the truth in order to fit the formula of his theology.

To sum up, Job's series of contradictory sayings in chapters 23-24 serve to broaden the audience's horizon, causing them to perceive the perplexity of life through Job's quest for divine justice. The theory of retribution and reward is not an answer to the existence of evil, either in Job's case or when facing social injustice. There are times when reality contradicts theology. Job is truthful in voicing these contradictions (Job 23-24), whereas Eliphaz is untruthful in twisting the facts to fit his theology (Job 22). The audience are also assumed to discern Job's misconception of God. The crux of Job's dilemma is that he does not know how to reconcile innocent suffering with the goodness of God. The process of such evaluations serves to stimulate the audience into seeking a resolution for Job's problem, and also prepares them to have "a fusion of horizons"[158] with the author's perspective later in the story, so that the exigency can be resolved.

V. *Job's Contradictory Sayings in Job 25-26*

Similarly to Job 24, Job 25 and 26 pose difficult interpretive problems too. Bildad's third speech in chapter 25 begins very abruptly,

---

[157] Gordis, *Book of Job*, 238; also Good, *In Turns of Tempest*, 273; and M. P. Matheney, Jr., "Major Purposes of the Book of Job," *SWJT* 14 (1971-72) 32.

[158] Combrink, "Rhetoric of Sacred Scripture," 116.

lacking an introduction and a personal challenge to Job, unlike his two previous rejoinders in 8:2-8 and 18:2-4. As the text stands, Bildad's speech consists of five verses only, and it is followed by Job's long speech (chs. 26-31), while Zophar's final speech is absent in the third speech cycle. In addition, the content of Job 26:5-14, like Job 24:18-24 and 27:13-23, sounds inappropriate from Job's lips because it is at variance with Job's previous standpoint. Therefore many scholars argue that the third speech cycle has suffered considerable disruption in the course of scribal transmission. They seek to rearrange these chapters to yield a complete third speech cycle. There are, however, great divergences among such reconstructions, as the following table shows:

Dhorme

Job	24:1-17, 25
Bildad	25:1-6; 26:5-14
Job	26:1-4; 27:2-12
Zophar	27:13; 24:18-24; 27:14-23

Rowley

Job	24:1-17, 25
Bildad	25:1-6, 26:5-14
Job	26:1-4; 27:1-6
Zophar	27:7-12; 24:18-24; 27:13-23

Gordis

Job	24:1-25
Bildad	25:1-6; 26:5-14
Job	26:1-4; 27:1-12
Zophar	27:13-23

Habel

Zophar	24:1-25
Bildad	25:1-6; 26:5-14
Job	26:1-4; 27:1-12
Zophar	27:13-23

Hartley

Job	24:1-25
Bildad	25:1-6; 27:13-23
Job	26:1-14; 27:1-12

Pope

Job	24:1-17, 21
Bildad	25:1-6; 26:5-14
Job	27:1, 26:1-4; 27:2-7
Zophar	27:8-23; 24:18-20, 22-25

Newsom

Job	24:1-25
Bildad	25:1-6
Job	26:1-4
Bildad	26:5-14
Job	27:1-23

Andersen/Clines/Good/Janzen/Whybray

Job	24:1-25
Bildad	25:1-6
Job	26:1-14; 27:1-23

In contrast to such reconstructions, this study proposes to read Job 25-26 as the text stands, retaining 26:5-14 as Job's speech. In addition, this study will not remove the contradiction caused by the juxtaposition of Job 26 to Job 25. Instead, contradictory juxtaposition is viewed as part of the author's rhetorical strategy to make a rhetorical impact upon the audience and to elicit a transformation of the exigency in due course.

This section firstly examines the content of Job 25-26. Secondly, the characteristics of Job's contradictory sayings in Job 26 are explored by comparing his hymn there with: a) Job's other hymnic materials; b) Job's other non-hymnic materials concerning his perceptions of God; and c) his three friends' hymnic materials. Thirdly, it proceeds to discuss how commentators resolve the issue of Job's contradictory sayings in Job 26. Finally, this study will argue that the juxtaposition of Job's contradictory sayings in Job 26 to Job 25 serves a positive rhetorical function in relation to the audience.

A. *The Content*

In 25:1-6 Bildad praises God's absolute power and majesty (vv.2-3) and affirms every creature's frailty and unworthiness before Him (vv.4-6). Bildad directs Job's thought to God's dominion (הַמְשֵׁל)[159] and fear (פַּחַד; v.2a). He makes peace (שָׁלוֹם) in His high places, resolving the conflicts in heaven (v.2b). God's armies (לִגְדוּדָיו) are uncountable and His light (אוֹרֵהוּ) penetrates everywhere (v.3). Before this awesome God, no human being can claim to be just (יִצְדָּק) and clean (יִזְכֶּה; v.4). If even the moon and stars cannot match with God's splendor and holiness (v.5), how much less can human beings (אֱנוֹשׁ "man" or בֶּן־אָדָם "son of man"), who are but maggot (רִמָּה) and worm (תּוֹלֵעָה)—symbols of death and decay (v.6).

Despite many scholars' comment that this hymn is too brief and fragmented, it displays a well-formed symmetrical structure. Hartley shows the chiastic pattern of this hymn as follows:[160]

> *Antithetical Parallel*: The greatness of God (v.2)// The insignificance of man (v.6)
> *Centre of the Chiasm*: No man can be just before God (v.4)
> *Heavenly Host*: God's troops (v.3)// The stars and moon (v.5)

After Bildad's short speech, Job gives his response, which can be divided into two sections. The first part consists of Job's rejection of Bildad's counsels (26:1-4),[161] while the second part highlights his praise of God's majestic power (26:5-14).

---

[159] הַמְשֵׁל is an Hiphil infinitive absolute, serving as a noun here.
[160] Hartley, *Job*, 355. Regarding the symmetry of this poem, Andersen points out the alternation between the heavenly bodies (vv.3, 5) and man (vv.4, 6). See Andersen, *Job*, 215.
[161] Job 26:2-4 is sometimes rejected as Job's speech because the pronouns

In the first section (26:1-4) Job complains that Bildad could not offer him any consolation, help or counsel to rescue him from the desperate situation. Job regards himself as one without power (לֹא־כֹחַ), without strength (לֹא־עֹז) and without wisdom (לֹא חָכְמָה; vv.2-3). He even questions the source of Bildad's sayings and the value of his instruction (v.4): "With whose (אֶת־מִי) help have you uttered words, and whose breath (נִשְׁמַת־מִי) has come out from you?" He implies that Bildad's advice is not divinely inspired.

The second section (26:5-14) is Job's hymn of praise, which highlights God's dominion over the underworld (vv.5-6), the heavens (vv.7-9; 12-13) and the earth (vv.10-11). Concerning God's governance over the underworld, 26:5-6 depicts the terror with which the shades (הָרְפָאִים)[162] in the underworld responds to God's awesome presence (v.5). Sheol (שְׁאוֹל) and Abaddon (אֲבַדּוֹן)[163] are completely exposed in God's holy presence (v.6).

Job 26:7-9 shifts the focus to God's divine rule in the heavens.[164]

"you" here are masculine singular, different from Job's frequent usage of plural to address his friends together (except 12:7ff.; 16:3 and 21:3). Some scholars thus claim that these verses are addressed to Job and once belonged to one of the friends, probably Bildad. Alternatively, the singular may better indicate that Job is not addressing all his friends, but just singling out Bildad alone. For the detail of the discussions, see Hartley, *Job*, 362; Andersen, *Job*, 217; Rowley, *Book of Job*, 171; Gordis, *Book of Job*, 286; Newsom, "Job," 517; and Driver and Gray, *Book of Job*, 216-7.

[162] According to Newsom, הָרְפָאִים (the shade) are "the dead who persist in shadowy form in Sheol" (Ps 88:11 [10]; Prov 2:18; 9:18; 21:16) or "the spirits of dead heroes and kings" (Isa 14:9; 26:14; Ps 88:11 [10]). See Newsom, "Job," 517; and Rowley, *Book of Job*, 172.

[163] אֲבַדּוֹן (Abaddon) which is derived from a Hebrew verb אָבַד (to perish), is a synonym for שְׁאוֹל (Sheol), a name for the place of the dead. The word "Abaddon" can only be found in the wisdom literature (Job 28:22; 31:12; Ps 88:12 [11]; Prov 15:11; 27:20). See Newsom, "Job," 518; Whybray, *Job*, 115; V. E. Reichert, *Job* (Soncino Books of The Bible; London; Jerusalem; New York: The Soncino Press, 1976) 133; and Rowley, *Book of Job*, 172. However, according to Habel, Sheol represents the extremity of the lower regions of the cosmos, while Abaddon refers to the deep mysterious world of death and decay; see Habel, *Job*, 370-1. Gordis suggests that the term Abaddon is later than Sheol. The former carries the meaning of "the land of destruction for the evil doer," while the latter refers to the undifferentiated domicile of all the dead; see Gordis, *Book of Job*, 278.

[164] All three verses of 26:7-9 begin with participles, with God as the implied subject:

נֹטֶה צָפוֹן עַל־תֹּהוּ	He stretches the north over the void (v.7a)
תֹּלֶה אֶרֶץ עַל־בְּלִי־מָה	He hangs the earth on nothing (v.7b)
צֹרֵר־מַיִם בְּעָבָיו	He binds up the waters in His thick clouds (v.8a)
מְאַחֵז פְּנֵי־כִסֵּה	He covers the face of (His) throne (v.9a)

God stretches His abode, i.e. the north (צָפוֹן),[165] over the void (תֹהוּ)[166] to set up a stable part of the firmament, and He hangs the earth over nothing (עַל־בְּלִי־מָה; v.7). In this way, "[t]he north above where God dwells and the earth below where humans reside are suspended mysteriously above empty space."[167] The heavy clouds, the floating reservoirs of rainwater, will not burst (נִבְקַע)[168] even under great weight (v.8). God spreads (פַּרְשֵׁז)[169] the clouds to hide His throne (כִּסֵּה; v.9).[170]

Regarding God's governance on the earth (vv.10-11), He drew a boundary (חֹק) as the horizon, at the end of the sea's waters, to di-

---

The participial form is characteristic of hymns of praise (cf. 5:9-13). See Whybray, *Job*, 116; Newsom, "Job," 518; and Dhorme, *Job*, 371-2.

[165] Habel points out that צָפוֹן (the north) is a designation for the dwelling place of gods (Job 23:9) and is connected with the cosmic mountain where the gods assemble (Isa 14:13). See Habel, *Job*, 371. Hartley claims that, according to Ugaritic mythology, the north is the place where gods gather, and Mount Saphon is the dwelling place of the chief god, Baal. Some OT passages borrow this imagery and use the term "the north" to refer to the place of God's supreme reign (Ps 48:3 [2]). Hartley further adds that "the north" symbolically refers to God's habitation (Isa 14:13-14). See Hartley, *Job*, 366; and Newsom, "Job," 518.

[166] Hartley considers תֹהוּ as the watery chaos (cf. Gen 1:2); see Hartley, *Job*, 366. Habel, however, renders תֹהוּ as the "void" or "nothing" over which the canopy of the north is pitched. Habel's rendering is preferable because תֹהוּ is parallel to אַיִן (nothing/nought) in Isa 40:17, 23 (cf. Isa 41:29; 44:9; 49:4). See Habel, *Job*, 371; and Dhorme, *Job*, 372.

[167] Habel, *Job*, 371.

[168] The Niphal of בָּקַע carries the sense of "crack open" or "burst open." It is especially used to describe the reservoirs of heaven which burst open (Gen 7:11). It is also used to describe the clouds as the wineskins of the sky which burst (Job 32:19; cf. 38:37). See Dhorme, *Job*, 372.

[169] MT פַּרְשֵׁז (spreading over), which occurs only once here in Scripture, is variously interpreted. Dhorme regards it as an error arising from the scribal conflation of פָּרַשׂ (spread) and פָּרַז (extend). He thinks that the original text should be פָּרַשׂ (unfurling); see Dhorme, *Job*, 373. Some scholars treat פַּרְשֵׁז as a quadriliteral form, an infinitive absolute of a Pil'el formation פַּרְשֵׁשׂ (from פָּרַשׂ "to spread out"), with a "euphonic" change of the first שׂ to שׁ and of the second to ז, or by dissimilation from פַּרְשֵׁשׂ. See E. Kautzsch and A. Cowley, *Gesenius' Hebrew Grammar* (2nd ed.; Oxford: Clarendon Press, 1910) 153-4, §56. But Driver-Gray find this explanation "highly artificial." See Driver and Gray, *Book of Job*, Philological Notes, 179-80. Hartley rightly comments: "The question of the correct form remains open, but the context accepts a meaning of 'spread out.'" See Hartley, *Job*, 364, n.5.

[170] Dhorme follows Ibn Ezra to consider כִּסֵּה (the throne) in MT as an erroneous vocalization of כֶּסֶה (full moon) (Ps 81:4, but כֶּסֶא in Prov 7:20); see Dhorme, *Job*, 373 and his translation on 372. Pope also reads כֶּסֶה (full moon); see Pope, *Job*, 184. Disagreeing with the above view, Gordis points out that the word כֶּסֶה does not mean "full moon", but "the day of full moon." See Gordis, *Book of Job*, 279; and Hartley, *Job*, 364, n.4.

vide the light from the darkness (v.10). Even the pillars of heavens
(עַמּוּדֵי שָׁמַיִם), i.e. the distant mountains,[171] which support the sky
tremble (רָפַף) at His rebuke (מִגַּעֲרָתוֹ; v.11).[172] When God expresses
His anger, even the supporting mountains will shake.

Repeating the idea in 25:2b-3 which highlights God's making
peace in heavens, Job depicts God's victory in the cosmic battle
(26:12-13).[173] With His wisdom and power, God defeated Rahab
(רָהַב) and the serpent (נָחָשׁ); He stilled (רָגַע)[174] the sea (הַיָּם) and made
the heavens fair (שָׁמַיִם שִׁפְרָה ; vv.12-13).[175]

Along with 26:12, v.13 continues the mythological motifs to depict God's power over the cosmic chaos as follows:

> By His power He stilled the sea (12a)//
> By His wind the heavens were made fair (13a)
>
> By His understanding He shattered Rahab (12b)//
> His hand pierced the fleeing serpent (13b)

Rahab (רָהַב) refers to the mythical sea monster in Scripture, personifying the raging pride of the sea (Job 9:13; Ps 89:11 [10]; Isa

---

[171] With reference to 2 Sam 22:8 and Ps 18:8, "the pillars of heaven" is parallel to "the pillars of mountains." Therefore many commentators (e.g. Dhorme, Driver-Gray, Gordis, Habel, Hartley and Pope) consider "the pillars of heavens" in Job 26:11 as "the distant mountains" which support the vault of heaven.

[172] "His rebuke" is expressed by a strong blast of wind (Job 26:13; Isa 50:2; Nah 1:3-4), or by a blast of the breath of His nostrils (Ps 18:16[15]; 2 Sam 22:16), or by a loud thunderclap (Ps 104:7). See Hartley, *Job*, 367.

[173] Habel, *Job*, 374.

[174] רָגַע has two diametrically opposite meanings: a) "disturb or stir up" (cf. Isa 51:15; Jer 31:35); and b) "still" (cf. Isa 34:14; Jer 31:2; 47:6; 50:34). In Job 26:12 NIV and NKJ pick up the first meaning, "stirred up," while NASB, RSV, NRSV and ESV the second meaning, "stilled." The "sea" is described as the aggressor in the cosmogonic battle. The rendering "stilled" is preferable because it signifies the subjugation of the chaotic forces. See Newsom, "Job," 518-9; Rowley, *Book of Job*, 173-4; and Hartley, *Job*, 367, n.20.

[175] שִׁפְרָה is differently interpreted. The root of שִׁפְרָה in Aramaic has the sense of "to be fair, beautiful, or bright." Driver-Gray translate v.13a as "By his wind the heavens are brightened"; see Driver and Gray, *Book of Job*, 223; Philological Notes, 181-2; and Hartley, *Job*, 364, n.9. Dhorme considers it as a Piel perfect and a cognate of Arabic verb *safara* (to shine/to sweep), and he translates v.13a as "His breath has swept the heavens." See Dhorme, *Job*, 375; and Hartley, *Job*, 364, n.9. Gordis vocalizes it as a Piel perfect שִׁפְּרָה and considers it as a cognate of Akkadian *šuparruru* (spread out). He renders this line as "His breath stretched out the heavens." See Gordis, *Book of Job*, 280. Pope relates שִׁפְרָה with the Akkadian *saparu* (net; bag/skin bottle in Ps 56:9 [8]). He separates שָׁמַיִם (heavens) into שָׂם יָם (he put the sea) and translates the line as "By his wind he put the sea (in) a bag." See Pope, *Job*, 185-6.

51:9).[176] The serpent (נָחָשׁ) is an alternative name for Leviathan (cf. Job 3:8; Isa 27:1: "Leviathan the fleeing serpent, Leviathan the twisting serpent").[177] Leviathan is also associated with the sea in Psalm 104:26; Job 41:23 [31] and Isaiah 27:1. Rahab and the serpent seem to be paralleled, both referring to the same sea-creature. The threat of chaos would not only bring the sea onto the land, but also replace light with darkness. Therefore stilling the sea and brightening or clearing the heavens would both result from defeating the sea monster.[178]

After depicting God's all-embracing rule and power, Job concludes that all we can know of His might are but the outskirts of His ways (קְצוֹת דְּרָכָו). How small a whisper (שֵׁמֶץ דָּבָר) we heard (נִשְׁמַע)[179] of Him (v.14)!

B. *The Characteristics of Job's Hymnic Material in Job 26*

Many scholars deny 26:5-14 to Job because they find it unlike Job's way of expressing God's negative aspects in his previous hymnic materials, and quite like the friends' hymns magnifying the great-

---

[176] See Newsom, "Job," 518; and Reichert, *Job*, 135. The ancient Near Eastern myths depict the god of order defeating the god(s) of chaos. In "Enuma Elish" Marduk defeats Tiamat, the deep sea. He mortally wounds her by extending her mouth with a blast of wind, and shooting an arrow into her heart (*ANET*, 66-67). In Ugaritic mythology Baal subdues his enemy Yamm, the Sea (*ANET*, 130-131). The OT borrows these mythical materials to describe God's total control over all the cosmic and terrestrial forces. See Hartley, *Job*, 367, n.19; and Habel, *Job*, 373-4.

[177] See J. Day, *God's Conflict with the Dragon and the Sea: Echoes of a Canaanite Myth in the Old Testament* (Cambridge: Cambridge University Press, 1985) 39; and Rowley, *Book of Job*, 174.

[178] Day notably points out the association of the serpent with darkness. According to Day, at first glance, we tend to conclude from v.13a ("By His wind the heavens were made clear") that the serpent is in the sky, even though the parallelism of Rahab and the sea in v.12 shows clearly that Rahab is a sea monster. However, compared with other references, Job 26 unfolds how the serpent is associated with darkness and why it relates to the sky. *KTU* 1.83.3-10 points out that the serpent in the sea reaches up into heaven before being defeated by Anat. In addition, Gen 1:2 indicates that Yahweh's wind hovering over the darkness is associated with the chaotic watery deep. According to Day, Job 3:8 implies that the rousing up of Leviathan brings darkness in its train. Therefore defeating the same monster will lead to the stilling of the sea and the brightening of the heavens. See Day, *God's Conflict with the Dragon and the Sea*, 39.

[179] נִשְׁמַע can be either a Niphal perfect 3ms "be heard" or a Qal imperfect 1cp "we heard." Therefore v.14b can either be translated as "and how (small) a whisper is heard of Him" or "and how (small) a whisper we heard of Him." We can choose either one, because both meanings are not different very much from each other.

ness of God, noting especially that its theme is quite similar to that of Bildad's hymn in chapter 25. To test such conclusion, a thorough investigation will be taken to compare 26:5-14 with: a) Job's other hymnic materials; b) Job's non-hymnic materials; and c) the friends' hymnic passages.

1. *Job 26:5-14 in Comparison with Job's Other Hymnic Passages*
Job has uttered four hymns of praise, namely 9:5-13, 10:8-13, 12:13-25 and 26:5-14. We now consider each of these in turn.

a) Job 9:5-13[180]
Job 9:5-13 links two traditional doxologies (vv.5-7 and vv.8-10), which are followed by two conditional statements both beginning with הן (vv.11-12) and by a concluding sentence (v.13).[181] Hartley proposes a three-part structure of the hymn: a) nature's response to God's appearance (vv.5-7); b) God's might and wisdom in creating the world (vv.8-10); and c) God's victory over all foes (vv.11-13). Each verse of 9:5-10 exhibits the Hebrew participial form (with the article in vv.5-7, but without it in vv.8-10).[182] Hartley further claims that this hymn is the expansion of v.4: "He is wise in heart and mighty in strength; who has hardened himself against Him and succeeded?" This idea is shown as follows:[183]

Deeds of power	(v.4a')	vv.5-7
Acts of wisdom	(v.4a)	vv.8-10
God's victory over foes	(v.4b)	vv.11-13

Gordis considers 9:5-10 as a hymn focusing on the destructive power of God. He states, "Job counters Eliphaz's glowing description of God's power (5:9-16) by emphasizing the negative aspects of God's might, as manifested in His overturning the mountains (v.5), shaking the earth (v.6), and shutting off the light of the sun and the stars (v.7)."[184] The theme of vv.8-10 is that God is the creator of the

---

[180] In regard to the unit division, some scholars treat Job 9:5-13 as a unit (Hartley, Habel, Westermann and Newsom), while some scholars consider Job 9:5-10 as a unit (Gordis, Janzen, Dell and Clines). Whedbee treats Job 9:2-10 as a unit. I choose Job 9:5-13 as a unit in this study for two reasons: 1) it constitutes a three-part structure (vv.5-7; 8-10; 11-13); and 2) it is large enough to cover most of the unit-demarcations.
[181] Newsom, "Job," 410.
[182] Clines, *Job 1-20*, 229; Newsom, "Job," 410; and Janzen, *Job*, 90.
[183] Hartley, *Job*, 169-70.
[184] Gordis, *Book of Job*, 522, Special Note 11.

heaven, sea and planets.¹⁸⁵ Gordis further points out that even if vv.8-10 do not depict the negative character of God, Job has cited older sources for a purpose far from their original context in order to "underscore the violent power of God."¹⁸⁶

Janzen thinks that Job reverts to the traditional laudatory form (Hebrew participial clauses) to express his suspicions about "the character of the divine wisdom and the ends of the divine strength: they are not creative and ordering, but destructive and bewildering (9:5-10)."¹⁸⁷ According to Janzen, in 9:10 Job gives Eliphaz's viewpoint in 5:9 a new and negative meaning. The unsearchability of God (אֵין חֵקֶר; 9:10a) is now no longer a positive mystery, but a negative and baffling enigma.¹⁸⁸

Dell holds that there is a parody contained in Job 9:5-10, which was originally a hymn depicting God's creative power.¹⁸⁹ She points out that usually in hymns, like Psalm 104 and Amos 5:6-9, God's unknowability and the wonders of His creation inspire human beings to praise Him. According to Dell, Job 9:5-10 expresses "reproaches against the unassailable God whose actions man cannot predict."¹⁹⁰ She further states that in chapter 9, contradictory to the friends' positive description of God's wisdom and might, Job focuses on the negative and destructive aspects of God's might in order to attack God's irresponsible and unjust power.¹⁹¹

Whedbee views Job's speeches as "a collage of brilliant parodies, where at almost every crucial juncture Job takes up diverse parts of

---

¹⁸⁵ Gordis points out that this section is sometimes deleted by scholars for two reasons: a) it does not depict the negative aspects of God as the rest of the passage does; and b) it is viewed as the reminiscences of other biblical passages (v.8a=Isa 44:24d; v.8b=Mic 1:3b [not identical]; v.9=Am 5:8; v.10=Job 5:9). See Gordis, *Book of Job*, 522, Special Note 11.

¹⁸⁶ Gordis, *Book of Job*, 522, Special Note 11.

¹⁸⁷ Janzen, *Job*, 90.

¹⁸⁸ Janzen, *Job*, 90-1.

¹⁸⁹ K. J. Dell, *The Book of Job as Sceptical Literature* (BZAW 197; Berlin; New York: De Gruyter, 1991). In her dissertation, Dell claims that the author of Job deliberately misuses literary forms from many areas of Israelite life—the traditional forms being used with a different content and context and thus having a different function—in order to convey his sceptical message (109-57). She terms this characteristic "misuse" as "parody", which is "parasitic on other genres and uses any genre for its own purposes" (148, 214-5). According to Dell, by using "parody", "the author deliberately stepped outside literary conventions to make a protest" (215). And parody becomes the dominant form of the Book of Job.

¹⁹⁰ Dell, *Book of Job*, 127.

¹⁹¹ Dell, *Book of Job*, 173-4. Here Dell analyses Job 9 and 10 by employing form-criticism.

his traditional heritage only to twist them and make them ludicrous."[192] He points out that Job's speech reaches a crescendo of bitter irony in his doxological hymn of Job 9:2-10, which portrays Yahweh as a God of terror rather than a God of justice and mercy.[193] According to Whedbee, Job "brings to a fitting climax his sardonic song to the God of chaos," when he concludes the divine attributes with an almost verbatim quotation of Eliphaz's words—"who does great things beyond understanding and wonders without number" (5:9; 9:10).[194]

Habel views 9:5-13 as a satirical hymn,[195] which highlights the characterization of God as Job's adversary who initiates chaos rather than maintaining just order.[196] According to Habel, the inscrutability of God's ways is reflected in His violent intervention in His created order, rather than reflected in His continual creative blessings. In Job's portrayal, God is powerful, aggressive, disruptive, elusive, invisible and wrathful, so that he is unable to comprehend God and to restrain His aggression. God's wrath was displayed when He subdued the forces of chaos. According to Habel, "Job's characterization of his adversary at law assumes the form of a doxology to the aggressive ways of the Maker."[197]

Westermann claims that the motif in 9:5-13 is the praise of the creator. He comments, "In chapter 9, the traditional praise of the creator in vv.8-9 is expanded in a customary way: the creator is lord of his creation (vv.5-7). But these clauses are already one-sided; what gets emphasized is the creator's ability to overturn mountains and cause the earth to quake. This theme is intensified even more in vv.12-13. If God deals with his creation in anger, then surely no one is in a position to withstand him."[198] Westermann thinks that in 9:5-13 the praise of God in His majesty is deliberately developed in a one-sided fashioned, mainly underscoring the negative aspects.

Clines views 9:5-10 as the hymnic doxology, which depicts the destructive or negative acts of God in vv.5-7, and His creative acts

---

[192] J. W. Whedbee, "The Comedy of Job," *Studies in the Book of Job* (Semeia 7; ed. Robert Polzin and David Robertson; Missoula: Scholars Press, 1977) 15.
[193] Whedbee, "Comedy of Job," 15-6.
[194] Whedbee, "Comedy of Job," 16.
[195] Habel, *Job*, 188.
[196] Habel, *Job*, 190-2, 366.
[197] Habel, *Job*, 190.
[198] Westermann, *Structure of Job*, 73-4.

in vv.8-10.[199] Clines recognises that the focus of vv.5-7 is on the negative aspect of God. However, he claims that "this emphasis, though perhaps one-sided, is not a satirical reversal of the psalmic motif" as Fullerton, Gordis and Whedbee claim.[200] According to Clines, the occurrence of the upheaval motif normally comes: a) as the worst disaster but without terrifying the pious (e.g. Ps 46:3-4 [2-3]; 75:4 [3]); or b) as an association with Yahweh's deliverance (e.g. Ps 18:8 [7]; 97:4; 114:5-7; Isa 13:13; 29:6; Hab 3:6, 10; Judg 5:4; cf. Ps18:16 [15]; Exod 19:18). With the latter emphasis, Yahweh's anger is often highlighted.[201] Clines further points out that the focus of the Psalms is upon God's deliverance, but in 9:5-10 it is upon God's sheer power. He claims that the depiction of God's destructive activity should not be the main thrust here.[202]

In the same vein as Clines, Newsom acknowledges that the negative aspects of God are depicted. Like Clines, she also disagrees with many commentators' claim that Job is parodying traditional doxologies to portray a violent and destructive God. According to Newsom, God's power is traditionally presented in a positive light because divine violence is associated with His victory over chaos and His deliverance. However, in 9:5-7 Job has contextualized the images of divine violence differently.[203] Newsom also denies any parody in the second doxology (9:8-10). She holds that Job sets the traditional hymn in a context that becomes a trouble rather than a comfort to him.[204]

Both Clines and Newsom deny 9:5-13 as a parody, because the "upheaval motif" is often associated with Yahweh's deliverance in the conventional psalms, but 9:5-13 illustrates the sheer power of God. But if 9:5-13 is used in a way different from the traditional one, might this not still be a satire on the psalmic motif?

---

[199] Clines, *Job 1-20*, 229.
[200] Clines, *Job 1-20*, 229-30. Clines disagrees with K. Fullerton, "On Job, Chapter 9 and 10," *JBL* 53 (1934) 321-49, [330-1]; Gordis, *Book of Job*, 522; and Whedbee, "Comedy of Job.". Clines especially disagrees with Whedbee's statement on pp.15-16: "[Job] catalogues examples of the pervasive chaos in creation.... What results is an ironic parody of a doxological hymn, which is used only in order to twist its intention....[it] portrays [God] as a God of terror who revels in destruction."
[201] Clines, *Job 1-20*, 229.
[202] Clines, *Job 1-20*, 229-30.
[203] Newsom, "Job," 410.
[204] Newsom, "Job," 411.

To decide whether Job 9:5-13 is parodying traditional doxologies by presenting God's power as violent and destructive, as Gordis, Westermann and the others claim, we need first to define the term "parody" and "satire". According to the *Oxford English Dictionary*,[205] "satire" refers to:

> A poem, or in modern use sometimes a prose composition, in which prevailing vices or follies are held up to ridicule. Sometimes, less correctly, applied to a composition in verse or prose intended to ridicule a particular person or class of person, a lampoon.

As far as "parody" is concerned, the *Oxford English Dictionary* gives the following definition:

> A composition in prose or verse in which the characteristic turns of thought and phrase in an author or class of authors are imitated in such a way as to make them appear ridiculous, especially by applying them to ludicrously inappropriate subjects, an imitation of a work more or less closely modelled on the original, but so turned as to produce a ridiculous effect.

In addition, *A Dictionary of Literary Terms* defines "parody" as "a literary composition that imitates the style of another work. Although it amuses us it need not make us devalue the original."[206]

Miles distinguishes "satire" from "parody" in the following way: "Satire is the exposure by comedy of behaviour which is standardized and, to that extent, foolish. Parody is that breed of satire in which the standardized behaviour to be exposed is literary."[207] According to Good, "parody is a form of satire that imitates its object by exaggeration in order to ridicule....There may be a certain irony in some parodies, but it is by no means constant, for parody is actually a form of sarcasm. Though it may produce a good laugh, the laugh is always tinged with bitterness."[208] Weisman rightly states that it is difficult to establish a clear-cut distinction between satire and irony, or between satire and humour. Their difference is in mood and tone, which are subjective. He further adds that hu-

---

[205] *The Oxford English Dictionary*. (Oxford: Clarendon, 1961).
[206] S. Barnet, M. Berman and W. Burbo, ed, *A Dictionary of Literary Terms* (London: Little Brown and Company, 1964).
[207] J. A. Miles, Jr., "Laughing as the Bible: Jonah as Parody," *JQR* 65 (1974-1975) 168.
[208] E. M. Good, *Irony in the Old Testament* (Sheffield: The Almond Press, 1981) 27-8.

mour and irony carry a mood of forgiveness, whereas satire brings out a tone of animosity and insult.[209]

Parody, then, is a form of satire. The purpose of both is to ridicule. Compared with other humorous writings, satire and parody evoke a sense of disdain and contempt.

I agree with Andersen that to interpret Job's trend of thought in Job 9:5-10, we need to discern his mood, because "we can no longer hear the tone of his voice, and the author has provided no comment on what kind of a temper he is in, we can only guess. Such guesswork can be dangerous, since it can lead us along a wrong track."[210] To resolve the problem, Weisman regards "wit" as "instrumental in moulding the mood which is typical of satire and which conveys its special message."[211] Concerning the function of "wit", Weisman further adds:

> By using wit, which is the most sophisticated linguistic device for imparting double entendre and even paradoxical meaning to ordinary words, the satirist stimulates his audience to share his sharp criticism against individuals and social institutions. Wit as a verbal and literary means (with a variety of artistic devices, such as puns, wordplays, etc.) is also employed in other genres, especially comedy. But whereas in comedy it arouses laughter and fun, in satire it evokes disdain and contempt.[212]

In 9:10 Job's quotation of Eliphaz's hymnic materials is a linguistic device of "wit", which may give us some clues in discerning Job's mood.

4:17a הַאֱנוֹשׁ מֵאֱלוֹהַּ יִצְדָּק
9:2b   וּמַה־יִּצְדַּק אֱנוֹשׁ עִם־אֵל

5:9   עֹשֶׂה גְדֹלוֹת וְאֵין חֵקֶר נִפְלָאוֹת עַד־אֵין מִסְפָּר:
9:10   עֹשֶׂה גְדֹלוֹת עַד־אֵין חֵקֶר וְנִפְלָאוֹת עַד־אֵין מִסְפָּר:

This verse of doxology is actually almost identical to Eliphaz's praise of God in 5:9. Job uses the same "wit" at 9:2b by quoting Eliphaz's sayings at 4:17a. However, similar language can be used for different purposes.[213] Eliphaz is presumably employing the conventional doxology in the traditional way, whereas Job is utilizing it in a different sense so as to bring about irony. For Eliphaz, God does "great

---

[209] Z. Weisman, *Political Satire in the Bible* (Georgia: Scholar Press, 1998) 7.
[210] Andersen, *Job*, 143.
[211] Weisman, *Political Satire*, 3.
[212] Weisman, *Political Satire*, 3.
[213] Whedbee, "Comedy of Job," 16.

things" and "wonders" to transform situations. But for Job, God's "great things" and "wonders" are "beyond understanding" and "without number" in the way that God eludes human comprehension. The strong connection between ...אֵין...אֵין... in 9:10 and ...לֹא...לֹא... in 9:11 helps unlock the meaning of 9:10. From Job's perspective, God is so elusive that he cannot see Him and perceive Him. Undeniably, Job really employs this verse of conventional doxology in an ironic way to bring out the negative sense of God's unfathomable wisdom.

To consider whether Job's hymn at 9:5-13 is a parody or not, it is necessary to detect whether Job cites these materials in order to ridicule with a strong sense of sarcasm. At this point, the immediate context can give a clue. Obviously, right after this magnificent hymn of praise, Job expresses his bitterness about how God turns against him. Job's ironic bitterness is evident in the following verses:

> For He crushes me with a tempest,
> and multiplies my wounds without cause.
> He will not let me get my breath,
> but fills me with bitterness. (9:17-18)
>
> It is all one; therefore I say,
> He destroys the blameless and the wicked.
> When disaster brings sudden death,
> He mocks at the calamity of the innocent.
> The earth is given into the hand of the wicked;
> He covers the faces of its judges.
> If it is not He, who then is it? (9:22-24)

The hymn of 9:5-13 is juxtaposed to the subsequent context of 9:17-18, 22-24, where Job accuses God of crushing him without cause and perverting justice. In addition, 9:24 seems to be a parody of God's "monotheistic" declarations (cf. Isa 40:25; 41:4). In brief, by looking at the immediate context of this hymn and the "wit" used at 9:10, it seems to me that 9:5-13 is parodying the traditional doxologies by displaying the negative aspects of God's power and wisdom.

Now we come to ask the next question: does Job use the hymn in 26:5-14, as he does in 9:5-13, to describe God's negative aspects? The hymn in chapter 26 ends at v.14, leaving no room for Job to add any comments to it. Then the new introductory formula in 27:1 implies that Job starts talking about another thing. Basically, unlike 9:5-13, the hymn in 26:5-14 has less obvious contextual indication that it is spoken satirically against God, but we will have further discussion in the flow of argument. Many scholars deny 26:5-14 to Job because it does not match Job's ways of depicting God as he does in his previous hymns (e.g. 9:5-13).

It is also noteworthy that Job's saying at 9:10 is almost identical to Eliphaz's saying at 5:9. It shows that speakers may use similar language to express different meanings. Many scholars attribute Job's speech to one of his friends on the ground of similar language. For example, they reallocate 26:5-14 from Job to Bildad because of the similar language in both 26:5-14 and Job 25. However, they overlook the fact that similar language can mean different things for different speakers.

To sum up, the comparison between 9:5-13 and 26:5-14 above shows us that the former hymn is satirical against God, while the latter has less obvious contextual indication that it is satirical against God. However, we have also shown that words may mean different things on the lips of different people. This leaves open the possibility that 26:5-14 may really be Job's words. For a final decision we must take the enquiry a step further.

b) Job 10:8-13

This hymn picks up the theme of 10:1-7, and continues to depict Job himself as the work of God's hands. In v.3 Job stresses God's effort in making man, while in v.8 he highlights that God has artfully designed man. Concerning the motif of this hymn, Westermann states:

> In this same speech of Job, within the accusation against God, we find praise of the creator of mankind. This motif first shows up in 10:3 and is then developed in 10:8-17 in such a way that the contrast between God's creative and his destructive activity vis-à-vis his creation is clearly brought out.[214]

In 10:8-9 Job complains that God, who made (עָשָׂה) and fashioned (עָצַב) him like clay (כַּחֹמֶר), is immoral to destroy him and turn him to dust (עָפָר). This section highlights the contradiction between God's creative and destructive acts. Verses 10-11 describe God's intimate divine work in Job's personal origins, from the formation of the embryo in the womb (v.10) to the development of the skeletal structure, soft tissues, and skin (v.11). Then there comes God's

---

[214] Westermann, *Structure of Job*, 74.

providential care for Job in v.12, emphasizing His granting of life and steadfast love, and special protection over Job's spirit. However, all God's tender care portrayed in vv.8-12 was just a façade. Job discerns that His true intentions are quite other—to play the spy and find fault in him (v.13).

Job utters this hymn to point out God's creative and providential deeds as a hidden plan to trap Job in sin (v.14). Job continues his charge against God in the following verses:

> If I sin, You watch me
> and do not acquit me of my iniquity. (10:14)
>
> And should my head be lifted up,
> You would hunt me like a lion;
> and again You would work wonders against me. (10:16)
>
> You renew Your witnesses against me,
> and increase Your anger toward me,
> You bring fresh troops against me. (10:17)

Job realises that his life serves one purpose—being God's target (vv.15-17).

Dell claims that Job 10:2-12 contains a parody whose background is found in Psalm 139. She points out that Psalm 139 is a prayer for deliverance from enemies (139:19-24), and that it highlights that God knows a man so thoroughly that escape from God is impossible (139:7-8). Here the psalmist praises God's all-seeing nature, and is pleased that he cannot escape from Him. Job 10:2-12 is also a request for God's deliverance, but Job turns the praise of God as creator to a reproach against Him. Not being able to escape from God is a bad thing in Job's eyes.[215]

Newsom thinks that Job is not parodying Psalm 139 itself, but just parodying "the complex of religious themes to which Psalm 139 gives expression."[216] She claims that understanding the background of Psalm 139 will certainly help understand the contrasting meaning in Job's hymn. She shows the parallels between Job 10 and Psalm 139 as follows:[217]

    10:4-7   Parodying God's complete knowledge of the individual (cf. Ps 139:2-6)

---

[215] Dell, *Book of Job*, 127-8.
[216] Newsom, "Job," 414.
[217] Newsom, "Job," 414.

> 10:8-12   Parodying Job himself as God's handiwork (cf. Ps 139:13-18)
> 10:13-14 Parodying God's true intention of inspecting for sin (cf. Ps 139:23-24)

I agree that in 10:8-13 Job is parodying the conventional doxology, though not necessarily Psalm 139 itself, to convey the satirical message that all the providential care and intimate love (cf. Ps 139: 13-18) God pours down upon Job are just His sinister purpose of trapping Job in sin and making him suffer for his guilt. Seemingly, Job 10:8-13 is used satirically to highlight the negative aspects of God's creation of mankind, whereas 26:5-14 has less obvious contextual indication that it is spoken satirically against God.

c) Job 12:13-25

Habel rightly considers Job 12:13-25 as a satirical doxology on God's wisdom and power.[218] This hymn is divided into three sections:[219]

> I.   To destroy the established orders   vv.13-16
> II. To deprive leaders of efficiency   vv.17-21
> III. To disorient nations and leaders   vv.22-25

The first section (vv.13-16) is bracketed by an inclusio which highlights God's capacities as a celestial ruler.

> 12:13   עִמּוֹ חָכְמָה וּגְבוּרָה לוֹ עֵצָה וּתְבוּנָה׃
> 12:16   עִמּוֹ עֹז וְתוּשִׁיָּה לוֹ שֹׁגֵג וּמַשְׁגֶּה׃

However, the second element of the inclusio includes "the misled" (שֹׁגֵג) and "the misleader" (מַשְׁגֶּה; v.16b), which pave the way to the development of the next theme. In the subsequent sections "leading astray" becomes God's way of disrupting society and disorienting its leaders.[220] Job alleges that wisdom belongs to God (v.13), not to mortals, regardless of their age (v.12). God's capacity to rule is demonstrated by the way He disrupts the social order (v.14) and the created order (v.15).

---

[218] Habel, *Job*, 216. Habel points out that the poet deliberately reverses the wisdom tradition reflected in Prov 8:14-16, where God guides earthly leaders. In Job 12:13-25 the same list of capacities is cited, but God nullifies the efficiency of the leaders.

[219] Habel, *Job*, 216-7. This is a simplified version of the structure Habel finds in the doxology.

[220] Habel, *Job*, 217.

The second section (vv.17-21) displays the parade of leaders: counselors, judges, kings, priests, the mighty, those who are trusted, elders, princes and the strong. God demonstrates His wisdom by depriving the earth's greatest potentates of their wisdom and authority, which they need to maintain the social order.

The last section (vv.22-25) is framed by an inclusio of the term "darkness" (חֹשֶׁךְ). God exposes the world to deep darkness. He leads nations astray and causes leaders to wander aimlessly in darkness like the drunken. God overwhelms them with devastating force, seemingly without any cause. Job seems to imply that the reason for his suffering lies in God, not himself.

In 12:13-25 Job uses phraseology and themes from conventional hymnic materials. This section is particularly close to Psalm 107 (Ps 107:40 = Job 12:21a, 24b). In addition, Isaiah 44:24-28 and Daniel 2:20-23 (Dan 2:22a almost = Job 12:22a) also have distinct similarities to this passage. Furthermore, Proverbs 8:14-16 shares many common words with Job 12:13-21.[221] According to Habel, Job satirizes the claim made by Proverbs 8:14-16 that God's wisdom is the source of just and effective human leadership and government.[222]

Gordis argues that 12:13-25 is a parody of descriptions by the friends of God's beneficent power (e.g. 5:9-16).[223] Andersen regards this hymn as a mock creed. He states that "If it is an imitation of Eliphaz's similar hymn in 5:18ff., it has been twisted into a parody. The positive side described there (healing after hurt, release after captivity) is either omitted by Job, or inverted."[224]

Clines suggests that "these verses must rather be seen as a deliberate reworking of... conventional hymnic material, blocking out the positive aspects of reversal of fortune."[225] He regards Job 12:13-25 as a parody of Psalm 107 because of its obvious dependence upon that psalm, especially vv.15, 21, 22 and 24.[226] Clines comments on this hymn: "Throughout this unarguably one-sided portrait of the

---

[221] Newsom, "Job," 429. See also Habel, *Job*, 216. The following words in bold type show how Prov 8:14-16 shares many common words with Job 12:13-21. In Proverbs, personified wisdom claims: "**Counsel** is mine and **sound wisdom**; I am **understanding**, **power** is mine. By me **kings** reign, rulers decree justice. By me princes rule, and **nobles**, all who **judge** rightly."
[222] Habel, *Job*, 216; also Newsom, "Job," 429.
[223] Gordis, *Book of Job*, 127, 524, Special Note 13.
[224] Andersen, *Job*, 163.
[225] Clines, *Job 1-20*, 297.
[226] Clines, *Job 1-20*, 287.

ways of God with humans, his subversive acts have been hymned. Only perhaps in v.23 are there allusions to any positive act of his, but they are immediately negated."[227] Westermann considers "God the Lord of history" as the motif of this hymn. However, when he compares Job 12:13-25 with other hymns sharing the same motif, he notes:

> Elsewhere, the motif "God the lord of history" is developed in a twofold manner: God exalts—God abases. The same is said in reference to the people in v.23, but only the negative side of the picture gets developed. The particularity of the praise of God on the part of Job is shown not only in this one-sided emphasis but even more clearly in a subtle and very deliberate distinction.[228]

All in all, 12:13-25 is not only a parody of the friends' depiction of God's beneficent power (e.g. 5:9-16; 5:18-26), but also a parody of conventional hymnic materials (e.g. Ps 107; Isa 44:24-28; Dan 2:20-23; Prov 8:14-16).[229] In the perplexity of his deep suffering, Job utters this hymn to expose God's fickle temperament. Job 12:13-25 is employed to depict God's use of wisdom and might to create chaos rather than order in nature and society. Beyond any doubt, Job uses these hymnic materials negatively to emphasize God's destructive way of governing. Comparatively speaking, however, 26:5-14 has less obvious contextual indication that it is spoken satirically against God.

Conclusion

To sum up, among the four hymns that Job utters in the book, the first three (9:5-13; 10:8-13; 12:13-25) are used in a different way from the last one (26:5-14). The former three negatively highlight God's destructive way of using His wisdom and creative power to govern nature, society and cosmos. In fact, Job uses these three hymns to argue against what the three friends claim about God's greatness. In those places Job has questioned God's way of governing, and queried whether God is the cause of his tremendous suffering. However, in 26:5-14, there is an absence of any obvious contextual indication that the hymn is spoken satirically against God. Many scholars reject this text as Job's speech because its de-

---

[227] Clines, *Job 1-20*, 304.
[228] Westermann, *Structure of Job*, 74-5.
[229] Dell, *Book of Job*, 129.

piction of God without explicit negative comments is at odds with Job's usual way of expressing God's character in his previous hymns. In conclusion, then, one of the striking characteristics of 26:5-14 is the lack of any apparent contextual evidence that it is expressing the negative aspects of God. The next section continues to examine the distinctive characteristics of 26:5-14 by comparing it with Job's non-hymnic materials.

2. *Job 26:5-14 in Comparison with Job's Non-Hymnic Materials*

Job makes some positive non-hymnic statements about God elsewhere in the book. For instance, his fervent desire to have a lawsuit with God through a third party[230] or to confront God in person implies that Job still keeps his confidence in God's justice. As far as the third party is concerned, 9:32-35 reflects Job's hope for an arbiter (מוֹכִיחַ) who can free Job from the intimidating presence of God's terror and present Job's case before God. In 16:19 Job continues to cry out for a heavenly witness (עֵד) who can testify to his integrity in the presence of God. Job's desire for a redeemer (גֹּאֵל) to witness for him is further expressed in 19:25. However, vindication after his death through the redeemer is only a second best for Job (19:25-26a), what he really yearns for is to have a face-to-face confrontation with God (19:26b-27). Such an expression recurs when Job affirms that he would be acquitted forever by his judge (שֹׁפֵט; 23:6-7), and that God knows his integrity (23:10-12). The above passages concerning Job's desire to confront God in person or through an arbiter are the only places where Job speaks positively about God, especially His divine justice. Elsewhere, most of Job's non-hymnic materials commenting on God's character depict God negatively, as his personal enemy. These passages are Job 6:4, 8-10; 7:12-21; 9:14-35; 10:2-7, 13-17; 13:20-28; 16:7-14; 19:7-12; 23:16-17; 27:2; and 30:19-23.[231]

Job complains that the arrows of the Almighty are in him and that God's terrors are marshalled against him (6:4). He accuses God of crushing him and cutting him off (6:9). Job also points out that

---

[230] Habel, *Job*, 274-6; and Newsom, "Job," 460, 477-9.

[231] J. L. Crenshaw, *A Whirlpool of Torment: Israelite Traditons of God as an Oppressive Presence* (Philadelphia: Fortress Press, 1984) 57-75. Here Crenshaw examines Job 13:24-28; 16:9-14 and 19:5-12, 22 to understand Job's perception of God as a personal enemy. He also lists all the other texts which depict God as Job's enemy in p.62, n.16.

God frightens him with dreams and terrifies him with visions (7:14). In such perplexity, he questions why God has made him His target (7:20) and treated him as His enemy (13:24). Job complains that God bruises him with a tempest, multiplies his wounds without cause, and saturates him with bitterness (9:17-18). Behind God's providential care, Job discovers that God's true intention is to play the spy and trap him in sin (10:14-17). God is regarded as Job's opponent, who tears and hunts him down in anger, and gnashes His teeth at him (16:9). God's archers surround him (16:13), and the Lord attacks him like a warrior (16:14). Again, in 19:7-12, Job charges God with indifference to his plight, with injustice and with an attack upon him. In Job's eyes it is God who has made his heart faint, and it is the Almighty who has dismayed him (23:16) and embittered his soul (27:2). With the might of His hand, God persecutes him (30:21).

Conclusion
Apart from the theme of arbiter, Job's non-hymnic materials reflect the fact that Job makes statements in a negative way to accuse God as his adversary, considering God as the cause of his suffering. In conclusion, the comparison of 26:5-14 with most of Job's non-hymnic statements once again affirms that one of the characteristics of 26:5-14 is the absence of any obvious contextual indication that it is satirically expressing the negative aspects of God. One of the reasons why scholars remove the hymn of praise in 26:5-14 from Job's lips is because they find that Job's way of expressing God's character (without explicitly negative comments) here is at odds with that in his non-hymnic passages mentioned above.

3. Job 26:5-14 in Comparison with the Friends' Hymnic Recitations
Another reason why many scholars attribute 26:5-14 to one of Job's friends is because this passage is quite like the friends' hymnic materials. In order to understand this similarity, a comparison between 26:5-14 and the friends' hymnic utterances is made in this section.

a) Job 5:9-16 (Eliphaz's)
Clines suggests "God as the reverser of fortunes" as the central theme of the doxology.[232] The hymn commences with a summary

---

[232] Clines, *Job 1-20*, 144-7. Newsom also suggests that this is a doxology in praise of God as the one who transforms situations; Newsom, "Job," 380.

acknowledging God as the maker of marvels and worker of wonders (v.9). There then comes the praise of God's sending of the rain (v.10). Clines points out that rain can make the landscape green and colourful in Near Eastern desert areas.[233] God establishes social justice by transforming the situation of the lowly and the socially afflicted (v.11). Verses 12-14 are the negative side of this "reversal of fortunes",[234] illustrating that God thwarts the plots of the crafty and prevents them from exploiting the weak. He delivers the poor from the strong, and gives them hope (vv.15-16). Eliphaz's doxology praises God as the transformer of situations.[235] Therefore, if Job turns to God, He can surely release him from his desperate situation. Eliphaz's intention in reciting this hymn can be seen in vv.17ff. He exhorts Job to seek God's face, so that he can be blessed and restored again (v.17).

According to Habel, this hymn contrasts drastically with Job's hymn in 12:13-25. Habel highlights their differences as follows:

> El is thus the wonder-worker, champion of social justice, rainmaker, and mastermind controlling all wisdom and strategies on earth. This image of God is precisely that which Job seeks to demolish in his reverse doxology (in 12:13-25): El is the master mind of drought, social disorder, and the promotion of deceit.[236]

Compared with other hymns in the book, 5:9 has almost the same wording as 9:10, depicting God's unfathomable wonders and uncountable miracles.

5:9 עֹשֶׂה גְדֹלוֹת וְאֵין חֵקֶר נִפְלָאוֹת עַד־אֵין מִסְפָּר
9:10 עֹשֶׂה גְדֹלוֹת עַד־אֵין חֵקֶר וְנִפְלָאוֹת עַד־אֵין מִסְפָּר

Seemingly, in 9:10, Job expresses a satirical message that contrasts with Eliphaz's perception of God in 5:9. Therefore, as mentioned in the last section, different speakers use similar language in quite different ways.

Concerning the limitation of human understanding, 5:9 makes a similar point to 26:14: "Behold, these are but the outskirts of His ways, and how small a whisper we hear of Him! But the thunder of His might who can understand?" Here, if 26:5-14 is from Job, there is a real similarity between Eliphaz's and Job's statements.

---

[233] Clines, *Job 1-20*, 144-5; also Newsom, "Job," 380.
[234] Clines, *Job 1-20*, 145.
[235] Newsom, "Job," 380-1.
[236] Habel, *Job*, 134.

In terms of the way of expression, there is no obvious contextual indication that 26:5-14 is spoken satirically against God. And the way of depicting God in 26:5-14, if spoken by Job, would be inconsistent with Job's earlier use of hymnic materials. In this respect Eliphaz's hymn in 5:9-16 is more like 26:5-14 than Job's other hymns. This raises the question, once again, of why Job might utter a hymn like 26:5-14.

b) Job 11:7-11 (Zophar's)
This hymn expounds the statement made in 11:6a: "And that He would tell you the secrets of wisdom!"[237] Zophar points out that human wisdom is so limited that he is not able to understand God's way of governing. This hymn starts with the hidden ways of God (v.7). The deep things of God and the limit of the Almighty are beyond human comprehension. God's inexhaustible wisdom (cf. 5:9 and 9:10) exceeds every boundary of the universe, i.e. sky, underworld, land and sea (vv.8-9). God's power is irresistible and His decision is irreversible (v.10). In addition, He can detect evil infallibly and take close notice of it (v.11). Job maintains that God's secret motive is to spy on him (7:8, 20; 10:14), while Zophar claims that God can discern the hidden sins of mortals. Zophar denounces Job's claim that God has misjudged him because Zophar believes that God can see the evil deeds of the wicked.

In general, 11:7-11 and 26:5-14 share one common point, namely the limitation of human understanding (11:7 and 26:14; cf. 5:9 and 9:10). Other than that, no further similarity is found between these two hymns in terms of their content. However, because of the absence of obvious contextual indication that 26:5-14 is spoken negatively against God, this hymn seems to be more similar to Zophar's hymn in 11:7-11 than to Job's other hymns. To some scholars, this sharpens the question of whether Job really utters the speech in 26:5-14.

c) Job 22:12-14 (Eliphaz's)
Eliphaz quotes a hymnic line to laud the all-seeing, all knowing God in His lofty dwelling (v.12; cf. Ps 33:13-14; Isa 40:22, 26-27). He aims to counter Job's claim that God's transcendence is such that He neither sees nor knows what happens on the earth (vv.13-14).

---

[237] Andersen, *Job*, 157.

In fact, Eliphaz has overinterpreted Job's complaints of God. For Job is not concerned about whether God is active in affairs on earth, but rather sees that God judges the wicked erratically and capriciously (cf. 9:22-24).[238]

The hymnic line of 22:12 underscores God's omniscience which is rooted in His power, while 26:5-14 extols God's majestic omnipotence over the underworld, heaven, earth and the chaotic forces. In terms of content, one common point is shared between these two hymns, namely the motif of clouds (22:13-14; 26:9). 22:13-14 points out that these dark clouds act as a big barrier to keep God from seeing and judging things on earth, whereas 26:9 brings out the idea that God uses thick clouds to cover His throne, so that the creatures are not consumed. Comparatively speaking, the lack of contextual indication that 26:5-14 is negatively depicting God's attributes and deeds, makes this hymn look more like Eliphaz's hymn in 22:12-14 than Job's other hymnic recitations.

d) Job 25:2-6 (Bildad's)

This hymn comprises two themes. The first theme (vv.2-3) highlights the absolute purity and majesty of God, while the second one (vv.4-6) pinpoints the imperfection of all creatures, especially human beings. Bildad utters this hymn to counter Job's complaint that God rules unjustly (24:1-17).[239]

Scholars have often noted similarities between Bildad's speech in Job 25 and the hymn attributed to Job in 26:5-14. Habel reallocates 26:5-14 to Bildad, linking it with 25:1-6 to form a longer speech. According to Habel, the coherence of this lengthened speech is reflected in the way in which it responds to the content of Job's speech in chapter 23. Habel sets out the terminological and thematic links between the speeches as follows:[240]

23:15	Job is dismayed (בָּהַל) and terrified (פָּחַד) before God
25:2a	"Awe" (פַּחַד) belongs to God
26:5	No one can escape God's terrifying presence, even the shades of the underworld writhe (יְחוֹלָלוּ) before Him
23:3, 8-9	Job wants to locate God's abode (v.3), but cannot discern (בִּין) His presence (vv.8-9)

---

[238] Hartley, *Job*, 329-30; Newsom, "Job," 501; and Habel, *Job*, 340-1.
[239] Hartley, *Job*, 355.
[240] Habel, *Job*, 367-8.

26:7	God stretches out the north over the void and hangs the earth on nothing.
	Therefore God's abode is inaccessible to humans
26:9	God's throne is covered by His celestial clouds
23:14	Job complains about the limit (חֹק) God has decreed for his life
26:10	The limit (חֹק) is important to the structure of the cosmos
23:10	God knows Job's way (דֶּרֶךְ)
23:11	Job has kept God's way (דֶּרֶךְ)
26:14	Mortals can barely discern (בְּיָן) the outskirts of His cosmic way (דֶּרֶךְ)

Habel draws the following conclusion from these links:

> Thus the speech of Bildad [25:1-6 and 26:5-14] taken as a whole emphasizes the holiness, transcendence, mystery, and awesome power of God in a way which counters the desire of Job (in chapter 23) to circumvent the laws of the cosmos, enter God's presence, and plead his innocence.[241]

These two speeches do share motifs, as Habel has shown, but they are used differently to express different views in different contexts.

Van der Lugt combines Job 25 and 26, and assigns these two whole chapters as Job's speech.[242] He divides this reconstructed unit into two cantos: a) 25:2-26:4; and b) 26:5-13. The first canto has 8 lines (25:2-3, 4-6, 26:2-4), while the second one has 9 lines (26:5-7, 8-10, 11-13). The mono-line strophe 26:14 functions as the conclusion of the speech.[243] Van der Lugt finds the thematic coherence of this reconstructed passage in two different patterns: a) a symmetric pattern; and b) a linear parallelism.

With respect to the symmetric pattern, van der Lugt observes that the motif of place links Job 25 and 26. In the first section (25:2-26:4) there is a movement of places downwards: from God's heavenly abode (25:2-3), to the position of man before the Almighty God (25:4-6), to the relationship of men among themselves (26:2-4). In the second section (26:5-13) the movement of places goes upwards: from the realm beneath the earth (26:5-7), to the realm of the firmament (26:8-10), to the heavenly realm (26:11-13).[244] In terms of

---

[241] Habel, *Job*, 368.
[242] Lugt, *Rhetorical Criticism and Job*, 295.
[243] Lugt, *Rhetorical Criticism and Job*, 292-3.
[244] Lugt, *Rhetorical Criticism and Job*, 293-4.

linear parallelism, the motif of God's power and holiness connects the two sections as follows:

God's dominion in heavens (25:2-3)	God's dominion beneath the earth (26:5-7)
The futility of mankind (25:4-6)	God's transcendent holiness and glory (26:8-10)
Empty human talk;	God's subjugation of cosmic chaos monsters;
man without strength and wisdom (26:2-4)	God with strength and understanding (26:11-13)

In addition, van der Lugt also singles out verbal repetitions and parallel word pairs between the two sections.[245]

Reduplication of ה (25:2a, 3a)[246]	//	The article ה (26:5a)
פַּחַד (fear; 25:2a)	//	יְחוֹלָלוּ (to be made to tremble; 26:5a)
לְלֹא־כֹחַ (without power; 26:2a)	//	בְּכֹחוֹ (with His power; 26:12a)
חָכְמָה (wisdom; 26:3a)	//	בִּתְבוּנָתוֹ (by His understanding; 26:12b)
נְשָׁמָה (spirit; 26:4b)	//	בְּרוּחוֹ (by His breath/wind; 26:13a)

After investigating the thematic links, verbal repetitions and parallel word pairs, van der Lugt concludes that both Job 25 and 26 are Job's words.[247]

Although van der Lugt has observed the linkages between Job 25 and 26 well, he does not explain how he deals with the introductory verse at 25:1, where Bildad is introduced as the speaker of chapter 25. Moreover, Habel's and van der Lugt's particular conclusions, which contradict each other, illustrate once more the difficulty of attributing these speeches, especially of trying to assign consistent differences among the speakers. However, their research on the linkages between Job 25 and 26 are noteworthy. Despite the difference in their reconstructions, both of them have shown concrete evidence that these two chapters, especially the hymnic materials, are quite alike. However, the problem of 26:5-14 as a speech of Job's remains unresolved.

---

[245] Lugt, *Rhetorical Criticism and Job*, 295.
[246] Here the reduplication of ה refers to "anaphora." In 25:2a הַמְשֵׁל is an Hiphil infinitive absolute of מָשַׁל, used as a noun. In 25:3a it refers to the interrogative ה. See Lugt, *Rhetorical Criticism and Job*, 295.
[247] Lugt, *Rhetorical Criticism and Job*, 295.

Conclusion

The characteristics of Job's saying in 26:5-14 are underscored by comparing this hymn with Job's other hymnic and non-hymnic materials, and with the friends' hymnic recitations. After such comparisons, we can conclude that Job's way of depicting God in 26:5-14 (without giving explicitly negative comments) is seemingly inconsistent with Job's earlier use of hymnic and non-hymnic materials. This way of describing God in 26:5-14 makes it sound more like the friends' hymns (5:9-16; 11:7-11; 22:12-14; 25:2-6) than Job's other hymns. In terminological and thematic terms, 26:5-14 is especially similar to Bildad's speech in 25:1-6. To resolve the issue of inconsistency in 26:5-14, scholars have developed different interpretations and reconstructions. These are examined in the next section.

C. *Commentators' Approaches to the Issue of 26:5-14*

There are four basic approaches resolving the issue of 26:5-14: 1) 26:5-14 is attributed from Job to Bildad (Habel, Dhorme, Rowley, Gordis, Pope and Newsom); 2) Job is the speaker, but in 26:5-14 he finishes Bildad's speech for him (Janzen); 3) 26:5-14 is considered as Job's speech (Hartley, Andersen, Whybray and Good); and 4) both Job 25 and 26 in their entirety are Job's speech (van der Lugt).

1. *Re-assigning from Job to Bildad*

Habel notes that the mood and perspective of 26:5-14 sound inconsistent with Job's previous use of hymnic materials to highlight God's creative power and governance. Comparing 26:5-14 with Job's previous hymns, Habel comments:

> In 9:5-13 Job cited God's cosmic power in order to highlight his violent and fickle character as an adversary at law. In 10:8-13 Job alleged that God's creative and providential deeds were but a façade which veiled his devious plan to catch Job in sin. Further, 12:13-25 is a satirical doxology hailing God's use of his wisdom and might for creating chaos rather than order in nature and society. Job uses these hymnic materials to expose God's insidious destructive mode of governing. In 26:5-14, however, the tone is positive and the hymnic materials are employed to emphasize the transcendent mystery and orderly design of the cosmos.[248]

For these reasons, Habel assigns 26:5-14 from Job to Bildad. He

---

[248] Habel, *Job*, 366.

brings 25:1-6 and 26:5-14 together because he finds a basic coherence between these two pieces. Furthermore, he identifies four themes of this reconstructed passage, key among which is v.9 as the pivot of its structure:[249]

(A) Opening hymnic formula: God's awe and dominion (25:2)
  (B) Contrasting the relative guilt of mortals and celestial powers (25:3-6)
    (C) God's awe and mystery (26:5-8)
      i. Underworld (5-6)
      ii. Suspended world (7)
      iii. Heavy clouds (8)
      (D) God's transcendence: His throne being hidden by the clouds (26:9)
    (C1) God's dominion and power (26:10-13)
      i. Establishment of structures for the heavens and waters (10-11)
      ii. Establishment of control over the chaos waters (12-13)
(A1) Interpretative summation: God's way beyond human comprehension (26:14)

Habel states that 26:14 sums up all the themes of the reconstructed speech. The extremities of God's cosmic way—the heights of heaven (25:2); the depths of the underworld (26:5-6); the celestial north where God dwells (26:7); or the horizon where light and darkness meet (26:10)—are just "the outskirts" and "a whisper" of His total world (26:14a, b). God's way is beyond human comprehension (26:14c).[250] Van der Lugt notably points out the weakness of Habel's design: that his second structural element (B) at 25:3-6 has no counterpart (i.e. B1). In Habel's structure the pattern is A–B–C–D–C1–A1. According to van der Lugt, the lack of the counterpart B1 makes Habel's design unbalanced.[251]

Dhorme also assigns 26:5-14 to Bildad and places this section after 25:1-6.[252] He states that the reconstructed doxology starts with the heavenly beings (25:2-3), and then goes on with the terrestrial beings (25:4-6) and the infernal beings (26:5-6). There then follows

---

[249] Habel, *Job*, 367.
[250] Habel, *Job*, 367.
[251] Lugt, *Rhetorical Criticism and Job*, 292, n.2.
[252] Removing the unnecessary formula of introduction in 27:1, Dhorme connects 26:1-4 with 27:2-12 to form Job's ninth speech, which is placed after Bildad's lengthened speech (25:1-6 and 26:5-14). See Dhorme, *Job*, xlviii, 377-85. For his reconstruction of Bildad's third speech, see pp.368-76.

the activity of God in the creation and organization of the world (26:7-10), and in extraordinary phenomena (26:11-13). Finally, 26:14 concludes with the agnosticism of divine mystery. Dhorme comments: "Hence it seems to us indisputable that the speech of Bildad, begun in 25:2-6, continues in 26:5-14."[253] Obviously, Dhorme's criterion of attributing a speech is on the basis of similar language. However, as we have seen, Job can use language and motifs similar to his friends', if only for different purposes.

Rowley too thinks that most probably Bildad's speech originally consisted of 25:2-6 and 26:5-14. Rowley points out that the theme of Bildad's reconstructed speech is the power of God and the universality of his dominion in the underworld, on earth and in heaven. This theme comprises two parts: a) God's power and purity (25:2-6); and b) God's all-embracing rule (26:5-14). However, these two sections are separated by Job's response (26:1-4; 27:2-6).[254]

Gordis reconstructs the speeches as follows: 25:1-6; 26:5-14 (Bildad's); and 26:1-4; 27:1-12 (Job's response).[255] After linking 26:5-14 with 25:1-6, Gordis sets out four aspects of God's greatness described by Bildad:[256]

a) His boundless sway over the heavenly bodies (25:3-6)
b) His rule of the subterranean regions (26:5-6)
c) The wonders of the natural order [using participles] (26:7-9)
d) God's might as revealed in creation [using perfect tense] (26:10-13)

Gordis believes that some parts of Bildad's reconstructed speech must be missing. Probably these lost materials are at the beginning or in the middle, which seem to be incomplete, while he finds that 26:14 is a very effective conclusion.[257]

Seeing the disruptions in chapters 25 and 26, Pope finds that the simplest and most satisfactory way to resolve the problem is to "augment Bildad's abbreviated discourse of chapter 25 with the beautiful paean to God's power in 26:5-14."[258]

Like all the above scholars, Newsom denies 26:5-14 to Job, and regards this passage as the second part of Bildad's speech. She claims that:

---

[253] Dhorme, *Job*, xlvii-xlviii.
[254] Rowley, *Book of Job*, 169-70.
[255] Gordis, *Book of Job*, 534-5, Special Note 20.
[256] Gordis, *Book of Job*, 276.
[257] Gordis, *Book of Job*, 276.
[258] Pope, *Job*, xx.

The body of the speech in 26:5-14, however, a description of God's creative power, lacks the ironic touches that characterize Job's previous use of that theme (e.g. 9:2-10; 12:13-25) and is not what one expects to hear from Job.[259]

Newsom believes that the text includes some interruptions. She claims that the interruption is not obvious in 26:1-4, but the change in style and content suggests that 26:5-14 has been dislocated.[260] Therefore she seeks to reconstruct the speech in the following way: "Bildad begins to speak in 25:1-6, but is interrupted by Job, who sarcastically mocks what Bildad has said (26:1-4). Undeterred, Bildad completes his speech (26:5-14), at which point Job resumes his discourse."[261] Newsom argues that the author deliberately displays the interrupted and overlapping speeches of the parties in order to show that the conversation has already totally broken down.[262]

To sum up, for those scholars who reassign 26:5-14 to Bildad, attribution of the speech is on the basis of similar language and ideas. However, they do not recognise that similar language can be used for different purposes by different speakers. Although they all consider 26:5-14 as Bildad's speech, their reconstructions of this passage vary in nuance. The difficulty of attributing a speech is again demonstrated.

2. *Job as Speaking Satirically against God*

Differently from many scholars, Dell considers this hymn as a parody of the psalms and prophets (e.g. Isa 40:9-11) to depict God negatively.[263] According to Dell, 26:5-6 originally extolled God's dominion over the underworld and 26:7-14 praised His power exhibited in His creative activity. She further adds: "However, the unorthodox note here is that God's power in creation is seen as frightening."[264] Concerning the pattern of parody in Job, she states:

> No misuse of forms [i.e. parody] can be found in the sections that are generally seen by scholars as inauthentic in the mouth of Job (those which rightly belong in the arguments of the friends in the third round of speeches—e.g. Job 27:7-23). This might provide support for the idea that they are inauthentic.[265]

---

[259] Newsom, "Job," 516.
[260] Newsom, "Job," 516.
[261] Newsom, "Job," 516.
[262] Newsom, "Job," 516.
[263] Dell, *Book of Job*, 132.
[264] Dell, *Book of Job*, 132.
[265] Dell, *Book of Job*, 138. In 136-8 Dell points out the pattern of the misuse of

Despite the fact that 26:5-14 is frequently seen by scholars as inappropriate from Job's lips, Dell considers it as Job's hymn, in which parody is employed to express his sceptical views about God. In my view, Dell's treatment of 26:5-14 seems to contradict her point about the pattern of parody in Job.

However, I agree with Dell that the hymn in chapter 26 may carry a certain satirical sense against God despite the fact that there is no obvious contextual indication in this chapter that the hymn is spoken satirically. We shall return to this in the next section.

3. Job as the Speaker, Finishing Bildad's Speech for him
Janzen assumes that Job is the speaker of chapter 26. According to Janzen, Job cuts Bildad's remarks (chapter 25) short with an impatient and sarcastic interruption (26:1-4). Then he mimics Bildad, finishing his speech for him (26:5-14). "The awed tone of Bildad's brief speech, as an invocation of God's grandeur, is reproduced with an angry sureness of eloquence and tone."[266]

Janzen considers 26:5-14 as an attack upon the friends' inspiration. In 26:4 Job challenges the source of the friends' inspiration: "With whose help have you uttered words, and whose breath has come out from you?" Janzen points out that Eliphaz explicitly makes claim to divine inspiration in 4:12-17, and he also indicates the revelatory source of his advice in the phrase "the comforts of God" (15:11). According to Janzen, although Bildad does not explicitly claim to speak by inspiration, Bildad's borrowed use of Eliphaz's argument (4:17-19; 15:14-16) in 25:4-6 indicates an implicit claim to inspiration.[267] Job strongly challenges any of these claims, says Janzen, adding: "Not all who claim the spirit possess it; or perhaps ... not all spirit phenomena are a guarantee of truth. To refute the claim to inspiration, Job proceeds to show that he can crank out the

---

forms in Job as follows: 1) all examples of this device in chapters 3-31 are found only in Job's speeches rather than the friends' (except 4:12-21; 5:3-7; 22:15-16); 2) this technique is only used in passages where Job is generalizing about life and man's lot, not in passages where he is simply describing his own condition, nor in judicial parts, nor in parts addressed to the friends, and nor in the two passages about the prosperity of the wicked (21:1-22; 24:1-17); and 3) this technique cannot be found in sections that are regarded by scholars as inauthentic in Job's mouth.

[266] Janzen, *Job*, 173.
[267] Janzen, *Job*, 174,177.

same sort of verbiage (26:5-14), and yet with a flair that shows up the rhetorically inferior quality of Bildad's words."[268]

Janzen also notes that the conclusion in 26:14 again ridicules the claim to inspiration. In 4:12 Eliphaz says: "Now a word (דָּבָר) was brought to me stealthily; my ear received the whisper (שֵׁמֶץ) of it." Job echoes this wording: "these are but the outskirts of His ways, how small a whisper (שֵׁמֶץ דָּבָר) we hear of Him" (26:14a,b). For Janzen, that שֵׁמֶץ occurs only in these two verses in the Hebrew Scripture underscores the connection between them,[269] and makes 26:5-14 a parody of Bildad's speech, used satirically to mock Job's friends.

I agree with Janzen that the hymn in 26:5-14 is mainly satirical against the friends. We shall return to this in the next section. However, I disagree that Job mimics and finishes Bildad's speech for him. Janzen's approach to the issue seems to be based solely upon grounds of similar language and ideas. His intention is to portray a consistent Job, who uses the same sort of language and ideas all the time. Janzen's approach tends to smooth the contradiction rather than wrestling with it. Again, this leads to the question: what points does Job try to make if the hymn is his own viewpoint?

4. Defending 26:5-14 as Job's Speech

Whybray and Good consider 26:5-14 as Job's speech, but do not give any reasons for doing so.[270] Differently from other scholars, Hartley expands Bildad's speech by joining 27:13-23 (instead of 26:5-14) to 25:1-6, and reducing Job's eighth response to 26:1-14; 27:2-12.[271] Hartley finds similarities between 9:5-13 and 26:5-14, concluding that 26:5-14 belongs to Job. He comments: "The majority of modern interpreters reassign the hymnic portion in praise of God's power (26:5-14) from Job to one of the comforters. But there is no serious obstacle to accepting this pericope as Job's."[272] In fact, these two speeches do share a lot of similarities. However, it may not be necessary to suppose that they should carry exactly

---

[268] Janzen, *Job*, 177.
[269] Janzen, *Job*, 178.
[270] Whybray, *Job*, 115-7; Good, *In Turns of Tempest*, 284-6.
[271] Hartley, *Job*, 25-6, 355-72.
[272] Hartley, *Job*, 26, n.18.

similar force. It remains to be seen if the differences can be accounted for.

Andersen defends 26:5-14 as Job's speech on the ground that no one else speaks quite like this. He argues that this passage is even more out of place in the mouth of Bildad. Andersen comments: "By tacking it on to the end of chapter 25, the impact of Bildad's last word (25:6) is lost. Furthermore, 26:2-4 makes sense as Job's retaliation to this insult, but it is inconceivable that Job would heap scorn on such a superb exposition of God's splendour as 26:5-14, if this is Bildad's final word."[273] According to Andersen, none of the friends says things like 26:5-14. Eliphaz's hymn in 5:9-16 is in line with 26:5-14, but less eloquent than Job's utterance in 9:4-10 and 12:7-25. He defends 26:5-14 as "Job's last and best treatment of this theme."[274]

However, Andersen's point about eloquence is rather subjective. He does not address the fact that 5:9-16 and 26:5-14 are quite similar regarding their shared theme. Again, Andersen's criterion of attribution is based on assumptions of similarity and consistency. However, as we have seen, different speakers may say similar things for quite different reasons. At the same time, the same speaker may also say something quite different or even contradictory to his previous speeches. In short, Andersen seeks to portray a consistent Job, but this only begs the question that we are asking.

5. *Assigning Both Job 25 and 26 to Job*

Van der Lugt finds that Job 25 and 26 in their entirety constitute a complete unit of Job's speech.[275] His argument is based (as we saw) on the grounds of poetic form.[276]

Despite van der Lugt's great efforts to display the thematic and terminological links within these two chapters,[277] he fails to deal with the issue of inconsistency. If this combined piece of Job 25-26 is Job's speech, why is it so different from his previous usage of hymnic forms? Van der Lugt also fails to deal with the inconsistency of the introductory formulae in 25:1 and 26:1, where Bildad and Job are introduced respectively. If both chapters are Job's sayings, why is

---

[273] Andersen, *Job*, 216.
[274] Andersen, *Job*, 216.
[275] Lugt, *Rhetorical Criticism and Job*, 286-96.
[276] Lugt, *Rhetorical Criticism and Job*, 292.
[277] Lugt, *Rhetorical Criticism and Job*, 293-5.

Bildad introduced at 25:1? Why is it necessary to introduce Job again at 26:1, the middle of the reconstructed passage? Apart from these, it seems bizarre that the reconstructed poem is interrupted by some non-hymnic lines (26:1-4), which highlight Job's rejection of his friends' counsel.

Conclusion
Those scholars who reject 26:5-14 as Job's speech assume that Job's and his friends' use of language and ideas should be more or less consistent throughout their dialogues. Job is expected to always use hymnic materials, together with explicitly negative comments, to depict God's destructive aspects and image. Therefore they try to reconstruct the speech in order to make Job continue to use the same expression against God, seeking to keep Job's use of language as consistent as possible.

On the other hand, some of those who defend 26:5-14 as Job's hymn attempt to smooth the contradiction caused by the juxtaposition of Job 26 to Job 25. However, the problem remains unsolved. And actually their intention to remove the contradiction reflects the same presupposition (as those scholars who reject 26:5-14 as Job's words): that Job's use of language and ideas must remain consistent.

Van der Lugt who attributes both Job 25 and 26 to Job sees the inconsistencies with other things Job has said, but fails to explain them. Although he has made a great effort to prove Job 25 and 26 as a whole to be Job's sayings, the inconsistency still cannot be resolved.

Both Dell and Janzen view 26:5-14 as satirical, but in different senses. The former holds that this hymn is satirical against God, while the latter maintains that it is satirical against Job's friends. However, this study combines these two ideas that the hymn in 26:5-14 is both satirical against God and his friends. But the main target that Job attacks is the friends.

D. *The Unity of Job 26*

This study proposes to read Job 26 as an integral part of the book and to retain 26:5-14 as Job's hymn. As we have seen, van der Lugt notes that the evidence of terminological correspondences within this chapter indicates to a certain extent its internal unity.[278] Hartley also

---

[278] Lugt, *Rhetorical Criticism and Job*, 295.

finds similarities between 9:5-13 and 26:5-14, concluding that 26:5-14 belongs to Job.[279]

Van der Lugt's and Hartley's studies do show some evidence that 26:5-14 is Job's speech and that Job 26 is a unitary whole. However, they are insufficient, as a single factor, to make such an argument convincing, because the odd juxtaposition of Job 26 to Job 25 remains.

E. *The Rhetorical Impacts of Job's Contradictory Sayings in Job 25-26*

Beyond any doubt, the juxtaposition of Job 26 to Job 25 seems very bizarre. But unlike Andersen and Janzen, this study does not smooth the contradiction caused by such juxtaposition. I disagree with Janzen's claim that in 26:5-14 Job is finishing Bildad's speech for him in an angry tone. Nevertheless, I argue that the contradictory juxtaposition in Job 25-26 is part of the author's strategy, serving a positive rhetorical function here in order to rectify the exigency. Like the treatment of Job 24, the discussion in this section focuses on two levels of analysis of Job's contradictory sayings in Job 26: a) the flow of argument in the story; and b) the rhetorical impacts upon the audience.

1. *The Flow of Argument*

In chapter 25 Bildad contrasts the absolute greatness and holiness of God with the insignificance and total depravity of mankind. Job frequently claims to be righteous (צָדֵק / צַדִּיק; 9:15, 20; 12:4; 13:18; 22:3), pure (זַךְ; 16:17) and blameless (תָּם; 9:20, 21). By uttering this hymn, Bildad intends to mock the absurdity of Job's claim to innocence before the absolutely holy God. In addition, the contrast between God's power and human moral unworthiness carries the implication that this all-powerful God cannot be ignorant of any human being's behaviour.[280]

This hymn is an "orthodox" praise of God's majesty, presenting the audience with conventional perceptions of God in Bildad's words. Bildad's points in Job 25 have already been made by Eliphaz in 4:17-21 and 15:14-16, and Job in 9:2-3 and 14:1-4. Notably, the centre of this hymn (25:4), which highlights that no human being can claim to be pure and righteous in the presence of this awesome

---

[279] Hartley, *Job*, 26, n.18.
[280] Whybray, *Job*, 113.

God, is a quotation of the rhetorical question posed by Eliphaz twice in 4:17 and 15:14.[281] In terms of content, it brings nothing new to the audience. However, Job 25 sets up an important backdrop for the upcoming contradictions in Job 26.

Job's subsequent rejection of Bildad's counsels (26:1-4) is made in a heavily ironic tone. Throughout vv.2-4 the second person masculine singular is used.[282] Most probably, here Job is addressing Bildad, rather than all his friends.[283] In 26:2-3 Job brings out a double irony. He regards himself as a person without power (לֹא־כֹחַ), without strenght (לֹא־עֹז) and without wisdom (לֹא חָכְמָה). At first glance, these words seem to describe Job himself, but they can also be used as a word-play to mock Bildad's advice. Regarding this word-play, Newsom offers the following translation:[284]

> How you have helped, without strength!
> How you have rescued, with a powerless arm!
> How you have counseled, without wisdom!
> And you have given your advice so abundantly!

In this irony the author employs the techniques of double-edged speech, "in which a character says one thing and his audience, with a wider context of knowledge, understands another."[285] "The ironic criticism requires of its hearers and readers the burden of recognition, the discovery of the relation between the ironist's 'is' and his 'ought'."[286] In 26:4 with the rhetorical questions "with whose help?" (אֶת־מִי, lit. "with whom?") and "whose spirit/breath?" (וְנִשְׁמַת־מִי), Job questions the value of Bildad's instruction and the source of its in-

---

[281] Whybray, *Job*, 113-4; and Hartley, *Job*, 355-7.

[282] In other speeches Job usually uses second person masculine plural forms to address the friends as a group. However there are some similar exceptions: a) once in Job's speech to Eliphaz (16:3); and b) twice in his speeches to Zophar (12:7-8; 21:3b).

[283] Hartley, *Job*, 362, n.2; Andersen, *Job*, 217; Newsom, "Job," 517; Rowley, *Book of Job*, 171; Gordis, *Book of Job*, 286; Driver and Gray, *Book of Job*, 216-7. All these scholars consider this as Job's address to Bildad. As far as Good is concerned, Job's address can be directed either to Bildad or to God. Good states: "Directed to Bildad, the opening tramples down whatever may be left of their sagacity to the unwise, he suggests that they would do better to disavow the sources of their talk. Directed to the god, the vitriol is more extreme, for Job addresses a deity who is not only absent but who has said absolutely nothing to him." See Good, *In Turns of Tempest*, 284.

[284] Newsom, "Job," 517. These verses are translated similarly by Habel, *Job*, 375.

[285] Good, *Irony in OT*, 31.

[286] Good, *Irony in OT*, 31.

spiration. Job's intention is to point out that Bildad's counsel is without wisdom and weight. Again, his rhetorical questions evoke a strong sense of bitter irony in this verse.

Hartley states that these verses (26:1-4) "contain Job's harshest rejection of a friend's counsel."[287] Their bitter irony can be perceived when Job pinpoints the incongruity between what Bildad's counsel actually "is" and what it "ought" to be. This is not the first time Job rejects his friends' counsels. However, the mood of Job's animosity and insult in 26:1-4 seems to be stronger than his in previous speeches (e.g. 12:2-3; 13:1-12; 16:2-5; 19:2-6; 21:2-3). The audience may expect Job to continue his argument against his friend in the sequel. In chapter 25 Bildad has uttered a hymn contrasting God's majesty and holiness with mankind's insignificance and depravity. Therefore the biting sarcasm in 26:1-4 may evoke the audience's expectation for Job's further refutation of Bildad's perceptions of God (25:2-6).

However, right after Job's strong rejection of Bildad's praise of God's majesty and awesomeness (26:1-4), he lauds God's majestic power as Bildad did in Job 25. Job's hymn in 26:5-14 is quite similar to Bildad's, and seems to continue Bildad's affirmation of God's omnipotence: dominion (הַמְשֵׁל) and fear (פַּחַד) are with Him (עִמּוֹ; 25:2a). Basically, the hymn in 26:5-14 highlights God's all-embracing rule over all areas: the lowest depth in the underworld (vv.5-6), the highest height in the heavens (vv.7-9, 12-13) and the farthest limits on the earth (vv.10-11). "Yet all we can know of his might is but a fragment of a vaster whole."[288] In addition, the conclusion in 26:14 that God's ways are mysterious and beyond human comprehension also echoes with Bildad's views in chapter 25 about the infinite distance between God and human beings.[289]

As mentioned above, when the text moves on from 26:1-4 to 26:5-14, the audience may expect Job to continue his rejection against Bildad's perceptions of God. But, quite unexpectedly, Job utters a hymn which sounds similar to Bildad's praise of God in chapter 25. Seemingly, the juxtaposition of Job 26 to Job 25 causes the following contradictions:

---

[287] Hartley, *Job*, 362.
[288] Rowley, *Book of Job*, 172. I adopt Rowley's analysis of the theme of this hymn, but do not agree with his reallocation of this section to Bildad.
[289] Whybray, *Job*, 115.

+ve 25:1-6	Bildad's praise of God's majestic power
-ve 26:1-4	Job's rejection of Bildad's counsels
+ve 26:5-14	Job's praise of God's majestic power

If both Job and Bildad praise God's supreme power, why does Job have to strongly repudiate Bildad's sayings in 26:1-4? If Job rejects Bildad's hymn of praise, why does he recite a similar hymn in 26:5-14? Job used to complain about God's destructive aspects (9:5-13; 10:8-13; 12:13-25), why does he not do so in 26:5-14? Furthermore, the abrupt shift from 26:4 to the hymn in 26:5-14, lacking any transition, has aroused some scholars' suspicion that some lines are missing (e.g. Hartley).[290] If the whole chapter of Job 26 is Job's words, what is the purpose of such suddenness? The juxtaposition of 26:5-14 to 25:1-26:4 does bring forth an uneasy feeling of contradiction and oddity here. Although Whybray considers chapter 26 as Job's speech, he expresses the following puzzle: "the problem is simply that these verses [26:5-14] are not particularly appropriate at this point: this confession of faith in God as Creator seems to serve no immediate purpose. No polemical use is made of it."[291]

Instead of eradicating the contradictions caused by the juxtaposition of 26:5-14 to 25:1-26:4, this study argues that it is exactly this contradictory juxtaposition that serves the author's strategy by facilitating rhetorical impacts upon the audience. But before exploring this authorial intent, we shall discuss the interpretive questions concerning the issues of 26:5-14 posed above.

Comparatively speaking, when Job utters his hymns in 9:5-13; 10:8-13; and 12:13-25, he always further describes God's negative aspects right after the hymns. In chapter 26, however, there is no contextual indication that Job describes God's character and His deeds negatively. Job 26:1-4 mainly focuses on refuting Bildad's counsels, and the hymn finishes abruptly at the end of the chapter, leaving no room for Job to make any further comments about God. Although in 27:2 Job accuses God of making his soul bitter, the new introductory formula "And Job again took up his discourse, and said" in 27:1 indicates that Job starts another topic at this point. This means that chapter 26 must be treated as a single unit, one in which there is no obvious contextual evidence in this chapter that Job quotes the hymn to mock God. According to the development of

---

[290] Hartley, *Job*, 363, n.2. See also Andersen, *Job*, 217.
[291] Whybray, *Job*, 115.

the story, both chapter 26 and chapter 27 seem to focus mainly upon the friends rather than God.

The linkage between vv.2-4 and v.14 gives a clue for unlocking the proper interpretation of Job's hymn in 26:5-14. As mentioned before, Bildad utters a hymn contrasting God's majesty and holiness with man's insignificance and moral unworthiness in chapter 25 in order to reveal Job's preposterous claim of innocence before God. Job's rejection of Bildad's counsels in 26:2-4 implies that Bildad's wisdom is limited and worthless. Job's challenge to Bildad's source of inspiration expresses a strong sense of disdain and contempt in 26:4. In such a context it is natural that Job's hymn in 26:5-14 must also carry some ironic sense. Job says the same kind of things as Bildad did in chapter 25, but his emphasis is on the fact that human beings have very limited understanding.

This theme of the limitation of human wisdom in 26:14 in fact serves as the "punch-line" of Job's hymn, echoing with Job's bitter irony in 26:2-4. It has an ironic aspect because it is the viewpoint that Bildad could be expected to agree with. In 26:14 Job's ironic use of שֵׁמֶץ דָּבָר corresponds with Eliphaz's language in 4:12. In addition, the theme of the limitation of human wisdom is also similar to Eliphaz's idea in 5:9 and Zophar's in 11:7. But Job actually uses the friends' viewpoint as a powerful weapon to attack them. If human understanding is so limited, how can they claim to have a right understanding of Job's situation? Therefore the rhetorical question at 26:14 acts as the "punch-line" of the hymn, and adds even further satirical bitterness to Job's expression in 26:2-4.

The close tie between 26:2-4 and 26:14 indicates that both 26:1-4 and 26:5-14 make the same point. It thus resolves the scholars' queries about the lack of transition between these two parts of the chapter. However, the absence of any obvious contextual indication that the hymn is spoken satirically against God does not necessarily rule out Job's satirical tone against God.

This is so because there are aspects of both hiddenness (26:14) and power (26:5-13) in this hymn, and this is bound to have echoes of what Job has already said about these topics (e.g. 9:5-15; 23:8-9, 13-16). Thus when we allow to Job all the speeches attributed to him, a cumulative picture is built up, and a series of speeches echo with each other. So we know that when Job speaks like this it is part of his debate with the friends.

In sum, 26:5-14 is counted as an insulting parody of the friends' viewpoints and the conventional hymns, but it also bears some satirical sense against God because it resonates with Job's other speeches in regard to God's power and hiddenness.

2. The Rhetorical Impacts upon the Audience

Habel comments: "The artist [i.e. the author of Job] combines literary techniques and traditional motifs to sustain theological suspense within a narrative boundary. The question of what will happen is continually bound up with what is right and true."[292] Before they discuss the intended impact of Job's hymn in 26:5-14, the audience has to judge whether Job's viewpoint here is right or not. If the audience listens to Job's doxology, they are expected to agree that God's way of governing is beyond human understanding. The audience is placed in a privileged position by having knowledge of the scene in heaven. They know that Job and his friends are totally ignorant of the reason for Job's suffering. Until this point God has remained elusive. Therefore they know that Job is speaking truly in his hymn that God's way of governing is beyond human understanding, although Job's doxology primarily aims at pointing out his friends' limited wisdom.

In addition, the audience is also expected to discern the double irony of Job's hymn in chapter 26. For Job as a speaker uses irony against the friends' lack of wisdom, but the narrator's intention is to show that Job speaks truly, yet without full knowledge. In the end Yahweh will turn this kind of argument against Job. Therefore Job's speech here prepares the audience to perceive how the irony is also against Job himself later in the divine encounter.

Job's doxology in 26:5-14 motivates the audience to sort out the problem of the friends' pride in playing God. Being an insider, Job is sure that he is innocent. But due to his ignorance of God's test, he does not understand why calamities befall him. Being honest with himself, Job admits the limitation of human wisdom. Therefore, in his doxology, he silences the friends with a remarkable depiction of "the outskirts of His ways." Job marvels that what is heard of Him is just a small whisper. He wonders, "But the thunder of His might, who can understand?" (26:14). If even Job as an insider has no clue about his own suffering, how can outsiders (his friends) claim to

---

[292] Habel, *Job*, 60.

know Job's situation? Instead of admitting their ignorance, the friends assume omniscience.[293] They boast of their wisdom (15:8-10; 20:3), and even play God, passing judgment on Job with their mechanical wisdom theology. As an insider, Job is so sure that his friends, the presumptuous wise men, are not really wise (12:2-4; 13:5; 17:10; 26:2-4). Their wrongdoing is finally corrected by Yahweh in 42:7-8. The evaluation of the friends' deeds prepares the audience to receive God's final verdict in due course.

To conclude, Job's hymn in 26:5-14 serves to provoke the audience to look back to the whole debate and recall how the friends fail to explain Job's situation with their rigid theology. Such failure symbolizes the limitation of human wisdom. Therefore the audience is expected to affirm that God's way of governance is far beyond human comprehension. In fact, from the very beginning of the story, the author has set up a persuasive plan to guide the audience step by step into perceiving the truth that "there are such testing experiences of life which transcend man's knowledge of them or ability to explain them, but which have valid reasons in the provident wisdom of God."[294] Such evaluation will be more clearly demonstrated when the story comes to the divine manifestation.

VI. *Job's Contradictory Sayings in Job 27*

Newsom rightly remarks: "Chapter 27, the final chapter in the third cycle of speeches, poses many of the same interpretive difficulties as chaps. 23-24 and 25-26."[295] For example, Job 27 commences with an unusual formula ("And Job again took up his discourse, and said") to introduce Job as speaker, although it immediately follows what has already been Job's speech (according to 26:1). On the one hand, some scholars query why two introductions are needed if both Job 26 and 27 are Job's words. On the other hand, the unusual heading in 27:1 (identical with that in 29:1) raises suspicions too, because it is different from the standard introductory formula ("Then Job answered and said") in the dialogue's other speeches (6:1; 9:1; 12:1; 16:1; 19:1; 21:1; 23:1; 26:1). Therefore some schol-

---

[293] Matheney, "Major Purposes of the Book of Job," 30.
[294] Matheney, "Major Purposes of the Book of Job," 36.
[295] Newsom, "Job," 522.

ars suspect that the text has been dislocated.[296] Furthermore, part of the content of Job 27 is at variance with Job's predominant standpoint, sounding again rather like the viewpoint of his friends. Scholars consider at least vv.13-23, and possibly vv.7-10, as more appropriate upon the lips of one of the friends than upon Job's.[297] Therefore they seek to reconstruct Job 27 in various ways:

Habel/Gordis
Job 26:1-4/ 27:1-12
Zophar 27:13-23

Dhorme
Job 26:1-4/ 27:2-12
Zophar 27:13/ 24:18-24/ 27:14-23

Pope
Job 27:1/ 26:1-4/ 27:2-7
Zophar 27:8-23/ 24:18-20, 22-25

Rowley
Job 26:1-4/ 27:2-6
Zophar 27:7-12/ 27:13/ 24:18-24/ 27:14-23

Driver-Gray
Job 27:2-6 (definitely);
   27:12 (probably);
   27:11 (perhaps)
Zophar 27:7-10/ 27:13-23

Whybray
No reattribution of Job 27; But views 27:7-10 as interpolation; and suspects 27:13-23 as Zophar's

Hartley
Bildad 25:1-6/ 27:13-23
Job 26:1-14/ 27:1-12

Andersen/Clines/Good
Job 27:1-23

Janzen/Newsom
Job 27:1-12
Job 27:13-23 (imitating Zophar's)

The above list shows that many scholars tend to re-assign 27:13-23 (sometimes even 27:7-12) from Job's lips to Zophar. In spite of the great divergence of reconstructions among the scholars, I propose to read Job 27 as the text stands. In the following textual analysis I consider vv.7-10 as Job's imprecation against his enemy rather than as a statement of fact, and view vv.13-23 as a contradictory juxtaposition, a part of the author's strategy to make a rhetorical impact upon the audience.

First of all, the content of Job 27 is investigated. Then Job's contradictory sayings in Job 27 are compared with: a) Job's other say-

---

[296] Rowley, *Book of Job*, 174; and Whybray, *Job*, 118.
[297] See Dhorme, *Job*, xlvii-l; Habel, *Job*, 37; Rowley, *Book of Job*, 174-8; and Whybray, *Job*, 118-20.

ings; and b) his friends' sayings in the dialogue. Next we discuss the commentators' approaches to the issue of Job's contradictory sayings in this chapter. Finally, these passages are interpreted by using rhetorical analysis to examine the contribution of Job's contradictory sayings to the flow of the argument within the story and their impact upon the audience. Once again, we shall argue that contradictory juxtaposition serves a positive rhetorical function to transform the exigency.

A. *The Content*

Job 27 is divided into four sections: a) Job's oath of innocence (vv.1-6); b) Job's imprecation against his enemy (vv.7-10); c) Job's intent to instruct his friends (vv.11-12); and d) Job's proclamation of the fate of the wicked (vv.13-23).

After the new heading "Then Job again took up his discourse (מָשָׁל) and said" (v.1), Job swears a series of oaths to defend the honesty of his speech, his integrity and his determination not to declare his friends to be innocent (vv.2-6). Verses 2-4 contain Job's first oath of innocence.[298] With the oath formula חַי־אֵל (v.2a) and שַׁדַּי (v.2c), Job swears the most solemn kind of oath by God's name,[299] and accuses God of two offences: a) God has set aside Job's right to pursue a litigation (v.2b); and b) God's unwillingness to hear Job has embittered Job's soul (v.2d). Ironically, "Job swears by the God who has wronged him. Once more the two conceptions of God, against whom and to whom he appeals, lie side by side in Job's thought."[300] Job acknowledges that God is the giver of life, and that Job will stand by his oath as long as he lives (v.3). There then comes the content of Job's oath: he will never speak falsehood (עַוְלָה) or deceit (רְמִיָּה; v.4). Job swears to speak the whole truth.

Job 27:5 introduces another exclamatory oath חָלִילָה לִּי (Far be

---

[298] Hartley, *Job*, 369. Hartley analyses the structure of Job's oath as follows: "It opens with an oath formula (v.2a, c), expanded by an accusation against God contained in a relative clause (v.2b, d), plus a parenthetical statement that God is the source of his life (v.3), and then the oath proper asserting that he has not lied at all in his affirmations of innocence (v.4)."

[299] To swear by God's life is the most solemn kind of oath, because the name of the deity is called upon to curse the speaker if the oath is not true (cf. Lev 19:12; Num 5:20-22). See Whybray, *Job*, 118.

[300] Rowley, *Book of Job*, 174-5. Concerning the two views of God, see also Newsom, "Job," 523; Andersen, *Job*, 220-1; Habel, *Job*, 379-80; Gordis, *Book of Job*, 287; and Hartley, *Job*, 369.

it from me).....עַד־אֶגְוָע (Till I die) to reject the counsels of Job's friends. The verb אַצְדִּיק (Hiphil of צדק) carries a declarative sense of "declare right/innocent" in a legal setting and thus connotes innocence (Deut 25:1; 1 Kg 8:32=2 Chron 6:23; Exod 23:7; Isa 5:23; Prov 17:15; Job 27:5). Its antonym is the Hiphil of רשע (prove or declare guilty). The Qal of צדק in the forensic context of Job means "be in the right or acquitted" (9:2; 9:15, 20; 13:18; 34:5). Very often, רשע and צדק are paired up together, carrying a legal and forensic meaning of "guilt and innocence." There are some examples of such pairing up in Job: צדק Qal + רשע Hi in 9:20; צַדִּיק adj ms + רשע Hi in 34:17; צדק Qal + רשע Hi in 40:8.³⁰¹ "Job would not declare his friends to be innocent" (27:5a) means that "he would declare them to be guilty." According to this legal metaphor, only one party can be in the right, i.e. either the friends or Job. Job declares that he is the innocent party. This implies that he has a case against the friends as well as against God. In 27:4 Job swears to speak the truth. At this point, speaking the truth means that Job will never declare his friends to be innocent (27:5a), because if he admits their innocence he would confess himself guilty, thus betraying his own integrity (תֻּמָּה). Therefore, till he dies, he will maintain his claim to integrity (27:5b). With firm determination, he will hold fast (חָזַק) to his righteousness and will not let it go (27:6a). Job examines his entire life with a clear conscience and has nothing to regret (27:6b).

After Job's oath of innocence in vv.1-6, there follows Job's imprecation against his enemy (vv.7-10).³⁰² יְהִי כְרָשָׁע אֹיְבִי (Let my enemy be as the wicked) is a kind of oath formula, bringing a curse

---

³⁰¹ With regard to the connotations of צדק and רשע, see Habel, *Job*, 380-1; F. Brown, S. Driver and C. Briggs, *The Brown-Driver-Briggs Hebrew and English Lexicon* (Peabody: Hendrickson, 1996) 842, 957; D. J. Reimer, "צדק," *NIDOTTE 3* (ed. Willem A. VanGemeren; Grand Rapids: Zondervan, 1997) 746-66; E. Carpenter and M. A. Grisanti, "רשע," *NIDOTTE 3* (ed. Willem A. VanGemeren; Grand Rapids: Zondervan, 1997) 1201; and B. K. Waltke and M. O'Connor, *An Introduction to Biblical Hebrew Syntax* (Winona Lake: Eisenbrauns, 1990) 438-9.

³⁰² One of the interpretative difficulties in this passage is to determine who the enemy is. Janzen considers vv.7-12 as Job's imprecation against his friends as a group; Janzen, *Job*, 185. Habel considers God as the enemy; Habel, *Job*, 381-2. Newsom comments that the enemy cannot be God, because "the content of the curse makes no sense on that supposition"; Newsom, "Job," 523-4. Newsom and Dhorme suggest that it is a rhetorical form of speech and that the content of the curse is more likely generic; Newsom, "Job," 523; and Dhorme, *Job*, 382. Dhorme points out, "instead of saying: 'May I not suffer the fate of the wicked! he says: 'May my enemy suffer the fate of the wicked!'"; Dhorme, *Job*, 382. In

against an opponent.³⁰³ The word רָשָׁע in vv.7-10 echoes the legal connotation of the same verb צדק in v.5, but it bears a more general meaning—the wicked. However, its implication is not far from "guilt." Job prays that the one who rises up against him may be punished as the wicked (v.7), for the godless has no hope when he is cut off (יִבְצָע)³⁰⁴ and when God takes away (יֵשֶׁל)³⁰⁵ his life (v.8). God will not hear his cry when distress befalls him (v.9). God will not deliver him because he cries out to God only to get out of his difficult situation, not because he delights in following God (v.10).

In vv.11-12 Job instructs his friends about the nature of God's power, and criticizes the futility of their counsels. He turns strongly on the friends, making himself their teacher, whereas they thought they were his.

Regarding the last section of the chapter, Habel has neatly demonstrated the structural design of 27:13-23, which is simplified as follows:³⁰⁶

---

agreement with Janzen, I interpret the enemy as Job's friends. Further explanation will be given later in this section.

³⁰³ See Hartley, *Job*, 371; Newsom, "Job," 522-4; Andersen, *Job*, 221; Habel, *Job*, 381-2; and Dhorme, *Job*, 382. All the above commentators read vv.7-10 as an imprecation rather than as a factual statement. NASB, ASV, KJV, NKJ, NIV, RSV, NRSV, NAB, NLT and NJB all render v.7 as "May my enemy be..." or "Let my enemy be..."

³⁰⁴ The verb יִבְצָע can either mean "to make gain by violence or wrongfully" (ASV, KJV and NKJ) or "to cut off." The latter meaning can be used as transitive "when God cuts him off" (RSV, NRSV, ESV and NLT) or intransitive "when he is cut off" (NIV, NASB, NAB, Habel, Hartley and Gordis). In order to make a formal passive, some scholars replace יִבְצָע by a Niphal יִבָּצַע or a Pual יְבֻצַּע or a Piel יְבַצַּע. See Dhorme, *Job*, 382-3; and Driver and Gray, *Book of Job*, Philological Notes, 185. Gordis treats it as Qal intransitive "when he is cut off," which seems to be the better alternative because it requires no modification of the text. See Gordis, *Book of Job*, 288; and Hartley, *Job*, 370, n.1.

³⁰⁵ The verb יֵשֶׁל can be interpreted variously: 1) reading יֵשֶׁל from נשל (cast off); 2) reading יֵשֶׁל from שׁלל (carry off/remove); 3) reading כִּי יִשָּׂא לֶאֱלוֹהַּ נַפְשׁוֹ (when God lifts up/raises his souls) where יִשָּׂא comes from נשא 4) reading יֵשֶׁל as a defective spelling of יִשְׁאַל (when God asks for his soul); and 5) deriving the verb from שלה (to draw/to pull). Gordis prefers the last two readings, because they require no modification of the text. See Gordis, *Book of Job*, 288-9; and Hartley, *Job*, 370, n.2. Dhorme sees that 27:9-10 highlights the prayer of the godless, but not on his last day. In order to harmonize with the context, he reads יִפְגַּע instead of יִבְצָע and יִשָּׂא לֶאֱלוֹהַּ instead of יֵשֶׁל אֱלוֹהַּ in v.8. His translation is "For what is the hope of the godless when he *prays*, when he *lifts up* his soul *to* Eloah (i.e. when he prays)." See Dhorme, *Job*, 383; Rowley, *Book of Job*, 176; and Hartley, *Job*, 370, n.2.

³⁰⁶ Habel, *Job*, 384.

Topic Statement on the Destiny of the Wicked	27:13
Elaboration of the Topic Statement	27:14-23
a. Destruction of their family by sword, famine and pestilence	vv.14-15
b. Ephemeral nature of the wealth of the wicked	vv.16-19
c. Annihilation by terrors, storms and east wind	vv.20-23

As this structure shows, 27:13-23 comprises two parts. The first part is the topic statement on the destiny of the wicked (v.13). In this verse Job stresses that God has set the penalty for the wicked (אָדָם רָשָׁע) and the tyrants (עָרִיצִים)[307] which are a standard pair of terms for the overt enemies of God (15:20). The second part (27:14-23) elaborates v.13, depicting the details of the destruction upon the wicked.

Job 27:14-15 illustrates the destruction of the offspring of the wicked, who suffer for the sins of their fathers and are destroyed by a succession of threefold disasters: war (v.14b), famine (v.14c) and pestilence (v.15a). It is ironical that the good fortune of having many children in v.14a only prepares for disasters. In times of disaster and pestilence, the destruction is so overwhelming that widows are not able to weep over the loss of their children. The formal funeral rites with wailing by women become impossible (v.15b).

Job 27:16-19 highlights the ephemeral nature of the wealth of the wicked: a) the inheritance of their wealth by the righteous (vv.16-17); b) the fragility of their houses (v.18); and c) the sudden, total loss of their wealth (v.19).[308] The covetous greed of the wicked drives them to pile up silver as dust (עָפָר) and clothing as clay (חֹמֶר; v.16). However, their wealth will be enjoyed by the righteous who were once exploited. The righteous will wear their clothing (v.17a) and divide their silver (v.17b).[309] The houses of the wicked are as flimsy as a booth (סֻכָּה) and the cocoon of a moth (עָשׁ; v.18). The wicked go to bed rich, but when they wake up all their wealth suddenly vanishes (v.19).

Job 27:20-23 focuses on the annihilation of the wicked by terrors, storm and east wind. Terrors like flood waters overtake them (v.20a), and by night the tempest snatches them from their place (v.20b). The scorching east wind lifts them up and sweeps them away from

---

[307] The plural ending of עָרִיצִים "tyrants" may be a dittography of עָרִיץ (singular) with מ in the next word מִשְּׁדַּי. See Hartley, *Job*, 358, n.2.

[308] Newsom, "Job," 524.

[309] Prov 13:22b; 28:8 and Eccl 2:20-21, 26 echo ideas similar to those in Job 27:16-17.

their place (v.21). The violent wind torments and pursues the wicked, who try to escape from its power (v.22). Seeing that the wicked are pursued by the wind, people will clap their hands at them and hiss them from their place (v.23).

The thrust of 27:13-23 is like other wisdom sayings on the fate of the wicked (e.g. Ps 73). As such it may be called "orthodox." It is also more like the friends' viewpoints than Job's. In addition, the juxtaposition of 27:13-23 with 27:1-12 seems jarring. Therefore 27:13-23 is frequently considered as inauthentic in Job's mouth. Most scholars reassign it as Zophar's missing third speech (Habel, Dhorme, Rowley, Gordis, Driver-Gray and Pope).

B. *The Characteristics of Job's Contradictory Sayings in Job 27*

In order to understand why most commentators think that 27:13-23 is more like the friends' words than Job's, it is important to examine the characteristics of Job's contradictory sayings in 27:13-23. In this section Job's sayings in vv.13-23 are compared with: a) his friends' sayings; and b) Job's other sayings in the dialogue.

1. *Job 27:13-23 in Comparison with the Friends' Sayings*
Comparatively speaking, the argument in Job 27:13-23 is similar to that of the three friends' first theodicy, but mainly focuses on the destiny of the wicked. The passages concerning the fate of the wicked are 4:8-11; 5:2-7 (Eliphaz); 8:11-19, 22 (Bildad); 11:20 (Zophar); 15:17-35 (Eliphaz); 18:5-21 (Bildad); 20:4-29 (Zophar); and 22:5-20 (Eliphaz). Job 27:13-23 shares the same general idea with the above passages: God will execute punishments upon evildoers. However, there are a number of points in common, above and beyond this general idea, between Job's speech in 27:13-23 and his friends' speeches on the fate of the wicked, as follows:

a) Job 4:8-11; 5:2-7 (Eliphaz's)

4:8	//	27:13	The evil reap what they sow
4:11	//	27:14	Famine
5:4	//	27:14	Fate upon their children
5:5	//	27:16-17	Their wealth enjoyed by the others

Job's speech in 27:13-23 shares two common points with Eliphaz's first speech in 4:8-11. Eliphaz states in 4:8, "As I have seen, those who plow iniquity and those who sow trouble reap the same." Job claims in 27:13, "This is the portion of a wicked man from God, and the inheritance which tyrants receive from the Almighty." Both Eliphaz and Job stress that the evil will reap what they sow. In 4:11 the wicked are depicted as the lion, which perishes because of a lack of prey. The cubs of the lioness are scattered because of this lack of food. Job 27:14 also shares the same "famine" motif—the offspring of the wicked lacking food.

There are two common points shared between 27:13-23 and 5:2-7. Both passages point out that calamities will fall upon the offspring of the wicked. Job 5:4 states that their children are far from safety, while 27:14-15 describes that their offspring are destined for the war, famine and pestilence. The second commonality is that the wealth of the wicked will be gone and taken away by others. Job 5:5 highlights that the hungry and the schemer will enjoy his wealth, while 27:16-17 claims that the righteous and the innocent will inherit his wealth.

b) Job 8:11-19, 22 (Bildad's)

| 8:15 // 27:18 | The fragility of the wicked's houses |
| 8:22 // 27:14-19 | All identified with the wicked will perish |

Here Bildad stresses that the houses of the wicked do not stand and endure (8:15). Similarly, Job points out that the houses of the wicked are just as flimsy as a moth's cocoon and a booth (27:18). In 8:22 Bildad claims that the tent of the wicked will be no more. "The tent" means the abode, wealth and family. All the things identified with the wicked will perish. In 27:14-19 Job specifically lists out the fate of the evildoer's offspring (vv.14-15), the inheritance of their wealth by the righteous (vv.16-17) and the fragility of their abodes and wealth (vv.18-19). All these things of the wicked will vanish.

c) Job 11:20 (Zophar's)

| 11:20 // 27:20-22 | No escape from destruction |

Job 11:20 generally states that the wicked will perish and that there is no escape for them. Job 27:20-22 specifically describes that the wicked are being pursued by the terrors of death, storms and east wind. Both passages stress that the wicked cannot escape from destruction.

d) Job 15:17-35 (Eliphaz's)

15:21, 24 //	27:20	The wicked tortured by terrors
15:22 //	27:14	Destined for the sword
15:23 //	27:14	Lacking food
15:29 //	27:19	Wealth not enduring

In 15:21, 24 the wicked are tortured by the sounds of terror (v.21). In addition, distress and anguish terrify and overpower them (v.24). Job expresses a similar idea in 27:20 that terrors overtake the wicked like a flood. Eliphaz says that the wicked are destined for the sword (15:22), while Job states that the children of the wicked are destined for the sword (27:14). Job 15:23 describes that the wicked wander about for food but cannot find it, whereas in 27:14 Job says that the descendants of the wicked suffer from famine. Both 15:29 and 27:19 emphasize that the wealth of the wicked will vanish.

e) Job 18:5-21 (Bildad's)

18:11, 14 //	27:20	Terrors (בַּלָּהוֹת)
18:12 //	27:14b	Famine
18:13 //	27:15a	Death
18:19 //	27:14-15	Offspring being cut off

Both 18:11, 14 and 27:20 stress that the wicked are frightened by terrors (בַּלָּהוֹת). Job 18:12 depicts that their strength is famished, while 27:14b describes that their descendants will not be satisfied with bread. Both 18:13 and 27:15a focus on how the wicked are devoured by pestilence and death. Finally, the offspring of the wicked are cut off and no survivor is left (18:19; 27:14-15).

f) Job 20:4-29 (Zophar's)

20:29	// 27:13	The portion of the wicked
20:26c	// 27:15	No survivor left
20:10, 15, 18-19 //	27:16-17	Their wealth taken back by the oppressed
20:21, 26a, 28	// 27:19	Poverty
20:25	// 27:20	Terrors
20:7-9	// 27:20-23	The wicked will perish

Job 20:29 and 27:13 share almost identical wording in regard to the portion and inheritance of the wicked:

20:29   זֶה חֵלֶק־אָדָם רָשָׁע מֵאֱלֹהִים וְנַחֲלַת אִמְרוֹ מֵאֵל
27:13   זֶה חֵלֶק־אָדָם רָשָׁע עִם־אֵל וְנַחֲלַת עָרִיצִים מִשַּׁדַּי יִקָּחוּ׃

Other than that, both passages point out that no survivor of the wicked will be left (20:26c; 27:15). Their wealth will be taken back by the poor and innocent, who were once oppressed (20:10, 15, 18-19; 27:16-17). Although they pile up their property, their riches and prosperity will vanish (20:21, 26a, 28; 27:19). The wicked are overtaken by terrors (20:25; 27:20). They will perish, and cannot escape annihilation (20:7-9; 27:20-23).

g) Job 22:5-20 (Eliphaz's)

22:10-11 //	27:20-23	Terrors and troubles
22:19-20 //	27:23	The wicked being mocked
22:20 //	27:19	Their wealth not enduring

Concerning the destiny of the wicked, 22:10-11 and 27:20-23 both emphasize that the wicked are overwhelmed by the terrors and troubles. The righteous and innocent rejoice when they see evildoers being punished (22:19-20; 27:23). The riches and abundance of the wicked will be consumed (22:20; 27:19).

Conclusion
In regard to the fate of the wicked, Job's speech in 27:13-23 is very similar to his friends' viewpoints in 4:8-11; 5:2-7; 8:11-19, 22; 11:20; 15:17-35; 18:5-21; 20:4-29 and 22:5-20. Basically, 27:13-23 shares a common general idea with these passages: the wicked will be punished by God.

Comparatively speaking, 27:13-23 is most similar to Zophar's words in 20:4-29, especially the almost identical wordings in 27:13 and 20:29. In view of the number of common points, and because Zophar's third speech is missing, many scholars consider that 27:13-23 is most probably Zophar's lost speech (Habel, Dhorme, Rowley, Driver-Gray, Gordis and Pope). The above comparisons indicate that 27:13-23 shares many common points with Bildad's speeches in 8:11-19, 22 and 18:5-21 too, which prompt Hartley to attribute 27:13-23 to Bildad. In short, the first characteristic of Job's contradictory sayings in 27:13-23 is that Job's statement about the fate of the wicked is quite similar to his friends' viewpoints, especially Zophar's in 20:4-29.

2. Job 27:13-23 in Comparison with Job's Other Sayings
To identify further characteristics of Job's sayings in 27:13-23, I now proceed to compare this passage with Job's other sayings. However,

I will omit 24:18-24, it too being a "suspect" saying, and will concentrate upon Job's "typical" sayings.

a) Job 21

21:8, 11-12	Offspring of the wicked are blessed
27:14-15	Offspring of the wicked are cut off
21:9	Their houses are secured
27:18	Their houses are unsecured
21:7, 13, 23-24	The wicked enjoy longevity and die in peace
27:15, 20-23	The wicked will perish soon
21:17	God's indifference to the evil deeds of the wicked
27:13	God's judgment upon the wicked
21:18	The wicked not being swept away by the wind and storm
27:20-23	The wicked being carried off by the tempest and east wind
21:30	The wicked being spared from the day of calamity
27:20-23	The wicked not being able to escape the judgment
21:32-33	Splendid funeral and memorial of the wicked
27:23	The wicked being mocked when they perish

When comparing Job's speech in 27:13-23 with his speech in chapter 21, the big contradiction between these two passages is immediately striking. In the former passage Job asserts that God executes judgment upon the evildoers, bringing destruction to them. But in the latter passage Job charges God with His indifference to the evil deeds of the wicked, which leads to them prospering.

b) Job 24:1-17

24:1, 12, 15	Time of judgment not being seen
27:13	God's judgment upon the wicked
24:2-17	The evil deeds of the wicked
27:14-23	The wicked tasting the fruit of their evil deeds
24:2-3, 9-10, 14, 16	The wicked snatching the properties of the poor
27:16-17	The wicked's wealth being enjoyed by the righteous
24:5, 11	The poor lacking food and drink
27:14	The descendants of the wicked suffering famine
24:7, 10	The poor being naked without clothing

27:16b, 17a	The wicked's garments being taken by the poor
24:8	The poor having no shelter
27:18	The wicked's houses being flimsy

Job's speech in 24:1-17 contrasts drastically with his speech in 27:13-23 too. In the former passage Job stresses that the time of judgment is not stored up by God, and His faithful servants do not see His days. It seems to Job that God pays no attention to that incongruity. But in the latter passage Job highlights that God has assigned a portion and inheritance for the wicked. The wicked and their offspring will be cut off. The righteous will be vindicated. For these reasons, 27:13-23 seems directly contradictory to Job's previous stance in 24:1-17 and chapter 21.

c) Job 27:1-12

27:2	Job complains about God's injustice upon him
27:13-23	Job affirms that God will bring judgment upon the wicked
27:5-6, 11-12	Job holds fast to his integrity and rejects his friends' arguments
27:13-23	Job adopts his friends' standpoints

The juxtaposition of 27:13-23 to the preceding text (27:1-12) is also unexpected. In 27:2-4, when Job swears an oath of innocence by God's name, he accuses God of two offences: 1) God takes away his right to litigation (v.2a); and 2) His unwillingness to hear Job has embittered him (v.2b). Job complains about God's injustice upon him in 27:2, but contrarily, he affirms that God will bring the portion and inheritance to the wicked (27:13-23). On the one hand, Job swears that he will never declare his friends to be innocent, otherwise he would betray his integrity (27:5-6), and he strongly rejects his friends' counsel as empty, foolish speech (27:11-12). But on the other hand, Job utters a speech about the destiny of the wicked (27:13-23), which coincides with his friends' opinions (4:8-11, 5:2-7; 8:11-19, 22; 11:20; 15:17-35; 18:5-21; 20:4-29; 22:5-20). So Job 27:13-23 is in tension not only with Job's general view, but with its immediate context.

Conclusion
To sum up, as 24:18-24, Job 27:13-23 appears to be more like the friends' than his own typical sayings.

C. Commentators' Approaches to the Issue of Job 27

The commentators employ three approaches to the issue of Job's contradictory sayings in Job 27: 1) denying both vv.7-10 and vv.13-23 to Job (Driver-Gray, Rowley, Pope and Whybray); 2) accepting vv.7-10 but rejecting vv.13-23 as Job's words (Dhorme, Gordis, Habel and Hartley); and 3) treating the whole of chapter 27 as Job's speech (Andersen, Good, Janzen and Newsom).

1. Denying Both vv.7-10 and vv.13-23 to Job

To start with, Driver-Gray deny 27:7-10 to Job, because the unhappy lot of the wicked sounds like the standpoint of the friends rather than Job. They make this comment on 27:7-10: "Such an execration would be intelligible in the mouth of the friends who hold the fate of the wicked to be the worst of fates, but not in the mouth of Job; for in his mouth it would mean: May my enemy prosper in life and be honoured in death...!" Driver-Gray find this section more appropriate as part of the apparent missing third speech of Zophar.[310]

Driver-Gray also deny 27:13-23 as Job's saying. The reasons for their rejection are as follows:

> For it would be remarkable (a) that Job should undertake to teach his friends what they had continuously maintained, viz. the evil fate which overtakes the wicked; (b) that he should himself affirm the opposite of what had been his previous position, viz. that an evil fate does not overtake the wicked (9:22-24; ch. 21; ch. 24); (c) that while coinciding with his friends in opinion, he should reproach them with folly (v.12).[311]

They conclude that "27:7-10, 13-23 would be perfectly suitable in Zophar's mouth, and consistent with what he has maintained before (ch. 20)."[312]

Rowley too thinks that 27:7-23 should be assigned to Zophar, and that 24:18-24 can best be inserted after 27:13.[313] He states that if 24:18-24 follows 27:13, thought about the fate of the wicked man himself passes naturally to thought of his family.[314] The whole reconstructed speech of Zophar is divided into two parts: a) the deso-

---

[310] Driver and Gray, *Book of Job*, 225, 226-8.
[311] Driver and Gray, *Book of Job*, 229.
[312] Driver and Gray, *Book of Job*, 229.
[313] Rowley, *Book of Job*, 175.
[314] Rowley, *Book of Job*, 177.

late state of the godless (27:7-12); b) the fate of the godless (27:13/ 24:18-24/ 27:14-23).³¹⁵ Rowley, therefore, looks for a strict logical development in the development of the speeches.

Pope rearranges 27:1/ 26:1-4/ 27:2-7 as Job's reply to Bildad. Then he reallocates 27:8-23/ 24:18-20, 22-25 as Zophar's third discourse, which he supplies with an introductory formula "Zophar the Naamathite answered:" between 27:7 and 27:8.³¹⁶ He too thinks 27: 8-23 presents the friends' view and cannot be attributed to Job. He further notes that the conclusion of Zophar's speech is found in 24:18-20, 22-25, which he ventures to transpose after 27:23.³¹⁷

Concerning 27:7-10, Whybray points out two interpretative difficulties: 1) the viewpoint about the fate of the wicked cannot be reconciled with Job's previous position; and 2) who is the enemy in v.7? Whybray finds it impossible that God is the enemy in view in vv.8-9, but does not think it refers to the "friends" either. Whybray considers that 27:7-10 is equally improbable as Job's or the friends' words. He suggests that: "It may be best to take the verses as an interpolation into the original book by someone who misunderstood Job's position and placed them inappropriately in his mouth."³¹⁸ Seeing that 27:13-23 speaks of the fate of the wicked, which is similar to the friends' views, especially Zophar's in 20:5-29, Whybray states: "They have been identified as part of Zophar's 'lost' third speech; but all that can be said with certainty is that the view that they express is not that of Job but of the friends."³¹⁹ Whybray therefore opposes treating 27:13-23 as Job's words, although he does not directly conclude that it is Zophar's speech. Despite Whybray's denying vv.7-10 and vv.13-23 as Job's speech, he does not propose any particular alternative.³²⁰ He claims that the text is an interpolation, but does not wrestle with its meaning or explain its incongruity.

Grammatically, I agree with Gordis' argument that the use of the first person singular in v.7 seems to be more appropriate upon Job's lips than upon his friends'. He rightly notes: "Being, like its predecessors, in the 1st person, v.7 links up with v.6. Moreover, v.8, in-

---

[315] Rowley, *Book of Job*, 176.
[316] Pope, *Job*, xx, 187-96.
[317] Pope, *Job*, 191.
[318] Whybray, *Job*, 119.
[319] Whybray, *Job*, 119.
[320] Whybray, *Job*, 118.

troduced by כִּי, gives the reason for v.7 and can hardly be the beginning of Zophar's address."[321] Gordis correctly observes that the close connection between v.6, v.7 and v.8 makes it unreasonable to reassign 27:7-10 to Zophar. In turn, Gordis considers 27:7-10 as a virtual quotation of Job's previous state of mind during his time of prosperity.[322] However, he does not give any reasons to explain why Job does this here.

Hartley's explanation seems to be more convincing. He rightly points out that vv.7-10 is more properly understood as Job's imprecation against the enemy rather than a statement of fact. In v.7 יְהִי כְרָשָׁע אֹיְבִי (Let my enemy be as the wicked) is a kind of oath formula, bringing a curse against an opponent.[323] Some scholars may also find that vv.7-10 seems out of place upon Job's lips because no one would expect Job to curse his enemy after his oath of innocence. But Hartley properly notes that praying for deliverance from an enemy is an important component of a personal psalm of lament (e.g. Ps 35, 69, 140).[324] Thus it is legitimate to have an imprecation against an enemy right after an oath. In short, I view 27:7-10 as Job's words, being in genre a curse, rather than a statement of fact.

2. *Accepting vv.7-10 but Rejecting vv.13-23 as Job's Words*

Concerning 27:13-23, Gordis finds that ideas about calamity coming upon the wicked and the ultimate prosperity of the righteous are "entirely congenial to the Friends but diametrically opposed to Job's standpoint."[325] He makes the following remarks:

> The position of this passage after Bildad's speech (25:1-6; 26:5-14) and Job's third response (26:1-4; 27:2-12) makes it most plausible to assign this passage to Zophar, the only surviving section of his final speech.[326]

---

[321] Gordis, *Book of Job*, 535, Special Note 21.
[322] According to Gordis, vv.7-10 should not be taken to mean that "Job suddenly finds his way to a new faith in God, because his rebellious attitude is expressed again later (30:20-23; 31:35-38)." Therefore he suggests that this passage should be seen as Job's virtual quotation of his previous state of mind during the time of his prosperity. See Gordis, *Book of Job*, 535.
[323] Hartley, *Job*, 370-1; also Newsom, "Job," 522, 523-524; Andersen, *Job*, 221; Habel, *Job*, 381-2; Dhorme, *Job*, 382.
[324] Hartley, *Job*, 370-1.
[325] Gordis, *Book of Job*, 534, Special Note 20.
[326] Gordis, *Book of Job*, 536. Gordis rejects the idea that Job is modifying his viewpoint and conceding that as a rule calamites fall upon the wicked. He also

Habel denies 27:13-23 as part of Job's speech because this passage depicts the destiny of the wicked. This is the viewpoint that Job's friends hold (18:5-21; 20:5-29), but which Job strongly rejects elsewhere (21:7-34).[327] Assigning the speech to Zophar, he points to the closing statement of Zophar's previous speech in 20:29 as the topic statement for this passage. According to Habel, in chapter 21 Job picks up several themes from Zophar's speech (ch. 20):[328]

a. Assigning the destined portion of the wicked (21:17)
b. The ominous "storm wind" sent to sweep away the wicked (21:18)
c. The set "days" or times of calamity reserved for the wicked (21:19, 30)

Then in 27:13-23 Zophar returns to the first two themes again: a) the portion of the wicked (27:13); and b) the ominous storm wind (27:20-23). Habel also assigns chapter 24 to Zophar. He points out that the "portion of the wicked" motif is also connected with the themes of the "days" and "times" of judgment, and this theme appears as the opening topic statement at 24:1. Therefore Habel concludes that there are connections between Job 21, Job 24 and Job 27:13-23 as follows:

> It is plausible, therefore, that ch. 24, as the continuation of the cluster of key themes raised by Job in ch. 21, originally followed 27:23 as the summative closure to Zophar's final speech, or to the speeches of the friends as a whole.[329]

Dhorme finds 27:13-23 out of place on Job's lips too, because this passage is the very contention of the friends which Job previously rejects. Its content goes back to the doctrine of Eliphaz (15:20-35), Bildad (18:11-21) and Zophar (20:4-29), but it is impossible to transfer it to one of the previous chapters because all these speeches are complete. According to Dhorme, Eliphaz has made a complete speech in chapter 22, and Bildad's speech has been recovered by combining chapter 25 with 26:5-14. There remain 24:18-24 and 27:13-23, both of which must have been Zophar's utterances.

Dhorme finds 27:13 a very natural introduction, for it is a repetition of Zophar's conclusion in 20:29. In terms of content, 27:13

---

rejects the idea that Job is ironically telling his friends that their accusations against Job make them subject to punishment, claiming that there is no indication that the punishment of the wicked is pointed at the friends, see 536, Special Note 22.
[327] Habel, *Job*, 377.
[328] Habel, *Job*, 385.
[329] Habel, *Job*, 385.

depicts the fate of the wicked and tyrants, while the subsequent passage (27:14-17) describes the fate of their sons and survivors. Job 24:18-24, which highlights the punishment on the wicked and tyrants, seems to be a continuation of the theme in 27:13. Therefore Dhorme interpolates 24:18-24 between 27:13 and 27:14 to form the final speech of Zophar. In this way the punishment and death of the wicked (27:13; 24:18-24) precedes the calamities of those who survive them (27:14-17). Furthermore, 24:18 contains the alternation of singular and plural. According to Dhorme, the most natural way of explaining it is that the singular הוּא (he) in 24:18 refers to the "wicked man," and the plural suffix of חֶלְקָתָם (their domain) refers to the tyrants of 27:13. In short, Dhorme reconstructs Zophar's final speech in this way: 27:13/ 24:18-24/ 27:14-23.[330]

Differently from other scholars, Hartley attributes 27:13-23 to Bildad rather than Zophar. Seeing that Bildad's speech (25:1-6) is too brief and lacking an introduction and conclusion, Hartley considers that it must have been cut off and a portion of it may have been dislocated in Job 24-28. According to Hartley, 27:13-23 sounds inappropriate from the lips of Job, because it rebuts Job's complaint that evildoers remain unpunished, owing to God's failure to keep the times of judgment (24:1-17). Therefore Hartley places 27:13-23 after 25:1-6 to fill out Bildad's brief speech. Hartley claims, "In support of this construction is the fact that 27:13-23 offers a direct rebuttal to the ideas Job was struggling with in chapter 24."[331] Then the reconstructed speech falls into two parts: a) hymn of praise to God (25:1-6) to contrast God's sovereign rule with the creature's frailty and unworthiness; and b) a discourse on the retribution of the wicked (27:13-23). This speech serves to repudiate Job's accusation of God's unjust rule (24:1-17) and his affirmation of innocence (27:4-6).[332]

Generally speaking, all the above scholars reject 27:13-23 as Job's speech because Job affirms the opposite of what has been his previous position and agrees with his friends. In addition, this passage also contradicts the preceding text (27:1-12), where Job swears not to concede his friends' viewpoint (vv.5-6) and regards their counsels as empty speech (vv.11-12). Furthermore, Job accuses God when

---

[330] Dhorme, *Job*, xlv-l; 386-398.
[331] Hartley, *Job*, 355.
[332] Hartley, *Job*, 25-6; 355-361.

he swears by His name (v.2), but he affirms God's justice by depicting His punishment upon the wicked (vv.13-23). Apart from Hartley, who attributes this section to Bildad, all the other scholars reassign it to Zophar.

In effect, the presupposition underlying their reconstructions of 27:13-23 is that Job's use of language and ideas must be consistent at all times. However, the scholars' attempts to resolve the problem by dividing up the material and assigning 27:13-23 to one of the friends (Zophar or Bildad) do not actually achieve a solution. In fact, the reconstructed pieces seem fragmented and incomplete. The removal of the problematic passage means that one does not wrestle with the incongruous text as it stands.[333] In contrast, the present study does not remove the inconsistencies from the text. Here too, contradictory juxtaposition is viewed as part of the author's rhetorical strategy to resolve the exigency. In the next section this study proceeds to examine the rhetorical impacts of Job's contradictory sayings in Job 27 upon the audience.

3. Treating the Whole of Chapter 27 as Job's Speech
Andersen defends chapter 27 as Job's closing statement to the third speech cycle. He claims that this closing remark is linked with Job's previous speech. In 21:34 Job considers his friends' answer as nothing but falsehood, and in 24:25 he challenges them to prove his speech worthless. These two thoughts surface again in 27:2-6. In chapter 26 Job lauds God's great power, which is beyond human comprehension. Similarly, God's justice cannot fully be perceived. According to Andersen, such limitation does not hinder Job from reaffirming God's justice in 27:7-23. He can only hold fast to his integrity (v.6) if he is confident that God will endorse it. To defend 27:7-23 as Job's speech, Andersen makes the following remark:

> Hence his prediction of judgment on the godless is not a belated conversion to his friends' point of view; nor is it a slice of orthodoxy put into the text long after it was finished, by some worried scribes....Nor need we relabel 27:7-23 as the lost third speech of Zophar, even though this proposal has enjoyed considerable prestige among scholars for two centuries. Since Job nowhere denies the justice of God, it is not inconsistent for him to affirm it here. The disagreement between Job and his friends is not over whether God is just or not; it is over how the justice of God is seen to work out in particular events, and specifi-

---

[333] Newsom, "Job," 522.

cally in Job's experiences. The friends think they know the answer, and they have offered it to Job. Job knows that they are wrong, not in affirming the justice of God, but in applying it to himself. But since he does not know how the justice of God is being fulfilled in his case, he is neither able to refute the friends nor able to satisfy his own mind.[334]

Andersen probably underplays the similarities of 27:13-23 with Zophar's speech, and its unexpectedness in Job's mouth. It is true in a sense that "Job nowhere denies the justice of God." Yet to say this overlooks the fact that this is the very thing that Job is now bringing into question. He may not "deny the justice of God," but it is still surprising to hear him simply affirm it.

Janzen claims that in chapter 27 Job starts with a solemn oath (vv.1-6), which is followed by the imprecation against his friends as a group (vv.7-12). There then comes Job's imitation of Zophar's speech (vv.13-23). According to Janzen, Job's oath in 27:1-6 is an answer to Zophar's sayings in 11:1-6, while 27:13-23 is a parody of what Job expects to hear from Zophar.[335] The idea of 27:13-23 has been initiated by Zophar in 11:13-20, and fully elaborated in Job 20.[336]

Newsom comments on scholars' tendencies to reassign 27:1-12 to Job and 27:13-23 to Zophar as follows:

> Such a solution does not solve all the problems, however. One is left with two fragments instead of two complete speeches, and even that surgical separation does not remove all the seeming inconsistencies from Job's speech. It is more appropriate to struggle with the text as it stands.[337]

In turn, Newsom claims that 27:13-23 is better understood as Job's satirical imitation of his friends' speaking. She points out that Job in effect preempts Zophar, who does not speak in the third cycle. In support of her argument, Newsom remarks:

> That these are not Job's own words but an imitation of the friends' speech is indicated by the way the introductory verse 13 mimics the last verse of Zophar's speech from the second cycle (20:29). As Janzen suggests, Job is in essence giving Zophar's speech for him.[338]

---

[334] Andersen, *Job*, 219-20.
[335] Janzen, *Job*, 185-6.
[336] Janzen, *Job*, 186.
[337] Newsom, "Job," 522.
[338] Newsom, "Job," 524.

Generally speaking, Andersen, Janzen and Newsom all defend 27:13-23 as Job's speech, although there are different nuances to their arguments. In my opinion, the three of them hold the same assumption as those scholars who reject 27:13-23 as Job's statement. That is to say, they too assume that Job's point of view has to remain consistent. Andersen tries to smooth the contradiction by explaining that Job nowhere denies the justice of God, so it is not inconsistent for Job to affirm it in 27:13-23. Similarly, Janzen and Newsom seek to resolve the contradiction by suggesting that though Job says these words, he does not mean them. They both recognise the contradiction, but try to avoid it. Although Newsom claims that it is more appropriate to wrestle with the text as it stands, she still falls into a trap of harmonizing the contradiction, leaving the problem unresolved. This begs the question: if these are Job's own ideas, what is the meaning and function of such contradictory sayings?

Good also reads 27:13-23 as Job's words, but his interpretation is quite different. He argues that Job redefines the deity as the "wicked enemy" (27:7a) and himself as "the godless" (חָנֵף; 27:8). Good suggests that Job has accepted the term "godless" that his friends have implicitly applied to him all along.[339] In the light of Job's redefinitions in vv.7-10, he interprets vv.13-23 as Job's depiction of his destruction at the hand of the wicked God.

According to Good, 27:13 is similar to 20:29, but the use of different prepositions makes a great difference in meaning. In 20:29 "the lot of evil humankind" (חֵלֶק־אָדָם רָשָׁע) is received "from God" (מֵאֱלֹהִים), and that is punishment. But in 27:13 "the lot of evil humankind" (חֵלֶק־אָדָם רָשָׁע) is received "with God" (עִם־אֵל), i.e. in the presence of God, and that is reward. Good points out that the plural עָרִיצִים (the oppressors) separate "evil humankind" who are on God's side, from the singular חָנֵף (godless) which refers to Job (27:8-10). Then 27:14-23 returns to the singular, that is Job himself. Good reads vv.14-23 as a topos on the destiny of the "godless."[340] According to Good, this passage is actually a parody of the friends' argument about the fate of the wicked. He writes: "Job describes his expectation of destruction at the hands of a wicked god

---

[339] These two redefinitions lead Good to a unique interpretation of 27:7-10. He says that the passage depicts Job's hopelessness because he will be destroyed by God (v.9). Furthermore, God will not alleviate Job's misery, nor will Job have any delight in God (v.10). See Good, *In Turns of Tempest*, 287-8.

[340] Good, *In Turns of Tempest*, 289.

exactly as the friends have described their expectation that he would be destroyed at the hands of a righteous god. That irony works at many depths."³⁴¹

But Good, in particular, does not convincingly explain how 27:13 is connected with 27:14-23 and why the terms "the oppressors" (עָרִיצִים) and "the wicked" (אָדָם רָשָׁע; v.13) are mentioned in this context. Simply based on the use of the preposition "with God" (עִם־אֵל), he cannot justifiably interpret "the lot of evil humankind" in v.13 as "reward" rather than "punishment." Gordis argues that "with God" (עִם־אֵל) means "in God's mind" or "stored up with him." The use of עִם־אֵל rather than מֵאֵל (20:29) might simply be because of the parallelism "with the Almighty" (עִם־שַׁדַּי) in v.11.³⁴² Furthermore, Good's idea about the redefinition of terms seems to be so artificial as to totally reverse meaning throughout the chapter. I doubt whether the audience could pick up so subtle a point. In addition, there is no contextual indication that Job has accepted the term "godless" (חָנֵף) that his friends have implicitly applied to him. In fact, in 27:5 Job swears not to declare his friends innocent and until he dies, he will not put away his integrity. Therefore it sounds inconceivable that Job could have accepted such a term and labelled himself as "godless." Finally, it makes no sense to imagine a "wicked god" punishing a "godless" man. Similarly to Andersen, Janzen and Newsom, Good's interpretation also avoids the sharp contradiction caused by the juxtaposition of 27:13-23 to 27:1-12. Good also portrays a Job who has to keep his hard-line ground to protest against God all along. In effect, his redefinition of terms in chapter 27 is just another attempt to remove the incongruities.

Conclusion
Contrary to Driver-Gray, Rowley and Pope, who read 27:7-10 as a statement of fact, I view it as Job's imprecation against his enemy. As many scholars have recognised, it is an oddity to juxtapose 27:1-12 and 27:13-23 together. Those who reject 27:13-23 as Job's speech (Driver-Gray, Rowley, Pope, Gordis, Habel, Dhorme, Hartley and Whybray) all hold the implicit assumption that Job's point of view has to remain consistent. Those who defend this passage as Job's words (Andersen, Janzen, Newsom and Good), in fact, also hold the

---

³⁴¹ Good, *In Turns of Tempest*, 289.
³⁴² Gordis, *Book of Job*, 294.

same assumption as those who reject it, though they conceive this differently. However, this study does not attempt to eradicate or smooth the contradictions as the above scholars do. Instead, it seeks to argue that contradictory juxtaposition is part of the author's rhetorical strategy. In the next section the rhetorical functions of Job's contradictory sayings in Job 27 are explored.

D. *The Rhetorical Impacts of Job's Contradictory Sayings in Job 27*

Before discussing how Job's contradictory sayings in Job 27 contribute to the flow of argument in the story, it is important to investigate the context of this chapter in order to understand the changes which have happened in the dialogue between Job and his friends in the third speech cycle. Here the friends' speeches become progressively shorter but Job's speeches become successively longer (from Job 23-24 to Job 26-31). Bildad's brief reply in chapter 25 contains only 5 verses, and Zophar's third speech is actually missing. According to Alter, this is one of the most common devices of contrastive dialogue employed in the biblical narrative by juxtaposing "some form of very brief statement with some form of verbosity."[343] The phenomenon of the friends' progressively shorter speeches and Job's successively longer speeches poses the question of why the friends fade off the stage, and what will happen next. Being the final chapter of the third speech cycle, Job 27, especially Job's contradictory sayings in this chapter, can provide some clues to answer the above question.

1. *The Flow of Argument*

After mocking the friends' limited wisdom by citing a hymn of praise in Job 26, Job continues to speak in the next chapter. Job 27 comprises four sections: a) Job's oath of innocence (vv.1-6); b) Job's imprecation against his enemy (vv.7-10); c) Job's intent to instruct his friends (vv.11-12); and d) Job's declaration of the destiny of the wicked (vv.13-23).

In the first section (27:1-6) the new heading at v.1 signifies a change of direction. Now, with the collapse of the debate, Job shifts his attention from the battle with his friends to the attempt to arouse God's response. Instead of using the standard introductory formula וַיַּעַן אִיּוֹב וַיֹּאמַר (Job answered and said; 6:1; 9:1; 12:1; 16:1; 19:1;

---
[343] Alter, *Biblical Narrative*, 72-3.

21:1; 23:1; 26:1), a new introductory formula, וַיֹּסֶף אִיּוֹב שְׂאֵת מְשָׁלוֹ וַיֹּאמַר (Then Job again took up his discourse and said) is used by the narrator in 27:1 (cf. 29:1). The heading "take up a מָשָׁל" is more than continuing a discourse.[344]

According to Alter, a shift in the introductory formula is an essential clue to the unfolding of the plot. It serves to forewarn and alert the audience to observe the kind of statement or response that the speaker goes on to make.[345] Habel rightly points out that the מָשָׁל statement is a weighty formal public "pronouncement" before the court, which initiates a direct confrontation with God.[346] The meaning of מָשָׁל may carry the sense of warning and admonition here.[347] It alerts the audience that something important, formal and legal is going to be pronounced.

After the heading (v.1), Job swears a series of oaths to defend the honesty of his speech, his integrity and his determination not to declare his friends to be innocent (vv.2-6). Hartley neatly analyses the structure of this oath as follows:

> It opens with an oath formula (v.2a, c), expanded by an accusation against God contained in a relative clause (v.2b, d), plus a parenthetical statement that God is the source of his life (v.3), and then the oath proper asserting that he has not lied at all in his affirmations of innocence (v.4).[348]

With the oath formula חַי־אֵל...וְשַׁדַּי (As God lives,...and the Almighty), Job makes his oath of innocence. To swear by God's life is the most solemn kind of oath, because the name of the deity is called upon to curse the speaker if the oath is not true (cf. Lev 19:12; Num 5:20-22).[349]

---

[344] According to Good, the new introductory formula suggests that Job pauses for Zophar to speak, if he will. But Zophar does not speak, and the field is thus left to Job; Good, *In Turns of Tempest*, 286.

[345] Alter, *Biblical Narrative*, 78.

[346] Habel, *Job*, 30,379.

[347] G. Wilson, "מָשָׁל" *NIDOTTE* 2 (ed. Willem A. VanGemeren; Grand Rapids: Zondervan, 1997) 1135. The syntactical construction "lifted up a מָשָׁל and said" occurs no less than 7 times in the Balaam narrative (Num 23:7, 18; 24:3, 15, 20, 21, 23). It also appears 3 times in the Latter Prophets (Isa 14:4; Mic 2:4; Hab 2:6) and twice in Job (27:1; 29:1). In the above passages, the great diversity of renderings, such as oracle, prophecy, discourse, parable, and taunt, reflects the fact that there is a lack of certain meaning for מָשָׁל. Apart from the passages in Job, these constructions bring forth prophetic warnings. But in Job the contexts are difficult, and the meaning of מָשָׁל is more uncertain. It may also carry some sense of warning and admonition.

[348] Hartley, *Job*, 369.

[349] See Whybray, *Job*, 118; Habel, *Job*, 379; and Dhorme, *Job*, 379.

Job makes his oath by the God whom Job charges with two offences. First, God has taken away Job's right to pursue litigation (27:2b), which Job has called on God many times to let him do (9:3-4, 32-35; 13:3, 15; 16:19, 20-22; 19:25-27; 23:3-4). However, God's elusiveness has denied Job's desire (23:8-9). Therefore Job takes the last resort of making an oath, by which he opens the hearing, no matter whether anyone is listening or not.[350] Job's second accusation against God is that His unwillingness to hear Job has embittered Job's soul (27:2d; cf. 3:20; 7:11; 10:1; 21:25). Ironically, "Job swears by the God who has wronged him."[351] Job's oath is paradoxical to the point of contradiction because God is both his accuser and the source of justice.[352]

With another formula of exclamatory oath ...חָלִילָה לִּי...עַד־אֶגְוָע (Far be it from me...Till I die), Job swears to condemn his friends and to hold fast to his integrity (27:5). If Brown claims that Job's oath of innocence here "represents a high-water mark in Job's self-defense,"[353] I would suggest that it also marks a high-point in Job's condemnation against his friends, which is well illustrated by אִם־אַצְדִּיק אֶתְכֶם (I will never declare you innocent) in 27:5. We have seen that the Hiphil of צדק in 27:5 carries forensic connotation, and that it affects the sense of רָשָׁע in 27:7. This oath reflects Job's strong condemnation of his friends. The forensic connotation of צדק sheds light on the interpretation of the subsequent text.

After Job's oath of innocence (vv.1-6), there follows Job's imprecation against his enemy (vv.7-10). One of the interpretive difficulties in this passage is to determine who the enemy is: God, Job's friends or someone else? Habel claims that the enemy refers to God (13:24; 16:9; 19:11ff).[354] However, Newsom rightly comments that in this context the enemy cannot be God, because "the content of the curse makes no sense on that supposition."[355] In addition, vv.8-

---

[350] Habel, *Job*, 379; and Dhorme, *Job*, 379.
[351] Rowley, *Book of Job*, 174-5.
[352] Regarding the two views of God, see Newsom, "Job," 523; Andersen, *Job*, 220-1; Habel, *Job*, 379-80; Gordis, *Book of Job*, 287; and Hartley, *Job*, 369.
[353] Brown, "Deformation of Character: Job 1-31," 77.
[354] Habel claims that it cannot be Job's friends because the enemy spoken of is in the singular (but the friends are addressed in the plural in vv.11-12), and Job considers his friends as his secondary adversaries, siding with God in pursuit of Job (19:22). Therefore Habel considers God as Job's primary enemy (13:24; 16:9; 19:11ff). See Habel, *Job*, 381-2. Good also considers the enemy as God. See Good, *In Turns of Tempest*, 287-8.
[355] Newsom, "Job," 523.

9 makes it impossible that the enemy is God.[356] More importantly, the use of אָדָם רָשָׁע indicates that the enemy cannot be God. Newsom points out that the curse is more probably generic, and Dhorme claims that it is a rhetorical form of speech—"Instead of saying: 'May I not suffer the fate of the wicked!' he says: 'May my enemy suffer the fate of the wicked.'"[357]

However, in my opinion, the use of אָדָם רָשָׁע and עָרִיצִים as a standard pair of terms for the overt enemies of God in 27:13 (cf.15:20) can help us interpret who אֹיְבִי (my enemy) refers to. The singular אָדָם רָשָׁע (a wicked man) in v.13a, which is parallel to the plural עָרִיצִים (tyrants/oppressors) in v.13b, is collective, referring to a group of people.[358] In my opinion, the singular אֹיְבִי (my enemy) in v.7 refers to Job's friends as a group.[359] Job addresses his friends in vv.11-12. Concerning the flow of the text, it seems very natural that vv.11-12 are connected with the preceding (vv.7-10) and subsequent verses (vv.13-23). Therefore it is more reasonable to interpret vv.7-10 as an imprecation against Job's friends.

With another kind of oath formula יְהִי כְרָשָׁע אֹיְבִי (Let my enemy be as the wicked) in v.7, Job invokes a curse against his friends. Then the imprecatory curse in 27:7 is supported by the sayings about the wicked in 27:8-10. Job says the sort of thing the friends usually say, but now he directs it, with heavy irony, at them. This is not just parody (as Janzen thought) but a powerful turning of the tables on the friends. Thus, after swearing a series of oaths in 27:1-6, Job utters an imprecation on his friends (vv.7-10).

By using the second person masculine plural suffixes (once in v.11 and 4 times in v.12), Job addresses his friends with an intent to instruct them about God's power (יַד־אֵל; v.11).[360] He will not conceal what is in God's mind and thought (אֲשֶׁר עִם־שַׁדַּי, lit. "what is with the Almighty").[361] God's power and what God has in mind ironically imply God's punishment upon the wicked, which Job will declare in vv.13-23. In v.12 Job concludes with a final rejection of

---

[356] Whybray, *Job*, 119.
[357] Newsom, "Job," 523; and Dhorme, *Job*, 382.
[358] Hartley, *Job*, 358, n.2; Gordis, *Book of Job*, 294; and Habel, *Job*, 383.
[359] Janzen, *Job*, 185.
[360] יַד (lit. "the hand") means "strength" or "power." See Hartley, *Job*, 371; Gordis, *Book of Job*, 289; and Newsom, "Job," 524.
[361] The idiom "what is with the Almighty" (v.11b) means "what is in His mind and thought" or "what God has in mind" (10:13b; 23:14b). See Dhorme, *Job*, 385; and Gordis, *Book of Job*, 289.

his friends' false speech about God. If they have seen God's power and purpose (v.12a), it is incomprehensible that they speak so vainly (v.12b).

In English, וְלָמָּה־זֶּה הֶבֶל תֶּהְבָּלוּ (v.12b) can literally be rendered as "Why do you become vain with vanity?"[362] However, the English translation cannot sufficiently express the original sense of the seriousness of the wrongdoing. In regard to the connotations of הֶבֶל Fredericks has given the following definition:

> This word functions as a metaphor for "insubstantial because false." הֶבֶל is used 32x to appraise the substantiality of personal action or heretical cults on the basis of their veracity or falsity. In a "Deuteronomic" sense, הֶבֶל refers to the components of false religions. In some passages הֶבֶל is nearly a synonym for "idol," e.g. Jer 10:8; 14:22.... Also false speech is of no value because of its deception or ignorance. Job and his friends exchange insults about their vain comments that lack wisdom (21:34; 27:12; 35:16; cf. Ps 94:11; Eccl 5:7 [6]; 6:11).[363]

From the above definition, the use of הֶבֶל indicates that the sin of false speech (Job 27:12) is as serious as worshipping false gods. הֶבֶל is actually used as an accusation of wickedness here. Fox also points out that הֶבֶל in Job 27:12 combines the connotations of both "vanity" and "deceit". "Vanity" means something worthless, while "deceit" means "lies," which makes הֶבֶל a fitting epithet for false gods.[364] Fox's definition also demonstrates that the English translation of הֶבֶל simply as "vanity" cannot express the connotation to its fullest sense. In what way have the friends acted so vainly? First, they did not speak truly of Job (v.5). Second, they did not speak truly of God either (vv.11-12), and this can be seen in God's comments on the friends in 42:7-8. Once again, Job turns the tables on the friends. They made themselves his teachers, but now he will teach them.

The final section of the chapter (vv.13-23) should be read as Job's speech. In addition, אָדָם רָשָׁע and עָרִיצִים should be understood as Job's friends for two reasons. First, it is in accordance with the

---

[362] Brown, Driver and Briggs, *BDB*, 211.
[363] D. C. Fredericks, "הֶבֶל," *NIDOTTE 1* (ed. W. A. VanGemeren; Grand Rapids: Zondervan, 1997) 1005-6.
[364] To sort out the meaning of הֶבֶל in the Hebrew Bible, Fox lists six meanings of this word: 1) ephermerality; 2) vanity; 3) nothingness; 4) incomprehensibility, mystery; 5) deceit; and 6) senselessness, nonsense. See M. V. Fox, *A Time to Tear Down and a Time to Build Up: A Rereading of Ecclesiastes* (Grand Rapids: Eerdmans, 1999) 28-9.

natural flow of the text to understand them in this way. Job addresses his friends in vv.11-12, strongly criticizing the wickedness of their false speeches, because they do not speak truly of God. In v.5 Job swears not to declare his friends to be innocent because they do not speak truly of him. In this context אָדָם רָשָׁע in v.13 corresponds with אִם־אַצְדִּיק in v.5. Both carry a forensic sense. Here רָשָׁע is better rendered "guilty" than "wicked." Previously, Job's friends falsely accused him of sin. Now Job claims that they are guilty of speaking falsely about him (v.5) and God (vv.11-12). Therefore Job turns the tables and proclaims God's judgment upon his friends in vv.13-23.

The use of עִם־אֵל in v.13 provides the second reason for reading אָדָם רָשָׁע and עָרִיצִים as Job's friends. עִם־אֵל (with God) meaning "in God's mind" or "stored up with Him"[365] in v.13 parallels עִם־שַׁדַּי (with the Almighty) in v.11. This suggests that vv.11-12 and vv.13-23 should be connected together. These catch-words serve as a linkage to bring out an ironical sense here. Job will teach his friends the power of God, and what is in the mind of the Almighty he will not conceal (v.11). Job is going to tell his friends what is in God's mind for them: the portion of the guilty (חֵלֶק־אָדָם רָשָׁע) and the inheritance of the tyrants (נַחֲלַת עָרִיצִים; v.13).

Job 27:13-23 focuses on the destiny of the wicked, depicting the destruction of their family by war, famine and pestilence; the ephemeral nature of their wealth; and the annihilation of the wicked by terrors, storms and east wind.

Besides the fact that Job's sayings in 27:13-23 are contradictory to his predominant stance in the first two cycles, there are other seeming contradictions between 27:1-12 and 27:13-23. Earlier Job swears not to concede his friends' viewpoint (vv.5-6) and regards their counsels as empty speech (vv.11-12), whereas in vv.13-23 Job confirms his friends' standpoint. Furthermore, Job accuses God when he swears by His name (v.2), but then affirms God's justice by depicting His punishment upon the wicked (vv.13-23). Again, as in Job 23-24 and Job 25-26, the author's use of contradictory juxtaposition as a rhetorical strategy is evident in Job 27.

–ve (vv.1-12)	a) Job accuses God of taking away his right to present his case, and of embittering his soul (v.2)

---

[365] Gordis, *Book of Job*, 289, 294.

                    b) Job rejects his friends' false speech about himself (vv.5-6)
                    c) Job rejects his friends' false speech about God (vv.11-12)

+ve (vv.13-23)   a) Job affirms God's justice by declaring the fate of the wicked
                    b) Job's viewpoint is the same as his friends'

The above contradictory juxtaposition in fact serves a crucial role in the flow of argument within the development of the story. By using contradictory juxtaposition, Job 27 marks the climax of condemnation regarding the friends' falsehood. Previously, the friends proclaimed the fate of the wicked to accuse Job as a evildoer. Now Job does the same to his friends by declaring the punishment of the wicked upon them (vv.13-23), who speak falsely of Job (vv.5-6) and of God (vv.11-12). Job turns the tables and uses his friends' argument as a weapon against them. This is heavily ironic. But it needs to be noted again that it is not mere parody. The crucial thing is that, in the flow of the argument, Job uses his friends' words against them. In so doing, he silences them, though we know that the issues are not yet settled. Such a declaration of punishment has driven them into total silence, a state Job requested of them in 13:5. They disappear from the stage until the epilogue's judgment against them at 42:7, and Job is allowed to have his say for four more continuous chapters (Job 28-31) as his final defence and call for God to appear.

2. *The Rhetorical Impacts upon the Audience*

Job's proclamation of judgment on his friends (27:13-23), together with his oath of innocence (27:1-12), serves to impact the audience in several ways. First, it provokes the audience to contrast Job's truthfulness and the friends' untruthfulness. As far as Job is concerned, throughout the three speech cycles, he holds fast to his integrity, and defends his innocence to the end. With great courage he questions the clash between reality and belief, challenges divine justice (e.g. Job 21; 24), and denies the friends' false allegations (e.g. Job 26; 27). The audience can affirm the consistency of Job's honesty. However, the friends' zealous attempts to defend their own theology have driven them to make unjust accusations about Job. At Job's expense they even twist the truth to fit their theology and falsely accuse Job of being sinful (e.g. Job 20; 22). The audience can thus recognise that the friends are not truthful, because from the very beginning of the story, they already know that Job is a blameless, upright man. The audience can confirm their judgment later, when the story comes to God's final verdict in 42:7-8, where God commends Job's truthfulness and denounces the friends' untruthfulness. The dialogue shows the audience that the road to "moral perfection no longer subsumes but opposes unquestioning acceptance."[366]

Secondly, Job's pronouncement of judgment upon his friends (27:13-23) shows a strong mockery of their misapplication of theology. Not based upon any evidence or fact, the friends apply the theodicies wrongly to explain Job's suffering. Ironically, based on the evidence of their folly and dishonesty, Job demonstrates to his friends how to apply their theology properly. Job's utterance of the destiny of the wicked is justified by God later in the epilogue, when Job is asked to intercede for the lives of his three friends. Job has to sacrifice a burnt offering for them, so that God's judgment will not befall them according to their folly (42:7-9). Therefore Job's ironical use of the orthodox saying in 27:13-23 reminds the audience that there are some experiences in real life which are beyond theological explanation, and that the misapplication of theology could bring disaster and judgment. To call the friends "the wicked" would shock the audience because the friends are supposed to be the wise in the community.

Thirdly, Job's declaration of the fate of the wicked (27:13-23) alerts the audience to perceive Job's two conflicting views of God. In Job's oath he complains that God has taken away his right, and embittered his soul (27:2). Job considers God as the cause of his suffering and questions His justice. However, his proclamation of the fate of the wicked to his friends in 27:13-23 assumes an assertion of God's justice. There is a kind of double irony in Job's words, therefore. In order to turn the tables on the friends, he has to assert what they assert, and what he otherwise questions. The audience may see this irony, but they also understand that Job's two conflicting views of God flow mainly from his ignorance of the scene in heaven. They know that God's silence is a test of his faith. "Whenever the audience is aware of elements of the plot of which the actors themselves are unaware, the suspense of true drama is present."[367] Such sus-

---

[366] Sternberg, *Poetics of Biblical Narrative*, 346.
[367] Matheney, "Major Purposes of the Book of Job," 35.

pense about the nature of God functions to arrest the audience's attention as they seek a resolution for Job's dilemma. The audience will always be concerned with whether Job can finally pass this test of faith, and how his problem can be resolved.

Finally, Job's utterance of judgment upon his friends is followed by their total silence. They seem to fade out from the scene after this point. The author deliberately lets the debate stop without giving any comment upon the friends. Alter highlights this rhetorical device:

> The more common biblical practice, as we shall have occasion to see elsewhere, is simply to cut off one speaker in a dialogue without comment, leaving us to ponder the reasons for the interrupted exchange. When someone's silence is actually isolated for narration, we may infer that the refusal or avoidance of speech is itself a significant link in the concatenation of the plot.[368]

The rhetoric of silence can produce an effect of suspense which arrests the audience's attention upon what happens next, and to sorting out who is right and true. The author suspends his evaluative point of view until the story comes to 42:7-8, where God vindicates Job by giving the final verdict upon his friends. Such evaluative suspense compels the audience to make their own judgment first, and motivates the audience to check their evaluation with God's verdict in due course.

Thus, the juxtaposition of Job's contradictory saying in 27:13-23 with his oath of innocence in 27:1-12 serves to remind the audience of the friends' folly, untruthfulness, misapplication of theology and lack of wisdom. This chapter marks the climax of the conflict between Job and the friends. In addition, the audience is assumed to realise that Job's problem here is his contradictory conception of God—a tyrant in 27:2, but a just God in 27:13-23. Furthermore, the total silence of and about the friends is the author's powerful rhetorical device: silence provokes a suspense which arrests the attention of the audience. In short, the use of contradictory juxtaposition serves to actively engage the audience in filling the gaps of ambiguity and incongruity in the story, and finding a resolution for Job's conflicts with his friends and God.

---

[368] Alter, *Biblical Narrative*, 79.

VII. *Job's Contradictory Sayings in Job 28-31*

Newsom comments on Job 28: "The poem on wisdom in chap. 28 is one of the most exquisite poetic compositions of the entire Bible. Precious jewels serve as an important image within the poem and might also serve as an image for the poem itself. Like a gemstone, this poem is beautifully crafted, clear and luminous, yet full of mysterious depths. Its unique literary form and meditative tone have led many commentators to conclude that it must be a late addition to the book, rather than an integral part of its composition..."[369] As mentioned in Chapter One, Job 28 is frequently regarded as secondary, because of its incongruity within its context and also because of the problems of 28:28.

The issues of Job 28 and the scholars' approaches to those issues were thoroughly discussed in Chapter One. The basic resolutions are as follows. Janzen, Childs, Good and Whybray hold that this chapter is Job's words and an integral part of the book. However, they cannot convincingly explain the incongruity of this wisdom poem in its surrounding context. Westermann, Andersen, Sawyer, Petersen, Newsom, Hartley and Habel defend Job 28 as integral, but they treat it as an interlude or authorial comment instead of Job's speech. This reflects their attempt to avoid contradictions. Scholars who consider this chapter as a later addition differ considerably in resolving the issues. Dhorme and Gordis treat Job 28 as an interlude, while Driver-Gray regard it as an independent poem. Clines attributes it to Zophar, but Szyczygiel, Tur-Sinai and Settlemire transpose it right after 42:6.

The present study proposes that Job 28 is Job's speech and an integral part of the book. It seeks to argue that Job 28 serves an important function in its present position, and that 28:28 functions as a catalyst for moving the wheel of the narrative plot. In approaching chapter 28, we continue from our analysis of chapters 22-27, in which we have found that Job's unexpected or "orthodox" speeches can be explained as part of his dialogue with the friends and the rhetorical strategy of the author. The contradictory sayings in this wisdom poem can also be seen as a possible guide to the author's method of conveying a meaning, and of persuading an audience of a point of view. The use of rhetorical questions in this poem (28:12,

---

[369] Newsom, "Job," 528.

20) is one way in which the audience is engaged to participate in the making of the meaning of Job. Therefore a rhetorical function is assumed in the author's design of the chapter in its present position. In short, this study will explore in what way Job 28 might contribute to the developing argument of the book, and will also investigate the intended rhetorical impacts of Job's contradictory sayings in this chapter upon the audience so as to bring change to the exigency.

Job 28's content is studied first. Next the characteristics of Job's sayings in Job 28 are set out by comparing this passage with the friends' sayings, Job's other sayings and the Yahweh speeches. There then follows a brief summary of the commentators' approaches to the issue of Job 28, thoroughly discussed in Chapter One. Finally, this study proceeds to argue that Job's contradictory sayings in Job 28 are part of the author's rhetorical strategy to convey a meaning, and to effect rhetorical impacts upon the audience.

A. *The Content*

Job 27:1 is marked by an introductory formula: "And Job again took up his discourse (מָשָׁל) and said", repeated exactly in 29:1. However, there is no separate introduction in either chapter 28 or chapters 30 and 31. This indicates that the author wants chapters 27-28 and chapters 29-31 to be understood as two distinct speeches of Job.[370]

The structure of Job 28 is clearly marked by the refrain: "But where shall wisdom be found? And where is the place of understanding?" (vv.12, 20),[371] which separates the poem into three sections: a) there is no known road to wisdom (vv.1-11); b) wisdom's value is beyond purchase (vv.12-19); and c) God alone has it (vv.20-27), and man can possess it only through submission to God (v.28).[372]

The opening כִּי[373] in v.1 functions as an asseverative particle,

---

[370] Whybray, *Job*, 18.
[371] Verse 20 is slightly different from v.12.
[372] Rowley, *Book of Job*, 179.
[373] The opening כִּי has led some scholars to think that there should have been some lines before v.1. Peake follows Duhm to move the refrain before v.1, while Szczygiel inserts Job 28 after 42:6, where he thinks כִּי has a better connection. See Peake, *Job*, 245-6; B. Duhm, *Das Buch Hiob Erklärt* (KHC; Tübingen: J. C. B. Mohr, 1897); and Szczygiel, *Job*, 234-5. Hartley rejects Duhm's reconstruction because it lessens the impact of the refrain. He suggests that the כִּי possibly works in conjunction with the *waw* of v.12. The כִּי introduces things accessible, while the *waw* introduces things inaccessible. See Hartley, *Job*, 373.

indicating a beginning with the stress "surely," "certainly," or "yea."[374] It is awkward to translate כִּי as "for/because" here as the causal relationship is not immediately obvious.[375] To render it as "surely" does not necessarily mean that Job 28 is out of context.[376] The relation between the poem and its context should not be conditioned by the particle כִּי. Job could quite easily have started his new speech with an affirmative like "surely." I will show the connection between chatpers 27 and 28 fully later.

In vv.1-2 Job's poem expresses the human ability of mining ores—silver, gold, iron and copper, and refining them. By emphasizing that the rare metals have their specified places, the poet paves the way for asking about the location of wisdom in vv.12 and 20.[377] מוֹצָא (mine, lit. "place of coming forth") and מָקוֹם (place) in v.1 parallel מָקוֹם (place) and מָצָא (Niphal, "be found") in v.12 too. Newsom comments: "Thus the contrast is established. There is a site where silver can be found and a place for gold, but where can wisdom be found, or where is the place of understanding?"[378]

The hymn proceeds to depict that, with lamps or torches, the miners put an end to darkness (v.3a). They even go to the farthest limit (לְכָל־תַּכְלִית) to search (חָקַר) for the stone hidden in the thick darkness (v.3b, c). The miners take the risk to probe to the edge and limit of the earth, but wisdom lies even further beyond (cf. 11:6-9). The poet uses the word "limit" to anticipate the human search for wisdom (28:12), which only God can probe (חָקַר; 28:27).

The metaphor of "putting an end to darkness" echoes the victory of God in overcoming the chaos when God made light, "putting an end" to the "darkness over the surface of the deep" in His first act. Geller rightly observes that the poet's tactic in v.3 is "to describe a human activity in terms which echo godhood. This form of hyperbole will culminate in verses 9-11."[379] Geller adds that the main purpose of this strategy is to prepare the audience to be aware of an ironic contrast between total human ignorance and perfect

---

[374] Brown, Driver and Briggs, *BDB*, 472; Dhorme, *Job*, 399; Gordis, *Book of Job*, 304; Hartley, *Job*, 373, n.1 of 28:1; and P. P. Zerafa, *The Wisdom of God in the Book of Job* (Rome: Herder, 1978) 137-8.
[375] Good translates כִּי as "for"; see Good, *In Turns of Tempest*, 123.
[376] Some scholars (REB, NIV, Hartley and Pope) simply leave it untranslated; see Pope, *Job*, 197; and Hartley, *Job*, 373.
[377] Habel, *Job*, 395.
[378] Newsom, "Job," 529.
[379] Geller, "Where is Wisdom?: Job 28," 159.

divine knowledge, which will not appear overtly until vv.13 and 23.³⁸⁰

The miners reach the place of precious minerals despite the remoteness and difficult accessibility of the mines (vv.4-6). In discovering the path to precious gems, human beings are superior over all earthly creatures: the bird of prey (עַיִט), the falcon (אַיָּה), and the proud beasts (בְּנֵי־שָׁחַץ) including the lion (שָׁחַל; vv.7-8). Here human beings are prized more than all of the earth's other admirable creatures.

The human achievement of delving into the earth reaches its pinnacle in vv.9-11.³⁸¹ Miners break through the hardest rocks (v.9a), and overturn mountains at the roots (הָפַךְ מִשֹּׁרֶשׁ הָרִים) in their search for treasures (v.9b). Man's power is like that of God, who also "overturns the mountains" (Job 9:5; cf. Hab 3:6). Verses 10-11 highlight human controls over mountains and waters. Here man's power is like that of God, who "splits" the earth with rivers (Hab 3:9; Ps 74:15). In addition, human success in seeing precious treasures (v.10b) and bringing hidden treasures out (v.11b) also echoes God's ability to bring things from darkness to light (12:22).³⁸²

The description of human success in vv.1-11 is, in fact, an important tactic to make a sharp contrast with the subsequent text. Newsom correctly points out: "In the overall strategy of the poem, however, the pinnacle of power and achievement that mining represents is used as a foil for the utter inability of human striving to find and secure something much more precious: wisdom."³⁸³

The second section of the poem (vv.12-19) commences with the *waw* "but wisdom..." (v.12), which carries a strong adversative force, alerting the audience that something contrasting will be brought out in the subsequent context. The double question in v.12 is the heart of the poem.³⁸⁴ It poses the pivotal question of the chapter.³⁸⁵ Different parts of the poem are closely tied with this pivotal question as follows. Humans are able to unearth precious stones and ores and bring them to light from their hidden places, where no bird or beast

---

³⁸⁰ Geller, "Where is Wisdom?: Job 28," 159.
³⁸¹ Andersen, *Job*, 226; also Newsom, "Job," 530.
³⁸² Newsom, "Job," 530.
³⁸³ Newsom's comment is similar to Geller's perspective. See Newsom, "Job," 531; and Geller, "Where is Wisdom?: Job 28," 159, 164.
³⁸⁴ See Dhorme, *Job*, 406; Hartley, *Job*, 379; and Newsom, "Job," 531.
³⁸⁵ Habel, *Job*, 397.

can reach them (vv.1-11). However, they are still asking the question: where can wisdom be found? (v.12). The way to wisdom cannot be discovered by humanity, in spite of their ingenuity, skill and knowledge (v.13); man cannot buy wisdom in exchange for valuable jewels (vv.13-19). From where, then, does wisdom come (v.20)? God alone knows its place and way (v.23) because of His all-seeing character (v.24). In the act of creation, God perceives wisdom (vv.25-27). Man can possess wisdom only through a dependent relationship with God—fearing God and shunning evil (v.28).[386]

With the use of rhetorical questions in v.12, the audience is addressed and engaged to find answers. Such rhetorical questions have prepared the audience to receive a negative answer: man does not know its place (עֶרְכָּהּ).[387] For human beings, the way to wisdom is untraceable and inaccessible (v.13a), and wisdom is not even found in the land of the living (בְּאֶרֶץ הַחַיִּים; v.13b).

Wisdom is not located in the deep (תְּהוֹם; v.14a), which is the primordial abyss of waters under the earth (cf. Gen 1:2). The deep was considered as a great reservoir of subterranean waters (Gen 7:11; 49:25) from which "the sea" (יָם) drew its supply of water and the floods emerged.[388] Nor is wisdom located in יָם "the sea" (v.14b), which is a symbol of chaos in Canaan and Israel (cf. Ps 89:10-11

---

[386] Habel, *Job*, 397.

[387] Many scholars find that the MT עֶרְכָּהּ (its price) seems out of place here, because the theme of wisdom's value is not developed until vv.15-19. They also find that the verb מָצָא in v.13 seems to fit better with "a place" or "a way" rather than "a price." Furthermore, the use of דַּרְכָּהּ (its way) in v.23 causes them to emend the MT עֶרְכָּהּ (its price) to דַּרְכָּהּ (its way). With the support of the LXX's rendering ὁδὸν αὐτῆς (its way), Dhorme and Habel prefer the reading דַּרְכָּהּ (its way); see Dhorme, *Job*, 406-7; and Habel, *Job*, 390. Reichert argues for retaining the MT עֶרֶךְ. He points out that the other ancient versions also corroborate MT, but unfortunately does not acknowledge which ancient versions they are. Reichert states: "Price must be understood in the sense that Wisdom is not an article to be found among the merchandise purchasable in a market-place. The second line establishes this meaning." However, he does not explain how the second line supports his interpretation; see Reichert, *Job*, 142-3. Gordis argues that it is unnecessary to make any emendation, because עֶרֶךְ may also mean "order, row, disposition" and here it means "place"; see Gordis, *Book of Job*, 308. Dahood, Pope and Hartley read עֶרֶךְ as "house" or "abode" on the basis of the Ugaritic parallel between עֶרֶךְ and בֵּית see J. Nougayrol et al., ed., *Ugaritica*, V (Paris: Imprimerie Nationale, 1968) 12:3-4; M. J. Dahood, "Hebrew-Ugaritic Lexicography VII," *Bib* 50 (1969) 355; Hartley, *Job*, 378; and Pope, *Job*, 203. I agree that emendation is unnecessary. Both Gordis' rendering as "its place" and the rendering of Dahood, Hartley and Pope as "its house" or "abode" sound acceptable.

[388] Dhorme, *Job*, 407; Reichert, *Job*, 143; Rowley, *Book of Job*, 182; and Andersen, *Job*, 227.

[9-10]; Deut 30:12-14; Job 38:16). According to Canaanite mythology, יָם is the primordial sea god which was conquered by the storm god Baal in the battle to establish cosmic order. The Israelite authors use יָם as a metaphor and tradition to describe the chaotic force or foe over which Yahweh was victorious.[389] Here, in v.14, "the deep" and "the sea" are personified to say: "Wisdom is not in/with me." Man is able to penetrate beyond the land of the living into the region of chaos. However, he cannot find wisdom even in those dark remote places, because it does not dwell there. The personification of "the deep" and "the sea" ironically brings out a sharp contrast that the primordial deep and the chaotic force "the sea" do not know wisdom; only the creator Yahweh knows it (v.23).

Newsom correctly notes that the passage of vv.15-19 "has a list-like quality, as the same point is made in subtly varying sentences."[390] There is a long list of precious gems and metals (silver, five expressions of gold and seven different gemstones), indicating both wealth and the technological skill of mining highly prized in vv.1-11. In addition, Newsom points out that there is "a list-like quality in the synonymous verbs for exchange or value"[391] in this passage—נָתַן (be given) and שָׁקַל (be weighed) in v.15; סָלָה (be weighed/valued) in v.16; עָרַךְ (compare/equal) in v.17; עָרַךְ (compare/equal) and סָלָה (be weighed/valued) in v.19. לֹא יְזֻכַּר (not be mentioned) in v.18 interrupts the sequence, but it carries more or less the same sense of meaning. The negative particle לֹא (not) is repeated in every verse, governing the whole section.[392] It reveals another aspect of the inaccessibility of wisdom: it cannot be acquired in exchange for precious stones and metals, no matter how rare or valuable they are.[393] In sum, the second section of the poem (vv.12-19) mainly points out that wisdom cannot be found and purchased.

The last section of the poem (vv.20-28) starts with a rhetorical question, which repeats that in v.12 with a little variation, asking how wisdom might be discovered or secured. This question being raised a second time marks the climax of the reality: "nowhere" can wisdom be found. The answer lies in the third strophe (vv.20-28):

---

[389] See Habel's commentary on Job 7:12; Habel, *Job*, 162; also Pope, *Job*, 60-1.
[390] Newsom, "Job," 531.
[391] Newsom, "Job," 531.
[392] Newsom, "Job," 531.
[393] Habel, *Job*, 398.

wisdom can be found only in God (v.23), while man can get it only by submission to God (v.28).

Verses 21-22 highlight that wisdom cannot be found among the living (v.21) or in the realm of the dead (v.22).[394] The poet makes a parallel between vv.21-22 and vv.13-14:

כָּל־חָי (all the living; v.21a) // בְּאֶרֶץ הַחַיִּים (in the land of the living; v.13b)

אֲבַדּוֹן (Abaddon) and מָוֶת (death; v.22) // תְּהוֹם (the deep) and יָם (the sea; v.14)

Verses 21-22 emphasize not only the inaccessibility of wisdom to mortals, but also its hiddenness (v.21): נֶעֶלְמָה (be hidden) and נִסְתָּרָה (be concealed). Human beings are able to bring to light the hidden things (תַּעֲלֻמָה; v.11b), which even the birds of prey and proud beasts cannot detect (vv.7-8). However, wisdom is hidden (נֶעֶלְמָה) from the eyes of all the living (v.21).[395]

Instead of the sea and the deep claiming the absence of wisdom in their domains (v.14), Abaddon and death state that they have only a rumour about wisdom's place, but they have no actual knowledge of it (v.22). "Abaddon" is a synonym of Sheol, meaning "destruction or dissolution" (Job 26:6; 31:12; Prov 15:11; 27:20).[396] מָוֶת (death) may refer to the Canaanite deity Mot, god of death and king of the underworld (cf. 18:13-14).[397] "To hear with the ears" means that it is just secondhand, hearsay evidence (cf. Job 42:5; 2 Sam 7:22; Ps 44:2 [1]).[398] In fact, 28:22 makes an ironic contrast with 28:23, 24, 27. Abaddon and the god of death/king of the underworld Mot have merely heard about (שָׁמַע) wisdom (v.22) by rumour, a shadow of the real thing. However, the creator Yahweh knows (יָדַע) the way to wisdom (v.23) because He sees (יִרְאֶה) everything under the whole heaven (v.24). He even sees (רָאָה) wisdom (v.27) in His act of creation. Obviously, Mot is ironically contrasted with the creator Yahweh, while "hearing" is contrasted with "seeing." שָׁמַע in v.22 thus serves as a transition to v.23.[399] Newsom correctly points out the function of vv.21-22, "These tantalizing words prepare for the

---

[394] Habel, *Job*, 398; and Newsom, "Job," 531.
[395] Habel, *Job*, 398.
[396] Habel, *Job*, 398; and Reichert, *Job*, 133, 144.
[397] Habel, *Job*, 398.
[398] Pope, *Job*, 205.
[399] Geller, "Where is Wisdom?: Job 28," 165.

climactic statement in v.23":[400] "Only God understands its way and He knows its place."

אֱלֹהִים (God) and הוּא (He) in v.23 are emphatic, marking the sharpest of contrasts between God's supremacy and human limitation.[401] God alone understands (הֵבִין) the way to wisdom and knows (יָדַע) its dwelling place (v.23). In contrast to man, God surveys (יַבִּיט) His entire universe and sees (יִרְאֶה) everything under the whole heaven (v.24). God is able to discern wisdom's place (v.23) because of His "all-seeing" character (v.24).[402] In v.24 the pronoun הוּא (He) is again emphatic, highlighting God as an "all-seeing" deity.[403] In short, the poet seems to connect the reason for God's knowledge of wisdom's place (v.23) with His ability to look to the ends of the earth and see everything under heaven (v.24).[404]

Verses 25-27 are linked together by an intricate grammatical structure, where v.25 and v.26 are subordinate clauses, introducing the clause v.27. בַּעֲשׂתוֹ לַמָּטָר חֹק (v.26a) ...לַעֲשׂוֹת לָרוּחַ מִשְׁקָל (v.25a)... אָז רָאָהּ (v.27a) is literally translated as "at (the time of) the making of a weight for the wind (v.25a)...in the setting of a limit for the rain (v.26a)...then He saw it (v.27a)..." More fluently, it can be rendered as "when...when...then..." Newsom further notes that the "when" clauses set up a relationship of simultaneity. That is to say, "in the act of" creating the world, לַעֲשׂוֹת (v.25a) and בַּעֲשׂתוֹ (v.26a), God perceived wisdom (v.27). According to Newsom, such grammatical structure sheds a new light on the references about wisdom's place: it is not a location, but is found in the act of creativity.[405] Geller rightly comments:

> But with lightning speed, almost before the reader can follow it, this lively poem makes a new swerve, this time from the spatial dimensions (vertical and horizontal) that have hitherto dominated it to the temporal. The "place" of wisdom is not where, but when, and "when" lies in the distant past, at the time of creation.[406]

In vv.25-26, God, who alone possesses wisdom, is seen to have carefully set the weight for the wind (v.25a), measured the amount of rainful (v.25b), regulated the law to govern the rain (v.26a), and

---

[400] Newsom, "Job," 532.
[401] Newsom, "Job," 532; and Reichert, *Job*, 144.
[402] Habel, *Job*, 399.
[403] Reichert, *Job*, 144.
[404] Newsom, "Job," 532; and Habel, *Job*, 399.
[405] Newsom, "Job," 532; and Janzen, *Job*, 197.
[406] Geller, "Where is Wisdom?: Job 28," 166.

made a way for the thunderbolt (v.26b). These wonders of nature demonstrate God's employment of wisdom in structuring the world order. In the acts of creating the world (vv.25-26), God saw and declared wisdom; He established it and searched it out (v.27). The tense of vv.25-26 is governed by the four perfect verbs of the main clause in v.27, which bring the reader back to the primeval past.

The suffixes of the four verbs in v.27—הֱכִינָהּ...יְסַפְּרָהּ...רָאָהּ... חֲקָרָהּ—refer to "wisdom."[407] These four verbs are chiastically parallel. God saw (רָאָה) wisdom. Contrasting with the "hearing" about wisdom in v.22, "seeing" here means the firsthand knowledge of wisdom. Next God declared (Piel of ספר) it and established (Hiphil of כון) it as the principle of His creation. The final verb חָקַר (search out/probe) is parallel with the first verb רָאָה (see/discover) and it echoes the earlier use of the verb חָקַר in v.3. Just as human beings "search out" the depths of the dark earth for the hidden treasures (v.3), God "searched out" wisdom to fathom her depths (v.27b).[408] Reichert comments on the four verbs of v.27: "The impressive array of verbs conveys the idea of God thoroughly examining and exploring Wisdom in all its manifold complexity as though it were a concrete object or idea with a separate task."[409] To sum up, the general sense of v.27 is that "God perfectly fathomed the nature of Wisdom."[410] Then the poem ends with God's promise that man can acquire wisdom only by fearing God and turning away from evil (v.28).

In sum, the first section (vv.1-11) highlights that despite the godlike power of human beings to search and mine precious minerals, man cannot find wisdom. The second section (vv.12-19) points out that in spite of human achievement in technical and research skills, no one knows where wisdom is. Nor can wisdom be acquired in exchange for all the precious metals and jewels in the world. The final section (vv.20-28) stresses that wisdom cannot be found among

---

[407] Scott L. Harris refers the 3rd feminine singular suffixes of these four verbs to "creation" rather than "wisdom" on the grounds that there is no reference in Hebrew where wisdom is used as the object of any of the four verbs, but these verbs have been employed in many places to depict God's role in creation. Harris states that "creation" is used as the object in vv.24-26. He adds that in Hebrew construction it is legitimate to refer the 3rd feminine singular suffixes in v.27 to the preceding content. See S. L. Harris, "Wisdom or Creation? A New Interpretation of Job XXVIII 27," *VT* 33 (1983) 419-27.

[408] Habel, *Job*, 400.

[409] Reichert, *Job*, 145.

[410] Rowley, *Book of Job*, 185.

the living or in the realm of the dead. God alone knows its way and place. Wisdom is found in the act of God's creation. Man can acquire wisdom only through submission to God.

B. *The Characteristics of Job's Contradictory Sayings in Job 28*

In order to understand why some scholars claim that Job 28 is more like the friends' speech (especially Zophar's) than Job's, and why they argue that the present position of Job 28 brings the book to a premature anticlimax, we will investigate the characteristics of this chapter by comparing it with Zophar's speech in 11:5-12, with the Yahweh speeches and with its nearest context (Job 27; Job 29-31).

1. *Job 28 in Comparison with Job 11:5-12*

Some scholars (e.g. Clines) reject this chapter as Job's speech because it sounds like the argument of Job's friends, especially Zophar's hymn in 11:5-12.[411] A comparison between these two passages can be summarized as follows.

Job 11:5-12 is Zophar's praise of God. The "mysteries/depths" (הַחֵקֶר) and the "limit" (תַּכְלִית) of God in v.7 are synonyms for the "secrets of wisdom" (תַּעֲלָמוֹת חָכְמָה) in v.6, which are beyond human understanding.[412] Therefore, when 11:7-9 depicts that the mysteries and limit of God are unfathomed in length, width, height and depth, it also means that wisdom is unfathomed and beyond all boundaries too.[413]

Similar keywords

    11:7   הַחֵקֶר (mysteries/depths, root of חָקַר "search out")...תַּכְלִית (limit)
    28:3   וּלְכָל־תַּכְלִית הוּא חוֹקֵר And to the farthest limit he (the miner) searches out.
    28:27   הֱכִינָהּ וְגַם־חֲקָרָהּ He (God) established it and also searched it out.

Wisdom beyond all boundaries

    11:8-9   It is higher than the heaven...deeper than Sheol... longer than the earth... broader than the sea.

---

[411] Clines, *Job 1-20*, lix.
[412] Habel, *Job*, 208.
[413] God's inexhaustible wisdom is beyond every boundary in the created order, expressed by the four dimensions—height, depth, length and breadth—which relate to heaven, Sheol, earth and sea. See Hartley, *Job*, 197-8.

28:13-14	It is not found in the land of the living...not in the deep...not in the sea.
28:22	Abaddon and death (similar to Sheol) have just heard of it.

Rhetorical questions bringing the theme of wisdom's inaccessibility

11:7-8	Can you discover the depths of God? Can you discover the limits of the Almighty? It is higher than the heaven, what can you do? Deeper than Sheol, what can you know?
28:12	But where can wisdom be found? And where is the place of understanding?
28:20	Where then does wisdom come from? And where is the place of understanding?

As the above comparisons demonstrate, both Job 28 and Zophar's speech in 11:5-12 stress the unsearchableness of wisdom by asking rhetorical questions. In addition, these two passages share some keywords and both highlight that wisdom is beyond all boundaries. One difference between the two passages may be noted however. In 11:5-12 Zophar is addressing Job in particular. He seems to be calling Job "an idiot" (v.12). However, Job 28 is about humanity in general—אֱנוֹשׁ (v.13) and אָדָם (v.28)—who cannot have access to wisdom.

2. Job 28 in Comparison with the Yahweh Speeches

Some scholars (e.g. Rowley) reject Job 28 as belonging to Job because its content is very similar to the Yahweh speeches (Job 38-41), making the rest of the book an anticlimax.[414] A comparison between Job 28 and the Yahweh speeches is made here to see how similar these two passages are.

Repetition of terminology and phraseology

28:8	בְּנֵי־שָׁחַץ	the proud beast
41:26 [34]	בְּנֵי־שָׁחַץ	the proud beast
28:24	תַּחַת כָּל־הַשָּׁמַיִם יִרְאֶה	He sees under the whole heaven

---

[414] See Andersen, *Job*, 223; Dell, *Book of Job*, 196, n.105; Gordis, *Book of Job*, 298; Hartley, *Job*, 26; and Rowley, *Book of Job*, 179.

41:3 [11]	תַּחַת כָּל־הַשָּׁמַיִם לִי־הוּא Whatever is under the whole heaven is Mine
28:26	וְדֶרֶךְ לַחֲזִיז קֹלוֹת And a way for the thunder bolt
38:25	וְדֶרֶךְ לַחֲזִיז קֹלוֹת And a way for the thunder bolt
28:14 // 38:16	תְּהוֹם (the deep)...יָם (the sea)
28:3 // 38:17	צַלְמָוֶת darkness/the shadow of the death
28:22 // 38:17	מָוֶת death
28:12, 20, 28	חָכְמָה (wisdom)...בִּינָה (understanding)
38:4	בִּינָה understanding
38:36	חָכְמָה (wisdom)...בִּינָה (understanding)
39:17	חָכְמָה (wisdom)...בִּינָה (understanding)

Passages on creation

28:25a // 38:24b	wind
28:25b // 38:8-11, 16, 34	waters
28:26a // 38:25a, 28a, 34, 37	rain
28:26b // 38:25b	thunderbolt

Descriptions of the living creatures

28:7, 21	bird of prey, falcon	38:39	the prey of lion
28:8	lion, the proud beast	38:41	the prey of the raven
28:21	all living creatures	Job 39	different kinds of wild lives
		Job 40-41	Behemoth & Leviathan

The use of a refrain in rhetorical question form

28:12	Where can wisdom be found? And where is the place of understanding?
28:20	Where then does wisdom come from? And where is the place of understanding?
38:19	Where is the way to the dwelling of light? And darkness, where is its place?
38:24	Where is the way that the light is provided, or the east wind scattered on the earth?

Personification

28:14	The deep says, "It is not in me"; And the sea says, "It is not with me."
28:22	Abaddon and death say, "With our ears we have heard a report of it."

38:35		Can you send forth lightnings that they may go and say to you, "Here we are"?
39:25		As often as the trumpet sounds he (the horse) says, "Aha!"

Submission to God

28:28	Fearing God and shunning evil
40:1-5	Job's first confession
42:1-6	Job's second confession

Wisdom beyond human limitations

28:13	Man does not know its way
28:21	Thus it is hidden from the eyes of all living
38:2	Who is this that darkens counsel by words without knowledge?
40:4	Behold, I am insignificant; what can I reply to Thee?
42:3	Who is this that hides counsel without knowledge? Therefore I have declared that which I did not understand, things too wonderful for me, which I did not know.

Job 28 and the Yahweh speeches share the same theme: man does not know the way to wisdom; God alone knows that. These two passages also share many commonalities. The expression of בְּנֵי־שָׁחַץ (the proud beast) in 28:8 is repeated only once in 41:26 [34] and nowhere else. The phrase תַּחַת כָּל־הַשָּׁמַיִם (under the whole heaven) in 28:24 recurs in the depiction of the Leviathan (41:3 [11]). In addition, the phrase וְדֶרֶךְ לַחֲזִיז קֹלוֹת (And a way for the thunderbolt) in 28:26b is repeated verbatim in 38:25b. The motifs of the deep and the sea in 28:14 have parallels in 38:16. The description of the netherworld appears in 28:3, 22 and 38:17. Furthermore, the synonyms of חָכְמָה (wisdom) and בִּינָה (understanding) in 28:12, 20 and 28 are used several times again in the Yahweh speeches (38:4, 36; 39:17). Basically, the content of creation (28:24-26) is expanded in chapter 38.[415] The illustration of nature being like the bird of prey, falcon, lion, the proud beast and all living creatures in 28:7-8, 21 is amplified in 38:39, 41 and Job 39-41.

In terms of style, Settlemire correctly notes that the refrain expressed in rhetorical question form in 28:12 and 28:20 also occurs in 38:19 and 38:24.[416] In addition, the style of personification in Job 28 can also be seen in the Yahweh speeches. In 28:14 both the deep

---

[415] Dhorme, *Job*, xcvii.
[416] Settlemire, "The Original Position of Job 28," 296.

and the sea speak. In 28:22 Abaddon and death speak. In 38:35 the lightnings are represented saying, "Here we are." In 39:25 the horse shows his readiness for battle by saying "Aha" when he hears the sound of the trumpet.[417]

In Job 28, after the description of the inaccessibility of wisdom to human (28:1-19) and God's access to wisdom in the act of creation (28:20-27), there comes the confession of fearing God and shunning evil as the human's only way of gaining wisdom (28:28). Similarly, in the divine speeches Yahweh demonstrates to Job the limitation of his wisdom, and how God's wisdom is revealed through His creation (38:1-39:30 and 40:15-41:26 [34]). Then follow Job's first confession in 40:1-5 and his second confession in 42:1-6. In terms of structure, Job 28 seems to be a miniature version of 38:1-42:6—a confession concerning God's wisdom in creation.

To sum up, Job 28 not only shares some of the terminologies and phraseologies with the Yahweh speeches, but more importantly, they both share a similar theme. In addition, the descriptions of God's creation and nature in Job 28 are amplified in the Yahweh speeches. Furthermore, they share similar styles such as the use of the refrain in rhetorical question form and personification. In terms of structure, the confessional statement at the end of Job 28 is similar to Job's confessions which follow Yahweh's speeches (40:1-5; 42:1-6). Based on these commonalities, some scholars find that Job 28 is so similar to the Yahweh speeches that it makes the latter an anticlimax. But actually, they overlook the fact that the most substantial difference between the two sections is their place in the book, which makes their function different in the plot of the story. We will return to it later in the chapter.

3. *Job 28 in Comparison with Job 27 and Job 29-31*

Settlemire makes this comment: "The non-relevance of chapter 28 to chapter 27 or to chapter 29 tells us that no explanation can satisfactorily justify its (Job 28) present position. Its appearance at this particular place and coming from the mouth of Job at this time would reduce the rest of the book into an illogical and unnecessary farce."[418] Settlemire's judgment prompts her to transpose Job 28 after 42:6. In order to understand the discrepancy caused by the

---

[417] Settlemire, "The Original Position of Job 28," 296.
[418] Settlemire, "The Original Position of Job 28," 299.

present position of chapter 28, we must compare it with its surrounding context.

  −ve   *Job's bitterness expressed in chapter 27*
           27:2   As God lives, who has taken away my right;
                     and the Almighty, who has embittered my soul.
           27:5   Far be it from me that I should declare you right;
                     till I die I will not put away my integrity from me.
           27:12 Behold, all of you have seen it;
                     why then do you act vainly?

  +ve   *Job's calm and orthodox reflection in chapter 28*
           28:28 And He said to man,
                     "Behold, the fear of the Lord, that is wisdom;
                     and to depart from evil is understanding."

  −ve   *Job's final defiant challenge to God in chapters 29-31*
          30:20-23 I cry out to You for help,
                     but You do not answer me;
                     I stand up, and You turn Your attention against me.
                     You have become cruel to me;
                     with the might of Your hand You persecute me.
                     You lift me up to the wind and cause me to ride;
                     and You dissolve me in a storm.
                     For I know that You will bring me to death
                     and to the house of meeting for all living.

          31:35-37 Oh that I had one to hear me!
                     Behold, here is my signature;
                     let the Almighty answer me!
                     And the indictment which my adversary has written, surely I would carry it on my shoulder;
                     I would bind it to myself like a crown.
                     I would declare to Him the number of my steps;
                     like a prince I would approach Him.

According to Settlemire, "chapter 28 was moved to the third cycle to relieve the strained tone of the speeches of Job. The bitterness expressed by Job in 27:2ff. and the egotistical self-righteousness of chapter 29ff. must have caused the editors great difficulty."[419] From the above comparison we can see how chapter 28 is often considered as incongruous in its present context, the poem being "calm" in tone and "orthodox" in content. In Job 28 there is no argumen-

---

[419] Settlemire, "The Original Position of Job 28," 299.

tation from the friends or Job. Petersen states, "In mood chapter 28 stands like a quiet pool in the midst of a raging storm."[420]

Chapter 28 is distinct from the surrounding chapters because it lacks direct address, personal reference and named speakers. This distinction is shown in the following table:[421]

Direct Address and Personal References in Chapters 22-31

* with named speaker   × without named speaker

	ch.22	ch.23	ch.24	ch.25	ch.26	ch.27	ch.28	ch.29	ch.30	ch.31
Direct Address	36	0	0	0	6	5	0	0	11	1
Personal References	3	35	2	0	0	21	0	50	52	84
Named Speaker	*	*	×	*	*	*	×	*	×	×

No introductory heading separating Job 28 from Job 27 indicates that it is a continuation of Job's speech, but the sudden shift of tone, topic and imagery it embodies arouses suspicion about whether the speaker is Job. Indeed, the introductory heading in Job 29 leads some scholars to think that Job is "resuming" his speech there, suggesting to them that Job 28 is not Job's word.[422] To sum up, the absence of direct address, personal references and introductory heading in Job 28 makes this chapter distinct from its surrounding speeches, thus causing suspicion about its speaker and originality.

Conclusion

Job 28 is frequently rejected as being Job's words because of its discrepancy in style and content from the surrounding context (Job 27; Job 29-31). In addition, this poem is often considered as an anticlimactic because of the resemblance of its style and content to the divine speeches. Furthermore, the statement in Job 28 seems out of place on Job's lips. The theme of the limitation of human wisdom in this poem is quite similar to Zophar's viewpoint in 11:5-12. However, as discussed above, although Job 28 is more like Zophar's than Job's characteristic speeches, it is not quite like Zophar's. Nor is it quite like Job 38-41. In fact, the study of Job's previous contradictory speeches in Job 24-27 shows us that Job sometimes uses language and ideas that are rather like those of his friends, and

---

[420] Petersen, "Job 28: Theological Center of Job," 100.
[421] Petersen, "Job 28: Theological Center of Job," 100.
[422] On the absence of an introductory heading in Job 28, see Newsom, "Job," 528.

unlike his predominant voice. So it is not surprising that he can utter contradictory sayings in Job 28. Job uses such language for special reasons, which will be investigated in the last part of this study.

C. *Commentators' Approaches to the Issue of Job 28*

The commentators' approaches to the issues of Job 28 have already been investigated in detail in Chapter One. We have examined the reasons for rejecting this chapter: 1) its variation from the author's style; 2) its unsuitability in Job's mouth; 3) its bringing of the book to a premature anticlimax; and 4) the problem of 28:28. It seems that those scholars who deny the authenticity of Job 28 assume that Job's language, ideas and emotion must remain consistent at all times.

But as we have seen (i.e. chs. 22-27), Job may use language and ideas which are quite like his friends', rather than his predominant stance. Despite the similarities between Job 28 and Job 38-41, Job 28 does not yet bring the book to its climax. In fact, these scholars fail to realise the special rhetorical function of 28:28 within the chapter and within its surrounding contexts, which will be examined later in this chapter.

This study argues that along with Job's other contradictory sayings in the third cycle, those in Job 28 are part of the author's strategy to make a rhetorical impact upon the audience. In the next section the contribution of Job's contradictory sayings in Job 28 to the flow of argument within the story and the intended rhetorical impact of such sayings are examined.

D. *The Rhetorical Impacts of Job's Contradictory Sayings in Job 28-31*

1. *The Flow of Argument*

a) The Wisdom Poem in Job 28

I am proposing that Job 28, as Job's speech in its present position, serves to develop the flow of argument in the story and to make a rhetorical impact upon the audience.

As we have seen, the key interpretive issues of Job 28 are: 1) the internal linkage between 28:1-27 and 28:28; and 2) the connection between Job 28 and its surrounding chapters. We need to resolve these interpretive problems in order to correctly understand the author's message, and thereby his intended impact upon the audience.

As mentioned before, some scholars deny 28:28 as an integral part of this chapter because they find it contradictory to the preceding poem. However, this verse serves to confirm vv.1-27, rather than contradicting that section.[423] More importantly, it gives an answer to, or a way of thinking about, the question expressed in vv.1-27. To properly understand the function of v.28 in this poem, it is necessary to discern the poet's literary techniques.

Habel correctly points out that the poet employs a number of polarities in this chapter. For instance, there is a site for silver and gold (vv.1-2), but nowhere can wisdom be found (vv.12, 20). In spite of their godlike power in the activity of mining (vv.3, 9-11), human beings do not find wisdom (v.13); God alone knows it (v.23). Despite its superiority over all earthly creatures in discovering precious gems (vv.7-8), mankind cannot find wisdom (v.13); only God perceives it (v.23).

Similarly, there are polarities between v.28 and other verses in the chapter. The deep, sea, Abaddon and death do not have actual knowledge of wisdom (vv.14, 22), only the creator does (v.23). Therefore, in v.28, "And He (God) said to man" (וַיֹּאמֶר לָאָדָם) stands in antithesis to the אָמַר of the deep, sea, Abaddon and death in v.14 and v.22. Thus this word of God stands as a polar opposite to the preceding text. God says to man with authority and promise: "Behold, the fear of the Lord, that is wisdom; and to depart from evil is understanding" (v.28). The poet uses this polarity to again affirm the statements made in vv.13 and 23, by declaring the only possible avenue for humanity to possess wisdom. God alone has access to wisdom, while human beings can only possess it through submission to God. Therefore v.28 serves as a direct counterbalance to vv.1-27,[424] but with the purpose of affirming the preceding poem, rather than contradicting it. It gives an answer to the questions posed in vv.1-27. This is the function of 28:28 within the chapter.

In addition, the hiddenness and availability of wisdom highlighted in Job 28 is in the same vein as in other wisdom literature. The Book of Proverbs, although for the most part it stresses the doctrine of retribution (righteousness rewarded and wickedness punished), does not neglect the perplexing and ambiguous side of life. In dealing

---

[423] Whybray, *Job*, 21.
[424] Habel, *Job*, 393.

with the more complicated way God works in creation, such as the "better-than" sayings in Proverbs (15:16-17; 16:16, 19), Van Leeuwen understands Proverbs in a different perspective:

> In general, the sages clearly believed that wise and righteous behaviour did make life better and richer, though virtue did not guarantee those consequences. Conversely, injustice, sloth, and the like generally have bad consequences. The editor-sages who structured Proverbs sought first to teach these basic "rules of life," thus the heavy emphasis on character-consequence patterns in both Proverbs 1-9 and 10-15. We must first learn the basic rules; the exceptions can come later. Though very aware of exceptions to the character-consequence rule, the sages insisted that righteousness is better than wickedness. The most fundamental and profound reason for this is that they believed that God loves the one and hates the other. For Israel's sages that sometimes seems the only answer...the sages knew that there are limits to human wisdom. General patterns may be discerned, but many particular events may be unjust, irrational, and ultimately inscrutable.[425]

Basically, then, Job 28 is in line with the teaching of Proverbs. The difference is that Job 28 starts with the limitations of human wisdom and ends with the accessibility of wisdom, while Proverbs starts with the accessibility of wisdom (the character-consequence rule) and then admits the limitations of it.

It follows that the message of Job 28 is basically in line with that of Proverbs. 28:1-27 is not necessarily contradictory to 28:28. This verse simply points out the fact that human beings have no access to wisdom, but that God alone possesses it. It gives an answer to the questions posed in vv.1-27: the only way for human beings to acquire wisdom is through their obedience to God.

The issue of how Job 28 hangs together with its surrounding chapters can now be investigated. As discussed above, some scholars reject Job 28 because they think that Job has already returned to "fearing God," renouncing his earlier outbursts, complaints and protests in this chapter. Therefore they consider that Job 28 lessens the effect of the Yahweh speeches and makes the rest of the book anti-climactic (e.g. Rowley). We have shown that Job 28, including v.28, is in line with mainstream wisdom. But Job is not merely affirming mainstream wisdom belief. The function of his utterance in chapter 28 can only be properly understood in the context of his (and the book's) argument. However, this does not satisfactorily

---

[425] R. C. Van Leeuwen, "Wealth and Poverty: System and Contradiction in Proverbs," *HS* 33 (1992) 32-3.

explain why Job's protest and complaint reappear in chapters 29-31. In my opinion, Job 28 has not reached the climax of what the author has to say. Westermann notes that this wisdom poem cannot "represent the high point of the book, as some interpreters assume, this is rendered impossible already by its location before the great concluding lament."[426] Habel claims: "The full significance of this chapter in the design of Job is only evident when due consideration is given to the closing verse (v.28)."[427] He further maintains:

> v.28 provides a formal closure which on the one hand is orthodox and traditional, but on the other stands in direct counterpoint to the poem which it precedes and serves as a deliberate foil for the climactic protestation of the hero which immediately follows (chs. 29-31). The poet thereby emphasizes once again that the traditional orthodox answer, while it may need to be said as a formal statement, is not acceptable to Job. He is no longer seeking traditional wisdom through piety; he is demanding direct personal access to God so that his integrity can be vindicated. He is no longer seeking access to wisdom as a means of understanding, but access to justice by confronting God in court.[428]

As Habel mentions above, 28:28 "stands in direct counterpoint to the poem which it precedes." Job 28:28 echoes with 1:1 and serves to remind the audience that Job has feared God and shunned evil in chapters 1 and 2. But "fearing God" and "shunning evil" have not saved Job from his present distress, nor have they given Job any wisdom to understand the crisis he faces. When Job recalls God's promise to man: "Behold, the fear of the Lord, that is wisdom; and to depart from evil is understanding," it creates rather than removes difficulty and tension for him.[429] This wisdom is what the friends believe and exhort Job to repent in line with throughout the dialogue (4:6-7; 8:20; 11:13-20; 22:21-30). However, Job denounces his friends' false accusations and defends his own integrity (9:20-22; 27:5). Job insists that he does "fear God" and "shun evil." Yet his suffering continues, and he cannot understand its cause. For Job, what is asserted in v.28 is at the root of the problem that he is voicing.

---

[426] Westermann, *Structure of Job*, 136.
[427] Habel, *Job*, 392.
[428] Habel, *Job*, 393. Wilson agrees with Habel; see L. Wilson, "The Book of Job and the Fear of God," *TynBul* 46 (1995) 69-79.
[429] Wilson, "Job and the Fear of God," 73.

The pondering over God's promise in v.28 creates further conflicts for Job, provoking even more furious outbursts in the subsequent chapters. That is why Habel thinks that 28:28 "serves as a deliberate foil for the climactic protestation of the hero which immediately follows (chs. 29-31)." Such conflict keeps the wheel of the plot in motion. Instead of seeking traditional wisdom, Job turns to pursue justice by confronting God directly in court, hoping that his integrity can be vindicated. Therefore 28:28 is a catalyst for the further development of the story in chapters 29-31. After understanding the function of 28:28 in relation to the following text, this study now turns to examine the flow of argument in chapters 29-31.

b) The Oath of Innocence in Job 29-31

The use of מָשָׁל in 29:1 indicates that chapters 29-31 are not simply a soliloquy reflecting the past and present situation, but a formal testimony addressed to a public assembly.[430] Job 29-31 "functions as a legal appeal for Job as defendant to gain a formal public hearing of his case."[431] In 27:1-6, where מָשָׁל is first used in v.1, Job has already made a public oath to defend his integrity and repudiate his friends' false sayings. In order to pursue litigation with God in court, Job makes his final testimony by swearing an avowal of innocence in chapters 29-31, challenging God, his adversary, to act.[432] Job's oath serves to compel God either to clear him or to activate the curses. Even God's continued silence will still be an answer for Job, because if the curses uttered by Job are not activated, the whole public assembly will know that Job is innocent.[433]

Reflection over the conclusion at 28:28 prompts Job to re-examine his life in the past and the present. According to Fohrer, "Die Herausforderungsreden Hiobs folgen dem Vorbild der Klagepsalmen, in denen der Beter die 'Erzählung' seiner Not und die eidliche Beteuerung seiner Unschuld vorbringt. Der 'Erzählung' liegt das Motiv des 'Einst und Jetzt' zugrunde, das aus dem Leichenlied stammt, in seinem ersten Teil (Kap. 29) aber mit Hilfe eines Weisheitsliedes ausgeführt wird."[434] In chapter 29 Job begins his

---

[430] Habel, *Job*, 404.
[431] Habel, *Job*, 408.
[432] Habel, *Job*, 404-5.
[433] Hartley, *Job*, 385.
[434] Fohrer states: "Job's challenges follow the model of the psalms of lament,

oath of integrity with the recollection of the past, in which he was considered as a paragon of righteousness. The speech of remembrance starts with Job's intimate relationship with God (vv.1-6). The community recognised God's blessings upon Job and highly respected him (vv.7-10). Job also strove for justice for the poor and the oppressed (vv.11-17). Confident that he was above reproach, Job hoped for a long, blessed life (vv.18-20). Job received extraordinary honour, like a king (vv.21-25). The core section of the speech (vv.11-17) "represents the heart of Job's expression of self-praise as a righteous ruler."[435]

The formula מִי יִתְּנֵנִי (Oh that/Oh, if only) highlights Job's progressive self-assertion in relation to God (cf. 19:23 and 23:3). Habel rightly observes that "this formula brackets Job's last extended speech (29:2 and 31:35) and identifies it as Job's final bold venture of faith as he moves from nostalgic recall to blatant confrontation."[436] In 29:2-6 Job expresses his longing for a return to the past, recalling the days when God had been his friend and had greatly blessed him. Whybray properly states that chapters 29-30 form an impressive lament. He adds that Job's description of the past in chapter 29, starting with the regretful words "Oh that I were..." is "in fact as much a lament over past glory as ch.30 is a lament over the misery of the present."[437]

The pondering over God's promise at 28:28 takes Job back to the days when he was respected in the community for his wisdom. He received great honour (vv.7-10) because equitable policy and just decisions characterized his rule (vv.11-17, where כִּי in vv.11, 12 gives the reasons). Throughout chapter 29 Job speaks of the way he lived, "fearing God" and "shunning evil." However, his fear of God did not save him from his present suffering or grant him any discernment about the cause of his plight. In fact, Job 29 serves to provoke God to action. Habel correctly states that: "In his speech of remembrance (ch.29), Job builds the level of his past importance and achievements as an ideal ruler to the point where he becomes a

---

in which the supplicant presents a 'narration' of his distress and a statement on oath of his own innocence. This 'narration' rests on the motif of 'then and now' which comes from the funeral lament but in its first part (ch. 29) is executed with the help of a wisdom poem." See G. Fohrer, *Das Buch Hiob* (KAT; Gütersloh: Gütersloher Verlagshaus Gerd Mohn, 1963) 51.

[435] Habel, *Job*, 407.
[436] Habel, *Job*, 408.
[437] Whybray, *Job*, 125.

mighty hero challenging God's administration of justice and usurping divine prerogatives."[438] Job's striving for justice for the underprivileged (29:12-17) refutes Eliphaz's unfounded allegations that Job had ignored the oppressed (22:5-9). On the other hand, Job's self-praise as a righteous ruler (vv.14, 25), as a father to the needy (v.16), and as a pastor to the mourners (v.25) also ironically attacks God's indifference to his cry for justice. Therefore chapter 29 is Job's provocative speech of remembrance.

However, all the evidence that Job has given in chapter 29 to prove his blamelessness is completely overthrown in chapter 30. All the blessing, honour and prosperity that have then confirmed Job's righteousness, now completely vanish. As Hartley states, "this remembrance serves to portray the depth of his shame as he will express it in his lament (ch.30)."[439]

The lament of chapter 30 comprises two sections.[440] In the first section Job cries out at the misery of his humiliation at the hands of different enemies, namely, the outcasts of society (vv.1-11), the terrors of death (vv.12-15) and God Himself (vv.16-19). Job's complaint in this section is underscored by the threefold וְעַתָּה (but now, vv.1, 9, 16), which forms a drastic and direct contrast with Job's glorious past in chapter 29, especially the pinnacle depicted at 29:25: "I chose a way for them and sat as chief, and dwelt as a king among the troops, as one who comforted the mourners."

The second section of this lament consists of Job's cry for justice and litigation (vv.20-31). The theme of Job's cry is marked by the threefold שָׁוַע in vv.20, 24 and 28. First, Job cries out for justice, but God does not respond to his repeated appeals for litigation (9:16-19; 13:19-24; 19:6-9; 23:3-9). Instead, God gives Job torments (vv.20-23). Secondly, Job complains that his administration of justice has not been rewarded by God. He strives for justice for the oppressed (cf. 29:12), but gets evils in return rather than blessings from God (vv.24-27). Finally, Job complains that he cries out his case in the public assembly but his appeal is treated like a jackal's or an ostrich's, which cry out in the wilderness but no one listens. Job uttered his self-lament just like a psalmist singing a dirge to the tune of the harp and flute (vv.28-31). Habel rightly comments: "Yet the boldness of Job's assertion that God has denied him justice when

---

[438] Habel, *Job*, 405.
[439] Hartley, *Job*, 387.
[440] Concerning the structure of Job 30, see Habel, *Job*, 417-8.

he was an acclaimed hero for justice is in itself a challenge for God to demonstrate otherwise."[441] While Job 29 is a provocative speech of remembrance, Job 30 is a provocative lament of present distress. They serve to provoke God to act. Again, the traditional conclusion of 28:28 serves as a deliberate foil for Job's protestation in chapters 29-31. God's promise at 28:28 provokes Job to respond that he does not accept such a conventional conclusion. Job tries to argue that he has already lived out the life of "fearing God" in chapter 29. However, his fear of God has not prevented his present distress (chapter 30).

The account of his past glory (Job 29) and the lament over his present humiliation (Job 30) drive Job to make a long chain of oaths for defending his innocence (Job 31). Habel discerns that Job's oath in chapter 31 is double-framed.[442] The outer frame (vv.1-3, 38-40) is formed by the covenant motifs. The opening one at vv.1-3 is Job's covenant with his eyes, highlighting Job's basic commitment to inner purity, which is the prerequisite of a righteous life.[443] The closing one at vv.38-40 is Job's summons to the earth to witness his innocence. If Job swears falsely, it will provoke an outcry of terror and a curse on his land.[444]

The inner frame (vv.4-6, 35-37) comprises two challenges to God.[445] The first one (vv.4-6) is Job's challenge to have God weigh his integrity on the scales of justice, since He has counted (סָפַר) Job's steps. The second one (vv.35-37) is Job's call for a written document to be presented to the court by his adversary (v.35). To express his certainty about the proof of his innocence, Job will carry the written accusation on his shoulder and bind it on his head (v.36), so that he can counteract the imprecatory power of the indictment in the document.[446] If the imprecatory power does not fall upon Job, he is innocent. This is the test of his oath of purity. With his opponent's document, Job will announce to God the count (מִסְפַּר) of steps in his perfect life, and confront God as proudly as a prince (v.37). Job's defence of his integrity reaches its climax here, and he is ready for the final confrontation with God.

---

[441] Habel, *Job*, 418.
[442] Habel, *Job*, 427-8.
[443] Habel, *Job*, 432.
[444] Habel, *Job*, 440.
[445] Habel, *Job*, 428.
[446] G. Fohrer, "The Righteous Man in Job 31," *Essays in Old Testament Ethics* (ed. James L. Crenshaw and John T. Willis; New York: KTAV, 1974) 3-4.

Between the double frames lies the core of Job's long chain of oaths (vv.7-34): a) impurity of heart and hands (vv.7-8); b) adultery (vv.9-12); c) disregard for the slaves' right (vv.13-15); d) hard-heartedness against the oppressed (vv.16-23); e) trust in wealth (vv.24-25); f) worship of the heavenly bodies (vv.26-28); g) hatred of enemies (vv.29-30); h) inhospitality (vv.31-32); and i) hypocrisy (vv.33-34). Such oaths of negative confession were taken before the deity when there was no witness to prove the accused party innocent. Fohrer points out that Job's oath is part of the legal process. The legal language takes three forms: a) an affirmation of innocence, by making a covenant בְּרִית, which requires an unconditional responsibility (vv.1-4); b) a conditional self-imprecation, in complete form with an imprecatory final clause (vv.5-23, 38-40a), intended to express the oath-taker's complete confidence in his righteousness; and c) a conditional self-imprecation in shortened form without a final clause, i.e. a real oath (vv.24-34).[447]

At first glance, the juxtaposition of Job 28 to the subsequent oath of innocence in Job 29-31 seems to be a stumbling block for interpretation, because such juxtaposition generates seeming contradictions within this context, as listed below:

+ve	28:28	God's promise: Man can gain wisdom by fearing God and shunning evil
−ve	30:20-23	Job's bitter complaints against God
	31:4-6	Job's challenge to God
	31:35-37	Job's challenge to God

However, as we have argued from the beginning, contradictory juxtaposition can be understood as part of the author's strategy to make a rhetorical impact upon the audience. But before exploring the author's intended impact upon the audience, it is necessary to recognise how Job's contradictory sayings in Job 28 contribute to the flow of argument within its context.

As mentioned above, the traditional conclusion at 28:28 plays an important role in accelerating the movement of the plot in chapters 29-31. God's promise to man that "the fear of the Lord, that is wisdom; and to depart from evil is understanding" (28:28) sounds contradictory to Job's experience. This conclusion of traditional wisdom is unacceptable to Job. Job does fear God and shun evil, but it does not save him from his present misfortunes. Therefore he

---

[447] Fohrer, "The Righteous Man in Job 31," 11.

decides to give up traditional wisdom, and turns to confront God directly. Job 28:28 catalyses Job's final defence of his innocence by swearing a series of oath in chapters 29-31.

In chapter 29 Job parades the evidence that he has lived in "the fear of God." However, his fear of God does not prevent his present distress (chapter 30). Job has tried many times to present his case before God, but God does not respond (9:16-19; 13:19-24; 19:6-9; 23:3-9; 30:20-31). Therefore, as a last resort, Job makes an oath of innocence (chapter 31), strongly intending to provoke God into act. Habel rightly states that "while Job's oath of purity may serve as a vehicle for the public vindication of Job's innocence, its reverse side is a barbed provocation like the formal challenges which frame the speech (vv.4-6, 35-37)."[448] Job has played his last card by making the vow of purity. If God remains silent, that means Job is innocent and God is the guilty party (cf. 40:8).

Conclusion
To conclude, this section has demonstrated two major functions of Job's contradictory sayings in Job 28 (especially the last verse 28:28) in the flow of argument within the story. First, 28:28 functions as a counterbalance to the preceding poem (vv.1-27). This final verse does not contradict the rest of the poem, but affirms it. It also gives an answer to the questions posed in vv.1-27. However, Job does not straightforwardly affirm the ideas expressed in this speech. Rather, 28:28 serves as a deliberate foil to accentuate Job's climactic protestation in chapters 29-31, keeping the wheel of the plot in motion. Based on this understanding of how Job's contradictory sayings in Job 28 make sense in the development of the story, this study continues to explore the intended rhetorical impacts of such contradictory sayings upon the audience.

2. *The Rhetorical Impacts upon the Audience*
In Job 28 Job's anger seems to have settled and he ponders over the issue of wisdom. Finally, he comes to the conclusion: "Behold, the fear of the Lord, that is wisdom; and to depart from evil is understanding" (28:28). At first glance, it seems that Job has found the resolution of his problem. However, right after the utterance of this wisdom poem, he falls back to defiant complainings and dissat-

---

[448] Habel, *Job*, 431.

isfaction again. The audience is expected to judge whether this is the real solution for Job. Job 28:28 serves to remind the reader that Job has already lived out the life of "fearing God." From the very beginning, the narrator depicts Job as a man who is "blameless, upright, fearing God and turning from evil" (1:1). Then Yahweh boasts of Job before the satan twice: "Have you considered My servant Job? For there is no one like him on the earth, a blameless and upright man, fearing God and turning from evil" (1:8; 2:3). In addition, the narrator gives the same verdict after each test of Job by Yahweh: "Through all this Job did not sin nor did he blame God" (1:22), and "In all this Job did not sin with his lips" (2:10). Therefore, when the friends urge Job in many ways to "fear God" as the solution to his problem (5:8, 27; 8:5-7, 20; 11:13-20; 22:21-30), the audience must realise that the friends' analysis of Job's problem is mistaken, and which is later corrected by God Himself (42:7-8).

Similarly, the audience will also perceive that "the fear of the Lord" in 28:28 cannot be the solution to Job's problem. Throughout the whole dialogue Job has defended his integrity (e.g. 6:14; 27:2-6), and thus he will certainly not accept "the fear of the Lord" as a satisfactory answer to his problem. In addition, the audience is assumed to trace the subsequent development of the story after 28:28. Seemingly, Job's strong outburst and his challenge to God in 30:20-23 and 31:35-37 reveal that his problem has still not been resolved. Therefore Job's saying in chapter 28 functions to provoke the audience to judge whether an affirmation of traditional wisdom has provided the key to Job's problem. After weighing all the data, comparing the dialogue between Job and his friends, and observing the flow of the story from chapter 28 to chapters 29-31, the audience ought to be able to conclude that Job 28 is a pseudo-climax. Such suspense is a powerful rhetorical device, stimulating the audience to search further for the resolution of Job's dilemma.

Furthermore, if the audience discovers that Job 28 is just a pseudo-climax, they will be triggered into figuring out the difference between a pseudo-climax and a real climax; discovering what makes a real climax real. Therefore Job 28 acts as an important base from which the audience can make such a comparison when the story comes to its climax. The audience is expected to ask what the difference between Job's response in Job 28:28 and his response after the divine encounter in Job 42:1-6 is. Job 42:3, 5 provides the clue.

Job's understanding is built upon the foundation of a first-hand encounter with God (Job 38-41), rather than upon traditional theodicies (Job 4-28). Therefore the author uses Job 28 to stimulate the audience's thought and to prepare them to adopt his evaluative worldview expressed by Job's final confession (42:2-6).

In addition, the structure of inclusio draws the audience's attention to the fact that the theme of "fearing God" and "shunning evil" in 28:28 is closely linked with the narrator's comment on Job's character in 1:1. Such structure alerts the audience to treat Job 1-28 as a block of text, where chapter 28 functions as the conclusion to its previous chapters, yet leaves open the question raised at the beginning. It also acts as a bridge for the further development of the rest of the story. Then the audience will observe what conclusion chapter 28 has made for the previous speech cycles. Corresponding to all Job's criticisms about the friends' lack of wisdom (12:1-4; 13:5; 17:10; 26:2-4; 26:5-14) and the total collapse of the debate in Job 27, Job 28 sums up that the reason for human suffering is beyond human comprehension. This poem in effect highlights the failed attempt on the part of both Job and his friends to account for his suffering. This forms a conclusion to the three speech cycles. It is the limitation of human understanding that prompts Job to address God directly.

To conclude, the inclusio linkage of 28:28 to 1:1 also alerts the audience about the place of Job 28 in the whole book—a conclusion to the previous chapters and a bridge to the development of the subsequent chapters. In addition, Job's saying in chapter 28 functions as a false climax to engage the audience in seeking the real resolution for Job's situation. Job 28 also serves as a base for the audience to make a comparison between a false climax and a real one later in the story. Such searching and comparing are crucial processes to guide the audience to take the evaluative worldview of the narrative later in the Yahweh speeches, so that the audience's perception of the world and God can be reconstructed.

VIII. *Job 28 Within the Context of Job 22-31*

As we have seen, Job 28 is more like Zophar's characteristic speeches than Job's, and quite like the Yahweh speeches. However, it does not surprise us that Job can use language and ideas that are rather like those of his friends, and unlike his predominant "voice," because this is not the first time Job has adopted contradictory sayings. In fact, he has used such language sporadically throughout the first two speech cycles for reasons that we have seen. But as the story comes to the third speech cycle, the frequency of Job's contradictory sayings reaches its peak, culminating in Job 28-31.

A. *Contradictory Juxtapositions as a Common Structure*

As we have observed, there is a series of contradictory juxtapositions in chapters 22-31, as follows:

	23:1-2	Introductory complaint
+ve	23:3-7	Hope: Having a litigation before God
−ve	23:8-9	Despair: Being unable to find God
+ve	23:10-12	Hope: God's knowledge of his integrity
−ve	23:13-16	Despair: Being frightened by God's overwhelming power
	23:17	Job's determination not to be silenced
−ve	24:1-17	God's absence leading to social injustice
+ve	24:18-24	God's judgment upon the wicked
	24:25	Job's challenging his friends to refute him if he is not telling the truth
	25:1-6	Bildad's praise of God's supremacy
−ve	26:1-4	Job's rejection of Bildad's counsel
+ve	26:5-14	Job's praise of God's supremacy
−ve	27:1-12	Job's condemnation of the friends' false speeches
+ve	27:13-23	Job's declaration of the fate of the wicked
+ve	Job 28	God's promise: Man can gain wisdom through submission to God
-ve	Job 29-31	Job's falling back to complaining and emotional outburst

Earlier in this chapter it has been argued that such contradictory juxtapositions are the author's deliberate design in the flow of the whole discourse, part of his strategy to make a rhetorical impact upon the audience. Now this study proceeds to give a panoramic view of how such contradictory juxtapositions function in the context of chapters 22-31, thereby recapturing the linkage between Job 28 and its surrounding chapters.

In response to Job's last speech in chapter 21, in which he turns the principle of retribution upside down, Eliphaz adopts the harshest of tones in his final speech of the third cycle. Without any introductory complaint about windy words, lack of wisdom or insulting speech, Eliphaz proceeds to argue that since God gains no advantage from human righteousness, Job's punishment proves his guilt (22:2-5). Eliphaz's accusation, that Job is "greatly wicked," has reached its climax (22:5a). To defend his theology of retribution, he even invents and imputes to Job various social crimes, falsely accusing him of oppressing the poor and the needy (22:6-9). Then he concludes that Job has been punished because of these sins (22:10-11). In his second argument Eliphaz proceeds to accuse Job of denying God's knowledge and judgment—sins that have led to ruin since ancient times (22:12-20). Finally, without losing hope in Job's restoration, he concludes his speech with an appeal to Job, exhorting him to return to God, in order to enjoy spiritual fellowship, material blessings and prosperity once again (22:21-30).

Although Eliphaz has advised Job to seek God (22:21-30), Job expresses his strong quest for personal vindication from God (23:2-7). However, Job's confidence oscillates between hope and despair. First, he despairs at his inability to find God (23:8-9). Job has been seeking God east, west, north and south, but he cannot see Him. Then Job's hope comes back, when he asserts that God knows his integrity (23:10-12). However, at the climax of his confidence, Job's dread returns again, as he thinks of the overwhelming power of God, who does what He has decreed (23:13-16). Job's determination to have a litigation before God reappears and he refuses to be silenced (23:17). Basically, Job 23 highlights that the absence of God has caused Job's plight, and has added to his personal pain and frustrations.

In Job 21 Job effectively argues that the prosperity of the wicked proves God's unjust governance in the world. Now, in Job 24:1-17, Job projects his personal experience upon the world of human beings in general in order to conclude that both his undeserved suffering and social injustice in the world prove God's irresponsibility and unjust moral governance. Acting as a righteous sufferer, Job declares God's judgment upon the wicked (24:18-24) to deliberately sharpen the contradiction between his actual experiences and the conventional theology of retribution. He has voiced such contradictions in Job 23, illustrating his own personal experiences of hope and despair before God. The contradiction between social injustice and the belief in retribution is then further exposed in Job 24. By asking a rhetorical question in 24:25, Job ends his speech with a strong assertion of his truthfulness—telling the whole truth of the contradictions between belief and experience (Job 23-24). He even challenges his friends to gainsay him and prove him a liar if he is speaking falsehood.

Bildad utters a hymn in chapter 25. But unlike in his first two speeches, Bildad does not here make any criticisms of Job (cf. 8:1-7; 18:1-4). Seemingly, Job's rhetorical question in 24:25 has asserted a truth that no one can easily deny. In addition, the brevity of this hymn also suggests the collapse of the debate. Bildad's doxology mainly contrasts the supreme power and complete perfection of God with the inferiority and total depravity of mankind. In fact, his point is the same as Eliphaz's in 4:17-21; 15:14-16, and as Job's in 9:2-3; 14:1-4. For example, Bildad's viewpoint in 25:4 is exactly Eliphaz's idea in 4:17, stressing that no one is more righteous than God. In addition, Bildad adds to it in 25:5 what Eliphaz mentioned in 15:5b: "and the sky is not pure in His eye." Bildad's return to Eliphaz's argument of humanity's total depravity reveals that he does not have any new ideas with which to attack Job, and that the discussion is nearly exhausted. When other explanations fail, the theodicy of human total depravity seems to be a "catch all" position that Job cannot escape without any blame for wrongdoing. Sticking rigidly to the ideology that only the guilty suffer, Bildad points out that Job's suffering is due to the sinful nature of mankind. Job's claim of innocence is proven to be ridiculous. Bildad shows no tendency to consider seriously the possibility that Job is innocent.

In response, Job sarcastically criticizes Bildad's (and other two friends') counsel as unhelpful and lacking in wisdom. He even queries the source and authority of Bildad's knowledge (26:1-4). Ironically, Job utters a hymn similar to Bildad's hymn in Job 25. But Job shifts the focus to contrast God's greatness with human beings' limited comprehension (26:5-14), in order to mock the friends' limited understanding. If God's way is beyond human comprehension, how can they claim to have knowledge of Job's situation and the reasons behind his problem?

In 27:1-6 Job makes an oath of innocence, the high point in the self-defence of his integrity. Job swears by the name of the God who Job accuses of taking away his right of litigation and embittering his soul. This vividly reflects Job's double concept of God: both his accuser and his source of justice. In this oath Job swears not to declare his friends to be innocent, and to hold fast to his integrity until he dies. In addition, Job's utterance in this chapter also marks the climax of the conflict between Job and his friends. First, Job charges his friends with their false speeches about himself (vv.5-6). Treating his friends as his enemies, he makes his imprecation against them (vv.7-10). There then comes his reproach against his friends' false speech about God (vv.11-12). To condemn his friends' untruthfulness, Job proclaims to them the fate of the wicked as their judgment (vv.13-23), which brings them to total silence. Step by step, Job's utterances push his condemnation against his friends to its climax, finally shutting their mouths. Their total silence may imply that they admit their guilt; or they might deny it, and simply give up speaking because they cannot convince Job. From then onward, the friends disappear from the stage until the divine judgment in 42:7.

The total collapse of the debate compels Job to probe into the mystery of wisdom and to seek God in person because he knows that his friends cannot help resolve his problem any further. Thus he proceeds to reflect upon the issue of wisdom in Job 28. Human beings are shown to be utterly unable to find wisdom in this poem, despite their godlike power to mine precious minerals (vv.1-11). In spite of their technical and research skills, they do not know the place of wisdom, which is not in the "deep" or the "sea." Wisdom cannot be acquired in exchange for all kinds of precious treasures, because it is beyond purchase (vv.12-19). Wisdom cannot be found among all the living or in the realm of the dead. God alone knows its way and place (vv.20-27). The only way man can obtain wisdom is to fear God and to turn away from evil (28:28). This is God's promise.

However, the remembrance of God's promise drives Job to recall his glorious past, and re-examine his life therein (Job 29). Such reminiscence triggers Job's anger, because he has lived out a life of fearing God and shunning evil, but it neither prevents his present plight, nor gives him any understanding of his suffering. Instead, what he faces now is humiliation from his enemies. Job strongly complains about God's inflictions upon him and His indifference to his cry for help (Job 30). Therefore Job seeks the last resort: to present his case before God by making a public oath of innocence which compels God to act. Job is confident that he can win the verdict and be vindicated. Even if God remains silent, the public will know that Job is innocent because the oath that he has sworn will not be worked out upon him. Job's oath indicates that both his challenge to God and the defence of his integrity have reached their climax (Job 31).

The seeming contradictions in the third speech cycle and chapter 28 have long been a perplexing issue for many interpreters. Instead of considering the third cycle as a dislocated chunk and chapter 28 as a secondary addition, this study proposes that the series of contradictory juxtapositions in Job 22-31 reflect a neat, orderly and articulate structuring of the text, contributing to the development of the flow of argument, as illustrated above. Concerning the interpretive key of the third speech cycle, Seitz notably remarks:

> Job moves to a position of defending the moral order, but this does not happen in such a way as to slacken his complaint. In fact, he is all the more resolute in defending his innocence and demanding a fair trial (27:1-6)....What happens in Round 3 is that the ground is effectively cut out from under the friends. In Round 2 they had all charged Job directly with being the justly punished, evil one. There was also a good deal of "if the shoe fits, wear it" argumentation, in hopes of getting Job to confess to prior sin. Now Job suggests the same for the friends. He defends the moral order—in support of his own position and against the friends. He emerges as the righteous sufferer after all, the one who asks God to vindicate him against evil-doers rising up against him, precisely as in the Psalter: "Let my enemy be as the wicked / and let him who rises up against me be as the unrighteous" (27:7). Apparently the "shoe fits," for the friends-become-enemies are driven into silence. Eliphaz speaks in lies (see 22:6-9). Bildad sputters for six verses (25:1-6). Zophar never appears.[449]

Closely linked with the third cycle, Job 28 serves as a conclusion to the preceding dialogue, underscoring the limitation of human comprehension, and pondering the way to acquire wisdom. On the other hand, reflection over the issue of wisdom in Job 28, especially 28:28, evokes Job's further determination to seek personal vindication from God (Job 29-31). Therefore, after recognising the distinctive structure of the contradictory juxtapositions in Job 22-31, this study claims that Job 28 makes sense as Job's speech, and functions as a bridge between the preceding cycles and the upcoming chapters.

---

[449] Seitz, "Job: Full-Structure, Movement, and Interpretation," 12-3.

B. *Contradictory Juxtapositions in Job 22-31 as Part of the Rhetorical Strategy*

As we discussed in Chapter Two, it is the rhetorical situation that motivates the author of the book to tell the story of Job. The rhetorical situation consists of three components: the audience, exigency and constraint. This study assumes that the audience may share some of the characteristics of the characters. Therefore the problems of the audience can be revealed by the problems of the characters.

The exigency of the book is the audience's misunderstanding of the relationship between innocent suffering and the justice of God. The audience may have different preconceptions, of course. The friends represent the audience who defend the theodicies and think that suffering proves one's guilt, whereas Job represents the audience who defend the innocent sufferer and think that undeserved suffering proves God's injustice. In fact, both parties hold the same presupposition: that only the guilty suffer. Basically, the exigency can be traced in the dialogue, which exposes Job's and the friends' misinterpretations of suffering.

Recognising that the traditional theological background is the constraint that he must work through in order to evoke changes, the author uses the evidence of Job's experience to bring out the contradiction between reality and belief, and thus exposes the inadequacy of the friends' theodicies for explaining Job's case. The author further also proves the inadequacy of Job's perspective by using God's corrections in the Yahweh speeches. This is the author's rhetorical strategy, directing the audience from a less to more adequate perspective.[450] The audience is expected to adopt God's perspective on reality, and to be transformed by it.

Job's contradictory sayings in chapters 22-31 are part of this "from less to more adequate perspectives" strategy, and aim to achieve the author's ultimate goal of positively modifying the exigency. The author uses Job's contradictory sayings to highlight the contradictions between reality and the theodicies, thus exposing the inadequacy of the friends' perspective. The contradictory juxtapositions in Job 22-31 serve to bring the urgency and acuteness of the exigency to full expression. The most furious conflict between Job and his friends (Job 22-27), the deepest internal reflection over wisdom (Job 28) and the strongest determination to compel God to act

---
[450] Newsom, "Job," 337.

(Job 29-31) have vividly marked the highest level of Job's bewilderment about the tension between innocent suffering and divine justice.

Contradictory juxtaposition in Job 22-31 reveals a certain degree of complexity and ambiguity, requiring the audience to play a more active role in making meaning than would a text in which the message was simple and transparent. Therefore contradictory juxtaposition functions primarily as a stimulus to the audience's own wrestling with the problems of each character, through evaluation of their viewpoints' reliability. Being able to figure out the problems of the characters is an essential step by which the audience is engaged in reflection over their own problems. Therefore contradictory juxtaposition is a powerful persuasive device, preparing the audience to adopt the author's evaluative worldview in the Yahweh speeches, which is the key to removing the exigency.

C. *Gap-Filling of the Contradictory Juxtapositions*

As we have mentioned, Job's contradictory sayings in Job 22-31 crack open the discrepancy between religious claims and stark reality—the clash between Job's undeserved suffering and the justice of God. Contradictory juxtapositions "open gaps, gaps produce discontinuity, and discontinuity breeds ambiguity."[451] Gaps direct the audience to move between the truth and the whole truth, finally achieving a full reading.[452] According to Sternberg, a literary work "establishes a system of gaps that must be filled in."[453] It is the contradictory juxtaposition "that pinpoints the incongruity and launches the quest for harmony by gap-filling."[454] This is a most effective device for actively engaging the audience to fill the gaps in the reading.

The need for gap-filling begs the question: what is the resolution to Job's problem? The above analysis of Job 28 in its immediate context makes it clear that Job 28 is not the climax of the book, otherwise the story would have stopped at 28:28. In addition, further contradictions follow this chapter, indicating that it is an inadequate solution to Job's problem.

---

[451] Sternberg, *Poetics of Biblical Narrative*, 236.
[452] Sternberg, *Poetics of Biblical Narrative*, 186-263.
[453] Sternberg, *Poetics of Biblical Narrative*, 186.
[454] Sternberg, *Poetics of Biblical Narrative*, 243.

The idea of "fearing God" in 28:28 is repeated at the conclusion of Elihu's speeches (37:24). If Elihu's role is to give a human verdict, his implied remedy of "fearing God" (37:24) does not lead to a resolution of Job's dilemma either, otherwise the story would have stopped at this point.[455] Job does not submit himself to God until he encounters God face to face (42:1-6). In terms of content, despite the similarities between Job 28 and the Yahweh speeches, the story does not reach its climax until Job's total submission to God in his final confession (42:1-6). Laurin rightly claims that:

> The clue to the author's intention is found in Job's final response to Yahweh in 42:5: "I had heard of thee by the hearing of the ear, but now my eye sees thee." Chapter 28 provides a summary of what Job had "heard" all his life, namely, the typical wisdom answer to life's problems—trust and obey Yahweh, for he alone has the wisdom by which the world was created and is to be run.[456]

A true faith does not simply proclaim certain facts about God, but finds its basic ground in a personal encounter with God (chs. 38-42).[457]

Therefore the Yahweh speeches are the answer to Job, and 42:5 is the summary of the answer to Job's problem. Furthermore, 42:6 is the climax, where Job repudiates and repents of his position of lamentation among the dust and ashes after he has met God. Comparatively speaking, Job's position in 28:28 is different from that in 42:1-6. He does not reach a state of complete obedience to God until 42:1-6.

The fact that the "fear of God" is not mentioned by Yahweh and the narrator again does not mean that the book seeks to overturn mainstream wisdom thinking. However, I would suggest that the "fear of God" is qualified through Job's wholehearted submissive response to Yahweh in 42:1-6, where Job actualizes and internalizes the true meaning of wisdom. Job admits that he has made ignorant accusations against God's governance of the cosmos (42:3). Job's concession here vindicates Yahweh's integrity.[458] He now gains a new, vibrant and direct knowledge of God in comparison with his previous "hand-me-downs" wisdom.[459] True faith is grounded on a

---

[455] Wilson, "Job and the Fear of God," 74.
[456] R. Laurin, "The Theological Structure of Job," *ZAW* 84 (1972) 87.
[457] Laurin, "Theological Structure of Job," 88.
[458] Habel, *Job*, 34.
[459] Brown, "Reformation of Character: Job 32-42," 108.

firsthand encountering of God, not "fossilized" wisdom claims.[460] Job's withdrawal of his case (42:6) indicates that God's appearance is a sufficient vindication for him.[461]

In conclusion, contradictory juxtaposition opens gaps, and gaps need to be filled. At first glance, the calm and contemplative tone of Job 28 may give a false impression that Job has resolved his problem. However, the strong emotional outburst in the subsequent passage indicates that Job has not yet reached resolution. Job 42:5, which is the summary of the Yahweh speeches, gives us a clue that God's appearance is the true resolution to Job's problem. It is the divine encounter that brings Job to total submission to God (42:6). Job 28 represents second-hand knowledge of God, while the Yahweh speeches represent first-hand experience. Therefore the Yahweh speeches serve to fill the gaps generated by the contradictory juxtapositions of chapters 22-31.

---

[460] G. Goldsworthy, "Job and the Hiddenness of Order," *Gospel and Wisdom: Israel's Wisdom Literature in the Christian Life* (Carlisle: Paternoster, 1995) 96.

[461] Habel, *Job*, 34.

CHAPTER FOUR

SUMMARY AND CONCLUSION

This study has presented arguments which lead to the conclusion that Job 28 is Job's words and an integral part of the book. Despite its seeming incongruities of tone and content, Job 28 fits in well with the whole book and with the context of chapters 22-31, when seen as Job's words. It is part of the entire book's plot design; it relates to the rhetorical situation of the book; and it is part of the author's "from less to more adequate perspectives" rhetorical strategy. Within the context of chapters 22-31, Job 28 shares the rhetorical device of contradictory juxtaposition with its surrounding chapters. All such contradictory sayings of Job serve to alert the audience to the inadequacy of their traditional theodicies.

The significant and integral role of Job 28 within the plot and purpose of the entire book cannot be seen unless the integrity of the piece as a whole is accepted: all the parts of Job are tightly knitted together. A removal of any single part will damage the entire plot structure. Despite the great variety of surface discrepancies throughout the book, including Job 28 itself, there is a continuous narrative plot giving underlying coherence to the book as a whole. It is the thread of the plot which knits Job 28 and the rest of the book closely together.

The collapse of the debate signifies the limitations of human understanding in probing the mystery of suffering. Within the plot design, Job 28 in its present position serves as a conclusion to and judgment upon the dialogue (Job 3-27). More importantly, "the fear of God" and "avoidance of evil" at 28:28 functions as a deliberate foil, triggering Job's actions in chapters 29-31. In fact, God's promise at 28:28 does not rescue Job from his present plight, nor does it grant him any understanding about the reason for his suffering. The answer of traditional wisdom in this verse seems to be so unacceptable to Job that it rouses him to finally present his case before God (Job 29-31). Therefore Job's contradictory sayings in chapter 28 serve as a catalyst to keep the wheel of plot in motion.

Job's characterization also provides an answer to the inconsistencies between Job 28 and its surrounding context. The central issue of the book is the conflict between Job's integrity and God's integrity, which motivates the progress of the story and keeps Job going through the whole journey of character and worldview. In the prologue Job is portrayed as a flat character with a single trait—a blameless and upright man who accepts his fate submissively. But in the dialogue Job is portrayed as a round character, which lays bare Job's inner life. Previously, Job appeared to strongly oppose his friends' interpretation of his suffering through theodicies. But now he uses his friends' standpoints to make his own argument. To read the text this way involves supposing that the words of the characters, especially Job, may not always be taken at face-value; they have sometimes to be taken as parody or satire. They can certainly be ironic. But the irony consists in how the sayings are used in the flow of the dialogue and the argument. Job's contradictory sayings in chapters 22-31 mark the climax of the conflict between Job and his friends. But at the same time, such sayings also reveal Job's contradictory views of God, bringing his highly complex inner life to its fullest expression.

The abrupt shift from "Job the silent" in the prologue to "Job the verbose" in Job 3-21, and then "Job the ambiguous" in Job 22-31 seems to threaten the unity of Job's character. However, it is actually Job's integrity which holds these three portrayals together, because the three "Jobs" all lay claim and hold fast to integrity. Therefore the inconsistency of tone and content between Job 28 and its context can be well understood in light of Job's characterization.

Job 28 relates to the rhetorical situation of the whole book, namely, the exigency, audience and constraint of the book. It is the rhetorical situation that motivates the author to tell the story. A rhetorical discourse specifies its audience, who are thus assumed to share some of the background and misconceptions of the protagonists. In regard to the exigency, neither Job nor his friends know how to reconcile the existence of evil and the goodness of God. Bound by the constraints of their traditional religious background, both parties assume that only the guilty suffer. Based on this shared presupposition, they go to different poles. To defend God's integrity the friends consider Job's suffering as evidence of his sins. To defend his own integrity Job charges God with injustice in governing the world. To rectify the exigency, the author needs to discover the constraint of the situation—the parameter of traditional religious background.

Job 28 exposes the exigency of the situation: the inadequacy of traditional theology to understand the relationship between suffering and the goodness of God. Furthermore, Job 28 reveals the constraint of the situation— traditional religious background—which shapes the audience's worldview. The traditional belief of "fearing God" and "shunning evil" as an answer to problems is questioned and re-evaluated at 28:28.

Job 28 is also part of the author's "from less to more adequate perspectives" strategy to modify the exigency. The author directs the audience from truth to whole truth. First, the inadequacy of the friends' perspective is exposed by Job's arguments from experience, which bring out the contradictions between belief and reality. Then the inadequacy of Job's perspective is disclosed by God's rebuke and instruction, which correct Job's wrong conceptions of God. Job 28 functions as a transition, concluding the disclosure of the inadequacy of the friends' perspective and setting the stage for God to reveal the inadequacy of Job's perspective.

Within the context of chapters 22-31, contradictory juxtaposition appears to be the predominant device linking Job 28 with its surrounding chapters. Job's contradictory sayings throughout this section seem to threaten the consistency of the text. But, in fact, the device of contradictory juxtapositions is part of the author's overall rhetorical strategy of "from less to more adequate perspectives." As we have said, the author guides the audience to perceive the inadequacy of the friends' theology by juxtaposing Job's arguments from the reality of his experience. The powerful employment of contradictory juxtapositions cracks open the contradictions between belief and experience, completely laying bare the limits of the traditional theodicies and bringing the friends to total silence. Contradictory juxtaposition in chapters 22-31 thus marks the climax of Job's rejection of his friends' arguments, and also reveals the deep perplexities of Job's inner life. In light of the common device of contradictory juxtaposition, it is not difficult to discern the close ties between Job 28 and chapters 22-31.

Contradictory juxtapositions open gaps, and gaps need to be filled. The disharmony and incongruity caused by contradictory juxtaposition actively engage the audience to seek the resolution of Job's dilemma. At first glance, the calm tone and contemplative content of Job 28 may give the audience a wrong impression that Job has found the answer to his problem. However, the subsequent emotional outburst in Job 29-31 indicates that Job 28 is just a pseudo-climax. The book does not reach its real climax until the Yahweh speeches (Job 38-41), where Job's inadequate perspective is corrected by God. The audience is expected to adopt God's evaluative points of view. From God's perspective the innocent can suffer. However, the existence of evil does not necessarily rule out the goodness and justice of God. Despite the existence of evil, God is still in control and He is loving. God's orderly governance of the world and His providence over nature reveal His love. This reminds the sufferer to hold fast to faith in God even though he does not know the reason for his suffering. Therefore the divine encounter, and not Job 28, functions to fill the gaps caused by the contradictory juxtapositions in chapters 22-31.

However, that the divine encounter brings resolution does not mean that the author is trying to overthrow the traditional value system of "fearing God" and "shunning evil." In fact, this wisdom value is qualified rather than nullified. Job 42:5 provides a clue for understanding the relationship between Job 28 and the Yahweh speeches. Job 28 represents Job's second-hand knowledge of God which he gains through hearing, whereas the divine encounter underscores the first-hand experience of God in which true and living faith takes root. True wisdom must be based upon first-hand knowledge of God.

In conclusion, this study has demonstrated that, as the text stands and as Job's words, Job 28 has a special function within the book and within the context of chapters 22-31. More importantly, this chapter is within the author's overall rhetorical strategy to alert the audience to the inadequacy of their traditional theodicies. Such an awareness paves the way to rectifying the exigency in due course.

APPENDIX

CONTRADICTORY JUXTAPOSITION IN OTHER BOOKS

I. *Introduction*

Contradictory juxtaposition is a common feature in biblical wisdom literature. The Book of Job is not the only book to use this device. In fact, Proverbs, Ecclesiastes, and the Psalms of Lament (Ps 9-10, 73) also employ similar unexpected juxtapositions. In order to back up my argument that contradictory juxtaposition in Job 22-31 is a deliberate authorial device to perform positive rhetorical functions, their use of this literary device is now investigated.

II. *Proverbs*

Many proverbs do positively highlight that righteousness and wealth go together, as do wickedness and poverty (12:3; 13:22; 13:25; 14:14; 14:19). However, there are also many sayings in Proverbs which recognise the failure of justice and equity, contradicting the above cause-and-effect doctrine. Such sayings acknowledge that the wicked can prosper while the righteous suffer (11:16; 13:23; 19:10; 28:15; 30:14). Seeing such contradictions, Van Leeuwen points out:

> In my judgment, it is mistaken to apply the term "dogmatism" to Proverbs or a class of sayings within the book. Such a label misconstrues the nature of the indicative sayings in collections by obscuring the fact that they are qualified by other, often contradictory sayings. Proverbs are inherently partial utterances. The widespread dogmatic misuse of retributive sayings or concepts (Job 42:7; Luke 13:1-5; John 9:1-2; cf. Prov 26:7, 9) does not itself render the sayings dogmatic.[1]

Contradictions within the Book of Proverbs reflect the fundamental

---

[1] Van Leeuwen, "Wealth and Poverty," 29. In this article, Van Leeuwen analyses sayings in Proverbs concerning wealth and poverty in relation to righteousness and wickedness by using a 4-quadrant chart. He points out that Proverbs not only highlights quadrant 1 (righteousness and wealth) and quadrant 4 (wickedness and poverty), but also quadrant 2 (righteousness and poverty) and quadrant 3 (wickedness and wealth) to show the contradictions.

tensions in the structure of Yahwistic faith. Fox has made the following comments:

> Intermixed with the proverbs formulated as absolutes are numerous sayings describing cases where the circumstances of one's life do not accord with the moral quality of one's behaviour. For although the writers of didactic wisdom emphasize the positive—which is what they think usually happens—they are well aware of exceptions: a good or industrious man may be poor or ill or mocked; a wicked or lazy one may be prosperous or respected.[2]

The "better than" sayings in Proverbs also illustrate the awareness of the contradictory situations, which reverse their usual worth and value: righteousness with wealth; and wickedness with poverty.[3] "Better is a little with the fear of the Lord than great treasure and trouble with it. Better is a dinner of herbs where love is than a fattened ox and hatred with it" (15:16-17). "Better is a little with righteousness than great revenues with injustice" (16:8). Other "better than" sayings are: 16:16; 16:19; 17:1; 19:22b; 21:3; 22:1 and 28:6. Usually, wealth is considered to be better than poverty (10:15; 13:8; 14:20; 18:23; 19:4, 6-7), and the gift of God as reward for the righteous (10:22). However, in the "better than" sayings, poverty with righteousness is "better than" wealth with wickedness. In this case, poverty is even better than wealth.

It is true that throughout most of Proverbs we can easily find the act-and-consequence connection—the basic wisdom doctrine that people reap what they sow. However, behind the cause-and-effect connection, there are exceptions and contradictions to the general rules of life. Van Leeuwen rightly comments on the contradictory proverbs:

> When proverbs are contradictory, it is not necessarily a sign of different origins or conflicting worldviews. Proverbs even from a single group or person can be contradictory, because life is complex.[4]

Therefore, although the Book of Proverbs is frequently regarded as

---

[2] M. V. Fox, *Qoheleth and His Contradictions* (Sheffield: Sheffield Academic Press, 1989) 134. See also J. A. Gladson, "Retributive Paradox in Proverbs 10-29," Ph.D. Dissertation. (Nashville: Vanderbilt University, 1978). Gladson presents evidence from Proverbs 10-29 to demonstrate that the sages took notice of the existence of injustice.

[3] Van Leeuwen, "Wealth and Poverty," 31-2.

[4] R. C. Van Leeuwen, "The Book of Proverbs," *NIB 5* (ed. Leander E. Keck et al.; Nashville: Abindon Press, 1997) 23.

orthodox, even it sounds "a minor chord in recognizing that the world does not operate in such a clear-cut manner,"[5] that real life includes contradictory situations. This book reflects the nature of wisdom literature as depicting the complexity of life; the co-existence of belief and doubt is a reality of life.

Comparatively speaking, the Book of Proverbs is by nature a collection of sayings that refer to a great range of circumstances and perspectives, whereas the Book of Job is by nature a coherent story. In addition, Proverbs 1-15 mainly focuses on the sayings of character-consequence patterns, and the contradictory sayings occur more sporadically from Proverbs 16 onwards, while in Job 22-31 the contradictory sayings appear in a rather orderly pattern. Despite the differences in nature and structure between the two books, however, one feature common to both is their use of contradictory sayings to bring out the tensions between reality and belief, to demonstrate the exceptions in actual experience, and to penetrate the depths of the perplexity of life. In sum, the use of contradictory sayings to express life's complexity is a common characteristic in the wisdom literature.

III. *Psalms 9-10*

The two incomplete acrostic hymns, Psalm 9 (aleph-kaph) and Psalm 10 (lamed-taw), seem to belong to one single literary unit,[6] although the pattern of letters is broken in the middle of the alphabet.[7] The

---

[5] T. I. Longman, *The Book of Ecclesiastes* (NICOT; Grand Rapids: Eerdmans, 1998) 106.

[6] There are a number of reasons for thinking thus: 1) the absence of a title in Psalm 10; 2) the continuity of the acrostic device (though partially obscured); 3) a shared vocabulary link; and 4) the LXX and the Vulgate's treatment of the two psalms as a unit. See P. C. Craigie, *Psalms 1-50* (WBC; Waco: Word Books, 1983) 116; W. A. VanGemeren, "Psalms," *The Expositor's Bible Commentary 5* (ed. Frank E. Gaebelein; Grand Rapids: Zondervan, 1991) 114; and J. C. McCann, Jr., "Psalms," *NIB 4* (ed. Leander E. Keck et al.; Nashville: Abingdon Press, 1996) 716-7. However, some commentators prefer to understand these psalms as two separate literary units. Concurring with Kirkpatrick's viewpoint that "The two psalms present an unsolved literary problem", VanGemeren claims that "the diverse elements in the two psalms caution us against treating the two psalms as one." See VanGemeren, "Psalms," 115.

[7] Craigie, *Psalms 1-50*, 118, 123. Psalm 9 covers the first 11 letters of the alphabet (אב), among which ד is missing. There is also some irregularity in the length of the strophes (118, 128). Psalm 10 carries the acrostic pattern from ל to

Psalm begins with an announcement of praise (vv.2-3 [1-2]), and an account of personal deliverance from enemies (vv.4-5 [3-4]). There then follows the contrast between the destruction of the wicked (vv.6-7 [5-6]) and the permanent enthronement of God (vv.8-9 [7-8]). On the basis of the reign of the Lord, the psalm affirms God's protection (vv.10-11 [9-10]) and raises a hymn of praise (vv.12-13 [11-12]) which then shifts to a petition (vv.14-15 [13-14]). Confidence is affirmed by God's judgment of the wicked and His deliverance of the afflicted (vv.16-19 [15-18]). Finally, the psalm ends with a renewed petition (vv.20-21 [19-20]).[8]

The petitions in Psalm 9:14-15 [13-14], 20-21 [19-20] anticipate the change of tone from praise (Psalm 9) to lament (Psalm 10). Psalm 10 starts with a complaint about God's hiddenness in times of trouble, when the wicked persecute the lowly (vv.1-2). There then comes a description of the evil deeds and prosperity of the wicked (vv.3-11): they deny accountability to God (vv.3-4; v.11); they are prosperous יָחִילוּ (lit. "are firm") in arrogant iniquity (vv.5-6); their mouths are evil (v.7); they crush the helpless and innocent (vv.8-10). The psalmist petitions God, urging Him not to forget the oppressed (vv.12-14). The psalm ends with a trusting conviction that God will enact the royal policy of justice—punishing the wicked and vindicating the afflicted (vv.15-18).[9]

Obviously, the juxtaposition of thanksgiving in Psalm 9 and complaint in Psalm 10 seems to be diametrically opposite. The psalmist becomes unsettled owing to the fact that 10:1 contradicts 9:9 [8], and 10:2b prays for what 9:15-16 [14-15] have already celebrated.

10:1	Why, O Yahweh, do you stand afar off? Why do you hide yourself in times of trouble?
9:9 [8]	And He will judge the world with righteousness; He will judge the people with equity.
10:2	let them be caught in the schemes that they have devised.
9:15-16 [14-15]	so that I may recount all your praises; that in the gates of the daughter of Zion, I may rejoice in your deliverance.

ה, but the letter מ is missing; צ, ס, and נ are restored tentatively; and the letters פ and ע are in a reversed order (123, 128).

[8] For the structure of Psalm 9, see J. L. Mays, *Psalms* (IBC; Louisville: John Knox Press, 1994) 71-2; and McCann, "Psalms," 717.

[9] For the structure of Psalm 10, see Mays, *Psalms*, 72; and McCann, "Psalms," 718-9.

> The nations have sunk in the pit that they made; in the net that they hid; their own foot has been caught.

The wicked continue to do evil deeds because they do not see God's intervention. They think that God does not call them to account בַּל־יִדְרֹשׁ (does not seek them) and even that there is no God (אֵין אֱלֹהִים; 10:4). The phenomenon of God's indifference to the prosperity of the wicked contradicts the assertion that God is the Avenger of blood (דֹּרֵשׁ דָּמִים, lit. "Seeker of blood"; 9:13 [12]).[10] In addition, the boasting of the wicked that "God has forgotten" (שָׁכַח אֵל; 10:11) contradicts the faith of the psalmist: "God does not forget the cry of the afflicted" (לֹא־שָׁכַח צַעֲקַת עֲנָיִים; 9:13 [12]) and "the needy will not always be forgotten" (לֹא לָנֶצַח יִשָּׁכַח אֶבְיוֹן; 9:19 [18]). Seemingly, tensions between complaint and confidence, between prayers for help and thanksgiving can clearly be shown by the juxtaposition of Psalms 9 and 10. Kraus recognises the sharp contradictions caused by such abrupt juxtaposition, and says:

> Godforsakenness and triumph are juxtaposed in one and the same psalm, and that quite abruptly. Jubilation and lament permeate the song. Two experiences lie adjacent to each other, just as they are met with under the world reign of God on Zion: wondrous rescue and incomprehensible delay.[11]

Apart from the tensions between Psalm 9 and Psalm 10, there are also contradictions within Psalm 10 itself. In 10:1-11 the psalmist complains about God's absence in times of trouble when the wicked oppress the afflicted. The psalmist's faith faces radical testing when he sees the prosperity of the wicked. However, in the second section (10:12-18), the psalm ends up with a trusting affirmation that God will surely enact His royal policy of justice to judge the evil and vindicate the afflicted. Internally, the juxtaposition of doubt (10:1-11) and certitude (10:12-18) creates tensions and disparities.

Psalms 9 and 10 reflect how the psalmist wrestles through the tension between his religious conviction about God's justice and his actual experience of injustice. This is the same as Job's struggle. Psalms 9 and 10 employ the device of contradictory juxtaposition similar to that in Job 22-31 for their rhetorical expressions.

---

[10] Craigie, *Psalms 1-50*, 124.
[11] H.-J. Kraus, *Psalms 1-59: A Commentary* (trans. H. C. Oswald; Minneapolis: Augsburg, 1988) 199.

+ve	Ps 9:1-21 [1-20]	Conviction about God's justice
–ve	Ps 10:1-11	Hiddenness of God (vv.1-2)
		Prosperity of the wicked (vv.3-11)
+ve	Ps 10:12-18	Affirmation of God's justice

The juxtaposition of Psalm 10:1-11 to Psalm 9:1-21 [1-20] creates tensions. Tensions open gaps, and gaps breed oddity and disharmony, which provoke the audience to actively engage in the perplexing issues at hand, especially when faith is threatened by harsh reality. However, gaps need to be filled and Psalm 10:12-18 is the turning point of the psalmist's faith in God, helping to fill the gaps of incongruity in the preceding psalm.

Comparatively speaking, the turning point of Psalms 9-10 is adjacent to the gap generated by the contradictions of 9:1-21 [1-20] and 10:1-11. Thus gap-filling quickly follows gap generation. However, in Job 22-31 the author seems to suspend the gap-filling process. Job 28 and Elihu's speeches (Job 33-37) serve as pseudo-climaxes to bring suspense in anticipation of the divine appearance (Job 38-41), the real climax of the story. The gaps in Job 22-31 are not filled until the story reaches the Yahweh speeches, giving the unsettled audience more time to search for their own resolution.

IV. *Psalm 73*

The literary structure of Psalm 73 is marked by the Hebrew particle אך (indeed/ truly/ surely) at the beginning of vv.1, 13 and 18. It seems best to divide this psalm into three main sections, beginning each with this אך marker.[12]

(1)	vv. 1-12	the problem (12 lines)
	1-3	the plight of the psalmist (3 lines)
	4-12	the prosperity of the wicked (9 lines)
(2)	vv. 13-17	the turning point
(3)	vv. 18-28	the solution (12 lines)
	18-20	the plight of the wicked (3 lines)
	21-28	the prosperity of the psalmist (9 lines)

In the first section (vv.1-12) the psalm commences with the traditional affirmation of faith (in the form of a creed):[13] surely (אך) God

---

[12] McCann, "Psalms," 968. See also Mays, *Psalms*, 240-1.

is good to Israel, to those who are pure in heart (v.1). But the prosperity or peace of the wicked (שְׁלוֹם רְשָׁעִים) brings the psalmist to crisis of faith (vv.2-3). There then follows a long, envious description of the success of the wicked (vv.4-12). The psalmist's religious convictions undergo fiery testing.

The central section (vv.13-17) serves as the turning point. When the psalmist sees that the wicked are not stricken (לֹא יְנֻגָּעוּ; v.5) but that he himself has been stricken all day long (וָאֱהִי נָגוּעַ כָּל־הַיּוֹם; v.14), he starts to question the purpose of keeping himself faithful to God (vv.13-14). When he ponders this enigma, he is overwhelmed by what he has seen and cannot understand (v.16). It is not until the psalmist enters the sanctuary and glimpses God's presence that his perspective is transformed and he understands the final destiny of the wicked (v.17). This is the turning point which carries the psalmist out of the crisis of faith.

Previously, the psalmist was on the slippery ground (vv.1-3), while the wicked were secure (vv.4-12). But now it is the other way round: the wicked are on slippery ground (vv.18-20), whereas the psalmist is secure (vv.21-28).[14] The turning point in the sanctuary of God sheds new insight on the destiny of the wicked and gives birth to renewed trust in God's goodness. Finally, the psalmist reasserts his faith in God: "But as for me, it is good to be near God; I have made Yahweh, the Lord, my refuge, that I may tell of all Your works" (v.28).

Verse 17 helps to link the theme of the psalm in v.1 and v.28 by repetition of "the goodness of God." The significance of v.1 and v.28 is not only underscored by their position as the first and last in the psalm, but through the inclusio of their common vocabulary: טוֹב (good). Concerning the theme of the psalm highlighted in v.1 and v.28, Crenshaw points out:

> The first verse announces the theme of the psalm...The psalm illustrates the manner in which religious convictions undergo radical testing and important reformulation. The final expression of the theme differs considerably from its original form. The weighty experiences

---

[13] J. L. Crenshaw, "Standing Near the Flame: Psalm 73," *A Whirlpool of Torment: Israelite Traditions of God as an Oppressive Presence* (Philadelphia: Fortress Press, 1984) 94.

[14] McCann, "Psalms," 969.

that the psalmist reflects on have transformed the meaning of divine goodness. Faith has matured in the process...The ultimate understanding of divine goodness soars to new spiritual heights. From this lofty perch the psalmist understands that the supreme good is the privilege of being near God.[15]

The first occurence of the phrase בָּרֵי לֵבָב (those who are pure in heart) in v.1 and the subsequent five occurences of the keyword לֵבָב (heart)[16] in vv.7, 13, 21, and 26 demonstrate the major purpose of this psalm: "to examine the traditional definition of purity of heart and the traditional understanding of the consequences of maintaining purity of heart."[17] The crisis of faith comes when the psalmist starts to question the conventional wisdom in keeping his heart pure and hands clean.

The struggle of the psalmist in Psalm 73 is quite similar to that of Job. Trust in God's goodness and justice is jeopardized by his own experience of injustice and the wickedness of the crooked world. In both Psalm 73 and Job this struggle is brought to full expression by the use of contradictory juxtaposition. This single psalm demonstrates some sharp and abrupt juxtapositions of doubt and belief, as listed below:

+ve	v.1	Confession of faith: the goodness of God
−ve	vv.2-16	Crisis of faith
		1) the prosperity of the wicked (2-12)
		2) the purpose of being faithful to God in question (13-16)
Gap-filling	v.17	Divine presence: the turning point
+ve	vv.18-28	Reaffirmation of faith: the goodness of God

Apparently, the envious reporting of the prosperity of the wicked in vv.2-16 is a severe threat to religious convictions regarding God's goodness (v.1). Such a juxtaposition creates a gap, which causes a sense of discontinuity, conflict and disharmony. The encounter with God in the sanctuary (v.17) acts as the turning point for the psalmist, filling the gap. After filling the gap, the religious confession is reasserted in vv.18-28.

---

[15] Crenshaw, "Psalm 73," 94.
[16] M. Buber, "The Heart Determines: Psalm 73," *Theodicy in the Old Testament* (ed. James Crenshaw; Philadelphia: Fortress Press, 1983) 111.
[17] J. C. McCann, Jr., "Psalm 73: A Microcosm of Old Testament Theology," *The Listening Heart: Essays in Wisdom and the Psalms in Honour of Roland E. Murphy, O. Carm* (JSOTSup 58; ed. Kenneth G. Hoglund et al.; Sheffield: JSOT Press, 1987) 250.

Similar to Job 22-31, Psalm 73 is another typical example of contradictory juxtaposition being employed to rhetorical effect, being aimed at the active engagement of the audience in wrestling through the faith crisis with the psalmist. However, the difference between them is that the gaps in Job 22-31 remain unresolved until the story gets to the divine appearance in Job 38-41, whereas the gap in Psalm 73 is filled right after its creation in the expression of contradictions. Despite the suspense caused by the delay in gap-filling in Job's case, divine encounter appears to be the resolution common to both Job and the psalmist.

V. *Ecclesiastes*

Many contradictory passages are placed together in Ecclesiastes. With special reference to Whybray's article and Bartholomew's dissertation, the seven texts listed below demonstrate the juxtapositions of all the contradictory pieces in the book.[18] Whybray suggests that the joy (*carpe diem*)[19] passages answer the central questions in Ecclesiastes. However, Bartholomew argues "that the questions are answered in two ways, that of הֶבֶל and that of joy, and that these contradictory answers are invariably juxtaposed, thereby creating a gap in the reading that needs to be filled."[20]

A. *Ecclesiastes 1:12-2:26*

In this section two contradictory passages are juxtaposed to each other. 1:12-2:23 brings out a long chain of הֶבֶל statements. There then comes the abrupt juxtaposition of טוֹב אֵין (*carpe diem* passage) in 2:24-26.

−ve	1:12-18	The vanity of wisdom
−ve	2:1-11	The vanity of self-indulgence
−ve	2:12-17	The vanity of living wisely
−ve	2:18-23	The vanity of toil
+ve	2:24-26	Seeking enjoyment

---

[18] C. G. Bartholomew, *Reading Ecclesiastes: Old Testament Exegesis and Hermeneutical Theory* (Rome: Editrice Pontificio Istituto Biblico, 1998) 237-54; and R. N. Whybray, "Qoheleth, Preacher of Joy," *JSOT* 23 (1982) 87-98.

[19] *Carpe diem* is a Latin term, meaning "seize the day."

[20] Bartholomew, *Reading Ecclesiastes*, 238.

The question posed at 1:3 is followed by two negative הֶבֶל conclusions in 2:11 (explicit) and 2:22 (implicit). The positive approach אֵין טוֹב (*carpe diem* passage) of 2:24-26 at the end seems to contradict these negative הֶבֶל statements as shown below:[21]

	1:3	What does man gain by all the toil at which he toils under the sun?
–ve	2:11	Then I considered all that my hands had done and the toil I had expended in doing it, and behold, all was vanity and a striving after wind, and there was nothing to be gained under the sun.
–ve	2:22	For what does a man get in all his toil and the striving of his heart with which he toils under the sun?
+ve	2:24-26	There is nothing better for a man than that he should eat and drink and find enjoyment (lit. make his soul see good) in his toil. This also, I saw, is from the hand of God, for apart from him, who can eat or who can have enjoyment? For to the one who pleases Him, God has given wisdom and knowledge and joy, but to the sinner He has given the task of gathering and collecting so that He may give to one who pleases God. This also is vanity and a striving after the wind.

In addition, there is also tension between 2:21 and 2:26,[22] which Qoheleth is aware of and wrestling with:

---

[21] Ogden sees 2:24-26 as the answer to the problems posed in 1:3-2:23; see G. Ogden, *Qoheleth* (Sheffield: Sheffield Academic Press, 1987) 48-9. However, Bartholomew argues that it sounds awkward for the question at 1:3 to flow, via two negative conclusions at 2:11 and 2:22, to its final, positive answer at 2:24-26. He suggests that there is a deliberate opposite juxtaposition here. See Bartholomew, *Reading Ecclesiastes*, 240-1. Whybray considers 2:24-26 as the answer to the problem in 2:22-23, and explains: "man should 'eat and drink and find enjoyment in his toil'; but this is possible only when it comes 'from the hand of God'. God may give joy and pleasure; man can never achieve it for himself, however hard he may try." See Whybray, "Preacher of Joy," 88-9.

[22] For a full discussion of the different approaches to this tension, see Bartholomew, *Reading Ecclesiastes*, 239-42. Whybray recognises that the contradiction between these two verses, both sides, needs to be included in order to encompass the whole truth; see R. N. Whybray, *Ecclesiastes* (NCB; Grand Rapids: Eerdmans, 1989) 64-5. Ogden states that neither v.21 nor v.26 can tell the totality of truth, but each may be true given certain circumstances; see Ogden, *Qoheleth*, 48-9. To resolve the tension, Murphy translates הוֹטֶא as "errant one" with no moral connotation, rather than as "sinner"; see R. E. Murphy, *Ecclesiastes* (WBC; Dallas: Word Books, 1992) 26-7. Fox, Crenshaw and Tremper Longman III also read הוֹטֶא in a non-moral sense. See Fox, *Qoheleth*, 188-90; J. L. Crenshaw, *Ecclesiastes* (OTL; London: SCM Press, 1988) 90-1; and Longman, *Ecclesiastes*, 109-10.

–ve	2:21	[B]ecause sometimes a man who has toiled with wisdom and knowledge and skill must give his inheritance to someone who did not toil for it. This also is vanity and a great evil.
+ve	2:26	For to the one who pleases Him, God has given wisdom and knowledge and joy, but to the sinner He has given the task of gathering and collecting so that He may give to one who pleases God. This also is vanity and a striving after the wind.

Apparently, the view of divine reward and punishment at v.26 contradicts the experience that Qoheleth observes at v.21. Then he discovers that even good gifts from God also appear to be vanity. Regarding to the הֶבֶל remark at the end of 2:26, Bartholomew rightly suggests that Qoheleth perceives the tension between these two contrasting perspectives, and is himself wrestling with this enigmatic dilemma.[23]

B. *Ecclesiastes 3:1-15*

The introductory statement at 3:1 is followed by a series of "time" (עֵת) sayings in 3:2-8, stating the right time for things to happen in God's created order. There then comes the programmatic question of 1:3 which surfaces again in 3:9: "What gain has the worker from his toil?"[24] This question is answered by two opposite responses:

–ve	vv.10-11	**I have seen** the task that God has given to the children of man to be busy with. He has made everything beautiful in its time. Also, he has put eternity into man's heart, yet so that *he cannot find out the work which God has done* from the beginning to the end.
+ve	vv.12-15	**I know that** *there is nothing better* for them than to rejoice and to do good as long as they live; also that everyone should eat and drink and take pleasure in his toil—this is God's gift to man. **I know that** whatever God does endures forever; there is nothing to add to it, nor anything to take from it. God has done it so that men should fear before Him. That which is, already has been; that which is to be, already has been; and God seeks what has been driven away.

---

[23] Bartholomew, *Reading Ecclesiastes*, 242.
[24] Ogden, *Qoheleth*, 51.

The negative observational response רָאִיתִי (I have seen) is the הֶבֶל statement in 3:10-11, focusing upon man's ignorance of God's plan. The two positive confessional responses יָדַעְתִּי כִּי (I know that) in vv.12-14 highlight God's calling to joy (*carpe diem*; vv.12-13), and His sovereignty which causes human reverance toward Him (v.14). Verse 15 reinforces the statement in v.14 about the immutability of God's determination of events. In brief, a tension is apparently generated by the juxtapositions of two contrasting passages—3:10-11 and 3:12-15.[25]

C. *Ecclesiastes 3:16-22*

Verse 16 states the problem of injustice in the world. It is followed by two reflections (v.17; vv.18-21), both of which begin with the same clause אָמַרְתִּי אֲנִי בְּלִבִּי (I said in my heart). Each reflection has a motive clause indicated by the כִּי (v.17b, v.19). The second reflection brings forth the closing observation in v.22.[26]

	v.16	Problem of injustice in the world
+ve	v.17	Traditional response—God has a time (עֵת) for judgment
–ve	vv.18-21	הֶבֶל response—Man and beast share the same fate (18-19)
		—Limitation of human knowledge after death (20-21)
+ve	v.22	Closing observation—אֵין טוֹב statement

The statement of the problem of injustice in v.16 evokes the first response, which positively confesses that God has His time of judgment (v.17). There then comes the juxtaposition of the negative response of vv.18-21, which is contradictory to v.17. In the הֶבֶל response Qoheleth reflects that man is no better than beast. Such a הֶבֶל response is further backed up by the fact that man does not even know anything after death. This negative reflection leads to the positive (*carpe diem*) conclusion: "So I saw that there is nothing

---

[25] Whybray claims that 3:1-15 highlights how human beings should behave in light of their ignorance of their future. He considers that v.13 provides the answer: "But once more the man who accepts what God gives finds happiness (v.13)." See Whybray, "Preacher of Joy," 89-90. Bartholomew notes that there are seeming contradictions between 3:10-11 and 3:12-15, and that the device of contradictory juxtaposition is employed here. See Bartholomew, *Reading Ecclesiastes*, 242-4.

[26] In this section I follow the structure suggested by Ogden; see Ogden, *Qoheleth*, 58-9.

better than that a man should rejoice in his work, for that is his lot. Who can bring him to see what will be after him?" (v.22).[27] The negative response (vv.18-21) is sandwiched by the positive confessional response (v.17) and the positive closing conclusion (v.22). Once again, a contradictory juxtaposition is demonstrated.[28]

D. *Ecclesiastes 5:9-19 [10-20]*[29]

This passage deals with the problem of the deceptiveness of money. The first part (5:9-16 [10-17]) depicts the reasons why wealth eventually brings no gain to its possessors:[30] a) wealth cannot bring satisfaction (v.9 [10]); b) wealth attracts greedy people to swallow it (v.10 [11]); c) wealth deprives the possessors of peace (v.11 [12]); d) wealth might be lost (vv.12-13 [13-14]); e) wealth cannot be taken beyond the grave (vv.14-15 [15-16]); and f) toil for wealth leads to vexation, sickness and anger (v.16 [17]). The second part (5:17-19 [18-20]) is the upbeat response to the problem of the toil for wealth—eating, drinking and enjoying life as the gift of God.[31]

–ve	vv.9-16 [10-17]	The toil for wealth
+ve	vv.17-19 [18-20]	Enjoying life as the gift of God

Apparently, the juxtaposition of these two contrasting passages demonstrates two ways of living life. This creates tensions, and thus sets up a gap, which remains unresolved at this point. The sharpest contrast in this section is the disparity between v.16 [17] and vv.17-18 [18-19]—two dramatically different circumstances of eating.[32]

–ve	v.16 [17]	Eating in darkness with great vexation, sickness and anger
+ve	vv.17-18 [18-19]	Eating and enjoying life as the reward from God

---

[27] According to Whybray, v.22 provides two reasons for Qoheleth's positive advice: "it is because 'that is his lot' and because no one can 'let him know what will happen to him next' that man should set himself to 'enjoy his work.'" See Whybray, "Preacher of Joy," 90.

[28] For more details about the analysis of contradictory juxtapositions and gaps in this section, see Bartholomew, *Reading Ecclesiastes*, 244-6.

[29] Tremper Longman III treats 5:9[10]-6:9 as one larger unit, whereas Murphy considers 5:9-19[10-20] as a portion within 4:17-6:9. See Longman, *Ecclesiastes*, 160; and Murphy, *Ecclesiastes*, 44-56. However, most commentators take 5:9-19[10-20] as a separate unit.

[30] Whybray, *Ecclesiastes*, 98-9.

[31] Whybray, "Preacher of Joy," 89.

[32] For the discussion of the contradictory juxtaposition in this section, see Bartholomew, *Reading Ecclesiastes*, 246.

E. *Ecclesiastes 8:10-15*

This section raises the issue of divine retribution. Verses 10-12a state that wickedness thrives because there is no sign of God's judgment on it. Then Qoheleth utters a statement in vv.12b-13 which reasserts God's reward to the righteous and His punishment upon the wicked. This passage sounds to be in conflict with the idea in vv.10-12a.[33] Interestingly enough, Qoheleth turns back to question justice again in v.14. Finally, in v.15, he recommends the joyful acceptance of what God sees fit to bestow.[34]

–ve	vv.10-12a	Prosperity of the wicked and delayed judgment (הֶבֶל statement)
+ve	vv.12b-13	Affirmation of God's justice and the fear of God
–ve	v.14	Reiteration of the issue of injustice (הֶבֶל statement)
+ve	v.15	Recommendation of enjoying life (אֵין טוֹב conclusion)

As shown above, there is a twofold tension in this section: a) how can a man assert God's justice and the fear of God (vv.12b-13) in the enigmatic plight of injustice (vv.10-12a; 14); and b) how can a man enjoy his life (v.15) when justice is perverted (vv.10-12a; 14). Qoheleth's statement in v.12: "Though a sinner does evil a hundred times and prolongs his life, yet I know that it will be well with those who fear God, because they fear before Him" demonstrates that he is aware of the contradiction, and that he has deliberately placed it here.[35]

F. *Ecclesiastes 9:1-12*

Quite correctly, Murphy notes that it is not coincidental that two inclusios appear in the text: אֵין יוֹדֵעַ הָאָדָם (man does not know) and לֹא־יֵדַע הָאָדָם (man does not know) in vv.1, 12; and מִקְרֶה (happening) and יִקְרֶה (happen) in vv.2, 11. Murphy also points out another

---

[33] Whybray summarizes three approaches to the contradiction caused by the juxtaposition of the passages, treating vv.12b-13: a) as a gloss by the later editor; b) as Qoheleth citing the view in order to refute it; and c) as Qoheleth not entirely rejecting the view, though neither can he accept it. See Whybray, *Ecclesiastes*, 135.

[34] For the structure of this section, see Longman, *Ecclesiastes*, 215-6. According to Whybray, v.15 brings out Qoheleth's conclusion that man should take the best opportunity given by God to eat, drink and enjoy his work; see Whybray, "Preacher of Joy," 90.

[35] Bartholomew, *Reading Ecclesiastes*, 247-8.

inclusio: גַּם־אַהֲבָה גַם־שִׂנְאָה (whether love or hate; v.1) and גַּם אַהֲבָתָם גַּם־שִׂנְאָתָם (their love and their hate; v.6).[36] Therefore 9:1-12 can justifiably be treated as an independent unit, and 9:1-6 as a subsection within it. Verses 7-10 form another sub-unit because of the multiple use of imperative throughout the passage.[37] Such structural analysis helps us to locate effectively certain contradictory juxtapositions as follows:

+ve   v.1a   Confessional statement about God's sovereignty
−ve   vv.1b-6   Human ignorance of whether God loves them or hates them (1b), because everyone faces the same fate of death (2-6)
+ve   vv.7-10   Qoheleth's command to enjoy pleasures of life (*carpe diem*)
−ve   vv.11-12 Human ignorance of the time of disaster

This passage commences with a confessional statement about God's sovereignty: that the just, the wise and their actions are in God's hand (v.1a). This is ironically juxtaposed to the enigmatic reality that nobody knows whether their actions will please God (v.1b), because all face the same destiny of death (vv.2-6). Life is better than death. To be a living dog is better than to be a dead lion. In vv.7-10 Qoheleth vigorously commands the enjoyment of the pleasures that life may provide.[38] Qoheleth concludes with the reflection that no one knows when calamity will strike (vv.11-12). Bartholomew remarks that the dilemma here is left unresolved: how can one enjoy his life while he is still living like a dog (v.4)?[39]

---

[36] For the form, structure and setting of the passage, see Murphy, *Ecclesiastes*, 89-90.
[37] Ogden, *Qoheleth*, 151.
[38] Ogden points out that the sentiment and mood of this *carpe diem* section has changed: "The most striking literary feature of this section is the sudden appearance of a series of imperatives bearing on enjoyment...What is new, however, in this section is the move from advice to imperative; it gives the enjoyment theme in this case a more authoritative presentation." See Ogden, *Qoheleth*, 151.
[39] Whybray considers that the human evils in v.3b are a common response to the problem of human ignorance about whether their deeds please God (v.1b), and to the problem of the common fate of death (v.2-3a). He claims that vv.4-10 represents a better response to the problem: to enjoy life as the gift of God. However, Bartholomew states that the exhortation to enjoyment should not be the answer to the problem of the universality of death. Instead, he sees the employment of contradictory juxtaposition as the author's deliberate literary device. He argues that the gap generated by such juxtaposition here remains unfilled. It means that the author has not yet disclosed the resolution to his audience. See Bartholomew, *Reading Ecclesiastes*, 248-50; and Whybray, "Preacher of Joy," 90-1.

G. *Ecclesiastes 11:7-12:8*[40]

The above six passages display juxtapositions of *carpe diem* passages with enigmatic הֶבֶל passages. Such juxtapositions create tensions and open gaps throughout the book. But gaps need to be filled. Regarding the resolution to these problems, Bartholomew notes that in all those passages the *carpe diem* statements come after the הֶבֶל statements. However, in 11:7-12:8 the reverse is true. He points out:

> This shift to having the *carpe diem* section preface and structure the enigmatic section about death is significant. Previously the two ways of seeing life tend to have been juxtaposed without resolution. This allowing of the *carpe diem* element to shape the whole suggests the possibility of integration and resolution ... Throughout Ecclesiastes תַּחַת הַשָּׁמֶשׁ is mainly a negative expression disparaging life. But here...life under the sun is assessed positively. The bridge element then between the הֶבֶל and *carpe diem* poles would be the *remembering* of one's creator in one's youth before (x3) encountering the death and הֶבֶל found throughout life.[41]

Therefore, according to Bartholomew, "remembrance of God" serves to fill all the gaps caused by Qoheleth's juxtapositions of enigma and joy in the previous six passages. To back up his argument, Bartholomew further adds that the conclusion of the Book in 12:13-14—"The end of the matter; all has been heard. Fear God and keep His commandments, for this is the whole duty of man. For God will bring every deed into judgment, with every secret thing, whether good or evil"—confirms his reading of 12:1 (remembrance of the creator) as the resolution which positively fill the gaps between the *carpe diem* and the enigma statements.[42]

After analysing the structure of the Book of Ecclesiastes, it is not difficult to discover that both Ecclesiastes and Job 22-31 employ the literary device of contradictory juxtaposition in their rhetorical ex-

---

[40] Whybray is aware that the advice to enjoy life appears at the beginning, and it is followed by the description of the brevity of life, expressed in a series of subordinate clauses with עַד אֲשֶׁר (before, until), which is dependent on the main imperative clause "Remember your creator in the days of your youth". He then claims that it is imperative to enjoy life, because this is the way to remember the creator, i.e. to do His will. Whybray further adds that the brevity of life is an additional reason for enjoying it here and now. He considers "the enjoyment of life" as a command of God and as an answer to the vanity of the brevity of life. See Whybray, "Preacher of Joy," 91.

[41] Bartholomew, *Reading Ecclesiastes*, 250.

[42] Bartholomew, *Reading Ecclesiastes*, 253.

pressions. In addition, the contradictory juxtapositions in Ecclesiastes appear to be in the pattern of a long series. All the gaps are deliberately left open until their final resolution at the end of the book. Comparatively speaking, this pattern is quite similar to that in Job. The gaps in Job 22-31 also remain unresolved until the story gets to the end of the book—the divine encounter (Job 38-41).

Of the significance of recognising contradictory juxtapositions in Ecclesiastes, Bartholomew remarks:

> Recognition of the juxtapositions grants the insight that he [Qoheleth] is skeptical and positive! His empiricist epistemology takes him towards skepticism, but his Jewish background and faith provide him with an undeniable, more shalomic perspective upon life.[43]

As far as the Book of Job is concerned, contradictory juxtapositions in Job 22-31 serve to crack open the contradictions between reality and theology so that the inadequacy of the friends' perspective can be fully exposed.

VI. *Conclusion*

After comparing Job 22-31 with Proverbs, Psalms 9-10, Psalm 73 and Ecclesiastes, we discover that contradictory juxtaposition is a typical rhetorical device for expressing the perplexity of life in the Old Testament wisdom literature and wisdom psalms. Thiselton highlights the primary function of biblical wisdom literature thus:

> Such texts as Job, Ecclesiastes, and the parables do not function primarily as raw-material for Christian doctrine....Their primary function is to invite or to provoke the reader to wrestle actively with the issues, in ways that may involve adopting a series of comparative angles of vision.[44]

Concurring with Thiselton, I add to his viewpoint that contradictory juxtaposition can achieve the primary function of biblical wisdom literature by engaging the reader "to wrestle actively with the issues, in ways that may involve adopting a series of comparative angles of vision."

---

[43] Bartholomew, *Reading Ecclesiastes*, 253.
[44] A. C. Thiselton, *New Horizons in Hermeneutics* (Grand Rapids: Zondervan, 1992) 65-6.

BIBLIOGRAPHY

Ackerman, James S.
1981   "Satire and Symbolism in the Song of Jonah." In *Traditions in Transformation: Turning Points in Biblical Faith*, 213-46. Edited by Baruch Halpern and Jon D. Levenson. Winona Lake: Eisenbrauns.

Aimers, Goeffrey J.
2000   "The Rhetoric of Social Conscience in the Book of Job." *JSOT* 91: 99-107.

Aiura, Tadao
1966   "Wisdom Motif in the Joban Poem." *Kwansei Gakuin University Annual Studies* 15: 1-20.

Albertson, R. G.
1983   "Job and Ancient Near Eastern Wisdom Literature." In *Scripture in Context II: More Essays on the Comparative Method*, 213-30. Edited by William W. Hallo, James C. Moyer and Leo G. Perdue. Winona Lake: Eisenbrauns.

Albertz, Rainer
1990   "The Sage and Pious Wisdom in the Book of Job: The Friends' Perspective." In *The Sage in Israel and the Ancient Near East*, 243-61. Edited by John G. Gammie and Leo G. Perdue. Winona Lake: Eisenbrauns.

Allen, Leslie C.
1982   "Psalm 73: An Analysis." *TynBul* 33: 93-118.

Alonso Schökel, Luis
1977   "Toward a Dramatic Reading of the Book of Job." In *Studies in the Book of Job*, 45-61. Edited by Robert Polzin and David Robertson. *Semeia* 7. Missoula: Scholars Press.
1983   "God's Answer to Job." In *Job and the Silence of God*, 45-51. Edited by Christian Duquoc and Casiano Floristián. Edinburgh: T. & T. Clark.
1988   *A Manual of Hebrew Poetics*. Rome: Editrice Pontificio Istituto Biblico.

Alonso Schökel, Luis, and J. L. Sicre Díaz
1983   *Job, Comentario Teológico y Literario*. Nueva Biblia Española. Madrid: Cristiandad.

Alter, Robert
1981   *The Art of Biblical Narrative*. London; Sydney: George Allen & Unwin.
1981   "Between Narration and Dialogue." In *The Art of Biblical Narrative*, 63-87. London; Sydney: George Allen & Unwin.
1981   "Biblical Type-Scenes and the Uses of Conventon." In *The Art of Biblical Narrative*, 47-62. London; Sydney: George Allen & Unwin.
1981   "Characterization and the Art of Reticence." In *The Art of Biblical Narrative*, 114-30. London; Sydney: George Allen & Unwin.
1981   "The Techniques of Repetition." In *The Art of Biblical Narrative*, 88-113. London; Sydney: George Allen & Unwin.
1983   "A Response to Critics." *JSOT* 27: 113-17.
1984   "The Voice from the Whirlwind." *Commentary* 77: 33-41.
1985   *The Art of Biblical Poetry*. Edinburgh: T. & T. Clark.
1985   "Truth and Poetry in the Book of Job." In *The Art of Biblical Poetry*, 85-110. Edinburgh: T. & T. Clark.

1992   "A Literary Approach to the Bible." In *Beyond Form Criticism: Essays in Old Testament Literary Criticism*, 166-85. Edited by Paul R. House. Winona Lake: Eisenbrauns.

1997   "The Characteristics of Ancient Hebrew Poetry." In *The Literary Guide to the Bible*, 611-24. Edited by R. Alter and F. Kermode. London: Fontana Press.

Amit, Yairah

2000   "The Test in the Frame Story of Job." In *Hidden Polemics in Biblical Narrative*, 241-49. Translated by Jonathan Chipman. Leiden; Boston; Köln: Brill.

Andersen, Francis I.

1976   *Job: An Introduction and Commentary*. TOTC. Downers Grove: InterVarsity Press.

Anderson, Bernhard W.

1974   "The New Frontier of Rhetorical Criticism. A Tribute to James Muilenburg." In *Rhetorical Criticism: Essays in Honour of James Muilenburg*, ix-xviii. Edited by J. J. Jackson and M. Kessler. Pittsburgh: Pickwick.

1979   "Biblical Structuralism: Method and Subjectivity in the Study of Ancient Texts (A Review)." *TToday* 35: 518-9.

Arnold, Carroll C.

1974   *Criticism of Oral Rhetoric*. Columbus: Charles E. Merrill.

1980   "Oral Rhetoric, Rhetoric, and Literature." In *Rhetoric in Transition: Studies in the Nature and Uses of Rhetoric*, 157-73. Edited by Eugene E. White. University Park; London: The Pennsylvania State University Press.

Aufrecht, Walter E., ed.

1985   *Studies in the Book of Job*. Ontario: Wilfrid Laurier University Press.

Aufrecht, Walter E.

1985   "Aramaic Studies and the Book of Job." In *Studies in the Book of Job*, 54-66. Edited by Walter E. Aufrecht. Ontario: Wilfrid Laurier University Press.

Baker, John A.

1979   "The Book of Job: Unity and Meaning." In *Studia Biblica 1978, 1: Papers on the Old Testament and Related Themes [6th International Congress on Biblical Studies, Oxford, April 1978]*, 17-26. Edited by Elizabeth A. Livingstone. Sheffield: JSOT Press.

Balentine, Samuel E.

1998   "'What Are Human Beings, That You Make So Much of Them?' Divine Disclosure from the Whirlwind: 'Look at Behemoth'." In *God in the Fray: A Tribute to Walter Brueggemann*, 259-78. Edited by Tod Linafelt and Timothy K. Beal. Minneapolis: Fortress Press.

Bar-Efrat, Shimon

1989   *Narrative Art in the Bible*. JSOTSup 70. Sheffield: The Almond Press.

1992   "Some Observations on the Analysis of Structure in Biblical Narrative." In *Beyond Form Criticism: Essays in Old Testament Literary Criticism*, 186-205. Edited by Paul R. House. Winona Lake: Eisenbrauns.

Barnet, S., M. Berman, and W. Burbo, eds.

1964   *A Dictionary of Literary Terms*. London: Little Brown and Company.

Barr, James

1971-72   "The Book of Job and Its Modern Interpreters." *BJRL* 54: 28-46.

1985   "Hebrew Orthography and the Book of Job." *JSS* 30: 1-33.

1988   "The Authority of Scripture: The Book of Genesis and the Origin of Evil in Jewish and Christian Tradition." In *Christian Authority. Es-*

says in Honour of Henry Chadwick, 59-75. Edited by G. R. Evans. Oxford: Clarendon Press.
 1989 "Philology and Exegesis: Some General Remarks, with Illustrations from Job." In *Questions Disputées D'Ancien Testament: Continuing Questions in Old Testament Method and Theology*, 39-61. Edited by C. Brekelmans. BETL 33. Leuven: Leuven University Press.

Barré, Michael L., ed.
 1997 *Wisdom, You Are My Sister: Studies in Honour of Roland E. Murphy, O. Carm., on the Occasion of His Eightieth Birthday*. Washington D. C.: Catholic Biblical Association of America.

Bartholomew, Craig G.
 1998 *Reading Ecclesiastes: Old Testament Exegesis and Hermeneutical Theory*. Rome: Editrice Pontificio Istituto Biblico.
 2001 *Reading Proverbs with Integrity*. Grove Biblical Series. Cambridge: Grove Book Limited.

Barton, George A.
 1911 "The Composition of Job 24-30." *JBL* 30: 66-77.

Barton, George Aaron
 1980 *The Book of Ecclesiastes*. ICC. Edinburgh: T. & T. Clark.

Barton, J.
 1984 "Classifying Biblical Criticism." *JSOT* 29: 19-35.
 1990 "History and Rhetoric in the Prophets." In *The Bible as Rhetoric: Studies in Biblical Persuasion and Credibility*. Edited by M. Warner. London: Routledge.
 1996 *Reading the Old Testament: Method in Biblical Study*. 2nd ed. London: Darton, Longman and Todd.

Barton, Stephen C., ed.
 1999 *Where Shall Wisdom be Found?: Wisdom in the Bible, the Church and the Contemporary World*. Edinburgh: T. & T. Clark.

Baskin, J. R.
 1992 "Rabbinic Interpretations of Job." In *The Voice from the Whirlwind: Interpreting the Book of Job*, 101-10. Edited by Leo G. Perdue and W. Clark Gilpin. Nashville: Abingdon Press.

Bastiaens, Jean Charles
 1997 "The Language of Suffering in Job 16-19 and in the Suffering Servant Passages in Deutero-Isaiah." In *Studies in the Book of Isaiah: Festschrift Willem A. M. Beuken*, 421-32. Edited by J. Van Ruiten and M. Vervenne. BETL 132. Leuven: Leuven University Press.

Beardslee, William A.
 1999 "Poststructuralist Criticism." In *To Each Its Own Meaning*. Revised edition, 253-67. Edited by Steven L. McKenzie and Stephen R. Haynes. Louisville: Westminster/John Knox Press.

Bergant, Dianne
 1982 *Job, Ecclesiastes*. Old Testament Message. Wilmington: Michael Glazier.
 1984 *What Are They Saying About Wisdom Literature?* New York: Paulist Press.

Berger, Klaus
 1993 "Rhetorical Criticism, New Form Criticism and New Testament Hermeneutics." In *Rhetoric and the New Testament: Essays from the 1992 Heidelberg Conference*, 390-96. Edited by Stanley E. Porter and Thomas H. Olbricht. JSNTSup 90. Sheffield: Sheffield Academic Press.

Berlin, A.
1985   *The Dynamics of Biblical Parallelism.* Bloomington: Indiana University Press.
1994   *Poetics and Interpretation of Biblical Narrative.* Orig. ed., Sheffield: The Almond Press, 1983. Winona Lake: Eisenbrauns.
Beuken, W. A. M., ed.
1994   *The Book of Job.* BETL 114. Leuven: Leuven University Press.
Beuken, W. A. M.
1994   "Job's Imprecation as the Cradle of a New Religious Discourse. The Perplexing Impact of the Semantic Correspondences Between Job 3, Job 4-5 and Job 6-7." In *The Book of Job*, 41-78. Edited by W. A. M. Beuken. BETL 114. Leuven: Leuven University Press.
Bimson, John J.
2000   "Who is 'This' in "Who is This..?" (Job 38:2)? A Response to Karl G. Wilcox." *JSOT* 87: 125-28.
Bitzer, Lloyd F.
1968   "The Rhetorical Situation." *Philosophy and Rhetoric* 1: 1-14.
1974   "The Rhetorical Situation." In *Rhetoric: A Tradition in Transition. In Honor of Donald C. Bryant*, 247-60. Edited by Walter R. Fisher. Michigan State University Press.
1980   "Functional Communication: A Situational Perspective." In *Rhetoric in Transition: Studies in the Nature and Uses of Rhetoric*, 21-38. Edited by Eugene E. White. University Park: The Pennsylvania State University Press.
Black, C. C.
1988-89 "Rhetorical Criticism and Biblical Interpretation." *ExpTim* 100: 252-58.
1995   "Rhetorical Criticism." In *Hearing the New Testament: Strategies for Interpretation*, 256-77. Edited by Joel B. Green. Grand Rapids: Eerdmans.
Black, Edwin
1978   *Rhetorical Criticism.* Madison: University of Wisconsin Press.
Blank, Sheldon H.
1950-51 "The Curse, Blasphemy, The Spell, And The Oath." *HUCA* 23: 73-95.
Blenkinsopp, Joseph
1995   *Wisdom and Law in the Old Testament: The Ordering of Life in Israel and Early Judaism.* Oxford: Oxford University Press.
Blommerde, A. C. M.
1969   *Northwest Semitic Grammar and Job.* BibOr 22. Rome: Biblical Institute Press.
Booth, Wayne C.
1961   *The Rhetoric of Fiction.* Chicago; London: The University of Chicago Press.
1975   *A Rhetoric of Irony.* Chicago; New York: The University of Chicago Press.
1983   "Rhetorical Critics Old and New." In *Deconstructing Literature.* Edited by L. Lerner. Oxford: Blackwell.
Bowers, John Waite, and Robert E. Sanders
1974   "Paradox as a Rhetorical Strategy." In *Rhetoric: A Tradition in Transition. In Honor of Donald C. Bryant.*, 300-15. Edited by Walter R. Fisher. Michigan State University Press.
Brenner, A.
1981   "God's Answer to Job." *VT* 31: 129-37.

1989 "Job the Pious? The Characterization of Job in the Narrative Framework of the Book." *JSOT* 43: 37-52.
Brinton, Alan
  1981 "Situation in the Theory of Rhetoric." *Philosophy and Rhetoric* 14: 234-48.
Brown, F., S. Driver, and C. Briggs
  1996 *The Brown-Driver-Briggs Hebrew and English Lexicon of the Old Testament.* Peabody: Hendrickson.
Brown, William P.
  1996 *Character In Crisis: A Fresh Approach to the Wisdom Literature of the Old Testament.* Grand Rapids: Eerdmans.
  1996 "The Deformation of Character: Job 1-31." In *Character in Crisis: A Fresh Approach to the Wisdom Literature in the Old Testament*, 50-82. Grand Rapids: Eerdmans.
  1996 "Introduction: The Ethics and Ethos of Biblical Wisdom." In *Character in Crisis: A Fresh Approach to the Wisdom Literature of the Old Testament*, 1-21. Grand Rapids: Eerdmans.
  1996 "The Reformation of Character: Job 32-42." In *Character in Crisis: A Fresh Approach to the Wisdom Literature in the Old Testament*, 83-119. Grand Rapids: Eerdmans.
  1999 "Introducing Job: A Journey of Transformation." *Int* 53: 228-38.
  2000 "Creatio Corporis and the Rhetoric of Defense in Job 10 and Psalm 139." In *God Who Creates: Essays in Honour of W. Sibley Towner*, 107-24. Edited by William P. Brown and S. Dean McBride Jr. Grand Rapids: Eerdmans.
  2000 *Ecclesiastes.* IBC. Louisville: John Knox Press.
Brueggemann, Walter
  1985 "Theodicy in a Social Dimension." *JSOT* 33: 3-25.
  1993 "The Book of Job as Sceptical Literature (Katharine J. Dell): A Review." *JBL* 112: 137-39.
  1993 "Response to James L. Mays, 'The Question of Context'." In *The Shape and Shaping of the Psalter*, 29-41. Edited by J. C. McCann. Sheffield: JSOT Press.
Bryant, Donald C.
  1974 "Rhetoric: Its Functions and Its Scope *Rediviva*." In *Rhetoric: A Tradition in Transition. In Honor of Donald C. Bryant.*, 231-46. Edited by Walter R. Fisher. Michigan State University Press.
  1974 "Rhetoric: Its Functions and Its Scope." In *Rhetoric: A Tradition in Transition. In Honor of Donald C. Bryant.*, 195-230. Edited by Walter R. Fisher. Michigan State University Press.
Buber, Martin
  1983 "The Heart Determines: Psalm 73." In *Theodicy in the Old Testament*, 109-18. Edited by James Crenshaw. Philadelphia: Fortress Press.
Burden, J. J.
  1991 "Decision by Debate: Examples of Popular Proverb Performance in the Book of Job." *OTE* 4: 37-65.
Burns, John Barclay
  1987 "The Identity of Death's First-Born (Job XVIII 13)." *VT* 37: 362-64.
  1991 "The Mythological Background to Job 18, 5-21." *BeO* 33: 129-40.
Burrows, Millar
  1928 "The Voice From the Whirlwind." *JBL* 47: 117-32.

Camp, Claudia V.
1987 "Woman Wisdom as Root Metaphor: A Theological Consideration." In *The Listening Heart: Essays in Wisdom and the Psalms in Honor of Roland E. Murphy, O. Carm.*, 45-76. Edited by Kenneth G. Hoglund et al. Sheffield: Sheffield Academic Press.
Carpenter, Eugene, and Michael A. Grisanti
1997 "רשע." In *NIDOTTE*. Vol. 3, 1201-4. Edited by Willem A. VanGemeren. Grand Rapids: Zondervan.
Carroll, Robert P.
1980 "Canonical Criticism: A Recent Trend in Biblical Studies?" *ExpTim* 92: 73-78.
Ceresko, A. R.
1980 *Job 29-31 in the Light of Northwest Semitic: A Translation and Philological Commentary*. BibOr 36. Rome: Biblical Institute Press.
1990 "The Sage in the Psalms." In *The Sage in Israel and the Ancient Near East*, 217-30. Edited by John G. Gammie and Leo G. Perdue. Winona Lake: Eisenbrauns.
Cheney, Michael
1994 *Dust, Wind and Agony: Character, Speech and Genre in Job*. Stockholm: Almqvist & Wiksell International.
Childs, Brevard S.
1979 *Introduction to the Old Testament as Scripture*. London: SCM Press.
Chin, Catherine
1994 "Job and the Injustice of God: Implicit Arguments in Job 13:17-14:12." *JSOT* 64: 91-101.
Clark, David J.
1982 "In Search of Wisdom: Notes on Job 28." *BT* 33: 401-05.
Classen, C. J.
1993 "St Paul's Epistles and Ancient Greek and Roman Rhetoric." In *Rhetoric and the New Testament: Essays from the 1992 Heidelberg Conference*, 265-91. JSNTSup 90. Sheffield: JSOT Press.
Clements, R. E.
1993 "The Good Neighbour in the Book of Proverbs." In *Of Prophet's Visions and the Wisdom of Sages: Essays in Honor of R. Norman Whybray on His Seventieth Birthday*, 209-28. Edited by Heather A. McKay and David J. A. Clines. Sheffield: Sheffield Academic Press.
1995 "Wisdom and Old Testament Theology." In *Wisdom in Ancient Israel: Essays in Honor of J. A. Emerton*, 269-86. Edited by John Day, Robert P. Gordon and H. G. M. Williamson. Cambridge: Cambridge University Press.
Clifford, Richard J.
1980 "Rhetorical Criticism in the Exegesis of Hebrew Poetry." In *Society of Biblical Literature Abstracts and Seminar Papers*, 17-28. Missoula: Scholars Press.
1984 *Fair Spoken and Persuading: An Interpretation of Second Isaiah*. New York: Paulist Press.
1997 "Introduction to Wisdom Literature." In *NIB*. Vol. 5, 1-16. Edited by Leander E. Keck et al. Nashville: Abingdon Press.
Clines, David J. A.
1981 "Job 5,1-8: A New Exegesis." *Bib* 62: 185-94.
1982 "The Arguments of Job's Three Friends." In *Art and Meaning: Rhetoric in Biblical Literature*, 199-214. Edited by David J. A. Clines, David

M. Gunn and Alan J. Hauser. JSOTSup 19. Sheffield: JSOT Press.
1985 "False Naivety in the Prologue to Job." *HAR* 9: 127-36.
1988 "Belief, Desire and Wish in Job 19:23-27: Clues for the Identity of Job's 'Redeemer'." In *"Wünschet Jerusalem Frieden": Collected Communications to the XIIth Congress of the International Organisation for the Study of the Old Testament, Jerusalem 1986*, 363-70. Edited by Matthias Augustin and Klaus-Dietrich Schunck. Frankfurt/am Main; Bern; New York; Paris: Peter Lang.
1989 *Job 1-20*. WBC. Dallas: Word Books.
1989 "The Wisdom Book." In *Creating the Old Testament: The Emergence of the Hebrew Bible*, 269-91. Edited by Stephen Bigger. Oxford: Basil Blackwell.
1990 "Deconstructing the Book of Job." In *The Bible as Rhetoric: Studies in Biblical Persuasion and Credibility*, 65-80. Edited by Martin Warner. London; New York: Routledge.
1994 "Why is There a Book of Job and What Does It Do to You If You Read It?" In *The Book of Job*, 1-20. Edited by W. A. M. Beuken. BETL 114. Leuven: Leuven University Press.
1996 "Varieties of Indeterminacy." *Semeia* 71: 17-27.
1998 "Quarter Days Gone: Job 24 and the Absence of God." In *God in the Fray: A Tribute to Walter Brueggemann*, 242-58. Edited by Tod Linafelt and Timothy K. Beal. Minneapolis: Fortress Press.

Clines, David J. A., D. M. Gunn, and A. J. Hauser, eds.
1982 *Art and Meaning: Rhetoric in Biblical Literature*. Sheffield: JSOT Press.

Cogan, Mordechai, Barry L. Eichler, and Jeffrey H. Tigay, eds.
1997 *Tehillah le Moshe: Biblical and Judaic Studies in Honour of Moshe Greenberg*. Winona Lake: Eisenbrauns.

Combrink, H. J. Bernard
1996 "The Rhetoric of Sacred Scripture." In *Rhetoric, Scripture and Theology: Essays from the 1994 Pretoria Conference*, 102-23. Edited by Stanley E. Porter and Thomas H. Olbricht. JSNTSup 131. Sheffield: Sheffield Academic Press.

Cook, Edward M.
1989 "Another Look at God's Watch Over Job (7:12)." *JBL* 108: 109-16.

Cook, Johann
1992 "Aspects of Wisdom in the Texts of Job (Chapter 28)—Vorlage(n) and / or Translator(S)?" *OTE* 5: 26-45.

Cooper, Alan
1982 "Narrative Theory and the Book of Job." *SR* 11: 35-44.
1990 "Reading and Misreading the Prologue to Job." *JSOT* 46: 67-79.
1997 "The Sense of the Book of Job." *Prooftexts* 17: 227-44.

Cooper, Burton Z.
1986 "Why, God? A Tale of Two Sufferers." *TToday* 42: 423-34.

Corbett, E. P. J.
1969 *Rhetorical Analysis of Literary Works*. New York: Oxford University Press.
1990 *Classical Rhetoric for the Modern Student*. 3rd ed. New York: Oxford University Press.

Cotter, D. M.
1992 *A Study of Job 4-5 in the Light of Contemporary Literary Theory*. SBLDS 124. Atlanta: Scholars Press.

Cox, Claude E.
1985 "Elihu's Second Speech According to the Septuagint." In *Studies in the Book of Job: Papers Presented at the Forty-Ninth Annual Meeting of the Canadian Society of Biblical Studies, May 1981*, 36-53. Edited by Walter E. Aufrecht. Ontario: Wilfrid Laurier University Press.
1987 "The Wrath of God Has Come to Me: Job's First Speech According to the Septuagint." *SR* 16: 195-204.

Cox, Dermot
1973 "The Desire for Oblivion in Job 3." *Liber Annuus* 23: 37-49.
1974 "Reason in Revolt: The Poetic Dialogues in the Book of Job." *Liber Annuus* 24: 317-28.
1981 "Structure and Function of the Final Challenge: Job 29-31." *PIBA* 5: 55-71.
1986 "A Rational Inquiry Into God: Chapters 4-27 of the Book of Job." *Greg* 67: 621-58.

Crafton, Jeffrey A.
1993 "The Dancing of an Attitude: Burkean Rhetorical Criticism and the Biblical Interpreter." In *Rhetoric and the New Testament: Essays from the 1992 Heidelberg Conference*, 429-42. Edited by Stanley E. Porter and Thomas H. Olbricht. JSNTSup 90. Sheffield: Sheffield Academic Press.

Craigie, Peter C.
1983 *Psalms 1-50*. WBC. Waco: Word Books.
1985 "Job and Ugaritic Studies." In *Studies in the Book of Job*, 28-35. Edited by Walter E. Aufrecht. Ontario: Wilfrid Laurier University Press.

Crenshaw, James L.
1976 "Studies in Ancient Israelite Wisdom: Prolegomenon." In *Studies in Ancient Israelite Wisdom*, 1-59. Edited by Harry M. Orlinsky. New York: KTAV.
1977 "In Search of Divine Presence." *RevExp* 74: 353-69.
1977 "The Twofold Search: A Response to Luis Alonso Schökel." In *Studies in the Book of Job*, 63-69. Edited by Robert Polzin and David Robertson. Missoula: Scholars Press.
1981 *Old Testament Wisdom: An Introduction*. Atlanta: John Knox Press.
1981 "Wisdom and Authority: Sapiential Rhetoric and Its Warrants." In *Congress Volume, Vienna 1980*, 10-29. Edited by J. A. Emerton. SVT 32. Leiden: Brill.
1983 "Introduction: The Shift from Theodicy to Anthropodicy." In *Theodicy in the Old Testament*, 1-16. Edited by James L. Crenshaw. Philadelphia: Fortress Press.
1984 "Murder Without Cause: Job." In *A Whirlpool of Torment: Israelite Traditions of God as an Oppressive Presence*, 57-75. Philadelphia: Fortress Press.
1984 "The Silence of Eternity: Ecclesiastes." In *A Whirlpool of Torment: Israelite Traditions of God as an Oppressive Presence*, 77-92. Philadelphia: Fortress Press.
1984 "Standing Near the Flame: Psalm 73." In *A Whirlpool of Torment: Israelite Traditions of God as an Oppressive Presence*, 93-109. Philadelphia: Fortress Press.
1984 *A Whirlpool of Torment: Israelite Traditons of God as an Oppressive Presence*. Philadelphia: Fortress Press.

1987	"The Acquisition of Knowledge in Israelite Wisdom Literature." *WW* 7: 245-52.
1988	*Ecclesiastes*. OTL. London: SCM Press.
1990	"The Sage in Proverbs." In *The Sage in Israel and the Ancient Near East*, 205-16. Edited by John G. Gammie and Leo G. Perdue. Winona Lake: Eisenbrauns.
1993	"The Concept of God in Old Testament Wisdom." In *In Search of Wisdom: Essays in Memory of John G. Gammie*, 1-15. Edited by Leo G. Perdue, Bernard Brandon Scott and William Johnston Wiseman. Louisville: Westminster/John Knox Press.
1993	"Wisdom Literature: Retrospect and Prospect." In *Of Prophets' Visions and the Wisdom of Sages: Essays in Honour of R. Norman Whybray on His Seventieth Birthday*, 161-78. Edited by Heather A. McKay and David J. A. Clines. Sheffield: Sheffield Academic Press.
1995	"Job." In *Urgent Advice and Probing Questions: Collected Writings on Old Testament Wisdom*, 426-48. Macon: Mercer University Press.
1995	*Urgent Advice and Probing Questions: Collected Writings on Old Testament Wisdom*. Macon: Mercer University Press.
1995	"When Form and Content Clash: The Theology of Job 38:1-40:5." In *Urgent Advice and Probing Questions: Collected Writings on Old Testament Wisdom*, 455-67. Macon: Mercer University Press.
1995	"Wisdom." In *Urgent Advice and Probing Questions: Collected Writings on Old Testament Wisdom*, 45-77. Macon: Mercer University Press.
1995	"Wisdom in Israel (Gerhard von Rad): A Review." In *Urgent Advice and Probing Questions: Collected Writings on Old Testament Wisdom*, 300-11. Macon: Mercer University Press.
1995	"The Wisdom Literature." In *Urgent Advice and Probing Questions: Collected Writings on Old Testament Wisdom*, 14-44. Macon: Mercer University Press.
1995	"Wisdom Literature: Biblical Books." In *Urgent Advice and Probing Questions: Collected Writings on Old Testament Wisdom*, 1-13. Macon: Mercer University Press.
1997	"Book Review: Rhetorical Criticism and the Poetry of the Book of Job." *JBL* 116: 342-4.
1999	"Flirting with the Language of Prayer (Job 14:13-17)." In *Worship and the Hebrew Bible. Essays in Honor of John T. Willis*, 110-23. Edited by M. Patrick Graham, Rick R. Marrs and Steven L. McKenzie. JSOTSup 284. Sheffield: Sheffield Academic Press.

Crüsemann, F.
1980	"Hiob und Kohelet: Ein Beitrag Zum Verständnis Des Hiobbuches." In *Werden und Wirken Des Alten Testaments*, 373-93. Edited by R. Albertz. Göttingen: Vandenhoeck & Ruprecht.

Curtis, John Briggs
1979	"On Job's Response to Yahweh." *JBL* 98: 497-511.
1983	"On Job's Witness in Heaven." *JBL* 102: 549-62.
1988	"Why Were the Elihu Speeches Added to the Book of Job?" *PEGLMBS* 8: 93-99.

Dahood, Mitchell J.
1962	"Northwest Semitic Philology and Job." In *The Bible in Current Catholic Thought*, 55-74. Edited by John L. McKenzie. New York: Herder & Herder.
1963-74	"Hebrew-Ugaritic Lexicography I-XII." *Bib* 44-55.
1969	"Hebrew-Ugaritic Lexicography VII." *Bib* 50: 337-56.

1989 "Northwest Semitic Texts and Textual Criticism of the Hebrew Bible." In *Questions Disputées D'Ancien Testament: Continuing Questions in Old Testament Method and Theology*, 11-37. Edited by C. Brekelmans. BETL 33. Leuven: Leuven University Press.

Dailey, Thomas F.
1993 "And Yet He Repents—On Job 42,6." *ZAW* 105: 205-09.
1993 "Theophanic Bluster. Job and the Wind of Change (Job 38:1-42:6)." *SR* 22: 187-95.
1994 *The Repentant Job: A Ricoeurian Icon for Biblical Theology*. Lanham: University Press of America.
1994 "The Wisdom of Divine Disputation? On Job 40:2-5." *JSOT* 63: 105-19.

Davidson, A. B.
1918 *The Book of Job*. Cambridge: Cambridge University Press.

Day, John
1985 *God's Conflict with the Dragon and the Sea: Echoes of a Canaanite Myth in the Old Testament*. Cambridge: Cambridge University Press.
1995 "Foreign Semitic Influence on the Wisdom of Israel and Its Appropriation in the Book of Proverbs." In *Wisdom in Ancient Israel: Essays in Honor of J. A. Emerton*, 55-70. Edited by John Day, Robert P. Gordon and H. G. M. Williamson. Cambridge: Cambridge University Press.

Day, John, Robert P. Gordon, and H. G. M. Williamson, eds.
1995 *Wisdom in Ancient Israel: Essays in Honour of J. A. Emerton*. Cambridge: Cambridge University Press.

Delitzsch, Franz J.
1866 *Biblical Commentary on the Book of Job*. 2 vols. Translated by F. Bolton. Edinburgh: T. & T. Clark.

Dell, Katharine J.
1991 *The Book of Job as Sceptical Literature*. BZAW 197. Berlin; New York: De Gruyter.

Dhorme, E.
1926 *Le Livre de Job*. Paris: Gabalda.
1967 *A Commentary on the Book of Job*. Translated by Harold Knight. London: Thomas Nelson and Sons.

Dick, Michael Brennan
1979 "Job XXVIII 4: A New Translation." *VT* 29: 216-21.
1979 "The Legal Metaphor in Job 31." *CBQ* 41: 37-50.
1983 "Job 31, the Oath of Innocence, and the Sage." *ZAW* 95: 31-53.

Dietrich, M., O. Loretz, and J. Sanmartin
1976 *Die Keilalphabetischen Texte Aus Ugarit*. AOAT 24. Neukirchen: Butzon & Bercker.

Diewert, David A.
1987 "Job 7:12: Yam, Tannin and the Surveillance of Job." *JBL* 106: 203-15.

Dozeman, Thomas B.
1992 "Old Testament Rhetorical Criticism." In *ABD*. Vol. 5, 712-15. Edited by D. N. Freeman et al. New York: Doubleday.

Driver, S. R., and G. B. Gray
1921 *A Critical and Exegetical Commentary on the Book of Job*. ICC. Edinburgh: T. & T. Clark.

Duhm, B.
1897 *Das Buch Hiob Erklärt*. KHC. Tübingen: J. C. B. Mohr.

Duke, R. K.
  1990   *The Persuasive Appeal of the Chronicler: A Rhetorical Analysis.* Sheffield: The Almond Press.
Duquoc, Christian, and Casiano Floristán, eds.
  1983   *Job and the Silence of God.* Edinburgh: T. & T. Clark.
Eagleton, T.
  1990   "J. L. Austin and the Book of Jonah." In *The Book and the Text: The Bible and Literary Theory.* Edited by R. M. Schwartz. Oxford: Blackwell.
  1996   *Literary Theory: An Introduction.* 2nd ed. Oxford: Blackwell.
Eaton, J. H.
  1996   *Job.* OTG. Sheffield: Sheffield Academic Press.
Ehninger, Douglas
  1980   "Toward a Taxonomy of Prescriptive Discourse." In *Rhetoric in Transition: Studies in the Nature and Uses of Rheotic*, 89-100. Edited by Eugene E. White. University Park; London: The Pennsylvania State University Press.
Eissfeldt, Otto
  1974   *The Old Testament: An Introduction.* Translated by Peter R. Ackroyd. Oxford: Basil Blackwell.
Fewell, Danna Nolan, and David M. Gunn
  1992   "Narrative, Hebrew." In *ABD.* Vol. 4, 1023-27. Edited by D. N. Freedman et al. New York: Doubleday.
Fiddes, Paul S.
  1996   "Where Shall Wisdom be Found? Job 28 as a Riddle for Ancient and Modern Readers." In *After the Exile: Essays in Honour of Rex Mason*, 171-90. Edited by John Barton and David J. Reimer. Macon: Mercer University Press.
Finnan, A. P.
  1988   "A Rhetorical Critical Analysis of Job 32-37." Ph.D. Dissertation. Louisville: The Southern Baptist Theological Seminary.
Fiore, Benjamin
  1992   "NT Rhetoric and Rhetorical Criticism." In *ABD.* Vol. 5, 715-19. Edited by D. N. Freedman et al. New York: Doubleday.
Fisch, H.
  1988   "Job: Tragedy is Not Enough." In *Poetry with a Purpose*, 26-42. Bloomington: Indiana University Press.
Fishbane, Michael
  1971   "Jeremiah IV 23-26 and Job III 3-13: A Recovered Use of the Creation Pattern." *VT* 21: 151-67.
  1992   "The Book of Job and Inner-Biblical Discourse." In *The Voice from the Whirlwind: Interpreting the Book of Job*, 86-98. Edited by Leo G. Perdue and W. Clark Gilpin. Nashville: Abingdon Press.
Fohrer, Georg
  1956   "Zur Vorgeschichte Und Komposition Des Buches Hiob." *VT* 6: 249-67.
  1959   "Form und Funktion in der Hiobdichtung." *ZDMG* 109: 31-49.
  1959   "Nun Aber Hat Mein Auge Dich Geschaut. Der Innere Aufbau Des Buches Hiob." *TZ* 15: 1-21.
  1962   "Gottes Antwort Aus dem Sturmwind, Hi. 38-41." *TZ* 18: 1-24.
  1963   *Das Buch Hiob.* KAT. Gütersloh: Gütersloher Verlagshaus Gerd Mohn.

1963 "Das Hiobproblem Und Seine Lösung." *WZ* 12: 249-58.
1974 "The Righteous Man in Job 31." In *Essays in Old Testament Ethics*, 3-22. Edited by James L. Crenshaw and John T. Willis. New York: KTAV.

Follis, Elaine R., ed.
1987 *Directions in Biblical Hebrew Poetry*. Sheffield: JSOT Press.

Fontaine, Carole R.
1987 "Folktale Structure in the Book of Job: A Formalist Reading." In *Directions in Biblical Hebrew Poetry*, 205-32. Edited by Elaine R. Follis. JSOTSup 40. Sheffield: Sheffield Academic Press.
1993 "Wisdom in Proverbs." In *In Search of Wisdom: Essays in Memory of John G. Gammie*, 99-114. Edited by Leo G. Perdue, Bernard Brandon Scott and William Johnston Wiseman. Louisville: Westminster/John Knox Press.

Forrest, R. W. E.
1988 "The Two Faces of Job: Imagery and Integrity in the Prologue." In *Ascribe to the Lord: Biblical and Other Essays in Memory of Peter C. Craigie*, 385-98. Edited by L. Eslinger and C. Taylor. JSOTSup 67. Sheffield: JSOT Press.

Fowler, Robert M.
1992 "Who Is 'The Reader' in Reader Response Criticism?" In *Beyond Form Criticism: Essays in Old Testament Literary Criticism*, 376-94. Edited by Paul R. House. Winona Lake: Eisenbrauns.

Fox, Michael V.
1981 "Job 38 and God's Rhetoric." *Semeia* 19: 53-61.
1989 *Qoheleth and His Contradictions*. Sheffield: Sheffield Academic Press.
1993 "Wisdom in Qoheleth." In *In Search of Wisdom: Essays in Memory of John G. Gammie*, 115-31. Edited by Leo G. Perdue, Bernard Brandon Scott and William Johnston Wiseman. Louisville: Westminster/John Knox Press.
1995 "The Uses of Indeterminacy." *Semeia* 71: 173-92.
1999 *A Time to Tear Down and a Time to Build Up: A Rereading of Ecclesiastes*. Grand Rapids: Eerdmans.

Fox, Michael V. et al., eds.
1996 *Texts, Temples, and Traditions: A Tribute to Menahem Haran*. Winona Lake: Eisenbrauns.

Frank, Jane
1990 "You Call That a Rhetorical Question? Forms and Functions of Rhetorical Questions in Conversation." *Journal of Pragmatics* 14: 723-38.

Franklyn, Paul
1983 "The Sayings of Agur in Proverbs 30: Piety or Scepticism?" *ZAW* 95: 238-52.

Fredericks, D. C.
1997 "הֶבֶל." In *NIDOTTE*. Vol. 1, 1005-6. Edited by Willem A. VanGemeren. Grand Rapids: Zondervan.

Freedman, David Noel
1968 "Notes and Observations: The Elihu Speeches in the Book of Job." *HTR* 61: 51-59.
1968 "The Structure of Job 3." *Bib* 49: 503-08.
1990 "The Book of Job." In *The Hebrew Bible and Its Interpreters*. Winona Lake: Eisenbrauns.

1997 "Orthographic Peculiarities in the Book of Job." In *Divine Commitment and Human Obligation: Selected Writings of David Noel Freedman. Volume Two: Poetry and Orthography*, 44-60. Edited by John R. Huddlestun. Grand Rapids: Eerdmans.

Frye, J. B.
1977 "The Use of Māšāl in the Book of Job." *Semitics* 5: 59-66.

Fullerton, K.
1924 "The Original Conclusion to the Book of Job." *ZAW* 42: 116-35.
1930 "Double Entendre in the First Speech of Eliphaz." *JBL* 49: 320-41.
1934 "On Job, Chapter 9 and 10." *JBL* 53: 321-49.

Fyall, Robert S.
2002 *Now My Eyes Have Seen You: Images of Creation and Evil in the Book of Job*. NSBT 12. Downers Grove: Inter Varsity Press.

Gammie, John G.
1978 "Behemoth and Leviathan: On the Didactic and Theological Significance of Job 40:15-41:26." In *Israelite Wisdom: Theological and Literary Essays in Honor of Samuel Terrien*, 217-31. Edited by John G. Gammie et al. Missoula: Scholars Press.
1987 "The Septuagint of Job: Its Poetic Style and Relationship to the Septuagint of Proverbs." *CBQ* 49: 14-31.

Gammie, John G., and Leo G. Perdue, eds.
1990 *The Sage in Israel and the Ancient Near East*. Winona Lake: Eisenbrauns.

Gammie, John G. et al., eds.
1978 *Israelite Wisdom: Theological and Literary Essays in Honor of Samuel Terrien*. Missoula: Scholars Press.

Geller, Stephen A.
1987 "'Where is Wisdom?': A Literary Study of Job 28 in Its Settings." In *Judaic Perspectives on Ancient Israel*, 155-88. Edited by Jacob Neusner, Baruch A. Levine and Ernest S. Frerichs. Philadelphia: Fortress Press.

Gese, H.
1982 "Die Frage Nach dem Lebenssinn: Hiob und die Folgen." *ZTK* 79: 161-79.

Geyer, J. B.
1992 "Mythological Sequence in Job XXIV 19-20." *VT* 42: 118-20.

Gitay, Yehoshua
1991 "Rhetorical Criticism and the Prophetic Discourse." In *Persuasive Artistry: Studies in New Testament Rhetoric in Honor of George A. Kennedy*, 13-24. Edited by Duane F. Watson. JSNTSup 50. Sheffield: Sheffield Academic Press.
1993 "Rhetorical Criticism." In *To Each Its Own Meaning: An Introduction to Biblical Criticisms and Their Application*, 135-49. Edited by Steven L. McKenzie and Stephen R. Haynes. Louisville: Westminster/John Knox Press.
1996 "The Realm of Prophetic Rhetoric." In *Rhetoric, Scripture and Theology: Essays from the 1994 Pretoria Conference*, 218-29. Edited by Stanley E. Porter and Thomas H. Olbricht. JSNTSup 131. Sheffield: Sheffield Academic Press.
1999 "The Failure of Argumentation in the Book of Job: Humanistic Language Versus Religious Language." *JNSL* 25/1: 239-50.

Givati, Meir
    1979   "Explicit and Implicit Irony in the Speeches of Job." In *The Ben-Zion Luria Volume*, 130-39. The Israel Society for Biblical Research. Jerusalem: Kiriath Sepher [in Hebrew].

Gladson, J. A.
    1978   "Retributive Paradox in Proverbs 10-29." PhD Dissertation. Nashville: Vanderbilt University.

Glatzer, Nahum N.
    1966   "The Book of Job and Its Interpreters." In *Biblical Motifs: Origins and Transformations*, 197-220. Edited by Alexander Altmann. Cambridge, Mass.: Harvard University Press.
    1969   *The Dimensions of Job*. New York: Schocken Books.

Goldsworthy, Graeme
    1995   "Job and the Hiddenness of Order." In *Gospel and Wisdom: Israel's Wisdom Literature in the Christian Life*, 89-105. Carlisle: Paternoster.

Good, Edwin M.
    1981   *Irony in the Old Testament*. Sheffield: The Almond Press.
    1990   *In Turns of Tempest*. Stanford: Stanford University Press.
    1992   "The Problem of Evil in the Book of Job." In *The Voice from the Whirlwind: Interpreting the Book of Job*, 50-69. Edited by Leo G. Perdue and W. Clark Gilprin. Nashville: Abingdon Press.

Goodman, L. E.
    1988   *The Book of Theodicy: Translation and Commentary on the Book of Job by Saadiah Ben Joseph al-Fayyumi*. New Haven: Yale University Press.

Gordis, Robert
    1939-40   "Quotations in Wisdom Literature." *JQR* 30: 123-47.
    1949   "Quotations as a Literary Usage in Biblical, Oriental and Rabbinic Literature." *HUCA* 22: 157-219.
    1964   "The Lord Out of the Whirlwind." *Judaism* 13: 48-63.
    1965   *The Book of God and Man: A Study of Job*. Chicago: The University of Chicago Press.
    1965   "Wisdom and Job." In *The Book of God and Man: A Study of Job*, 31-52. Chicago; London: The University of Chicago Press.
    1968   *Koheleth: The Man and His World*. 3rd ed. New York: Schocken Books.
    1978   *The Book of Job: Commentary, New Translation and Special Studies*. New York: Jewish Theological Seminary of America.
    1985   "Job and Ecology (And the Significance of Job 40:15)." *HAR* 9: 189-202.

Gordon, Cyrus H.
    1966   "Leviathan: Symbol of Evil." In *Biblical Motifs: Origins and Transformations*, 1-9. Edited by Alexander Altmann. Cambridge, Mass.: Harvard University Press.

Gowan, Donald E.
    1985-86   "God's Answer to Job: How is It an Answer?" *HBT* 7-8: 85-102.
    1992   "Reading Job as a 'Wisdom Script'." *JSOT* 55: 85-96.

Gray, G. Buchanan
    1968   "The Purpose and Method of the Writer." In *Twentieth Century Interpretations of the Book of Job: A Collection of Critical Essays*, 36-45. Edited by Paul S. Sanders. Englewood Cliffs: Prentice-Hall.

Greenberg, Moshe
    1997   "Job." In *The Literary Guide to the Bible*, 283-304. Edited by Robert Alter and Frank Kermode. London: Fontana Press.

Greenstein, Edward L.
- 1996 "A Forensic Understanding of the Speech from the Whirlwind." In *Texts, Temples, and Traditions: A Tribute to Menahem Haran*, 241-58. Edited by Michael V. Fox et al. Winona Lake: Eisenbrauns.
- 1999 "In Job's Face/Facing Job." In *The Labour of Reading: Desire, Alienation, and Biblical Interpretation*, 301-17. Edited by Fiona C. Black, Roland Boer and Erin Runions. Alanta: SBL.

Greidanus, Sidney
- 1988 *The Modern Preacher and the Ancient Text*. Grand Rapids: Eerdmans.

Grossberg, Daniel
- 1998 "The Literary Treatment of Nature in Psalms." In *Boundaries of the Ancient Near Eastern World: A Tribute to Cyrus H. Gordon*, 69-87. Edited by Meir Lubetski, Claire Gottlieb and Sharon Keller. Sheffield: Sheffield Academic Press.

Gruber, Mayer I.
- 1998 "Human and Divine Wisdom in the Book of Job." In *Boundaries of the Ancient Near Eastern World: A Tribute to Cyrus H. Gordon*, 88-102. Edited by Meir Lubetski, Claire Gottlieb and Sharon Keller. Sheffield: Sheffield Academic Press.

Guillaume, A.
- 1962-63 "The Unity of the Book of Job." *ALUOS* 4: 26-46.
- 1968 *Studies in the Book of Job with a New Translation*. Leiden: Brill.

Gutiérrez, Gustavo
- 1994 *On Job: God-Talk and the Suffering of the Innocent*. Translated by Mattthew J. O'Connell. Maryknoll; New York: Orbis Books.

Habel, Norman C.
- 1975 *The Book of Job: Commentary*. Cambridge Bible Commentary. Cambridge: Cambridge University Press.
- 1981 "'Naked I Came..': Humanness in the Book of Job." In *Die Botschaft und die Boten: Festschrift Für Hans Walter Wolff Zum 70. Geburtstag*, 373-92. Edited by Jörg Jeremias and Lothar Perlitt. Neukirchen-Vluyn: Neukirchen Verlag.
- 1983 "The Narrative Art of Job: Applying the Principles of Robert Alter." *JSOT* 27: 101-11.
- 1983 "Of Things Beyond Me: Wisdom in the Book of Job." *CurTM* 10: 142-54.
- 1984 "The Role of Elihu in the Design of the Book of Job." In *In the Shelter of Elyon: Essays on Ancient Palestinian Life and Literature in Honor of G. W. Ahlström*, 81-98. Edited by W. Boyd Barrick and John R. Spencer. Sheffield: JSOT Press.
- 1985 *The Book of Job*. OTL. London: SCM Press.
- 1992 "In Defense of God the Sage." In *The Voice from the Whirlwind: Interpreting the Book of Job*, 21-38. Edited by Leo G. Perdue and W. Clark Gilpin. Nashville: Abingdon Press.

Hadley, Judith M.
- 1995 "Wisdom and Goddess." In *Wisdom in Ancient Israel: Essays in Honor of J. A. Emerton*, 234-43. Edited by John Day, Robert P. Gordon and H. G. M. Williamson. Cambridge: Cambridge University Press.

Harris, Scott L.
- 1983 "Wisdom or Creation? A New Interpretation of Job XXVIII 27." *VT* 33: 419-27.

Hartley, John E.
  1988   *The Book of Job*. NICOT. Grand Rapids: Eerdmans.
  1994   "From Lament to Oath: A Study of Progression in the Speeches of Job." In *The Book of Job*, 79-100. Edited by W. A. M. Beuken. BETL 114. Leuven: Leuven University Press.
Hermission, Hans-Jürgen
  1978   "Observations on the Creation Theology in Wisdom." In *Israelite Wisdom: Theological and Literary Essays in Honour of Samuel Terrien*, 43-57. Edited by John G. Gammie et al. Missoula: Scholars Press.
Hill, Robert C.
  1993   "Job in Search of Wisdom." *ScrB* 23: 34-38.
Hoffman, Yair
  1981   "The Relation Between the Prologue and the Speech-Cycles in Job: A Reconsideration." *VT* 31: 160-70.
  1983   "Irony in the Book of Job." *Immanuel* 17: 7-21.
  1996   *A Blemished Perfection: The Book of Job in Context*. JSOTSup 213. Sheffield: Sheffield Academic Press.
Hoglund, Kenneth G.
  1987   "The Fool and the Wise in Dialogue." In *The Listening Heart: Essays in Wisdom and the Psalms in Honor of Roland E. Murphy, O. Carm.*, 161-80. Edited by Kenneth G. Hoglund et al. Sheffield: Sheffield Academic Press.
Hoglund, Kenneth G. et al., eds.
  1987   *The Listening Heart: Essays in Wisdom and the Psalms in Honour of Roland E. Murphy, O. Carm.* Sheffield: Sheffield Academic Press.
Holbert, John C.
  1981   "'The Skies Will Uncover His Iniquity': Satire in the Second Speech of Zophar (Job XX)." *VT* 31: 171-79.
  1983   "The Rehabilitation of the Sinner: The Function of Job 29-31." *ZAW* 95: 229-37.
Holladay, William L., ed.
  1988   *A Concise Hebrew and Aramaic Lexicon of the Old Testament*. Grand Rapids: Eerdmans.
Holland, J. A.
  1972   "On the Form of the Book of Job." *AJBA* 1/5: 160-77.
Holman, J.
  1994   "Does My Redeemer Live or Is My Redeemer the Living God? Some Reflections on the Translation of Job 19, 25." In *The Book of Job*, 377-81. Edited by W. A. M. Beuken. BETL 114. Leuven: Leuven University Press.
Horst, F.
  1960-63   *Hiob*. BKAT. Vol. 1 (chaps. 1-19). Neukirchen: Neukirchener Verlag.
Howard, David M., Jr
  1994   "Rhetorical Criticism in Old Testament Studies." *BBR* 4: 87-104.
Hölscher, G.
  1937   *Das Buch Hiob*. HAT. Tübingen: J. C. B. Mohr (Paul Siebeck).
Humphreys, W. L.
  1985   *The Tragic Vision and the Hebrew Tradition*. OBT 18. Philadelphia: Fortress Press.
Illman, Karl-Johan
  1998   "Did God Answer Job?" In *"Lasset Uns Brücken Bauen..": Collected Communications to the 15th Congress of the International Organization for the*

Study of the Old Testament, Cambridge 1995, 275-85. Edited by Klaus-Dietrich Schunck and Matthias Augustin. BEATAJ 42. Frankfurt am Main; Berlin; New York; Paris; Wien: Peter Lang.

Irwin, William A.
1933 "The First Speech of Bildad." *ZAW* 51: 205-16.
1937 "The Elihu Speeches in the Criticism of the Book of Job." *JR* 17: 37-47.
1962 "Job." In *Peake's Commentary on the Bible*. Revised edition, 391-408. Edited by M. Black and H. H. Rowley. London: Thomas Nelson and Sons.
1962 "Job's Redeemer." *JBL* 81: 217-29.

Jacobson, R.
1981 "Satanic Semiotic, Jobian Jurisprudence." *Semeia* 19: 63-71.

Jamieson-Drake, David W.
1987 "Literary Structure, Genre and Interpretation in Job 38." In *The Listening Heart: Essays in Wisdom and the Psalms in Honor of Roland E. Murphy, O. Carm.*, 217-35. Edited by Kenneth G. Hoglund et al. JSOTSup 58. Sheffield: Sheffield Academic Press.

Janzen, J. Gerald
1985 *Job*. IBC. Atlanta: John Knox Press.
1987 "The Place of the Book of Job in the History of Israel's Religion." In *Ancient Israelite Religion: Essays in Honour of Frank Moore Cross*, 523-37. Edited by Patrick D. Miller, Jr. et al. Philadelphia: Fortress Press.
1994 "On the Moral Nature of God's Power: Yahweh and the Sea in Job and Deutero-Isaiah." *CBQ* 56: 458-78.

Jastrow, Morris, Jr.
1906 "A Babylonian Parallel to the Story of Job." *JBL* 25: 135-91.

Jenks, Alan W.
1985 "Theological Presuppositions of Israel's Wisdom Literature." *HBT* 7: 43-75.

Jobling, David
1983 "Robert Alter's, The Art of Biblical Narrative." *JSOT* 27: 87-99.

Joüon, Paul S. J.
1996 *A Grammar of Biblical Hebrew*. 2 vols. Translated by T. Muraoka. Rome: Editrice Pontificio Istituto Biblico.

Jung, C. G.
1969 *Answer to Job*. Translated by R. F. C. Hull. Princeton: Princeton University Press.

Kaiser, Otto
1995 "Qoheleth." In *Wisdom in Ancient Israel: Essays in Honor of J. A. Emerton*, 83-93. Edited by John Day, Robert P. Gordon and H. G. M. Williamson. Cambridge: Cambridge University Press.

Kaiser, Walter C., Jr.
1986 "Integrating Wisdom Theology Into Old Testament Theology: Ecclesiastes 3:10-15." In *A Tribute to Gleason Archer*, 197-209. Edited by Walter C. Kaiser, Jr. and Ronald F. Youngblood. Chicago: Moody Press.

Kaufmann, H. E.
1983 *Die Anwendung das Buchs Hiob in der Rabbinischen Agadah*. Frankfurt am Main: Slobotzky.

Kautzsch, E., and A. Cowley
    1910   *Gesenius' Hebrew Grammar*. 2nd edition. Oxford: Clarendon Press.
Kelly, Balmer H.
    1961   "Truth in Contradiction: A Study of Job 20 and 21." *Int* 15: 147-56.
Kennedy, George A.
    1980   *Classical Rhetoric and Its Christian and Secular Tradition from Ancient to Modern Times*. Chapel Hill: University of North Carolina Press.
    1984   *New Testament Interpretation Through Rhetorical Criticism*. Chapel Hill: University of North Carolina Press.
    1984   "Rhetorical Criticism." In *New Testament Interpetation Through Rhetorical Criticism*, 3-38. Chapel Hill; London: The University of North Carolina Press.
Kidner, Derek
    1985   *The Wisdom of Proverbs, Job & Ecclesiastes: An Introduction to Wisodm Literature*. Downers Grove: Inter-Varsity Press.
Kinet, Dirk
    1983   "The Ambiguity of the Concepts of God and Satan in the Book of Job." In *Job and the Silence of God*, 30-35. Edited by Christian Duquoc and Casiano Floristán. Edinburgh: T. & T. Clark.
Kinnier Wilson, J. V.
    1975   "A Return to the Problem of Behemoth and Leviathan." *VT* 25: 1-14.
Kirkpatrick, A. F.
    1930   *The Book of Psalms*. Cambridge Bible For Schools and Colleges. Cambridge: Cambridge University Press.
Knight, Harold
    1956   "Job." *SJT* 9: 63-76.
Koehler, L., and W. Baumgartner
    1983   *Hebräisches und Aramäisches Lexikon*. 3rd ed. Leiden: Brill.
    1996   *The Hebrew and Aramaic Lexicon of the Old Testament: The New Koehler-Baumgartner in English*. Translated and edited by M. E. J. Richardson. Leiden; New York; Köln: Brill.
Koops, R.
    1988   "Rhetorical Questions and Implied Meaning in the Book of Job." *BT* 39: 415-23.
Kraus, Hans-Joachim
    1986   *Theology of the Psalms*. Translated by Keith Crim. Minneapolis: Augsburg.
    1988   *Psalms 1-59: A Commentary*. Translated by H. C. Oswald. Minneapolis: Augsburg.
    1989   *Psalms 60-150: A Commentary*. Translated by H. C. Oswald. Minneapolis: Augsburg.
Kubina, V.
    1979   *Die Gottesreden Im Buche Hiob*. Freiburger Theologische Studien 115. Freiburg: Herder.
Kuntz, J. Kenneth
    1992   "Psalm 18: A Rhetorical-Critical Analysis." In *Beyond Form Criticism: Essays in Old Testament Literary Criticsm*, 70-97. Edited by Paul R. House. Winona Lake: Eisenbrauns.

Kuyper, Lester J.
    1959   "The Repentance of Job." *VT* 9: 91-4.
LaCocque, André
    1981   "Job or the Impotence of Religion and Philosophy." *Semeia* 19: 33-52.
    1996   "Job and Religion at Its Best." *BibInt* 4: 131-53.
Lambert, Wilfred G.
    1960   *Babylonian Wisdom Literature*. Oxford: Clarendon Press.
    1995   "Some New Babylonian Wisdom Literature." In *Wisdom in Ancient Israel: Essays in Honor of J. A. Emerton*, 30-42. Edited by John Day, Robert P. Gordon and H. G. M. Williamson. Cambridge: Cambridge University Press.
Lasine, Stuart
    1995   "The King of Desire: Indeterminacy, Audience, and the Solomon Narrative." *Semeia* 71: 85-118.
Laurin, Robert
    1972   "The Theological Structure of Job." *ZAW* 84: 86-89.
Lawrie, Douglas
    2001   "How Critical is It to be Historically Critical? The Case of the Composition of the Book of Job." *JNSL* 27: 121-46.
Lenchak, Timothy A.
    1993   *"Choose Life!" A Rhetorical Critical Investigation of Deuteronomy 28,69-30,20*. Roma: Editrice Pontificio Istituto Biblico.
Lévêque, Jean
    1983   "Tradition and Betrayal in the Speeches of the Friends." In *Job and the Silence of God*, 39-44. Edited by Christian Duquoc and Casiano Floristán. Edinburgh: T. & T. Clark.
Lillie, William
    1956-57   "The Religious Significance of the Theophany in the Book of Job." *ExpTim* 68: 355-58.
Linafelt, Tod
    1996   "The Undecidability of ברך in the Prologue to Job and Beyond." *BibInt* 4: 154-72.
Linblom, Johannes
    1969   "Wisdom in the Old Testament Prophets." *VT*Sup 3: 192-204.
Livingstone, Elizabeth A., ed.
    1979   *Studia Biblica 1978, 1: Papers on Old Testament and Related Themes [6th International Congress on Biblical Studies, Oxford, April 1978]*. Sheffield: JSOT Press.
Loader, J. A.
    1984   "Job—Answer or Enigma?" *OTE* 2: 1-38.
    1992   "Seeing God with Natural Eyes: On Job and Nature." *OTE* 5: 346-60.
Longman, Tremper III
    1998   *The Book of Ecclesiastes*. NICOT. Grand Rapids: Eerdmans.
Loyd, Douglas Emory
    1986   "Patterns of Interrogative Rhetoric in the Speeches of the Book of Job." PhD Dissertation. The University of Iowa.
Lubetski, Meir, Claire Gottlieb, and Sharon Keller, eds.
    1998   *Boundaries of the Ancient Near Eastern World: A Tribute to Cyrus H. Gordon*. Sheffield: Sheffield Academic Press.

Luc, Alex
 2000 "Storm and the Message of Job." *JSOT* 87: 111-23.
Lugt, Pieter van der
 1988 "The Form and Function of the Refrains in Job 28: Some Comments Relating to the 'Strophic' Structure of Hebrew Poetry." In *The Structural Analysis of Biblical and Canaanite Poetry*, 265-93. Edited by W. van der Meer. JSOTSup 74. Sheffield: Sheffield Academic Press.
 1988 "Stanza Structure and Word Repetition in Job 3-14." *JSOT* 40: 3-38.
 1995 *Rhetorical Criticism and the Poetry of the Book of Job*. Leiden; New York; Köln: Brill.
Mack, Burton L.
 1970 "Wisdom Myth and Mythology." *Int* 24: 46-60.
MacKenzie, R. A. F.
 1959 "The Purpose of the Yahweh Speeches in the Book of Job." *Bib* 40: 435-45.
MacKenzie, Roderick
 1983 "The Cultural and Religious Background of the Book of Job." In *Job and the Silence of God*, 3-7. Edited by Christian Duquoc and Casiano Floristán. Edinburgh: T. & T. Clark.
Malchow, Bruce
 1982 "Nature from God's Perspective: Job 38-39." *Dialog* 21: 130-33.
Marcus, Joel
 1997 "Blanks and Gaps in the Markan Parable of the Sower." *BibInt* 5: 247-62.
Marguerat, Daniel
 1993 "The End of Acts (28:16-31) and the Rhetoric of Silence." In *Rhetoric and the New Testament: Essays from the 1992 Heidelberg Conference*, 74-89. Edited by Stanley E. Porter and Thomas H. Olbricht. JSNTSup 90. Sheffield: Sheffield Academic Press.
Martin, James D.
 1995 *Proverbs*. OTG. Sheffield: Sheffield Academic Press.
Matheney, M. Pierce, Jr.
 1971-72 "Major Purposes of the Book of Job." *SWJT* 14: 17-42.
Mays, James Luther
 1994 *Psalms*. IBC. Louisville: John Knox Press.
McCann, J. Clinton, Jr.
 1987 "Psalm 73: A Microcosm of Old Testament Theology." In *The Listening Heart: Essays in Wisdom and the Psalms in Honour of Roland E. Murphy, O. Carm*, 247-57. Edited by Kenneth G. Hoglund et al. JSOTSup 58. Sheffield: JSOT Press.
 1993 *A Theological Introduction to the Book of Psalms: The Psalms as Torah*. Nashville: Abingdon Press.
 1996 "Psalms." In *NIB*. Vol. 4, 641-1280. Edited by Leander E. Keck et al. Nashville: Abingdon Press.
 1997 "Wisdom's Dilemma: The Book of Job, the Final Form of the Book of Psalms, and the Entire Bible." In *Wisdom, You Are My Sister— Studies in Honour of Roland E. Murphy, O. Carm., on the Occasion of His Eightieth Birthday*, 18-30. Edited by Michael L. Barré. Washington D. C.: The Catholic Biblical Association of America.

McKay, Heather A., and David J. A. Clines, eds.
    1993   *Of Prophets' Visions and the Wisdom of Sages: Essays in Honour of R. Norman Whybray on His Seventieth Birthday*. Sheffield: Sheffield Academic Press.

McKeating, Henry
    1970-71   "Central Issue of the Book of Job." *ExpTim* 82: 244-47.

Meer, Willem van der, and Johannes C. De Moor, eds.
    1988   *The Structural Analysis of Biblical and Canaanite Poetry*. Sheffield: JSOT Press.

Mettinger, Tryggue N. D.
    1992   "The God of Job: Avenger, Tyrant, or Victor?" In *The Voice from the Whirlwind: Interpreting the Book of Job*, 39-49. Edited by Leo G. Perdue and W. Clark Gilpin. Nashville: Abingdon Press.
    1993   "Intertextuality: Allusion and Vertical Context Systems in Some Job Passages." In *Of Prophets' Visions and the Wisdom of Sages: Essays in Honour of R. Norman Whybray on His Seventieth Birthday*, 257-80. Edited by Heather A. McKay and David J. A. Clines. Sheffield: Sheffield Academic Press.

Meynet, Roland
    1998   *Rhetorical Analysis: An Introduction to Biblical Rhetoric*. JSOTSup 256. Sheffield: Sheffield Academic Press.

Michel, W. L.
    1987   *Job in the Light of Northwest Semitic. I. Prologue and First Cycle of Speeches: Job 1:1-14:22*. BibOr 42. Rome: Biblical Institute Press.
    1994   "Confidence and Despair: Job 19, 25-27 in the Light of Northwest Semitic Studies." In *The Book of Job*, 157-81. Edited by W. A. M. Beuken. BETL 114. Leuven: Leuven University Press.

Miles, John A., Jr.
    1974-75   "Laughing as the Bible: Jonah as Parody." *JQR* 65: 168-81.

Miller, Douglas B.
    2002   *Symbol and Rhetoric in Ecclesiastes: The Place of Hebel in Qohelet's Work*. Atlanta: SBL.

Miller, James E.
    1991   "Structure and Meaning of the Animal Discourse in the Theophany of Job (38,39-39,30)." *ZAW* 103: 418-21.

Miller, Patrick D., Jr.
    1986   *Interpreting the Psalms*. Philadelphia: Fortress Press.

Miller, Ward S.
    1989   "The Structure and Meaning of Job." *Concordia Journal* 15: 103-20.

Moberly, R. W. L.
    1999   "Solomon and Job: Divine Wisdom in Human Life." In *Where Shall Wisdom Be Found?: Wisdom in the Bible, the Church, and the Contemporary World*, 3-17. Edited by Stephen C. Barton. Edinburgh: T. & T. Clark.

Moore, Rick D.
    1983   "The Integrity of Job." *CBQ* 45: 17-31.

Morrow, William
    1986   "Consolation, Rejection, and Repentance in Job 42:6." *JBL* 105: 211-25.

Mowinckel, Sigmund
    1969   "Psalms and Wisdom." *VTSup* 3: 205-24.

Möller, Karl
1999 "Presenting a Prophet in Debate: An Investigation of the Literary Structure and the Rhetoric of Persuasion of the Book of Amos." Ph.D. Dissertation. Cheltenham and Gloucester College of Higher Education.
2003 *A Prophet in Debate: The Rhetoric of Persuasion in the Book of Amos.* JSOTSup 372. London: Sheffield Academic Press.
Muecke, D. C.
1969 *The Compass of Irony.* London: Methuen & Co. Ltd.
Muenchow, Charles
1989 "Dust and Dirt in Job 42:6." *JBL* 108: 597-611.
Muilenburg, James
1969 "Form Criticism and Beyond." *JBL* 88: 1-18.
1992 "Form Criticism and Beyond." In *Beyond Form Criticism: Essays in Old Testament Literary Criticism*, 49-69. Edited by Paul R. House. Winona Lake: Eisenbrauns.
Murphy, Roland E.
1962 "A Consideration of the Classification, 'Wisdom Psalms'." *VT*Sup 9: 156-67.
1965 *Introduction to the Wisdom Literature of the Old Testament.* Collegeville: Liturgical Press.
1977 "What and Where is Wisdom?" *CurTM* 4: 283-87.
1978 "Wisdom—Thesis and Hypothesis." In *Israelite Wisdom: Theological and Literary Essays in Honor of Samuel Terrien*, 35-42. Edited by John G. Gammie et al. Missoula: Scholars Press.
1981 *Wisdom Literature: Job, Proverbs, Ruth, Canticles, Ecclesiastes, Esther.* The Form of the Old Testament Literature. Grand Rapids: Eerdmans.
1983 *Wisdom Literature and Psalms.* Nashville: Abingdon Press.
1984 "The Theological Contributions of Israel's Wisdom Literature." *Listening* 19: 30-40.
1987 "Religious Dimensions of Israelite Wisdom." In *Ancient Israelite Religion: Essays in Honor of Frank Moore Cross*, 449-58. Edited by Patrick D. Miller, Paul D. Hanson and S. Dean McBride. Philadelphia: Fortress Press.
1990 "The Sage in Ecclesiastes and Qoheleth the Sage." In *The Sage in Israel and the Ancient Near East*, 263-71. Edited by John G. Gammie and Leo G. Perdue. Winona Lake: Eisenbrauns.
1992 *Ecclesiastes.* WBC. Dallas: Word Books.
1995 "The Personification of Wisdom." In *Wisdom in Ancient Israel: Essays in Honour of J. A. Emerton*, 222-33. Edited by John Day, Robert P. Gordon and H.G.M. Williamson. Cambridge: Cambridge University Press.
1999 *The Book of Job: A Short Reading.* New York: Paulist Press.
Nel, P. J.
1991 "Cosmos and Chaos: A Reappraisal of the Divine Discourses in the Book of Job." *OTE* 4: 206-26.
Neusner, Jacob, Baruch A. Levine, and Ernest S. Frerichs, eds.
1987 *Judaic Perspectives on Ancient Israel.* Philadelphia: Fortress Press.
Newsom, Carol A.
1992 "Job." In *The Women's Bible Commentary*, 130-36. Edited by C. A. Newsom and S. L. Ringe. Louisville: Westminster/John Knox Press.
1993 "Considering Job." *CR:BS* 1: 87-118.
1993 "Cultural Politics and the Reading of Job." *BibInt* 1: 119-38.

1994 "The Moral Sense of Nature: Ethics in the Light of God's Speech to Job." *PSB* 15: 9-27.
1996 "The Book of Job." In *NIB*. Vol. 4, 319-637. Edited by Leander E. Keck et al. Nashville: Abingdon Press.
1999 "Job and His Friends: A Conflict of Moral Imaginations." *Int* 53: 239-53.
2002 "The Book of Job as Polyphonic Text." *JSOT* 97: 87-108.

Nichols, Helen Hawley
1911 "The Composition of the Elihu Speeches (Job, Chaps. 32-37)." *AJSLL* 27: 97-186.

Nicholson, E. W.
1995 "The Limits of Theodicy as a Theme of the Book of Job." In *Wisdom in Ancient Israel: Essays in Honour of J. A. Emerton*, 71-82. Edited by John Day, Robert P. Gordon and H. G. M. Williamson. Cambridge: Cambridge University Press.

Nida, E. A. et al.
1983 *Style and Discourse: With Special Reference to the Greek New Testament*. Cape Town: Bible Society.

Nougayrol, J. et al., eds.
1968 *Ugaritica, V*. Paris: Imprimerie Nationale.

Oblath, Michael D.
1999 "Job's Advocate: A Tempting Suggestion." *BBR* 9: 189-201.

O'Connor, Daniel J.
1983-84 "Job's Final Word—'I Am Consoled..'." *ITQ* 50: 181-97.
1985 "The Futility of Myth—Making in Theodicy: Job 38-41." *PIBA* 9: 81-99.
1991 "The Cunning Hand: Repetitions in Job 42:7, 8." *ITQ* 57: 14-25.

O'Connor, Donal
1996 "'Bless God and Die' (Job 2:9): Euphemism or Irony?" *PIBA* 19: 48-65.

O'Connor, K. M.
1988 *The Wisdom Literature*. Collegeville: Liturgical Press.

Odell, David
1993 "Images of Violence in the Horse in Job 39:18-25." *Prooftexts* 13: 163-73.

Ogden, Graham
1987 *Qoheleth*. Sheffield: Sheffield Academic Press.

Olbricht, Thomas H.
1999 "Classical Rhetorical Criticism and Historical Reconstructions: A Critique." In *The Rhetorical Interpretation of Scripture: Essays from the 1996 Malibu Conference*, 108-24. Edited by Stanley E. Porter and Dennis L. Stamps. JSNTSup 180. Sheffield: Sheffield Academic Press.

Oorschot, J. van
1987 *Gott Als Grenze*. BZAW 170. Berlin; New York: De Gruyter.
1994 "Hiob 28: Die Verborgene Weisheit und die Furcht Gottes Als Ueberwindung einer Generalisierten חכמה." In *The Book of Job*, 183-201. Edited by W. A. M. Beuken. BETL 114. Leuven: Leuven University Press.

Orlinsky, Harry M., ed.
1976 *Studies in Ancient Israelite Wisdom*. New York: KTAV.

Owens, John Joseph
　1991　　　*Analytical Key to the Old Testament*. Vol. 1-4. Grand Rapids: Baker.
Parsons, Gregory W.
　1981　　　"Literary Features of the Book of Job." *BSac* 138: 213-29.
　1981　　　"The Structure and Purpose of the Book of Job." *BSac* 138: 139-57.
Patrick, Dale
　1976　　　"The Translation of Job 42:6." *VT* 26: 369-71.
　1979　　　"Job's Address of God." *ZAW* 91: 268-82.
Patrick, Dale, and Allen Scult
　1990　　　"Finding the Best Job." In *Rhetoric and Biblical Interpretation*, 82-102. JSOTSup 82. Sheffield: The Almond Press.
　1990　　　*Rhetoric and Biblical Interpretation*. JSOTSup 82. Sheffield: The Almond Press.
　1990　　　"Rhetorical Criticism and Biblical Exegesis." In *Rhetoric and Biblical Interpretation*, 11-27. JSOTSup 82. Sheffield: The Almond Press.
　1999　　　"Rhetoric and Ideology: A Debate Within Biblical Scholarship Over the Import of Persuasion." In *The Rhetorical Interpretation of Scripture: Essays from the 1996 Malibu Conference*, 63-83. Edited by Stanley E. Porter and Dennis L. Stamps. JSNTSup 180. Sheffield: Sheffield Academic Press.
Patte, Daniel
　1993　　　"Structural Criticism." In *To Each Its Own Meaning: An Introduction to Biblical Criticisms and Their Application*, 153-70. Edited by Steven L. McKenzie and Stephen R. Haynes. Louisville: Westminster/John Knox Press.
Peake, A. S.
　1905　　　*Job*. The Century Bible. Edinburgh: T. C. & E. C. Jack.
Penchansky, David
　1990　　　*The Betrayal of God: Ideological Conflict in Job*. Louisville: Westminster/John Knox Press.
Perdue, Leo G.
　1986　　　"Job's Assault on Creation." *HAR* 10: 295-315.
　1991　　　"The Return to First Naïveté: The Search for Wisdom and the Speeches of Elihu." In *Wisdom in Revolt: Metaphorical Theology in the Book of Job*, 242-59. Sheffield: JSOT Press.
　1991　　　*Wisdom in Revolt: Metaphorical Theology in the Book of Job*. Sheffield: The Almond Press/JSOT Press.
　1993　　　"Wisdom in the Book of Job." In *In Search of Wisdom: Essays in Memory of John G. Gammie*, 73-98. Edited by Leo G. Perdue, Bernard Brandon Scott and William Johnston Wiseman. Louisville: Westminster/John Knox Press.
　1994　　　"Metaphorical Theology in the Book of Job: Theological Anthropology in the First Cycle of Job's Speeches (Job 3; 6-7; 9-10)." In *The Book of Job*, 129-56. Edited by W. A. M. Beuken. BETL 114. Leuven: Leuven University Press.
Perdue, Leo G., and W. Clark Gilpin, eds.
　1992　　　*The Voice From the Whirlwind: Interpreting the Book of Job*. Nashville: Abingdon Press.

Perdue, Leo G., Bernard Brandon Scott, and William Johnston Wiseman, eds.
    1993   *In Search of Wisdom: Essays in Memory of John G. Gammie.* Louisville: Westminster/John Knox Press.
Perelman, C.
    1979   *The New Rhetoric and the Humanities: Essays on Rhetoric and Its Applications.* Synthese Library 140. Dordrecht: Reidel.
    1982   *The Realm of Rhetoric.* Notre Dame: Notre Dame University Press.
Perelman, C., and L. Olbrechts-Tyteca
    1969   *The New Rhetoric: A Treatise on Argumentation.* Notre Dame: Notre Dame University Press.
Petersen, Mike
    1995   "Job 28: The Theological Center of the Book of Job." *Biblical Viewpoint* 29: 99-111.
Pfeiffer, Robert H.
    1927   "The Priority of Job Over Is. 40-55." *JBL* 46: 202-6.
    1941   *Introduction to the Old Testament.* New York: Harper & Brothers.
Polzin, Robert M.
    1974   "The Framework of the Book of Job." *Int* 28: 182-200.
    1977   *Biblical Structuralism: Method and Subjectivity in the Study of Ancient Texts.* Philadelphia: Fortress Press.
Polzin, Robert M., and David Robertson, eds.
    1977   *Studies in the Book of Job.* Missoula: Scholars Press.
Pope, Marvin H.
    1964   "The Word שחת in Job 9:31." *JBL* 83: 269-78.
    1973   *Job.* 3rd edition. AB. Garden City: Doubleday.
Porter, Stanley E.
    1991   "The Message of the Book of Job: Job 42:7b as Key to Interpretation?" *EvQ* 63: 289-304.
Powell, Mark Allan
    1990   *What Is Narrative Criticism?* Minneapolis: Fortress Press.
    1995   "Narrative Criticism." In *Hearing the New Testament: Strategies for Interpretation,* 239-55. Edited by Joel B. Green. Grand Rapids: Eerdmans.
Priest, John F.
    1976   "Where is Wisdom to be Placed?" In *Studies in Ancient Israelite Wisdom,* 281-8. Edited by Harry M. Orlinsky. New York: KTAV.
    1984   "Wisdom and Humanism." In *The Answers Lie Below: Essays in Honor of Lawrence Edmund Toombs,* 263-77. Edited by Henry O. Thompson. Lanham; New York; London: University Press of America.
Pritchard, J. B.
    1969   *ANET.* 3rd ed. Princeton: Princeton University Press.
Rad, Gerhard von
    1970   "The Self-Revelation of Creation." In *Wisdom in Israel,* 144-76. Translated by James D. Martin. London: SCM Press.
    1972   *Wisdom in Israel.* Translated by James D. Martin. London: SCM Press.
    1976   "Job XXXVIII and Ancient Egyptian Wisdom." In *Studies in Ancient Israelite Wisdom,* 267-91. Edited by Harry M. Orlinsky. New York: KTAV.
Ray, J. D.
    1995   "Egyptian Wisdom Literature." In *Wisdom in Ancient Israel: Essays in Honor of J. A. Emerton,* 17-29. Edited by John Day, Robert P. Gordon and H. G. M. Williamson. Cambridge: Cambridge University Press.

Redditt, Paul L.
    1994   "Reading the Speech Cycles in the Book of Job." *HAR* 4: 205-14.
Reddy, Mummadi Prakasa
    1978   "The Book of Job—A Reconstruction." *ZAW* 90: 59-94.
Regt, Lénart J. de
    1994   "Functions and Implications of Rhetorical Questions in the Book of Job." In *Biblical Hebrew and Discourse Linguistics*, 361-73. Edited by Robert D. Bergen. Dallas: Summer Institute of Linguistics.
    1994   "Implications of Rhetorical Questions in Strophes in Job 11 and 15." In *The Book of Job*, 321-8. Edited by W. A. M. Beuken. BETL 114. Leuven: Leuven University Press.
Reichert, Victor E.
    1976   *Job*. Soncino Books of The Bible. London; Jerusalem; New York: The Soncino Press.
Reimer, David J.
    1997   "צדק." In *NIDOTTE*. Vol. 3, 744-69. Edited by Willem A. VanGemeren. Grand Rapids: Zondervan.
Rensburg, J. F. J. van
    1991   "Wise Men Saying Things by Asking Questions: The Function of the Interrogative in Job 3 to 14." *OTE* 4: 227-47.
Renz, Thomas
    1999   *The Rhetorical Function of the Book of Ezekiel*. SVT 76. Leiden; Boston; Köln: Brill.
Reyburn, William D.
    1992   *A Handbook on the Book of Job*. New York: United Bible Societies.
Ricoeur, Paul
    1975   "Biblical Hermeneutics." *Semeia* 4: 29-148.
Roberts, J. J. M.
    1975   "SĀPÔN in Job 26,7." *Bib* 56: 554-57.
Robertson, David
    1973   "The Book of Job: A Literary Study." *Soundings* 56: 446-69.
Ross, James F.
    1975   "Job 33:14-30: The Phenomenology of Lament." *JBL* 94: 38-46.
Rowley, H. H.
    1958   "The Book of Job and Its Meaning." *BJRL* 41: 167-207.
    1963   "The Book of Job and Its Meaning." In *From Moses to Qumran: Studies in the Old Testament*, 141-83. London: Lutterworth Press.
    1970   *Job*. NCB. London: Thomas Nelson and Sons.
    1980   *The Book of Job*. Revised edition. NCB. Grand Rapids: Eerdmans.
Rowold, Henry
    1985   "Yahweh's Challenge to Rival: The Form and Function of the Yahweh-Speech in Job 38-39." *CBQ* 47: 199-211.
Sacks, Robert
    1999   *The Book of Job with Commentary*. Atlanta: Scholars Press.
Sanders, Paul S., ed.
    1968   *Twentieth Century Interpretations of the Book of Job: A Collection of Critical Essays*. Englewood Cliffs: Prentice-Hall.
Sanders, Paul S.
    1968   "Introduction." In *Twentieth Century Interpretations of the Book of Job: A Collection of Critical Essays*, 1-19. Edited by Paul S. Sanders. Englewood Cliffs: Prentice-Hall.

Sarna, Nahum M.
- 1957 "Epic Substratum in the Prose of Job." *JBL* 76: 13-25.
- 1963 "The Mythological Background of Job 18." *JBL* 82: 315-18.
- 1996 "Notes on the Use of the Definite Article in the Poetry of Job." In *Texts, Temples, and Traditions: A Tribute to Menahem Haran*, 279-84. Edited by Michael V. Fox et al. Winona Lake: Eisenbrauns.

Sasson, Victor
- 2001 "In Defence of Job." *UF* 32: 465-74.

Sawyer, John F.
- 1979 "The Authorship and Structure of the Book of Job." In *Studia Biblica 1978, 1: Papers on Old Testament and Related Themes [6th International Congress on Biblical Studies, Oxford, April 1978]*, 253-57. Edited by Elizabeth A. Livingstone. Sheffield: JSOT Press.

Schlobin, Roger C.
- 1992 "Prototypic Horror: The Genre of the Book of Job." *Semeia* 60: 23-38.

Scholnick, Sylvia Huberman
- 1975 "Lawsuit Drama in the Book of Job." Ph.D. Dissertation. Brandeis University.
- 1982 "The Meaning of Mišpat in the Book of Job." *JBL* 101: 521-29.
- 1987 "Poetry in the Courtroom: Job 38-41." In *Directions in Biblical Hebrew Poetry*, 185-204. Edited by Elaine R. Follis. JSOTSup 40. Sheffield: Sheffield Academic Press.

Schreiner, Susan E.
- 1989 "Exegesis and Double Justice in Calvin's Sermons on Job." *CH* 58: 322-38.
- 1992 "'Why Do the Wicked Live?': Job and David in Calvin's Sermons on Job." In *The Voice from the Whirlwind: Interpreting the Book of Job*, 129-43. Edited by Leo G. Perdue and W. Clark Gilpin. Nashville: Abingdon Press.
- 1994 *Where Shall Wisdom be Found?: Calvin's Exegesis of Job from Medieval and Modern Perspectives*. Chicago; London: The University of Chicago Press.

Schultz, Carl
- 1996 "The Cohesive Issue of Mišpāt in Job." In *"Go to the Land I Will Show You": Studies in Honour of Dwight W. Young*, 159-75. Edited by Joseph E. Coleson and Victor H. Matthews. Winona Lake: Eisenbrauns.

Schultz, Richard L.
- 1997 "Unity or Diversity in Wisdom Theology? A Canonical and Covenantal Perspective." *TynBul* 48: 271-306.

Scott, R. B. Y.
- 1965 *Proverbs, Ecclesiastes*. AB. Garden City: Doubleday.
- 1970 "The Study of the Wisdom Literature." *Int* 24: 20-45.
- 1971 *The Way of Wisdom in the Old Testament*. New York: Macmillan.
- 1971 "Wisdom in Revolt: Agur and Qoheleth." In *The Way of Wisdom in the Old Testament*, 165-89. New York: Macmillan.

Scott, Robert L.
- 1980 "Intentionality in the Rhetorical Process." In *Rhetoric in Transition: Studies in the Nature and Uses of Rhetoric*, 39-60. Edited by Eugene E. White. University Park; London: The Pennsylvania State University Press.

Seitz, Christopher R.
    1989   "Job: Full-Structure, Movement, and Interpretation." *Int* 43: 5-17.
Selms, A. van
    1982-83   *Job*. Prediking OT. 2 vols. Nijkerk: Callenbach.
Settlemire, Clara C.
    1984   "The Original Position of Job 28." In *The Answers Lie Below: Essays in Honour of Lawrence Edmund Toombs*, 287-317. Edited by Henry O. Thompson. Lanham; New York; London: University Press of America.
Sewall, Richard B.
    1968   "The Book of Job." In *Twentieth Century Interpretations of the Book of Job: A Collection of Criticial Essays*, 21-35. Edited by Paul S. Sanders. Englewood Cliffs: Prentice-Hall.
Shelley, John C.
    1992   "Job 42:1-6: God's Bet and Job's Repentance." *RevExp* 89: 541-46.
Shelton, Pauline
    1999   "Making a Drama Out of a Crisis? A Consideration of the Book of Job as a Drama." *JSOT* 83: 69-82.
Ska, Jean Louis
    1990   *"Our Fathers Have Told Us": Introduction to the Analysis of Hebrew Narratives*. Rome: Pontifical Biblical Institute.
Skehan, Patrick W.
    1964   "Job's Final Plea (Job 29-31) and the Lord's Reply (Job 38-41)." *Bib* 45: 51-61.
Smick, Elmer B.
    1986   "Architectonics, Structured Poems, and Rhetorical Devices in the Book of Job." In *A Tribute to Gleason Archer*, 87-104. Edited by Walter C. Kaiser, Jr. and Ronald F. Youngblood. Chicago: Moody Press.
Smith, Gary V.
    1992   "Is There a Place for Job's Wisdom in Old Testament Theology?" *Trinity Journal* 13: 3-20.
Snaith, Norman H.
    1968   *The Book of Job: Its Origin and Purpose*. Studies in Biblical Theology. London: SCM Press.
Sonnet, Jean-Pierre
    1997   *The Book Within the Book: Writing in Deuteronomy*. Leiden; New York; Köln: Brill.
Spiegel, Shalom
    1991   "Noah, Danel, and Job, Touching on Canaanite Relics in the Legends of the Jews." In *Essential Papers on Israel and the Ancient Near East*, 193-241. Edited by Frederick E. Greenspahn. New York; London: New York University Press.
Stamps, Dennis L.
    1999   "The Theological Rhetoric of the Pauline Epistles: Prolegomenon." In *The Rhetorical Interpretation of Scripture: Essays from the 1996 Malibu Conference*, 249-59. Edited by Stanley E. Porter and Dennis L. Stamps. JSNTSup 180. Sheffield: Sheffield Academic Press.
Steinmann, Andrew E.
    1995   "The Graded Numerical Saying in Job." In *Fortunate the Eyes That See: Essays in Honor of David Noel Freedman in Celebration of His Seventieth Birthday*, 288-97. Edited by Astrid B. Beck et al. Grand Rapids: Eerdmans.

Stek, John H.
    1997   "Job: An Introduction." *CalTJ* 32: 443-58.
Sternberg, Meir
    1985   *The Poetics of Biblical Narrative: Ideological Literature and the Drama of Reading*. Bloomington: Indiana University Press.
    1985   "Going from Surface to Depth." In *The Poetics of Biblical Narrative: Ideological Literature and the Drama of Reading*, 342-64. Bloomington: Indiana University Press.
    1985   "The Play of Perspectives." In *The Poetics of Biblical Narrative: Ideological Literature and the Drama of Reading*, 153-85. Bloomington: Indiana University Press.
Swanepoel, M. G.
    1991   "Job 12—An(Other) Anticipation of the Voice from the Whirlwind?" *OTE* 4: 192-205.
Szczygiel, P
    1931   *Das Buch Job*. HSAT. Bonn: Peter Hanstein.
Talstra, E.
    1994   "Dialogue in Job 21: 'Virtual Quotations' or Text Grammatical Markers?" In *The Book of Job*, 329-48. Edited by W. A. M. Beuken. BETL 114. Leuven: Leuven University Press.
Tate, Marvin E.
    1990   *Psalms 51-100*. WBC. Dallas: Word Books.
Terrien, Samuel
    1954   "The Book of Job: Introduction and Exegesis." In *IB*. Vol. 3, 875-1198. New York; Nashville: Abingdon Press.
    1963   *Job*. Commentaire de l'Ancien Testament. Neuchâtel: Delachaux et Niestlé.
    1971   "The Yahweh Speeches and Job's Responses." *RevExp* 68: 497-509.
    1978   *The Elusive Presence*. New York: Harper and Row.
    1990   "Job as a Sage." In *The Sage in Israel and the Ancient Near East*, 231-42. Edited by John G. Gammie and Leo G. Perdue. Winona Lake: Eisenbrauns.
    1993   "Wisdom in the Psalter." In *In Search of Wisdom: Essays in Memory of John G. Gammie*, 51-72. Edited by Leo G. Perdue, Bernard Brandon Scott and William Johnston Wiseman. Louisville: Westminster/John Knox Press.
Thiselton, A. C.
    1992   *New Horizons in Hermeneutics*. Grand Rapids: Zondervan.
Thomas, Daniel
    1971   "Types of Wisdom in the Book of Job." *IndJT* 20: 157-65.
Thompson, Henry O., ed.
    1984   *The Answers Lie Below: Essays in Honour of Lawrence Edmund Toombs*. Lanham: University Press of America.
Tilley, Terrence W.
    1989   "God and the Silencing of Job." *Modern Theology* 5: 257-70.
Towner, W. Sibley
    1997   "The Book of Ecclesiastes." In *NIB*. Vol. 5, 267-360. Edited by Leander E. Keck et al. Nashville: Abingdon Press.
Trible, Phyllis
    1994   *Rhetorical Criticism: Context, Method, and the Book of Jonah*. Minneapolis: Fortress Press.

Tsevat, Matitiahu
- 1966 "The Meaning of the Book of Job." *HUCA* 37: 73-106.
- 1980 *The Meaning of the Book of Job and Other Biblical Studies*. New York: KTAV.

Tur-Sinai [Torczyner], N. Harry
- 1957 *The Book of Job: A New Commentary*. Jerusalem: Kiryath Sepher.

Unknown *Biblical Hapax Logomena in the Light of the Akkadian and Ugaritic*.
- 1978 Missoula: Scholars Press.

Urbrock, William J.
- 1972 "Formula and Theme in the Song-Cycle of Job." *SBL, Proceedings* 2: 459-87.
- 1976 "Oral Antecedents to Job: A Survey of Formulas and Formulaic Systems." *Semeia* 5: 111-37.

Vall, Gregory
- 1995 "'From Whose Womb Did the Ice Come Forth?' Procreation Images in Job 38:28-29." *CBQ* 57: 504-13.

VanGemeren, Willem A., ed.
- 1997 *New International Dictionary of Old Testament Theology & Exegesis*. Vol. 1-5. Grand Rapids: Zondervan.

VanGemeren, Willem A.
- 1991 "Psalms." In *The Expositor's Bible Commentary*. Vol. 5, 1-880. Edited by Frank E. Gaebelein. Grand Rapids: Zondervan.

Van Leeuwen, Raymond C.
- 1992 "Wealth and Poverty: System and Contradiction in Proverbs." *HS* 33: 25-36.
- 1993 "Scribal Wisdom and Theodicy in the Book of the Twelve." In *In Search of Wisdom: Essays in Memory of John G. Gammie*, 31-49. Edited by Leo G. Perdue, Bernard Brandon Scott and William Johnston Wiseman. Louisville: Westminster/John Knox Press.
- 1997 "The Book of Proverbs." In *NIB*. Vol. 5, 19-264. Edited by Leander E. Keck et al. Nashville: Abindon Press.
- 2001 "Psalm 8.5 and Job 7.17-18: A Mistaken Scholarly Commonplace?" In *The World of the Aramaeans I: Biblical Studies in Honour of Paul-Eugène Dion*, 205-15. Edited by P. M. Michèle Daviau, John W. Wevers and Michael Weigl. JSOTSup 324. Sheffield: Sheffield Academic Press.

Vawter, Bruce
- 1980 "Prov. 8:22: Wisdom and Creation." *JBL* 99: 205-16.

Viviers, Hendrik
- 1997 "Elihu (Job 32-37), Garrulous But Poor Rhetor? Why Is He Ignored?" In *The Rhetorical Analysis of Scripture: Essays from the 1995 London Conference.*, 137-53. Edited by Stanley E. Porter and Thomas H. Olbricht. JSNTSup 146. Sheffield: Sheffield Academic Press.
- 1997 "How Does God Fare in the Divine Speeches (Job 38:1-42:6)?" *OTE* 10: 109-24.

Waltke, Bruce K., and David Diewert
- 1999 "Wisdom Literature." In *The Face of Old Testament Studies: A Survey of Contemporary Approaches*, 295-328. Edited by David W. Baker and Bill T. Arnold. Grand Rapids: Baker.

Waltke, Bruce K., and M. O'Connor
- 1990 *An Introduction to Biblical Hebrew Syntax*. Winona Lake: Eisenbrauns.

Walton, Steve
 1996 "Rhetorical Criticism: An Introduction." *Themelios* 21: 4-9.
Waterman, L.
 1952 "Notes on Job 28:4." *JBL* 71: 167-70.
Watson, Duane F.
 1999 "The Contributions and Limitations of Greco-Roman Rhetorical Theory for Constructing the Rhetorical and Historical Situations of a Pauline Epistle." In *The Rhetorical Interpretation of Scripture: Essays from the 1996 Malibu Conference*, 125-51. Edited by Stanley E. Porter and Dennis L. Stamps. JSNT Sup 180. Sheffield: Sheffield Academic Press.
Watson, Duane F., and Alan J. Hauser, eds.
 1994 *Rhetorical Criticism of the Bible: A Comprehensive Bibliography with Notes on History and Method*. Leiden; New York; Köln: Brill.
Watts, James W.
 1995 "Rhetorical Strategy in the Composition of the Pentateuch." *JSOT* 68: 3-22.
Webster, Edwin C.
 1983 "Strophic Patterns in Job 3-28." *JSOT* 26: 33-60.
 1984 "Strophic Patterns in Job 29-42." *JSOT* 30: 95-109.
Weeks, Stuart
 1999 "Wisdom in the Old Testament." In *Where Shall Wisdom be Found?: Wisdom in the Bible, the Church and the Contemporary World*, 19-30. Edited by Stephen C. Barton. Edinburgh: T. & T. Clark.
Weiser, A.
 1959 *Das Buch Hiob*. ATD. Göttingen: Vandenhoeck & Ruprecht.
Weisman, Ze'ev
 1998 *Political Satire in the Bible*. Georgia: Scholar Press.
Weiss, M.
 1983 *The Story of Job's Beginning*. Jerusalem: Magnes.
West, Marjory S.
 1928-29 "The Book of Job and the Problem of Suffering." *ExpTim* 40: 358-64.
Westermann, Claus
 1956 *Der Aufbau Des Buches Hiob*. BHT 23. Tübingen: J. C. B. Mohr.
 1980 *The Pslams: Structure, Content and Message*. Minneapolis: Augsburg.
 1981 *Praise and Lament in the Psalms*. Atlanta: John Knox Press.
 1981 *The Structure of the Book of Job: A Form-Critical Analysis*. Translated by Charles A. Muenchow. Philadelphia: Fortress Press.
Whedbee, J. William
 1977 "The Comedy of Job." In *Studies in the Book of Job*, 1-39. Edited by Robert Polzin and David Robertson. Semeia 7. Missoula: Scholars Press.
White, Hugh C.
 1991 *Narration and Discourse in the Book of Genesis*. Cambridge; New York; Port Chester; Melbourne; Sydney: Cambridge University Press.
Whitley, C. F.
 1979 *Koheleth: His Language and Thought*. BZAW 148. Berlin: De Gruyter.
Whybray, R. Norman
 1965 "Proverbs VIII 22-31 and Its Supposed Prototypes." *VT* 15: 504-14.

1974	*The Intellectual Tradition in the Old Testament.* BZAW 135. Berlin; New York: De Gruyter.
1982	"Qoheleth, Preacher of Joy." *JSOT* 23: 87-98.
1983	"ON ROBERT ALTER'S The Art of Biblical Narrative." *JSOT* 27: 75-86.
1989	*Ecclesiastes.* NCB. Grand Rapids: Eerdmans.
1995	"The Wisdom Psalms." In *Wisdom in Ancient Israel: Essays in Honor of J. A. Emerton,* 152-60. Edited by John Day, Robert P. Gordon and H. G. M. Williamson. Cambridge: Cambridge University Press.
1996	"The Immorality of God: Reflections on Some Passages in Genesis, Job, Exodus and Numbers." *JSOT* 72: 89-120.
1997	"Psalm 119: Profile of a Psalmist." In *Wisdom, You Are My Sister: Studies in Honor of Roland E. Murphy, O. Carm., on the Occasion of His Eightieth Birthday,* 31-43. Edited by Michael L. Barré. Washington D. C.: The Catholic Biblical Association of America.
1998	*Job.* A New Biblical Commentary. Sheffield: Sheffield Academic Press.

Wiesel, E.
1979 *The Trial of God.* New York: Schocken Books.

Wilcox, John T.
1989 *The Bitterness of Job.* Ann Arbor: University of Michigan Press.

Wilcox, Karl G.
1998 "'Who is This..?': A Reading of Job 38:2." *JSOT* 78: 85-95.

Wilde, A. de
1981 *Das Buch Hiob.* OTS 22. Leiden: Brill.

Williams, James G.
1971	"'You Have not Spoken Truth of Me' Mystery and Irony in Job." *ZAW* 83: 231-55.
1977	"Comedy, Irony, Intercession: A Few Notes in Response." In *Studies in the Book of Job,* 135-45. Edited by Robert Polzin and David Robertson. Missoula: Scholars Press.
1978	"Deciphering the Unspoken: The Theophany of Job." *HUCA* 49: 59-72.
1984	"Job's Vision: The Dialectic of Person and Presence." *HAR* 8: 259-72.
1992	"Job and the God of Victims." In *The Voice from the Whirlwind: Interpreting the Book of Job,* 208-31. Edited by Leo G. Perdue and W. Clark Gilprin. Nashville: Abingdon Press.
1993	"On Job and Writing: Derrida, Girard, and the Remedy-Poison." *SJOT* 7: 32-50.

Williams, Ronald J.
1985 "Current Trends in the Study of the Book of Job." In *Studies in the Book of Job: Papers Presented at the Forty-Ninth Annual Meeting of the Canadian Society of Biblical Studies, May 1981,* 1-27. Edited by Walter E. Aufrecht. Ontario: Wilfrid Laurier University Press.

Wilson, Gerald
1997 "משל." In *NIDOTTE.* Vol. 2, 1134-36. Edited by Willem A. VanGemeren. Grand Rapids: Zondervan.

Wilson, Lindsay
1990 "The Place of Wisdom in the Old Testament Theology." *The Reformed Theological Review* 49: 60-69.

1995 "The Book of Job and the Fear of God." *TynBul* 46: 59-79.
1996 "Realistic Hope or Imaginative Exploration? The Identity of Job's Arbiter." *Pacifica* 9: 243-52.

Wolde, Ellen J. van, ed.
2003 *Job 28: Cognition in Context*. BIS 64. Leiden; Boston; Köln: Brill.

Wolde, Ellen J. van
1994 "Job 42, 1-6: The Reversal of Job." In *The Book of Job*, 223-50. Edited by W. A. M. Beuken. BETL 114. Leuven: Leuven University Press.

Wolfers, David
1989-90 "The Volcano in Job 28." *Jewish Biblical Quarterly* 18: 234-40.
1994 "The Stone of Deepest Darkness: A Mineralogical Mystery (Job XXVIII)." *VT* 44: 274-76.
1995 *Deep Things Out of Darkness: The Book of Job*. Grand Rapids: Eerdmans.

Wolters, Al
1990 "A Child of Dust and Ashes." *ZAW* 102: 116-19.

Wright, Addison G.
1997 "The Poor But Wise Youth and the Old But Foolish King." In *Wisdom, You Are My Sister: Studies in Honor of Roland E. Murphy, O. Carm., on the Occasion of His Eightieth Birthday*, 142-54. Edited by Michael L. Barré. Washington D. C.: The Catholic Biblical Association of America.

Wright, J. Stafford
1991 "Ecclesiastes." In *The Expositor's Bible Commentary*. Vol. 5, 1135-97. Edited by Frank E. Gaebelein. Grand Rapids: Zondervan.

Wuellner, Wilhelm
1987 "Where Is Rhetorical Criticism Taking Us?" *CBQ* 49: 448-63.

Yaffe, M. D., ed.
1989 *Thomas Aquinas's Literal Exposition on Job*. Translated by A. Damico. Atlanta: Scholars Press.

Yaffe, M. D.
1992 "Providence in Medieval Aristotelianism: Moses Maimonides and Thomas Aquinas on the Book of Job." In *The Voice from the Whirlwind: Interpreting the Book of Job*, 111-28. Edited by Leo G. Perdue and W. Clark Gilpin. Nashville: Abingdon Press.

Youngblood, Ronald F.
1986 "Qoheleth's 'Dark House' (Eccles. 12:5)." In *A Tribute to Gleason Archer*, 211-27. Edited by Walter C. Kaiser, Jr. and Ronald F. Youngblood. Chicago: Moody Press.

Zemach, Eddy
1989 "What Did God Answer Job?" *Moznayim* 61/9: 14-17 [in Hebrew].

Zerafa, Peter Paul
1978 *The Wisdom of God in the Book of Job*. Rome: Herder.

Zimmerli, Walther
1964 "The Place and Limit of the Wisdom in the Framework of the Old Testament Theology." *SJT* 17: 146-58.

Zimmermann, Ruben
1994 "Homo Sapiens Ignorans Hiob 28 Als Bestandteil der Urspruenglichen Hiobdichtung." *BN* 74: 80-100.

Zink, James K.
 1965 "Impatient Job: An Interpretation of Job 19:25-27." *JBL* 84: 147-52.
Zuck, Roy B., ed.
 1992 *Sitting with Job: Selected Studies on the Book of Job.* Grand Rapids: Baker.
Zuck, Roy B.
 1992 "Job's Discourse on God's Wisdom: An Exposition of Job 28." In *Sitting with Job: Selected Studies on the Book of Job.* Edited by Roy B. Zuck. Grand Rapids: Baker.
Zuckerman, Bruce
 1991 *Job the Silent: A Study in Historical Counterpoint.* New York: Oxford University Press.

ADDITIONS TO BIBLIOGRAPHY

Eisen, Robert
    2004   *The Book of Job in Medieval Jewish Philosophy.* New York: Oxford University Press.

Kelly, Joseph F.
    2005   *The Problem of Evil in the Western Tradition: From the Book of Job to Modern Genetics.* Collegeville: Liturgical Press.

Nam, Duck-woo
    2003   *Talking about God: Job 42:7-9 and the Nature of God in the Book of Job.* New York: Peter Lang.

Newsom, Carol A.
    2003   *The Book of Job: A Contest of Moral Imaginations.* Oxford; New York: Oxford University Press.

Pfeffer, J. I.
    2005   *Providence in the Book of Job: The Search for God's Mind.* Brighton: Sussex Academic Press.

INDICES

INDEX OF AUTHORS

Alter, R., 38-39, 43, 87-88, 91, 187-188, 195
Andersen, F. I., 2, 8, 115-118, 127, 138, 143, 152, 158, 160, 167, 178, 183-186, 196
Arnold, C., 59

Bar-Efrat, S., 38, 41
Bartholomew, C. G., 245, 247, 251-253
Beardslee, W. A., 35
Bitzer, L. F., 58
Booth, W. C., 61, 91
Brown, W. P., 34, 37, 42, 45, 50, 52-55, 189

Childs, B. S., 2-5, 28-29, 196
Clines, D. J. A., 2, 7-8, 35-37, 42, 60, 63, 66, 121, 127, 135-136, 143, 146-147, 167, 196, 205
Combrink, H. J. B., 91
Crenshaw, J. L., 18, 243
Culler, J., 35

Dell, K. J., 134, 141, 155-156, 159
Dhorme, E., 2-3, 6-7, 9, 12, 105, 112-113, 117, 127, 152-154, 167, 172, 175, 178, 181-182, 186, 190, 196
Driver, S. R. & G. B. Gray, 2-3, 5-7, 9, 11-12, 23-24, 113, 115, 117, 167, 172, 175, 178, 186, 196

Fiddes, P. S., 13-14
Fiore, B., 18
Fohrer, G., 216, 220
Fox, M. V., 75, 191, 238
Fredericks, D. C., 191
Fullerton, K., 136

Geller, S. A., 3, 12, 198, 203
Gitay, Y., 19
Good, E. M., 2-5, 27-28, 116-118, 127, 137, 152, 157, 167, 178, 185-186, 196

Gordis, R., 2, 9, 12-13, 26, 60, 75, 114, 117-118, 126-127, 133-134, 136-137, 143, 152, 154, 167, 172, 175, 178-180, 186, 196
Greenberg, M., 27
Greidanus, S., 61
Gutiérrez, G., 33

Habel, N. C., 1-2, 8, 12-15, 37-39, 42-43, 46, 50, 54-56, 105, 109-111, 114, 117, 119, 127, 135, 142-143, 147, 149-153, 165, 167, 170, 172, 175, 178, 181, 186, 188-189, 196, 213, 215-218, 221
Hartley, J. E., 2, 8, 13, 60, 115-118, 127-128, 133, 152, 157, 159-160, 162-163, 167, 175, 178, 180, 182, 186, 188, 196, 218

Irwin, W. A., 27

Janzen, J. G., 2-5, 127, 134, 152, 156-157, 159-160, 167, 178, 184-186, 190, 196
Joüon, P. S. J., 101

Kennedy, G. A., 17, 92
Koops, R., 88-89
Kraus, H.-J., 241

Laurin, R., 231
Lugt, P. van der, 17-18, 110-112, 117, 150-153, 158-160

Miles, J. A., Jr., 137
Muilenburg, J., 17
Murphy, R. E., 250

Newsom, C. A., 2, 8, 13-14, 68, 73, 114-118, 127, 136, 141, 152, 154-155, 161, 166-167, 178, 184-186, 189-190, 196, 198-199, 201-203
Nicholson, E. W., 53, 95

Patrick, D., 33

Patrick, D. & A. Scult, 16, 19, 118, 120
Patte, D., 34
Peake, A. S., 109, 117
Petersen, M., 2, 8, 196, 211
Pfeiffer, R. H., 60
Polzin, R. M., 22, 29-32, 34-35
Pope, M. H., 2-3, 7, 11-12, 32, 105, 113, 117, 127, 152, 154, 167, 172, 175, 178-179, 186
Porter, S. E., 94
Powell, M. A., 62, 84

Regt, L. J. de, 89
Reichert, V. E., 204
Renz, T., 19
Rowley, H. H., 2, 9, 27, 32, 113, 127, 152, 154, 167, 172, 175, 178-179, 186, 206, 214

Sawyer, J. F., 2, 8, 196
Seitz, C. R., 25, 27, 118, 123, 228
Settlemire, C. C., 2, 6, 10-12, 196, 208-210
Ska, J. L., 85
Snaith, N. H., 26
Sonnet, J.-P., 93-94
Sternberg, M., 38, 44, 50, 54, 79-82, 91, 230
Szczygiel, P., 2, 10-11, 196

Thiselton, A. C., 253
Tur-Sinai, N. H., 2, 10-11, 196

Van Leeuwen, R. C., 214, 237-238

Walton, S., 19
Weisman, Z., 137-138
Westermann, C., 2-3, 8, 12, 24, 135, 137, 140, 144, 196, 215
Whedbee, J. W., 134-136
Whybray, R. N., 2-3, 5, 13, 123, 127, 152, 157, 163, 167, 178-179, 186, 196, 217, 245

INDEX OF BIBLICAL TEXTS

Old Testament (Hebrew Text)

Genesis
1:2	200
7:11	200
49:25	200

Exodus
6:2-3	70
19:18	136
23:7	169
32:12	33
32:14	33

Leviticus
19:12	188

Numbers
5:20-22	188

Deuteronomy
4:35	70
4:39	70
6:2	71
6:13	71
6:24	71
19:14	100
22:1-3	100
23:24-25	101
24:17	100
24:19-21	100
25:1	169
25:4	101
27:17	100
28:1-14	1, 72
28:15-68	1, 72
30:12-14	201

Judges
5:4	136

2 Samuel
7:22	202

1 Kings
8:32	169

Isaiah
5:23	169
13:13	136
27:1	132
29:6	136
40:9-11	155
40:22	148
40:25	139
40:26-27	148
41:4	139
44:6-8	70
44:24-28	143-144
46:9	70
51:9	131-132

Jeremiah
10:8	191
14:22	191
18:8	33
18:10	33
23:6	70

Ezekiel
14:14	59
14:20	59

Amos
5:6-9	134
7:3	33
7:6	33

Habakkuk
3:6	136, 199
3:9	199
3:10	136

Psalms
1:1-3	1, 72
1:1	12
1:4-6	1, 72
1:4	12
8	74
8:5-6	74
9-10	237, 239, 242, 253

INDEX OF BIBLICAL TEXTS

9	239-242	73:5	243
9:2-3	240	73:7	244
9:4-5	240	73:13-17	242-243
9:6-7	240	73:13-16	244
9:8-9	240	73:13-14	243
9:9	240	73:13	242, 244
9:10-11	240	73:14	243
9:12-13	240	73:16	243
9:13	241	73:17	243-244
9:14-15	240	73:18-28	242, 244
9:15-16	240	73:18-20	242-243
9:16-19	240	73:18	242
9:19	241	73:21-28	242-243
9:20-21	240	73:21	244
10	239-241	73:26	244
10:1-11	241-242	73:28	243
10:1-2	240, 242	74:15	199
10:1	240	75:4	136
10:2	240	89:10-11	200
10:2b	240	89:11	131
10:3-11	240, 242	94:11	191
10:3-4	240	97:4	136
10:4	241	104	134
10:5-6	240	104:26	132
10:7	240	107	143-144
10:8-10	240	107:40	143
10:11	240-241	111:10	71
10:12-18	241-242	112:1-9	1, 72
10:12-14	240	112:10	1, 72
10:14-15	1, 72	114:5-7	136
10:15-18	240	119:1-2	1, 72
15:1-5	1, 72	139	141-142
18:8	136	139:2-6	141
18:16	136	139:7-8	141
33:13-14	148	139:13-18	142
33:18-19	1, 72	139:19-24	141
35	180	139:23-24	142
37:35-36	1, 72	140	180
44:2	202		
46:3-4	136	*Job*	
50:16	12	1-37	30
69	180	1-28	223
73	172, 237, 242, 244-245, 253	1-2	22, 25-26, 36, 92
		1	215
73:1-12	242	1:1-2:10	39, 41
73:1-3	242-243	1:1-8	36
73:1	242-244	1:1-5	39
73:2-16	244	1:1	3, 14, 39, 41, 43, 55, 71, 86-88, 126, 215, 222-223
73:2-12	244		
73:2-3	243		
73:4-12	242-243	1:5	41

INDEX OF BIBLICAL TEXTS

1:6-22	40	4:17-21	65, 66, 160, 226
1:8	3, 40-41, 43, 55, 71, 85, 88, 126, 222	4:17-19	156
		4:17	65, 161, 226
		4:17a	138
1:9	40, 43	4:18	65-66
1:13-19	88	4:19	65-66
1:20-21	40	5:1-7	47
1:21	41, 46	5:2-7	105, 115, 172-173, 175, 177
1:22	40-41, 43, 71, 86, 222		
		5:2-3	71
2	4, 215	5:3	67
2:1-10	40	5:4	172-173
2:3	3, 40-43, 55, 71, 85, 88, 125-126, 222	5:5	172-173
		5:6	71
		5:8-18	70
2:3b	40	5:8	47, 63, 222
2:4-5	43	5:9-16	133, 143-144, 146, 148, 152, 158
2:6-7	41		
2:9	43, 88		
2:9a	41	5:9	134-135, 138, 140, 147-148, 164
2:9b	41		
2:10	41, 43, 71, 86, 89, 222	5:10	147
		5:11	147
2:11-31:40	39, 45	5:12-14	147
2:11-13	39, 46	5:15-16	147
3:1-42:6	22, 36, 92-93	5:17-27	66
3-27	14, 18, 25-26, 233	5:17ff	147
		5:17	147
3-21	55, 234	5:18-26	144
3	18, 34, 46-47	5:18ff	143
3:1	46	5:27	47, 67, 222
3:4-5	70	6-7	47
3:8	132	6:1	166, 187
3:20-23	47	6:3-11	34
3:20	70, 189	6:4	47, 145
3:25-26	99	6:8-10	145
4-28	223	6:9	145
4-14	18	6:14	222
4:2-6	46	6:25	34
4:6-7	47, 215	6:29	34
4:6	43, 46, 63-64, 71, 88	7:5	66
		7:8	148
4:7-11	63	7:11	34, 189
4:7-8	64	7:12-21	145
4:7	46	7:12	47, 74
4:8-11	47, 105, 172, 175, 177	7:14	146
		7:16	32
4:8	46, 67, 71, 172	7:17-21	74
4:11	172-173	7:17-20	68
4:12-17	156	7:17-19	99
4:12-16	67	7:20	146, 148
4:12	157, 164	7:21	112

INDEX OF BIBLICAL TEXTS

8	64	9:11-13	133
8:1-7	226	9:11-12	133
8:2-8	127	9:11	50, 139
8:2	111	9:12-13	135
8:3	64, 66, 68, 70	9:13	131, 133
8:4	64	9:14-35	145
8:5-7	47, 64, 222	9:14-16	70, 121
8:5-6	63	9:15	160, 169
8:5	111	9:16-19	218, 221
8:6-7	64	9:17-19	70
8:6	46	9:17-18	139, 146
8:8-22	63	9:19	121
8:8-19	47, 115	9:20-22	215
8:8-10	67	9:20	160, 169
8:11-19	105, 172-173, 175, 177	9:21-22	43, 88
		9:21	97, 160
8:13	71	9:22-24	139, 149, 178
8:15	173	9:22	70
8:20-21	47	9:24	139
8:20	43, 88, 215, 222	9:32-35	98, 121, 145, 189
8:21-22	64	9:33-35	34, 51
8:22	47, 105, 111, 172-173, 175, 177	9:33a	51
		9:34-35	99
9-10	47	10	34, 141
9	134-135	10:1-17	74
9:1	166, 187	10:1-7	140
9:2-10	135, 155	10:1	189
9:2-3	160, 226	10:2-12	141
9:2	169	10:2-7	70, 145
9:2b	138	10:3	73, 140
9:3-4	121, 189	10:4-7	99, 141
9:3	121	10:8-17	140
9:4-13	70	10:8-13	68, 133, 140, 142, 144, 152, 163
9:4-10	158		
9:4	121, 133	10:8-12	70, 141-142
9:4a'	133	10:8-9	140
9:4a	133	10:8	140
9:4b	133	10:9	89
9:5-15	164	10:10-11	140
9:5-13	68, 133, 135-137, 139-140, 144, 152, 160, 163	10:10	140
		10:11	140
		10:12	141
9:5-10	133-136, 138, 157	10:13-17	145
9:5-7	133, 135-136	10:13-14	142
9:5	133, 199	10:13	141
9:6	133	10:14-17	146
9:7	133	10:14	141, 148
9:8-10	133, 136	10:15-17	141
9:8-9	135	10:16	141
9:10	134-135, 138-140, 147-148	10:17	141
		11	8, 64
9:10a	134	11:1-6	184

INDEX OF BIBLICAL TEXTS

11:5-12	205-206, 211	13:1-12	162
11:6-9	198	13:2	67
11:6	47, 64, 205	13:3	70, 121, 189
11:6a	148	13:4-5	32
11:6c	64	13:4a	63
11:7-20	7-8	13:4b	63
11:7-11	148, 152	13:5	67, 166, 193, 223
11:7-9	64, 205	13:7	63
11:7-8	206	13:15-24	70
11:7	148, 164, 205	13:15-22	68
11:8-9	148, 205	13:15	121, 189
11:10-11	64	13:17-19	47
11:10	148	13:18	51, 160, 169
11:11	89, 148	13:19-24	218, 221
11:12	8, 206	13:20-28	145
11:13-20	47, 184, 215, 222	13:20-22	51
11:13-19	47	13:20-21	99, 121
11:13-14	64	13:21	99
11:15-19	64	13:23-28	71
11:20	47, 64, 105, 172-173, 175, 177	13:23-27	47
		13:24	51, 146, 189
12-14	47	14	47, 51
12	114	14:1-4	160, 226
12:1-4	223	14:13-17	51
12:1	166, 187	14:13	34
12:2-4	166	15-26	18
12:2-3	67, 162	15	47
12:2	86	15:2-6	47
12:4	160	15:4	71
12:6	73	15:5	48
12:7-25	158	15:5b	226
12:12	89, 142	15:8-10	67, 166
12:13-25	52, 68, 133, 142-144, 147, 152, 155, 163	15:11	156
		15:14-16	66, 156, 160, 226
		15:14	66, 161
12:13-21	143	15:15	66
12:13-16	142	15:16	66
12:13	70, 142	15:17-35	48, 63-64, 115, 172, 174-175, 177
12:14	142		
12:15	142-143	15:17-19	67
12:16	142	15:20-35	105, 181
12:16b	142	15:20	171, 190
12:17-21	142-143	15:21	174
12:21	143	15:22	174
12:21a	143	15:23	174
12:22-25	142-143	15:24	174
12:22	143, 199	15:29	174
12:22a	143	16-17	105
12:23	144	16	48
12:24	143	16:1	166, 187
12:24b	143	16:2-5	162
13	121	16:2-3	63

INDEX OF BIBLICAL TEXTS

16:6-17	48	20:4-11	105
16:7-14	145	20:5-29	179, 181
16:9-14	68	20:5-11	65
16:9	146, 189	20:5	106, 110
16:11-18	70	20:6	110
16:13	146	20:7-9	110, 174-175
16:14	146	20:10	106, 110, 174-175
16:17	97, 160	20:11	106
16:19-21	70	20:12-23	65
16:19	48, 51, 121, 145, 189	20:12-18	105
		20:15	174
16:20-22	121, 189	20:18-19	174-175
17:4b	89	20:19	105, 110
17:10	166, 223	20:20-29	105
17:14	66	20:21	106, 174-175
18:1-4	65, 226	20:24-29	65
18:2-4	47, 127	20:25	174-175
18:2	111	20:26-28	106
18:5-21	48, 63, 65, 105, 115, 172, 174-175, 177, 181	20:26a	174-175
		20:26c	174-175
		20:27	110
18:11-21	181	20:28-29	106
18:11	174	20:28	110, 174-175
18:12	174	20:28a	110
18:13-14	202	20:29	48, 110, 112, 174-175, 181, 184-186
18:13	174		
18:14	174		
18:19	174	21	48, 97, 104-111, 114, 121, 176-178, 181, 193, 224-225
19	48, 105, 121		
19:1	166, 187		
19:2-6	162		
19:2-3	63	21:1	166, 188
19:6-12	70	21:2-3	162
19:6-9	218, 221	21:3	86
19:7-22	48	21:7-34	181
19:7-12	145-146	21:7-16	106
19:11ff	189	21:7-13	73
19:23	217	21:7	106-107, 176
19:25-27	70, 121, 189	21:8-12	107
19:25-26a	121, 145	21:8-9	106
19:25	48, 51, 145	21:8	106, 176
19:26b-27	121, 145	21:9-10	106
19:28-29	49	21:9	176
20	8, 65, 105, 110, 112, 178, 181, 184, 193	21:11-12	106, 176
		21:13	106-107, 176
		21:14-16	71, 98
20:1	112	21:15	97
20:2-3	48	21:17-21	106
20:3	8, 67, 166	21:17	106-107, 115, 176, 181
20:4-29	48, 63, 105, 115, 172, 174-175, 177, 181	21:18	176, 181
		21:19	181

21:22-26	106	22:20	175
21:23-26	106, 115	22:21-30	48, 65, 98, 215, 222, 225
21:23-24	176		
21:25	189	23-24	34, 56, 93, 96, 120-123, 125-126, 166, 187, 192, 226
21:26	66		
21:27-33	106		
21:28	106		
21:30-33	68	23	15, 48, 56, 97, 107, 111, 122-123, 149, 211, 225
21:30	176, 181		
21:32-33	107, 176		
21:32	107		
21:34	183, 191	23:1-2	122, 224
22-31	16, 20-21, 24, 36, 54, 57, 72, 77-80, 83, 85, 90, 92-94, 96, 211, 223-224, 228-230, 232-237, 239, 241-242, 245, 252-253	23:1	166, 188
		23:2-7	225
		23:2	98
		23:3-9	218, 221
		23:3-7	68, 70, 98, 122, 124, 224
		23:3-4	189
22-27	196, 212, 229	23:3	98, 149, 217
22-24	94, 97, 120	23:4	98
22	93, 96, 98, 105, 111, 126, 181, 193, 211	23:5	98
		23:6-7	145
		23:6	51, 98
22:2-5	225	23:8-9	51, 99, 122, 124, 149, 164, 189, 224-225
22:2-3	97		
22:3	160		
22:4	97	23:10-12	122, 124, 145, 224-225
22:5-20	48, 63, 172, 175, 177		
		23:10	150
22:5-9	105, 218	23:10a	99
22:5	65, 97	23:10b-12	99
22:5a	97, 225	23:11	150
22:6-9	63, 65, 97, 126, 225, 228	23:13-16	99, 122, 124, 164, 224-225
22:6	97	23:13-14	111
22:7	97	23:13	99
22:9	97	23:14	99, 150
22:10-20	65	23:15-16	99
22:10-16	105	23:15	149
22:10-11	98, 175, 225	23:16-17	145
22:12-20	98, 225	23:16	146
22:12-14	98, 148-149, 152	23:17	99, 122, 224-225
22:12	148-149	24-28	182
22:13-14	148-149	24-27	211
22:15-18	71	24	48, 55-56, 73, 96, 99, 104, 110-111, 114, 116, 119, 122, 126-127, 160, 178, 181-182, 193, 211, 225
22:15-16	98		
22:16-18	98		
22:17	98		
22:18-20	105		
22:18	98		
22:19-20	98, 175		

INDEX OF BIBLICAL TEXTS

24:1-17	15, 23, 48, 55-56, 68, 73, 97, 100, 102, 104, 107-108, 110, 113-116, 119, 122-125, 127, 149, 176-177, 182, 224-225
24:1-12	111
24:1-3	113
24:1	99-100, 102, 107-108, 110-111, 176, 181
24:1a	108
24:1b	108
24:2-17	100, 102, 110, 176
24:2-12	110-111
24:2-4	100
24:2-3	176
24:2	119
24:2a	100
24:2b	100, 103
24:3	101, 119
24:4-8	113
24:4	101
24:5-8	100-101
24:5	101, 111, 176
24:6	101
24:7	101, 176
24:8	101, 177
24:9-10	176
24:9	100-101, 113, 119
24:9a	103
24:10-14b	113
24:10-12	100-101
24:10	176
24:10a	101
24:10b	101
24:11	101, 119, 176
24:11b	101
24:12	108, 176
24:12a	101
24:12b	102, 108
24:13-25	111
24:13-17	100, 102
24:13	116
24:13a	102
24:13b	102
24:14	102, 119, 176
24:14c	113
24:15	102, 113, 176
24:16-17	113
24:16	102, 176
24:17	102
24:18-25	15, 23, 48, 55-56, 73
24:18-24	27, 36, 79, 96-97, 102, 104-119, 121-125, 127, 167, 176-179, 181-182, 224-225
24:18-21	109, 113, 117
24:18-20	104-105, 113, 116-117, 127, 167, 179
24:18	97, 107, 110, 112-113, 116-117, 119, 182
24:18a	102, 106, 108, 110, 117
24:18b	102, 106, 108, 117
24:18c	103, 106, 117
24:19-25	111
24:19	103, 117, 119
24:19b	108
24:20	66, 107-108, 110, 117
24:20a	103
24:20b	103
24:20c	103
24:20d	103
24:21-25	113
24:21-24	116-117
24:21	103-105, 113, 117, 119, 127
24:22-25	113, 127, 167, 179
24:22-24	104-105, 107, 113, 117
24:22	103, 110, 119
24:23	103, 108, 110
24:23a	117
24:23b	117
24:24	107-109, 111, 117
24:24a	103, 108, 110, 117
24:24b	103, 108, 117
24:24c	103
24:25	90, 103, 114, 122-124, 126-127, 183, 224, 226
25-26	96, 111, 126-128, 158, 160, 166, 192

25	15, 23, 26, 48, 56, 66, 93, 114, 116, 123, 126-128, 133, 140, 149-164, 167, 180-181, 187, 211, 224, 226, 228	26:5-13 26:5-8 26:5-7 26:5-6 26:5	144-160, 162-166, 180-181, 223-224, 226 150, 164 153 150-151 129, 153-155, 162 129, 149
25:1	111, 151, 158-159	26:5a	151
25:1-26:4	163	26:6	129, 202
25:2-26:4	150	26:7-14	155
25:2-6	149, 152, 154, 162	26:7-10 26:7-9	154 129, 154, 162
25:2-3	128, 149-151, 153	26:7	130, 150, 153
25:2	128, 153	26:8-10	150-151
25:2a	128, 149, 151, 162	26:8 26:9	130, 153 130, 149-150, 153
25:2b-3	131	26:10-13	153-154
25:2b	128	26:10-11	129-130, 153, 162
25:3-6	153-154	26:10	131, 150, 153
25:3	128	26:11-13	150-151, 154
25:3a	151	26:11	131
25:4-6	66, 128, 149-151, 153, 156	26:12-13	129, 131, 153, 162
25:4	66, 128, 160, 226	26:12	131
25:5	128, 226	26:12a	131, 151
25:6	66, 128, 158	26:12b	131, 151
26-31	56, 93, 127, 187	26:13	131
26-27	56	26:13a	131, 151
26	15, 56, 93, 126-128, 132, 139, 150-152, 154, 156-167, 183, 187, 193, 211	26:13b 26:14	131 32, 48, 132, 139, 147-148, 150, 153-154, 157, 162, 164-165
26:1-4	23, 127-129, 154-156, 159, 161-164, 167, 179-180, 224, 226	26:14a 26:14b 26:14c 27-31	153, 157 153, 157 153 18
26:1	158-159, 166, 188	27-28	3, 5, 197
26:2-4	32, 86, 150-151, 158, 161, 164, 166, 223	27	3-5, 7, 10, 15, 49, 56-57, 93, 96, 127, 164, 166-168, 172, 178, 183-184, 186-187, 192-193, 198, 205, 209-211, 223
26:2-3	129, 161		
26:2a	151		
26:3a	151		
26:4	129, 156, 161, 163-164	27:1-12	15, 23, 55, 56, 127, 154, 167,
26:4b	151		172, 177, 182,
26:5-14	23, 27, 34, 48, 55-56, 79, 127-129, 132-133, 139-140, 142,	27:1-6	184, 186, 192-193, 195, 224 118, 127, 168-

302 INDEX OF BIBLICAL TEXTS

	169, 184, 187, 189-190, 216, 226, 228	27:11	167, 186, 190, 192
27:1	127, 139, 163, 166-168, 179, 187-188, 197, 216	27:12	32, 112, 167, 178, 190-191, 210
		27:12a	191
		27:12b	191
27:2-12	127, 157, 167, 180	27:13-23	15, 23, 27, 34, 36, 48-49, 55-56, 79, 112, 114, 127, 157, 167-168, 170-173, 175-187, 190-195, 224, 227
27:2-7	127, 167, 179		
27:2-6	68, 154, 167-168, 183, 188, 222		
27:2-4	168, 177		
27:2-3	70	27:13	112, 117, 127, 167, 171-176, 178-179, 181-182, 184-186, 190, 192
27:2ff	210		
27:2	57, 68, 145-146, 163, 177, 183, 192, 194-195, 210		
		27:13a	190
27:2a	168, 177, 188	27:13b	190
27:2b	168, 177, 188-189	27:14-23	5, 112, 116, 127, 167, 171, 176, 179, 182, 185-186
27:2c	168, 188		
27:2d	168, 188-189		
27:3	168, 188	27:14-19	173
27:4-6	182	27:14-17	112, 182
27:4	168, 169, 188	27:14-15	171, 173-174, 176
27:5-6	43, 88, 177, 182, 192-193, 227	27:14	112, 172-174, 176, 182
27:5	32, 63, 168-170, 186, 189, 191-192, 210, 215	27:14a	171
		27:14b	171, 174
		27:14c	171
27:5a	169	27:15	174-176
27:5b	169	27:15a	171, 174
27:6	50, 179-180, 183	27:15b	171
27:6a	169	27:16-19	171
27:6b	169	27:16-17	3, 171-176
27:7-23	155, 178, 183	27:16	171
27:7-12	127, 167, 179, 184	27:16b	177
		27:17a	171, 177
27:7-10	167-170, 178-180, 185-187, 189-190, 227	27:17b	171
		27:18-19	173
		27:18	171, 173, 176-177
27:7	4, 49, 170, 179-180, 189-190, 228	27:19	171, 174-175
		27:20-23	171, 174-176, 181
27:7a	185	27:20-22	173
27:8-23	113, 127, 167, 179	27:20	174-175
		27:20a	171
27:8-10	185, 190	27:20b	171
27:8-9	179, 189-190	27:21	172
27:8	170, 179-180, 185	27:22	172
27:9	170	27:23	172, 175-176, 179, 181
27:10	170		
27:11-12	168, 170, 177, 182, 187, 190-193, 227	28-31	34, 93, 96, 193, 196, 212, 224

INDEX OF BIBLICAL TEXTS

28	1-12, 14-15, 20-22, 24-29, 36-38, 49, 51, 56-58, 71-72, 77-80, 87, 195, 197-198, 205-206, 208-215, 220-224, 227-236, 242	28:20-27	197, 209, 227
		28:20	6, 13, 90, 197-198, 200, 206-208, 213
		28:21-22	202
		28:21	202, 207-208
		28:21a	202
		28:22	12, 202, 204, 206-209, 213
28:1-27	2, 10-14, 71, 212-214, 221	28:23	199-203, 213
28:1-19	209	28:24-26	208
28:1-11	3, 197, 199-201, 204, 227	28:24	200, 202-203, 206, 208
28:1	10, 197	28:25-27	14, 200, 203
28:1-2	198, 213	28:25-26	203-204
28:3	198, 204-205, 207-208, 213	28:25	203
		28:25a	203, 207
28:3a	198	28:25b	203, 207
28:3b	198	28:26	203, 207
28:3c	198	28:26a	203, 207
28:4-6	199	28:26b	204, 207-208
28:7-8	199, 202, 208, 213	28:27	198, 202-205
		28:27a	203
28:7	207	28:27b	204
28:8	5-6, 206-208	28:28	1-3, 5, 10-15, 36, 49, 51, 56, 71, 77, 87, 196-197, 200, 202, 204, 206-210, 212-217, 219-223, 227-228, 230-231, 233, 235
28:9-11	198-199, 213		
28:9a	199		
28:9b	199		
28:10-11	199		
28:10b	199		
28:11b	199, 202		
28:12-19	197, 199, 201, 204, 227	28:28a	11
		28:28bc	11
28:12	5-6, 13, 90, 196-201, 206-208, 213	29-31	1, 3-5, 7, 14-15, 22, 25-26, 34, 56-57, 68, 70, 77, 197, 205, 209-211, 215-216, 219-222, 224, 228, 230, 233, 236
28:13-19	200		
28:13-14	202, 206		
28:13	199-200, 206, 208, 213		
28:13a	200		
28:13b	200, 202		
28:14	12, 201-202, 207-208, 213	29-30	217
		29ff	210
28:14a	200	29	3, 7, 10, 49, 51, 57, 209, 211, 216-219, 221, 227
28:14b	200		
28:15-19	201		
28:15	6, 201	29:1-6	217
28:16	5-6, 201	29:1	166, 188, 197, 216
28:17	201		
28:18	5-6, 201	29:2-6	217
28:19	201	29:2	217
28:20-28	201, 204	29:7-10	217

304 INDEX OF BIBLICAL TEXTS

29:11-17	217	31:38-40	219
29:11	217	31:38-40a	220
29:12-17	218	32:1-42:17	39, 51
29:12	217-218	32-37	23, 25-26
29:14	218	32:1-5	39
29:16	218	32:4	83
29:18-20	217	32:6	83
29:21-25	217	33-37	242
29:25	218	33:5	52
30	3, 49, 51, 57, 197, 211, 217-219, 221, 227	33:13-30	66
		33:14-33	67
		33:19-33	51
30:1-11	218	33:32b	51
30:1	218	34	109
30:9	218	34:5	169
30:12-15	218	34:17-18	70
30:16-19	218	34:17	169
30:16	218	34:23-28	70
30:19-23	145	34:31-33	66
30:20-31	218, 221	35:16	191
30:20-23	1, 4, 7, 57, 210, 218, 220, 222	36	109
		36:7-12	66
30:20	218	36:15-16	66
30:21	146	37:2	52
30:24-27	218	37:14	52
30:24	218	37:23	52, 70
30:28-31	218	37:24	231
30:28	218	38-42	231
31	43, 49, 51, 57, 97, 197, 211, 219, 221, 228	38:1-42:6	10, 25-26, 30, 209
		38-41	8, 10, 15, 18, 29-30, 77, 95, 206, 211-212, 223, 236, 242, 245, 253
31:1-4	220		
31:1-3	219		
31:4-6	219-221		
31:5-23	220		
31:7-34	220	38-39	52, 75, 209
31:7-8	220	38	95, 208
31:9-12	220	38:2	52, 75-76, 95, 208
31:12	202		
31:13-15	220	38:4-38	75
31:16-23	220	38:4	207-208
31:24-34	220	38:5	75
31:24-25	220	38:5a	89
31:26-28	220	38:8-11	207
31:29-30	220	38:8	89
31:31-32	220	38:12-15	109
31:33-34	220	38:16	201, 207-208
31:35-37	1, 4, 7, 51, 57, 210, 219-222	38:17	207-208
		38:19	6, 207-208
31:35	51, 217, 219	38:24	6, 207-208
31:36	219	38:24b	207
31:37	219	38:25	75, 207

INDEX OF BIBLICAL TEXTS

38:25a	207	42:7	30, 193, 227, 237
38:25b	207-208	42:7b	79, 83, 94-96
38:28a	207	42:10-17	30, 32
38:31-35	75	42:12-16	39
38:34	207		
38:35	109, 208-209	*Proverbs*	
38:36	75, 207-208	1-15	239
38:37	207	1-9	214
38:39-39:30	75	1:7	1, 71
38:39	207-208	3:7	71
38:41	75, 207-208	3:33	1, 72
39-41	208	4:4	12
39	207	8:14-16	143-144
39:5	75	9:10	1, 71
39:17	207-208	10-15	214
39:25	208-209	10:15	238
40-41	207	10:22	238
40	114	10:27	1, 13, 71-72
40:1-5	208-209	10:30	1, 72
40:2	95	11:16	237
40:3-5	52	12:3	237
40:4	10, 52, 208	12:21	1, 72
40:6-41:26	52, 76	13:8	238
40:8-9	10	13:22	237
40:8	52, 76, 95, 125, 169, 221	13:23	237
		13:25	237
40:15-41:26	209	14:14	237
40:15-24	23, 76, 125	14:19	237
40:24	89	14:20	238
40:25-41:26	23, 76, 125	14:26	13
40:25	89	14:27	13
41:2-6	114	15:11	202
41:3	207-208	15:16-17	214, 238
41:23	132	15:29	1, 72
41:26	206, 208	15:33	71
42:1-6	18, 52, 208-209, 222, 231	16ff	239
		16:8	238
42:2-6	10, 46, 223	16:16	214, 238
42:2-3	52	16:19	214, 238
42:3	76, 208, 222, 231	17:1	238
42:3b	32	17:15	169
42:5	76, 202, 222, 231-232, 236	18:23	238
		19:4	238
42:6	2, 7, 10-11, 32-33, 196, 209, 232	19:6-7	238
		19:10	237
42:6a	33	19:22b	238
42:6b	33	21:3	238
42:7-17	22, 25-26, 36, 92	22:1	238
42:7-9	30, 32, 194	22:8	71
42:7-8	29-30, 53, 95, 126, 166, 191, 194-195, 222	22:28	100
		23:10	100
		26:4-5	81

26:7	237	5:9-16	249
26:9	237	5:9	249
27:20	202	5:10	249
28:6	238	5:11	249
28:15	237	5:12-13	249
30:14	237	5:14-15	249
		5:16	249
Ecclesiastes		5:17-19	249
1:3	246-247	5:17-18	249
1:12-2:26	245	6:11	191
1:12-2:23	245	8:10-15	250
1:12-18	245	8:10-12a	250
2:1-11	245	8:12	250
2:11	246	8:12b-13	250
2:12-17	245	8:14	250
2:18-23	245	8:15	250
2:21	246-247	9:1-12	250-251
2:22	246	9:1-6	251
2:24-26	245-246	9:1	250-251
2:26	246-247	9:1a	251
3:1-15	247	9:1b-6	251
3:1	247	9:1b	251
3:2-8	247	9:2-6	251
3:9	247	9:2	250
3:10-11	247-248	9:4	251
3:12-15	247-248	9:6	251
3:12-14	248	9:7-10	251
3:12-13	248	9:11-12	251
3:14	248	9:11	250
3:15	248	9:12	250
3:16-22	248	11:7-12:8	252
3:16	248	12:13-14	252
3:17	248-249	12:1	252
3:17b	248		
3:18-21	248-249	*Daniel*	
3:18-19	248	2:20-23	143-144
3:19	248	2:22a	143
3:20-21	248		
3:22	248-249	*2 Chronicles*	
5:7	191	6:23	169
5:9-19	249		

New Testament

Luke		*John*	
13:1-5	237	9:1-2	237

INDEX OF SUBJECTS

Abaddon, 12, 129, 202, 207, 209, 213
Abelian Group, 31
Acceptance as Job's Speech:
  Job 24   114-117
  Job 25-26   158-159
  Job 26   157-158
  Job 27   183-186
  Job 28   3-5, 15, 20-21, 28-29, 37, 196
Acrostic Hymn, 239
Act-Consequence Nexus, 42, 214, 237-239
All-Seeing Character, 203-204
Anacrusis, 12
Anticlimax, 9-11, 206, 214
Approaches to the Literary Issues:
  Job 24   108-118, 120-126
  Job 26   152-159, 160-166
  Job 27   178-187, 187-195
  Job 28   2-21, 196-197, 212-223
Aramaism, 6
Arbiter, 51, 145
Asseverative Particle, 197
Assumptions for Approaching a Story, 83-84
Audience, 18-19, 58-62, 69, 72, 229
Audience-Elevating Strategy, 45
Authenticity of 28:28, 2, 11-15
Authorial Comment, 8-9, 196
Authorial Intent, 18-19
Authorial Style, 2, 5-6, 12

Baba Bathra, 60
Babylonian Exile, 60
Behemoth, 23-24, 52, 76, 125, 207
Better-Than Sayings, 214, 238
Birthday Curse, 46
Blamelessness, 40, 42-43, 56, 88
Blank, 81

Canonical Shaping/Final Form, 4, 28, 37, 118
Carpe diem Passage, 245-246, 248, 251-252

Catchwords, 111, 119, 192
Characterization of God, 42, 135
Characterization of Job, 41, 50, 54-57
Claims to Knowledge, 67, 72
Climax, 222, 231, 242
Complexity of Life, 50, 55-57, 124-125, 213, 239, 253
Compositional Development of Job, 26-27
Confessions of Job, 32-33, 52, 208, 231
Conflict in the Plot, 40-41, 43-45, 50, 52-54
Constituent-Pieces, 25
Constraints, 58-59, 70-72, 229
Content of the Text:
  Job 22-24   97-103
  Job 25-26   128-132
  Job 27   168-172
  Job 28   197-205
Contradictory Juxtaposition, 15-16, 55-57, 77, 79-82, 120-126, 160-166, 187-195, 212-223, 224-232, 237-253
Contradictory Sayings, Characteristics of:
  Job 24   104-108
  Job 26   132-152
  Job 27   172-177
  Job 28   205-212
Contrastive Dialogue, 187
Covenant Motif, 219

Dating of Job, 60-61
Death, The, 12, 202, 207, 209, 213
Deceptiveness of Money, 249
Deconstructionist Approach, 35-37
Deep, The, 12, 200-202, 207-208, 213
Denial as Job's Speech:
  Job 24:18-24   109-113
  Job 26:5-14   152-155
  Job 27:7-10, 13-23   178-183
  Job 28   5-15
Discourse (מָשָׁל), 188, 197, 216

INDEX OF SUBJECTS

Divine Chastisement, Concept of, 66-67, 74
Divine Counsel, 75
Divine Encounter, 76, 223, 231-232, 244-245, 253
Divine Hiddenness, 44, 99, 124, 240-241
Divine Holiness, 149, 160
Divine Inspiration, 129, 156, 161-162
Divine Justice, 70-71, 76, 250
Divine Names, 11-13, 70
Divine Testing, 42, 124-125
Dogmatism, 237
Dominion of God, 128-132
Dramatic Presentation, 91-94

Elihu Speech, 23, 51-52
Empiricist Epistemology, 253
Evaluative Points of View, 16, 84-86, 93-96, 195, 230
Evil, Existence of, 76, 125-126
Exigency, 58, 62-69, 72, 229

Fate of the Wicked, 64-65, 102-108, 171-177, 178-183, 191-194, 240, 243
Fearing God, 1, 5, 13-14, 71, 215, 217, 220-223, 231, 250, 252
Final Verdict of God, 94-96, 126, 166, 194-195
First Speech Cycle, 46-47, 64
Flat Character, 49, 55
Form-Critical Approach, 29
"From Less to More Adequate Perspectives", 73-77, 229

Gap/Gapping, 80-82, 230-232, 242, 244-245, 252-253
Gap-Filling, 82, 230-232, 242, 244-245, 252-253
God as Enemy, 145-146
Godlike Power of Man, 198-199, 213
Goodness of God, 243-244
Guide to Interpretation, 84-91
Guilt, Forensic Meaning of, 169-170, 192

Heavenly Council, 40
Historical-Critical Approach, 25-29
Historicity, 61
Holistic Reading, 4
Human Depravity, Concept of, 65-66, 74, 160

Humour, 137-138
Hypothesis of This Study, 15

Imitation of Friends' Speaking, 156-157, 184
Implicit Auditor, 88
Implied Author, 61-62
Implied Reader, 61-62
Imprecation, 169, 180, 189-190
Inclusio, 14, 87, 142-143, 223, 243, 250-251
Incongruities, cf. Literary Issues
Independent Poem, 2, 5-6, 28, 109, 196
Injustice, 99-102, 105-108, 176-177, 240-243, 250
Innocence, Forensic Meaning of, 169, 189, 192
Integrity of God, 40, 42, 50, 52-55
Integrity of Job, cf. Blamelessness, 40-43, 50, 52-57
Interlude, 2, 8-9, 196
Introductory Formula/Headings, 3, 7, 11-12, 92, 163, 166, 187-188, 197, 211
Irony, 45-46, 86-87, 137-138, 161-162, 164-165, 190

Job the Ambiguous, 57
Job, The Impatient, 4, 29
Job, The Patient, 4, 29
Job the Silent, 50, 54
Job the Verbose, 50, 54

Klein Group, 31

Lawsuit with God, 51, 98, 121
Leitwort, 42-43, 88
Leviathan, 23-24, 52, 76, 125, 132, 207-208
Linear Progression, 88, 93
Literary Issues:
    Prologue-Epilogue-Dialogue, 22
    3rd Speech Cycle, 22-23, 27
    Job 24   96-97
    Job 25-26   126-127
    Job 27   166-167
    Job 28   1-2, 196
    Elihu Speeches, 23
    Yahweh Speeches, 23-24
Literary-Rhetorical Markers, 87-91

INDEX OF SUBJECTS

Majestic Power, 128, 149, 160, 162-163
Misconceptions of God, 67-69, 99, 124-125, 168, 177, 189, 192, 194
Misuse of Forms, 155
"Monotheistic" Declaration, cf. One God, Idea of, 139
Muilenburg School, 17

Narration, 38-39, 92
Narrative, 20
Narrative Criticism, 20
Narrative Plot, 38
Narrator, 41, 85-86, 91-93

Oath Formula, 168-169, 180, 188-190, 217
Oath of Innocence, 49, 168-169, 188-189, 216-221
Oath of Negative Confession, 220
Oddity in Job's Mouth, cf. Denial as Job's Speech, 2, 7
One God, Idea of, 70
Optative Reading, 115-116
Oral Presentation, 87
Orthodox Statement, 1, 55, 114, 160, 172, 194, 196, 210, 239
Ostensible Auditor, 88

Parody, 134, 136-145, 155-157, 184-185
Personification, 201, 207-208
Pious Gloss, 109
Pivot Statement, 153, 199
Play of Perspectives, 44
Plot Development, 37-57
Polarity, 213
Practical Persuasion, 17-18
Pragmatic Criticism, 18
Premature Climax, 2, 9-11
Primacy of Dialogue, 38-39, 45, 91
Privilege of Omniscience, 85
Psalms of Lament, 81, 180, 237
Pseudo-Climax, 222, 231, 242
Punch-Line, 164
Purity of Heart, 244

Quotations of the Friends' Position, 113-114

Rabbinic Tradition, 60
Rahab, 131-132

Reader-Response Criticism, 18
Redefinition of Terms, 185-186
Refrain, 5-6, 197, 207-208
Remembrance of the Creator, 252
Repetition, 43, 87-88
Retributive Concept, cf. Fate of the Wicked, 29, 36, 63-65, 73-74, 104-105, 250
Reverser of Fortunes, God as, 146
Rhetoric, 16-17, 120
Rhetoric of Silence, 44, 46, 193, 195
Rhetorical Criticism, 17-20
Rhetorical Impact upon:
    Flow of Argument, 16, 121-123, 160-165, 187-193, 212-221
    Audience, 16, 83-96, 123-126, 165-166, 193-195, 221-223
Rhetorical Questions, 6, 88-90, 122, 161, 196, 199-201, 206-208
Rhetorical Situation, 57-72, 229
Rhetorical Strategy, 16, 73-77, 80-82, 229-230
Rhetorical Unit, 92-93, 96
Round Character, 49, 55

Satire, 137-138
Satire Against God, 133-136, 155-156, 164
Satirical Doxology/Hymn, 135, 142, 152
Scene-Types, 88
Sea, The, 12, 74, 131-132, 200-202, 207-209, 213
Second Speech Cycle, 47-48, 64-65
Second Temple, 60
Serpent, 131-132
Sheol, 31, 129, 202
Shunning Evil, 1, 14, 71, 215, 217, 220-223
Skepticism, 253
Source-Critical Approach, 29
Speech-Reattribution, 2, 7-8, 110-113, 118, 152-155, 167, 178-179, 180-183
Structuralist Approach, 29-35
Stylistics, 17-18, 112
Systematization of Point of View, 94

Talmud, 60
Text, 18-19
Theodicies, 62-67, 72, 73-74, 104-105, 194

Third Speech Cycle, 22-23, 48-49, 54-57, 65, 223-230
"Time" (עֵת) Sayings, 247
Transformation, 32-34, 52
Truthfulness, 53, 95, 124, 126, 193-194

Undermining, 35-36
Unity of the Text, 119-120, 159-160
Upheaval Motif, 136

Vanity, 191
"Vanity" (הֶבֶל) Statement, 245-248, 250, 252
Verbatim, 135, 208
Vindication, 50-53, 98, 121-122, 221, 232

Wisdom, 1, 13, 14-15, 71-72, 207-208, 215
Wisdom, Limit of, 4, 8, 13-15, 71-72, 147-148, 162, 164-166, 200-206, 208-209, 213-214, 223
Wisdom Literature, Nature of, 239, 253
Wisdom, Temporality of, 203-204
Wisdom Traditions, 1, 69, 71, 214-215, 220, 231-232
Wit, 138-140

Yahweh Speeches, 9-11, 23-24, 52, 75-76, 206-209, 231-232
Yahwism, 1, 69, 71, 238